PAKISTAN

THE SOCIAL SCIENCES' PERSPECTIVE

PAKISTAN

THE SOCIAL SCIENCES' PERSPECTIVE

Edited by

Akbar S. Ahmed

KARACHI
OXFORD UNIVERSITY PRESS
OXFORD   NEW YORK   DELHI
1990

Oxford University Press
OXFORD NEW YORK
TORONTO MELBOURNE AUCKLAND
PETALING JAYA SINGAPORE HONG KONG TOKYO
DELHI BOMBAY CALCUTTA MADRAS KARACHI
NAIROBI DAR ES SALAAM CAPE TOWN
and associates in
BERLIN IBADAN

OXFORD is a trademark of Oxford University Press

First Edition, 1990

ISBN 0 19 577388 8

Printed at
Mueid Packages, Karachi
Published by
Oxford University Press
5-Bangalore Town, Sharae Faisal
P.O.Box 13033, Karachi-8, Pakistan.

Contents

Acknowledgement

Some of the papers published in this volume have been previously published and are reprinted with permission.

Foreword

Pakistan inherits a rich tradition of social sciences (defined broadly as sociology and anthropology). Yet, the state of its contemporary social sciences is in a shambles and therefore the social sciences' perspective virtually absent from analysis.

The detailed and extant works of Al-Beruni, Ibn-Batuta, and Ibn-Khaldun provide a legitimate base for Pakistani social sciences.[1] There is another, more recent, tradition. With the coming of the British about two centuries ago a sharp impetus was provided to the social sciences' perspective. Colonial authority wished to know as much as it could about the history, tribes, customs, rituals, and languages of each of its districts. Thus were the district gazetteers born. Written with a keen eye and a lively style they still remain an unrivalled mine of information for the flora and fauna of the districts.

For the areas that would form Pakistan from British India the gazetteers, like the one for Makran at one end of Pakistan and for Hazara, at the other end, are still unmatched sources of sociological information. Their freshness belies their age of 80 years. In addition political officers contributed what they called 'monographs' on the tribes they administered or lived among. Elphinstone—the first Briton to know and write of the Pathans—Burnes and Burton, in the first half of the last century, and Ibbetson, Raverty, Merk, and King in the second half, established a high standard and tradition of socio-political commentary. The tradition was followed into this century by officers like Howell and Caroe in the North-West Frontier Province, Lambrick in Sind, and Darling in the Punjab. It is, therefore, surprising that the social sciences have not flourished in Pakistan.

Sociological and anthropological studies in Pakistan have been few and far between. Alavi, Eglar, and Saghir Ahmad studied rural Punjab (in the sixties). The Pastners studied Makran and the Pehrsons the Marris in Baluchistan. Barth wrote of the Swat Pathans of the Frontier Province and over the years made numerous trips to Swat.[2]

The evidence points to the lack of success that has been the fate of the social sciences' perspective in Pakistan. While economic and Islamic centres/academies — sometimes two rooms and two members of staff — have proliferated no such institutions exist for the social sciences. Sociology, social work, and anthropology are often lumped together in one department at the universities. There is only one department of anthropology in Pakistan at the Quaid-e-Azam University in Islamabad. Many of the bright anthropologists graduating from Islamabad disguise themselves as 'economic investigators' or 'rural development experts' to find jobs, in the process unlearning their discipline. The Planning Commission, the most powerful and established arm of government for planning and development, hires dozens of highly qualified economists, but it does not boast a single sociologist or anthropologist among its designated experts or luminaries (although its model, the World Bank, has established the post of a senior sociologist a few years ago). While Pakistani economists such as Dr. Mahbub-ul-Haq and Javed Burki have made names for themselves, with a base in the World Bank, and written extensively on Pakistan there is no counterpart to them among the sociologists and anthropologists. The Pakistan Sociological Association and the Pakistan Institute of Anthropology are moribund institutions working in fits and starts. Not a single worthwhile journal of the social sciences is published in Pakistan. The arguments justifying this bleak picture are false: to counter them it may be said that 'practical' subjects, like economics, cannot depict social reality without sociology and anthropology (as the World Bank concedes); the social sciences are not a 'luxury' when serious ethnic clashes, a feature of the eighties, create severe stress in society and lie unexamined.[3]

It is not surprising that Pakistan society has been traditionally analysed with an undeveloped sociological perception.[4] One result is the assumption that it possesses a largely uniform social structure with common values and norms. As the papers in this volume indicate this is an inaccurate picture of society. It points to the retarded growth of the sociological perspective.

Another consequence has been the blurred sociological vision in Pakistan at all levels of planning and execution. In particular the social sector, which includes projects for women and education, has always suffered from faulty designing and poor implementation. The endemic failure with women's projects in Baluchistan or those of dacoity in Sind clearly expose the inadequacy of sociological planning or analysis. Other major problems — ethnic strife, costing lives and property worth millions, or women's processions demanding rights — are dealt with in the traditional, colonial, law and order manner, mainly in the form of police wielding sticks. These defects arise in spite of the efforts of some of the outstanding economists and administrators available in Pakistan.

A collection like the present one is therefore to be doubly welcomed. Like most collections it may be uneven in quality and interest. Why an article has been included or left out may well be asked. Some already published articles are included along with fresh ones. The time warp for the older articles is 'corrected', from the time they were written, by the generally slow pace of change in the rural areas.[5] From this perspective each tribal society or ethnic group is in some sense unique and the papers attempt to capture this uniqueness. But at another level the state, national ideology and the major religion of the country also matter, providing the larger frame within which people order their lives.[6] The past, too, matters.[7] The authors represent a wide range of nationalities (USA to USSR). They write of their area and in their discipline with authority, many having spent years studying their 'group'. In order not to disturb the preference and style of the contributors, especially in view of their diverse backgrounds, editing has been kept to a minimum, even leaving spellings to their choice (for example, Pakhtun, Pukhtun, Pashtun, Pathan, etc. for the same ethnic group.) The entire gamut of Pakistan society — saints in Sind, Afghan refugees in Peshawar, chiefs in Gilgit, rural groups in Faisalabad, Punjab, tribalism in Baluchistan — is presented in detail. Together, the collection underlines the complex and diverse features that add up to make Pakistan society; the book thus fills an important vacuum in Pakistan studies.

10 March 1989

Akbar S. Ahmed
The Allama Iqbal Fellow
Chair in Pakistan Studies,
and Fellow of Selwyn College,
University of Cambridge

NOTES

1. Ahmed, A. S., *Toward Islamic Anthropology: Definition, Dogma and Directions,* International Institute of Islamic Thought, U.S.A., 1986(a) reprinted in Pakistan by Vanguard Books Ltd., Lahore, Pakistan, 1987.

2. Barth, F., *The Last Wali of Swat,* Columbia University Press, U.S.A., 1985, is his latest work on the subject.

3. Ahmed, A. S., *Pakistan Society: Islam, Ethnicity and Leadership in South Asia,* Oxford University Press, Karachi, 1986(b); and 'Pakistan's Social Ethnic Dilemma: 1947-1988', *Dawn (Magazine),* 12 August 1988(b).

4. Ali, T., *Can Pakistan Survive? The Death of a State,* Penguin Books, Harmondsworth, 1983; Binder, L., *Religion and Politics in Pakistan,* University of California Press, U.S.A, 1961; Bolitho, H., *Jinnah: Creator of Pakistan,* John Murray, London, 1964; Braibanti, R., *Research on the Bureaucracy of Pakistan,* Duke University, Durham, U.S.A. 1966; Burki, S. J., *Pakistan Under Bhutto, 1971-1977,* Macmillan, London, 1980; Callard, K., *Pakistan: A Political Study,* Allen and Unwin, London, 1958; Sayeed, K. B., *Pakistan: The Formative Phase,* Oxford University Press, London, 1960; Stephens, I., *Pakistan,* Penguin Books, Harmondsworth, 1964; Wilcox, W. A., *Pakistan: The Consolidation of a Nation,* Columbia University Press, New York, 1963; and Williams, R.L.F., *The State of Pakistan,* Faber and Faber, U.K., 1962.

5. Ahmed, op. cit., 1986(b) and 1988(b).

6. A useful collection discussing these issues is to be found in Banuazizi, A. and Myron Weiner (editors), *The State, Religion , and Ethnic Politics: Pakistan, Iran and Afghanistan,* Syracuse University Press, 1987, published simultaneously by Vanguard Books Ltd., Pakistan.

7. For the continuing impact of Hinduism, the major religion of South Asia, on Muslim society, see Ahmed, A. S., *Discovering Islam: Making Sense of Muslim History and Society,* Routledge and Kegan Paul, London, 1988(a).

About the Contributors

Ahmed, A.S., Scholar-administrator, was Commissioner Baluchistan, Pakistan, and is now The Allama Iqbal Fellow/Chair in Pakistan Studies at the University of Cambridge, U.K.

Chaudhry, H.R., is Assistant Professor, Department of Anthropology, Quaid-i-Azam University, Islamabad, Pakistan.

Edward, D.B., is engaged with the Department of Anthropology, The University of Michigan, U.S.A.

Emerson, R.M., (late) was Professor of Sociology and South Asian Studies, University of Washington, U.S.A.

Ewing, K., is Visiting Scholar in the Committee on Southern Asian Studies, University of Chicago and Research Candidate, Institute of Psychoanalysis, Chicago.

Gankovsky, Y., is Head, Near and Middle East Department, Institute of Oriental Studies, USSR Academy of Sciences, Moscow.

Gilmartin, D., is engaged with the University of California, Berkeley.

Hart, D.M., is an American Anthropologist living and working in the Maghreb, North Africa.

Kurin, R., is Deputy Director, Office of Folk Life Programs, Smithsonian Institute, Washington D.C.

Lindholm, C., is associated with the Departments of Anthropology and Social Studies, Harvard University, Cambridge, Massachusetts, U.S.A.

Pastner, C.Mc.C., is Professor at the University of Vermont, Burlington, U.S.A.

Pastner, S.L., is also Professor at the University of Vermont.

Waseem, M., is associated with the International Relations Department, Quaid-i-Azam University, Islamabad, Pakistan.

1

The Afridi of the Khaibar Tribal Agency and the Kohat Frontier Region[1]

David M. Hart

It is a striking fact that ethnic and national frontiers fail signally to coincide in a good many parts of the world; and one of these is the Afghanistan-Pakistan frontier, with an estimated 6.5 million Pukhtun tribesmen on each side of it. Not only this, but ethnic plurality and diversity is a keynote of both countries, with a major difference that although Pukhtuns are traditionally the dominant ethnic group in Afghanistan as a whole, they are by no means so in Pakistan. Yet, they are unquestionably a dominant group in the North-West Frontier Province and there are even indications that they may be coming to be the same in Baluchistan. We refer here, of course, to the period prior to the brutal Soviet invasion of Afghanistan at the end of 1979 and the new and major problems created for Pakistan by the arrival of 2.5 million Afghan refugees, the great bulk of whom are currently located in camps in precisely these two provinces.

Another striking fact is that in the midst of this ethnic diversity in both Afghanistan and Pakistan, the relative cultural and structural homogeneity of the Pukhtuns stands out sharply: their tribal organization and values, and the fact that they tend to look alike, dress alike, talk alike and to project, very consciously, the same set of images. These are embodied by the triad of patrilineal descent, Islam, and *Pukhtunwali* or Pukhtun Custom, as Barth[2] and others have noted. A prototypical case of this maintenance of Pukhtun identity, probably the most famous one in the North-West Frontier in terms of legend, song, and story, is that provided by the Afridi (in Pakhtu, *Apriday*) of the Khaibar Tribal Agency and the Kohat Frontier Region.

The Afridi live entirely within Pakistani territory, although two of their immediate neighbours, the Shinwari to the west and the Mohmand to the north, also extend west across the border into Afghanistan. The Khaibar Agency, established by the British in the Peshawar Cantonment in 1879, is the senior of what were formerly the five, and today, the seven Federally Administered Tribal Areas of the North-West Frontier Province in Pakistan; and although the Afridi are not the only tribal group located within it (for the eastern Shinwari and several smaller groups are encompassed by it as well), they are unquestionably the dominant one, with a population of about 350,000 in an area of 990 square miles, according to the *Pakistan Census of 1972,* while an additional 38,000 in an area of 160 square miles — and all from one major section, the Adam Khayl — were counted in that same year in the Kohat Frontier Region, mostly in and around Darra Adam Khayl where the majority of the Afridi rifle factories are located. The Khaibar Agency accounts for the other seven major Afridi clans or sections, and its seniority alone is a source of Afridi pride.

Despite administrative differences between the Tribal Agencies on the one hand and the Frontier regions on the other, Afridi land is not geographically discontinuous, but forms a single unit, with the Khaibar Pass at its northern neck and the North Tirah, the cool and well-watered Afridi heartland, totally forbidden and inaccessible to all non-Afridi, where most of the tribesmen spend the summer, with its Maydan and its congregational mosque at Bagh ('garden'), the Afridi 'capital', at its west-centre and at a height of 6000 to 7000 feet. To the south-west are the Kajuri Plain, the Bara and Bazar Valleys, Waran, Rajgal, and the Kohat Pass, all of which are also Afridi territorial holdings. The central fact of Afridi history is their guardianship and control of the Khaibar Pass as far back as adequate historical records or even historical memory exist ('as far back as Alexander the Great, who did not want to pay his toll fees', tribal wags like to say). Because the Afridi, and no one else, can always fall back on their North Tirah heartland — for the South Tirah is held by their southern neighbours the Orakzai — they have literally been able to force any would-be conqueror coming through the Pass to pay toll. The most notable single example was in 1672, when under the leadership of an Adam Khayl man named Aymal Khan they decimated a Mughal Army under the Emperor Aurangzeb. The toll system, levied on any form of transport, whether human, animal or mechanical, is still very much in effect to this day. The fee may be minimal, but it is still paid, both as a matter of principle and as a matter of augmenting the tribal allowances — paid them both by the British and today by the Pakistanis on a bi-annual basis — for the tribal Pukhtuns pay no taxes. Not only this, but the Afridi are able to back up their Pass toll-fees through force of arms: for every able-bodied Pukhtun tribesman, the Afridi of course included, carries a rifle (*topak*) and is exceptionally adept in its use.

* * *

A notable feature of the Tribal Agencies in general is the very feeble development in them of anything resembling urban life or settlements. The Khaibar Agency is in this respect atypical only in that the Political Agent's residence, which still looks exactly as it did in Victorian times, is located in Peshawar Cantonment, only a short distance by motorized rickshaw from the North-West Frontier Provincial capital. Even so, the Political Agent must hold meetings in Landi Kotal, at the west end of the Khaibar Pass, in summer, as Peshawar is too hot and most of the Afridi are in the Tirah anyway.

The fact that the Afridi move up into the Tirah in spring and down toward the Peshawar valley in the autumn, without, however, ever leaving their tribal territory is the answer, called *dwa kora* or 'two houses', which in common with other Tribal Agency Pukhtuns, they give to the dictates of their ecology and climate: for all of them have houses both in the Tirah and the various valleys to the south-west. Neither this fact nor their bi-annual moves back and forth, however, makes transhumants of them: they are in fact sedentary agriculturalists with too little land to cultivate, and their permanent holdings in arable land and movable holdings on the hoof, in livestock, are both slender in the extreme. Such cultivated land as there is (*zmaka* or *jaidad* and producing mainly wheat, potatoes, and maize) falls invariably into the category of *milk* or individual private property, while hillsides are generally used as grazing land (*banjar*), by meagre flocks of goats and sheep, and a few scrawny zebu cattle, less than half the size of the big zebu oxen and the water buffaloes to be seen pulling immensely heavy cartloads in Peshawar. And rice is cultivated under irrigation in the Bara valley, the only part of Afridi land where irrigation exists at all.

The small fields under cultivation are close to the villages (*kilay*) which are to be seen scattered here and there through the Khaibar. Stark, fortified mud-and-stone house compounds with feud towers (*burj*, *tapu*) three or four storeys high, blend right into the rocky landscape. If big enough, they are divided into quarters (*kandi*), each one with its separate *hujra* or guesthouse. But the village — which is generally named for its *malik*, its headman who is usually also its senior agnatic lineage member (for instance, Malik Sarwar Khan Kilay in Darra Adam Khayl, Malik 'Ali-Manshah Kilay near Jamrud, at the eastern entrance to the Khaibar) — although it may be the unit of residence, is not that of kinship. For there is none of the mystique of a peasantry associated with agriculture, and its attendant ritual, or with the land here. This is a truly tribal situation. Generally speaking, too, the winter village in the plain (although some Afridi sections live in caves in the Kajuri Plain near Peshawar when they go there) is more or less a replica of the one in the mountains, and, as the Afridi are not accompanied by their animals on their moves from one to the other and as they never live in tents, they disqualify as transhumants even more than they do as purely sedentary agriculturalists. They have to supplement their income, and the legitimate ways for this have long been through toll-fees and tribal allowances, while the less legitimate ways have also long been through raiding and contraband, (for the Tirah is also notorious for poppy cultivation).[3] And today additional supplements are provided through the transportation industry (for trucking and bus lines in Pakistan are almost entirely in the hands of tribal Pukhtuns), labour migration to Saudi Arabia and the Gulf States and, for the more prosperous, ownership of considerable urban real estate in Peshawar itself.

* * *

The main features of the Afridi kinship system, of a 'Modified Sudanese' type in conformity with the like systems of neighbouring tribes,[4] are rapidly summed up: although terms for aunts are characterized by merging (Father's Sister, and Mother's Sister called by the same term), and although the same is true not only of their offspring but of those of Mother's Brother, the same Mother's Brother and Father's Brother show bifurcation and distinctive terminology, as do their offspring. Those of Mother's Brother are merged with those of Mother's Sister and Father's Sister. This is one major feature of the system. The other, despite the fact that some informants played it down is that while Father's Brother's Daughter, *tarla* is regarded as a potential or even preferential spouse, Father's Brother's Son, *tarbur*, is equally regarded as a potential and preferential enemy. There is no question at all of any merging here, for indeed *tarbur* means not only male patrilateral parallel cousin but, even more so, above and beyond this, enemy. The implications of this issue, which are intimately bound up with the agnatic lineage structure and with succession and inheritance, are of crucial importance to Pukhtun social structure generally, and have been documented in detail by Ahmed for the Mohmand in particular.[5] The Pukhtun kinship system as exemplified by the Afridi thus retains the merging factor in all but the most important collateral instance, that of Father's Brother (*tray*) and his offspring, who are at once apart, marriageable, and hostile. It is here that its patrilineal bias is most evident.

For various reasons, in-depth genealogies or household census data in the field could not be collected and thus what is presented here about marriage results are mere normative statements by informants. Foremost among these reasons, of course, is the excellent one that one simply does not ask heavily armed Afridi or any other tribesmen any questions about their women.[6]

First, 'except for a few *maliks*' (community or clan and sectional headman), the great majority of Afridi are monogamous. Secondly, although divorce does occur, it is looked upon with disfavour. Finally, widow inheritance (marriage of a widow to her husband's younger brother) is normally practised, as elsewhere in Islam, if the widow is fairly young. If not, and if she has grown children, she is generally not remarried but remains in the household all the same. Shame and pride are both major considerations here, aside from the economic one of wanting to keep the widow's property in the family.

An estimated 20 per cent of the total marriages in any given village community (*kilay*) is with the female patrilateral parallel cousin. Again, this estimate was provided by informants, who also volunteered the information that marriage with one's *tarla* is no bar whatsoever to institutionalized hostility with one's *tarbur*, her brother. It was also made known on the offchance that a man and his *tarbur* get on well together, they refer to each other reciprocally not as *tarbur*, which carries built-in implications of enmity, but as *trayzwi* (literally Father's Brother's Son), which, evidently, does not. But we are also unfortunately unable to corroborate any cases of Father's Brother's Daughter marriage which were at the same cases of *tarbur* vengeance, although Ahmed has vividly outlined, for the Mohmand, the dilemma and the anguish

inherent in the offspring of such a relationship. We are fully in agreement with Ahmed that the problem is a crucial one in Pukhtun society,
not only with respect to the quandaries and paradoxes it poses to the
offspring of such unions but also with respect to the preservation of
the formal though essentially non-corporate lineage structure of the
Afridi.

There remain the remaining 80 per cent or so of marriages, alleged
by informants to occur in their great majority within the same sub-sec-
tion or sub-clan, whether this be physically located within the village
or, probably more likely, in another one outside it but not too far outside. It is also very common for such locally exogamous marriages to
be effected through direct exchange of sisters, among the Afridi, as no
bridewealth is paid thereby, and the only financial outlay is a negligible
one, on clothing. But intersectional or interclan marriage — among the
eight Afridi clans is rare, while extra-tribal marriage is impossible and
unthinkable. Although the *mahr* or brideprice as of 1977 was only a
token figure, Rs. 200 to 300, save among wealthier tribesmen, Ashraf's
notation that tribal Pukhtuns are generally reluctant to accept girls of
other tribes as wives owing to higher bridewealth may provide an
economic underpinning to what the Afridi might conceive as a social
unthinkability.[7]

* * *

It has been noted earlier that the quality of 'Pukhtun-ness' of 'doing
Pukhtu' as opposed to merely 'speaking Pukhtu', rests on three pillars:
agnatic or patrilineal descent (and its concomitant, a segmentary
lineage organization), Islam and Pukhtun Customary Law or *Pukhtunwali*. Here are the formal features and properties of the first of these,
based on the existence and acceptance by all concerned of a master
genealogy for all the Pukhtun tribes.

In brief, this master genealogy holds that all Pukhtuns are descended from a certain Qays, who is held to have lived in Arabia at the time
of the Prophet Muhammad. The latter, so the story goes, found him
in Medina, personally converted him to Islam and afterwards renamed
him 'Abd al-Rashid, after which he married the daughter of the famous
Arab Muslim general Khalid ibn al-Walid. As these events are believed
to have taken place only thirty generations ago, one can only conclude
that the longevity of the members forging the intermediate ancestral

links in the genealogy must have been incredible or, and far more likely, that considerable genealogical telescoping and foreshortening has
taken place here and there, to weed out the less consequential or
productive ancestors. In any case, according to one version of the overall genealogy (and there are several), this 'Abd al-Rashid (or Qays bin
'Abd al-Rashid) left three sons, from whom most of the Pukhtun tribes
in Afghanistan are descended, including the Mohmand and the Shinwari on both sides of the Pakistan-Afghanistan border. But there was,
ironically enough, also a foundling involved, named Karlanr, who ac-
creted or grafted himself into the genealogy. Karlanr himself left sons,
and one of the grandsons of the first son, Faridun, became the ancestor of the Afridi, while one of the grandsons of the second son, Wazir,
became the ancestor of the Wazir and Mahsud.[8] And these more than
any others are the prototypical Pukhtun tribes of today.

Among all Pukhtuns, and not only among the Afridi, a fundamental characteristic of their segmentary organization is that each tribe, at
whatever level of segmentation, has its common patrilineal and
patrilateral ancestor; and even if tribesmen may in fact greatly fore-
shorten the genealogical distance separating themselves from him, this
fact in no way invalidates their claim to such descent.

The second characteristic of this segmentary organization is that
these tribes, the Afridi very much included, are segmentary in their
composition. This is to say that the whole corpus or body of the tribal
society is made up of segments which are related to each other, or, to
express it in their own idiom, their genealogical lines resemble the
branches of a tree which lead to its main trunk. We may explore this
crucial and fundamental point more closely by looking at the internal
composition of one of the eight Afridi clans or maximal segments: the
Adam Khayl, Aka Khayl, Kuki Khayl, Qambar Khayl, Malik Din Khayl,
Kamar Khayl, Sipah and Zakha Khayl. Before doing so, however, we
may note in passing that the term *khayl*, denoting a lineage segment at
virtually any level, permeates the whole pyramidal edifice, or, perhaps
better, scaffolding, of Afridi social structure and has been referred to
by Ahmed as an integral feature of *nang*-type ('honour-type', as embodied by free tribesmen in the Agencies), as opposed to *qalang*-type
('tax-type', as embodied by the strongman Khanats to the north, Swat,
Dir, Bajaur, etc.), Pukhtun tribal organization. The suffix-*zai* (such as
Yusufzai, Barakzai) is generally identified with the *qalang* end of the
scale on which Pukhtun socio-political structure perpetually oscillates,
while the use of the *khayl* suffix clearly puts the Afridi into the *nang*

bracket – a fact independently confirmed by most if not all other features of their socio-political organization.[9]

The example pursued in depth is that of the Zakha Khayl, for historical reasons which will become apparent later, as they reflect integrally, in microcosmic form, the macrocosm of the whole Afridi segmentary system. If the Afridi as a whole can be regarded as Segmentary Level I, then the eight clans or maximal sections, the Zakha Khayl among them, may be regarded as Segmentary Level II.

Figure 1.1

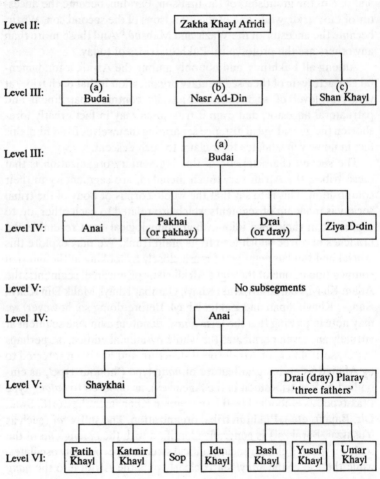

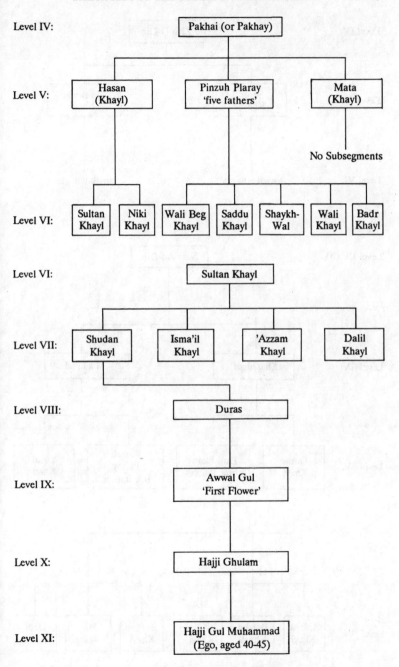

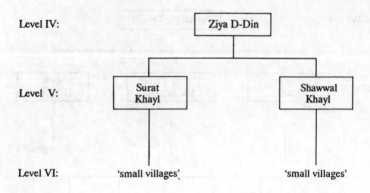

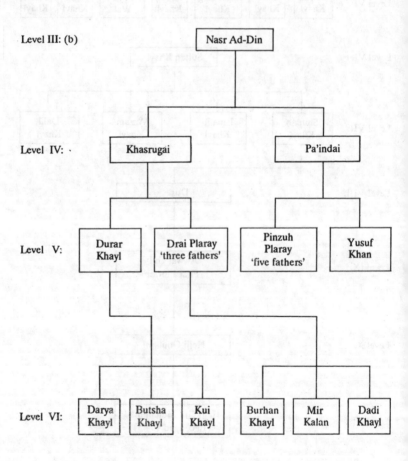

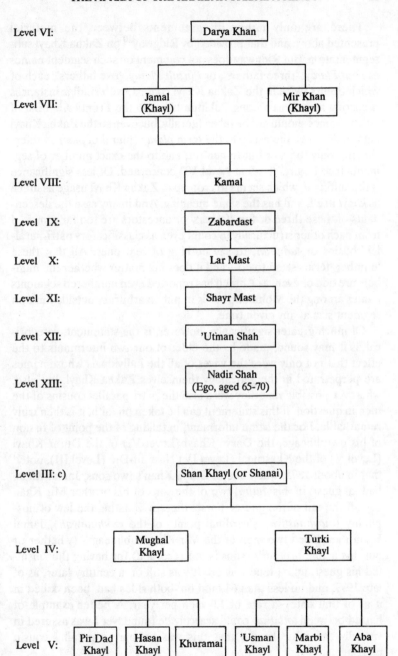

There are only minor disagreements between the material presented above and that provided by Ridgway[10] on Zakha Khayl sub-segmentation. But Ridgway does not comment on such segment names as *Drai Plaray*, 'three fathers', or *Pinzuh Plaray*, 'five fathers', each of which occurs twice in the Zakha Khayl context, with similar instances occurring as well as among Pukhtun tribes in the Frontier.[11] First of all, the names should not be taken literally, but even so the Zakha Khayl data underscore the usage of the term *plaray* (plural of *plar*) as referring not only to pater but to genitor, and to the exact number of segments (see Figure1.1, all at Level VI) concerned. Of less significance is the suffix *-ai*, which seems to crop up in Zakha Khayl usage as much as *khayl* itself, and has the same meaning. And in any case the descendants of these three or five 'fathers' or ancestors are too far removed from each other structurally to count even as classificatory patri-parallel cousins or *tarburan*, to say nothing of real ones. All that these 'number' terms seem to do — and it does not matter whether the numbers are odd or even, as Ahmed has reported even numbered segments names among the Mohmand[12] — is to put an arbitrary outside limit on segment size at any given time.

Of much greater significance, however, is the statement, categorical as it may sound, made by the elder of our two informants to the effect that not only were the wives of all the individuals whose names are perpetrated in the genealogy themselves Zakha Khayl, but also, wherever possible that they were also the patri-parallel cousins of the men in question. If this statement can be taken on faith, it is then truly remarkable. For the same informant, in talking of the point of fission of his own lineage, the Darya Khayl (Level VI) of the Durar Khayl (Level V) of the Khasrugai (Level IV) Nasr ad-Din (Level III), noted that in about 1875, when one of Darya Khan's two sons, Jamal Khan, had a guest in his *hujra*, two of the sons of his brother Mir Khan cut off the tail of the guests' horse, thereby violating the law of hospitality (*maylmastiya*, a cardinal point of the *Pukhtunwali*), Jamal Khan then killed two men of the Mir Khan sublineage (whether or not his actual brother's sons is not recorded) for having thus insulted his guest, and a feud was on. It was still on a century later, as of late 1977, and no less than 61 men on both sides had been killed in it as of that date — a rate of 1.6 men per year. A better example of hatred between *tarburan* could scarcely be found, yet I was assured in virtually the same breath that this was no bar to parallel cousin marriage.

Another and more important reason for having selected the Zakha Khayl as our segmentary example is the fact that early in 1908 the British carried out the last in a series of at least eight 'punitive expeditions' against the Afridi (since 1850), and in this instance, the Zakha Khayl, who had been raiding the settled districts around Peshawar with more than their normal wont. Although this final expedition was more a footnote to the major Frontier conflagration of 1897-8, when the British had actually invaded the Afridi heartland of the Tirah, where they encountered the most savage resistance they had experienced up to that time on the Frontier, what is noteworthy about it is precisely that it was directed against the Zakha Khayl alone. The other seven Afridi clans were fed up with the behaviour of the Zakha Khayl who in any case had never even made a token surrender in 1898, and in a major council meeting or *jirga*, numbering 600 men from each clan except the Adam Khayl and the Aka Khayl, or 3000 men all told, on 28 February 1908, they agreed to hold themselves jointly and severally responsible for the future good behaviour of every section and subsection of the Zakha Khayl. In translation, this was a masterpiece both of tribal justice and of segmentary organization, and it is worth recording in detail.[13] This *jirga* visited all the Zakha Khayl settlements and finally returned to Jamrud on 3 April. Except for a particularly notorious Zakha Khayl raider named Multan, who had taken refuge as a *mafrur* or proclaimed offender across the Afghan border in Jalalabad, they brought with them every other Zakha Khayl raider of the day as well as all the loot (rifles, jewellery, and money) that they had forced them to disgorge, amounting to Rs. 53,03,994/9. Now the fine which had been imposed on the Zakha Khayl for their share in the 1897 uprising was Rs. 9000, which was eventually paid for them by the other clans, whose members had never recovered any of it, in itself an indication of their success in doing so on this occasion. The *jirga* deposited with Major (later Sir) George Roos-Keppel, the British Political Agent for the Khaibar and later the Governor of the North-West Frontier Province, thirteen rifles, valued at Rs. 5000 to 6000, as a guarantee that it would not allow Multan to return to the Tirah until he had been properly punished. On 19 April, they made a written statement to this effect, again in *jirga*.

Furthermore — and this is a point of particular interest — at the same original *jirga* of 28 February, the spelling out of the shared responsibility for future good behaviour on the part of the Zakha Khayl meant that:(1) the Malik Din Khayl Afridi were to be responsible for the Sahib

Khayl half of the Anai, the Pa'indai and the Jamal Khayl Khasrugai; (2) the Qambar Khayl Afridi were to be responsible for the Shan Khayl Zakha Khayl of Bara and the Tirah; (3) the Kuki Khayl and the Niki Khayl Pakhai Afridi (the latter evidently Zakha Khayl themselves as well) were to be responsible for the Muhibb Khayl half of the Anai Zakha Khayl; (4) the Sipah Afridi were to be responsible for the Ziya d-Din Zakha Khayl; (5) the Kamar Khayl were to be responsible for all the Khasrugai Zakha Khayl subsections save the Jamal Khayl (discussed in (1) earlier); and (6) the Khaibar Pakhai Zakha Khayl were to be responsible for the Bara Pakhai Zakha Khayl. Apart from indicating that probably two-thirds of the Pakhai Zakha Khayl subsections (located in two different areas) were innocent of the charges levelled at the rest of them and the rest of their fellow clansmen, this division of internal tribal responsibility provides us with an unrivalled example of balance and opposition at work and in action in a highly segmentary system. Aside from the fact (which is not of very great importance) that Roos-Keppel's information on Zakha Khayl segmentation is not entirely in agreement with our own, as given in Figure1.1, there is, unfortunately, no indication in the report about how long this shared responsibility may have lasted. We may, however, hazard the guess that it was probably unique in the annals of Frontier history.

Roos-Keppel notes, finally, that there was a deposit of 53 rifles in the Zakha Khayl *jirga*'s petition, and that these had to be extracted from them, 'a tedious exercise, as each person was most anxious that his brother's rifle, and not his own, be given up, while efforts were also made to induce the British to accept arms of local manufacture, with a very small market value'.[14] He concludes his report on the proud but paternalistic note that during the expedition not a man of the Khaibar Rifles force (organized originally by his predecessor Colonel Sir Robert Warburton) deserted, even though brother may have been fighting brother.[15] But then, unlike the conflagration of 1897-8, this was hardly a millenial uprising, and if any *mulla*-s (Qur'an teachers and readers) were involved, they were far from the centre of the stage. It was, rather, a totally secular exercise in chastisement, fully approved by the other clans, as the active participation in it of all of them save the Adam Khayl and the Aka Khayl (who are both too far away to have been affected) shows; they felt they had a legitimate grievance against the Zakha Khayl because the latter had wriggled out of paying their share of the collective fines accrued from the 1897-8 uprising, and that they had been left holding the Zakha Khayl baby.

Here the matter might be said to have ended: certainly from this point on the Kiplingesque references in the colonial literature and archives to the propensity for theft and raiding among the Zakha Khayl drop sharply. Indeed, it is pleasing to note that in the post-colonial period they have died completely, to the extent that the individual Zakha Khayl Afridi may even be regarded today as just one more Pakistani going about his business. But, as Roos-Keppel well knew, few matters of this sort ever ended among the Afridi, particularly at the time in question, and he provides a somewhat unexpected denouement, dated June 1912 and referring us to Yar Muhammad Khan, one of the 'big men' of the Malik Din Khayl.[16] Early that month one Safdar of the Malik Din Khayl attempted to poison an entire dinner party assembled at the house of 'Abd al-Rahman, also of the Malik Din Khayl, the rival and enemy of Malik Yar Muhammad Khan of Tshura in the Tirah. (Whether or not he stood in a *tarbur* relationship to Yar Muhammad Khan is not indicated.) One of the dinner guests was 'Usman of the Jamal Khayl subsection of the Khasrugai Zakha Khayl, described in the report as a prime cause of the British expedition to Zakha Khayl territory in 1908, a notorious raider and the most trusted Afridi agent of the Amir of Afghanistan, to which country a later Zakha Khayl *malik* in post-Independence times was also to defect, over the 'Pukhtunistan' issue, the Afghan claims to which were not recognized by Pakistan. However, the poison failed to have fatal effects and so Safdar quickly took refuge with Yar Muhammad Khan, to whom the instigation of the crime was widely (and probably correctly) attributed. On 13 June, 'Usman was killed at Tshura by Yar Muhammad Khan's men, who also put an end to Safdar shortly afterwards. 'Usman's murder caused considerable excitement among the Zakha Khayl of the Bara valley and aroused much animosity against Yar Muhammad Khan. Yet nothing could be actually proven, and as attested by Molesworth,[17] Malik Yar Muhammad Khan was still very much alive — and far more anti-British — at the time of the Third Anglo-Afghan War in 1919. Yet the case under review here shows him to have been a master in the art of killing two birds with one stone: a dangerous Zakha Khayl raider, possibly in order to win British approbation, and a lower-order lineage-mate or sectional or factional hanger-on who knew too much and whose presence might therefore have proven embarrassing. The whole scenario and script, indeed, would also have won the approval of a certain Sicilian organization which shall remain nameless.

*   *   *

We have dwelt at length on the segmentary organization of the Zakha Khayl Afridi, as it illustrates a number of cardinal points about that of Pukhtun tribesmen in general. But aside from the fact that an extraordinarily high percentage of Afridi (certainly over 90 per cent) are resident male members of the agnatic lineage or lineages associated with any given territory, a third major characteristic of Afridi society, and of Pukhtun tribal society in general, is its acephaly. The diffusion of power is extreme. As Emilio Blanco Izaga sagaciously observed about the Berber tribesmen of a very similar area, the Moroccan Rif, 'in a region where everyone is a personality, only a political order based on masses and not on individuals can produce results'.[18] The same is the case here, and very much so, for among the Afridi and their neighbours, the *jirga*, the council, which may literally consist of all the tribesmen, and certainly all the able-bodied ones, is the repository of power. Every family headman regards himself as a *malik* and is so regarded by others, even though there are only two hereditary *maliks* officially recognized as such by the Pakistani administration of the North-West Frontier Province for the Kuki Khayl, Malik Din Khayl, and Kamar Khayl in the Khaibar Agency while the Qambar Khayl and the Zakha Khayl, each had three until, as noted, one of the Zakha Khayl *maliks* defected to Afghanistan in the sixties as a result of the 'Pukhtunistan' issue — which has now in any case been completely killed by the Soviet invasion of that country. The Aka Khayl, Sipah and the Adam Khayl resident in the Khaibar Agency, on the other hand, have only one official *malik* apiece. The Afridi *jirga*, however, does not go to quite the extremes that the Mahsud one does, for a Mahsud proverb has it that if that tribe traditionally had 18,000 warriors, it also had 18,000 potential *maliks*.[19] Yet the 3000-man *jirga* of 1908 referred to earlier is nothing if not representative: it bespeaks an almost absolute state of egalitarianism, an egalitarianism rendered all the more striking by the fact that among the Afridi as among other Pukhtun tribes there is not a single man able to bear arms who does not bear them. Everyone is armed, and to the teeth, even if the great majority obtain their arms from the two or three hundred little factories which line both sides of the Peshawar-Kohat road as it runs through Darra Adam Khayl. The Afridi provide a very close approximation to the popular (and inaccurate, as it happens) American image of 'All Chiefs and No Indians'!

* * *

All major Afridi *jirgas* are held in the Jum'a Masjid, or Friday Congregational Mosque, at Bagh, in the Tirah, right after the noon prayer and after any oaths, which must be sworn on the Qur'an by accused individuals with one of their agnates to support their claim to innocence, are over. An elderly and respected spokesman, a *mashar* as opposed to a *kashar* or 'young hothead', is always selected in advance by the participants in order to officiate at any *jirga*. Nobody may refuse to attend a *jirga*, for if he does, a *lakhkar* or raiding party is formed at once to descend on his house and burn it, a fact which insures 100 per cent participation. Likewise, any murders which break a general truce or peace, *tiga* (literally, 'stone'),[20] are heavily sanctioned by the *jirga* through the levying of prohibitive fines, *nagha*, on the murderer or the burning of his house; and sometimes both.

Contending parties to any dispute sit apart from each other but near the main body of the *jirga* in order to air their grievances. When each side has done so, the *jirga* appoints some ten to twenty of its members as arbiters, and when they come to an agreement, the number of arbiters is then generally reduced to four or five. They now inform the *jirga* of their decision; and this decision is final. *Jirga* members are of course all armed, but no one would dare to fire his rifle or even threaten to do so. The Afridi take their *jirga*-s very seriously.

Each contending party has also had to give a certain number of rifles to the *jirga* as security or *damana*; and if either party does not accept the decision, it forfeits these rifles. If it accepts the decision, the rifles are of course returned to it. Every individual at feud has in his own interest a *damin* or guarantor, a man he can trust who represents him when he cannot himself be present. This guarantor is unpaid, but if he sees some default in the security, he may then collect. He must also avenge the death of the individual whom he is sponsoring should the latter be killed.

It is here worth introducing another concept, that of *sarishta*. This refers to the executive branch or arm of the *jirga* once a decision has been made; and it is formed either from among the members of a single clan, in the regulation of its internal affairs, or from several or indeed all eight of the Afridi clans jointly in order to enforce collective decisions of importance, especially those with respect to other clans or tribes. The *sarishta* is appointed primarily to ensure the *tiga* that the *jirga* has established. A *jirga* meeting over the hostility between two *tarburan*, for instance, is made up of men from other neutral lineages or communities and makes its collective decision after hearing each contending viewpoint.

A truce or *tiga*, realistically regarded by the Afridi as temporary in character, is effected in any area contested by two hostile factions. The *jirga* arranges it and then appoints a neutral but strong individual to see that the truce is kept. At the same time the *jirga* also establishes the amount to be paid to the *damin*, the guarantor of the truce. Should anyone break the *tiga* by committing a murder, the *damin* and the victim's agnates must jointly take vengeance on the killer's lineage; and the amount agreed in the *tiga*, known as *mutshalga*, is then paid by the killer's lineage-mates to the *damin*. However, if retaliation has already been exacted, the *jirga* then usually reduces the amount of the *mutshalga* by about half. But if the victim's agnates are willing to accept *saz* or bloodwealth, and usually they are not (it amounted to Rs.20,000 to 30,000 in 1977), then the full amount of the *mutshalga* is insisted upon and is generally paid. Both the Kuki Khayl and the Kamar Khayl clans were pointed out to the author as invariably insisting on the full amount even if revenge has been taken.

A commentary on factional hostility is now in order. Factions are known as *gundi*, and informants were unanimous in saying that at some unspecified time in the past, all eight of the Afridi clans as well as all fifteen of the Orakzai ones were grouped around the bitter rivalry between the Malik Din Khayl and the Qambar Khayl, and were either on one side or the other. It should be noted too that the Malik Din Khayl and the Qambar Khayl are both held to be descended from brothers who were themselves the sons of a single father, Miramat Khan; and hence they are both, logically, Miramat Khayl. However, with the passage of time, the two brother clans, in good *tarburwali* style, began to fight bitterly against each other. What happened was that two *gundi*-s as factions were formed around each of the participants, and that these factions acquired names, the Samil faction which crystallized around the Malik Din Khayl and the Gar faction which did so around the Qambar Khayl, (Figure 1.2, page 19).

These two factions, Samil and Gar, were conceived as permanent and as existing, under different names, all over the present day Pukhtun tribal territory. In Waziristan and that part of eastern Afghanistan immediately adjacent to it (Paktya Province), the Samil faction is held to be called *Spin Gund*, 'white faction', while the Gar faction is known as *Tor Gund* 'black faction', recapitulating the white-black dichotomy which is most crucially embodied in the concept of female honour, even

Figure 1.2:

FACTION A: SAMIL OR SAMAL	FACTION B: GAR
1) MALIK DIN KHAYL	QAMBAR KHAYL
2) Other AFRIDI Clans	Other AFRIDI Clans
ZAKHA KHAYL	ADAM KHAYL
SIPAH	KUKI KHAYL
AKA KHAYL	
KAMAR KHAYL	
3) ORAKZAI Clans:	ORAKZAI Clans:
'ALISHAYRZAI	MAMUZAI
MULA KHAYL	'ALI KHAYL
SHAY KHAN	MASUZAI
FAYRUZ KHAYL	A-KHAYL
'ABD AL-'AZIZ KHAYL	MANI KHAYL (Shi'a)
BAR (Lower) MUHAMMAD KHAYL(Shi'a)	SIPAYA (Shi'a)
	STURI KHAYL
4) Settled Districts:	Settled Districts:
MOHMAND of Peshawar	KHALIL (Paykan)
(Landai, Arbab)	

the attempted violation of which is punishable by the death of both parties.

At any rate, such is the situation as presented by informants. To what extent, however, it actually corresponded, whether totally or partially, to a real situation on the ground may very well be another matter. Here a further consideration is in order: that of size. If we go by the 1910 population estimates given by Ridgway at a time when these factions may still have been active,[21] it is patently obvious that for the Afridi at least, the manpower of the Gar faction (with three clans and 13,700 men) was only two-thirds that of the Samil faction (with five clans and 19,200 men). As for the involvement of the Orakzai, although the number of clans was almost equal on each side, informants specifically stipulated that two-thirds of their total manpower was pulled into the Samil orbit, with only one-third in the Gar one. So whatever may be said of the *de jure* equality, plus balance and opposition of clans between the factions, this was certainly not the case in a *de facto* sense.

Nonetheless, even if the Samil-Gar factions can no longer be truth-fully said to exist today, there is still little love lost between the Malik Din Khayl and the Qambar Khayl. As late as 1967, the two clans had a clash over land ownership in Arjali Nadi, in the Kajuri Plain area near Bara Fort. According to the Malik Din Khayl, the land in ques-tion was acquired illegally by the Qambar Khayl, who had started to build houses on it. It was this housebuilding in particular which the Malik Din Khayl contested. The Qambar Khayl villages were or had been regularly attacked and set on fire by the Malik Din Khayl, and in colonial times the British often had to intervene, not through choice but because the scene of battle was dangerously close to the Settled Districts. But since Independence many tribesmen have purchased land in the Settled Districts and go back and forth to their Tribal Agency houses as per the *dwa kora* or 'two houses' principle. It might also be added that the Settled Districts were also a major point of refuge if either side was getting the worst of it in a feud; and it was normal to send women and children there if a feud was raging.

Any permanent alliance, as conceived by informants, of the clans within the Samil faction *vis-a-vis* those within the Gar faction by no means completely precluded fighting within the faction. At about the end of World War II, heavy fighting broke out between the Zakha Khayl and the Aka Khayl over the Matrai area, a pass between two mountains which borders a big forest and which is hence of some strategic importance. What seems to have happened in fact is that the stronger Zakha Khayl had simply 'muscled in' on the territory of the weaker Aka Khayl, and the latter were not strong enough to fend them off. Nearly fifty people were killed and the case was only settled about 1950-1 by a full-scale tribal *jirga*. But in the settlement of the case, the Zakha Khayl wound up with the lion's share, two-thirds of the Matrai forest as opposed to the one-third of the Aka Khayl. We might add that the Zakha Khayl informants who were present grinned when this was mentioned. Consistent with this is the fact that, wherever possible, a major objective in feud is to capture one's opponents' water supply.[22]

A further note on feuds,(not a final one, as the subject is inter-minable), is that the Malik Din Khayl informants — and the Malik Din Khayl are generally regarded as the most peaceful and level-headed of the Afridi clans — estimated that there is normally only about one death every six months resulting from them. They opined that the same is true of all other Afridi clans save the Zakha Khayl, among whom the death rate through violence and feud may be somewhat higher. As noted, most feuds are intra-village in that they are restricted to the village of the participants and/or occur between men who stand in a *tarbur* relationship to each other. Inter-village feuds, those between two villages, occur but are less common; for the wider any dispute becomes the longer it takes to settle. Sometimes, informants noted, a feud may break out between full brothers, of the same mother and father. As noted constantly and consistently, it is the norm for them to do so between the sons of these brothers: while in no way impending parallel cousin marriages, the problem, with its core issue of 'We marry our enemies', can indeed become a major dilemma for the actors. The uterine kinsmen and the affines of the members of a feuding lineage or sublineage only tend to give it moral support rather than active support — unless the affines in question also happen to be agnates through Father's Brother's Daughter marriage. In this case the involvement of all parties concerned is automatic and total.

* * *

The cardinal principles of the *Pukhtunwali*, or Pukhtun Customary Law, one hospitality *(maylmastiya)*, the right of asylum for anyone who seeks it *(nanawati)* and vengeance *(badal*, from an Arabic root meaning 'to exchange'), for the pursuit of which, as we have seen, the Afridi show a very marked predilection. Its causes are generally reducible to money, women and land; and in theory, unless *tarburwali* rules it out, any member of a feuding lineage may avenge the death of an agnate. If A kills B, all the agnatic members of both lineages are automatically involved; but an informant noted that the agnates of B, the victim, make it, typically, a practice not to gun down A himself but rather the most influential or wealthy member of his lineage or lineage segment. They recognize the stipulation by the Shari'a that the law of talion may be exercised and that the original killer be killed in return, but often some license is taken here, thus underscoring the thoroughly agnatic character of the feud.

Wounding is indemnified according to the degree of the wound, while threatening a person with a knife or drawing a bead on him and then not pulling the trigger is considered *sharmana*, shameful on all counts. It is made good only by enforced hospitality, in which the *jirga* forces the guilty party to slaughter one or more sheep in order to ask his would-be victim for pardon. The number of sheep required for sacrifice is directly proportional to the number of *jirga* members present, as all must eat .

Among the Afridi, fines or *nagha* have always been imposed and payable in money, in contrast to the situation prevailing among the Wazir and the Mahsud, among whom they may also be levied in rifles, livestock or any other marketable commodity, allowing theoretically for greater latitude. But as noted, if any fine, as stipulated, is not paid, an assembled *lakhkar* burns the house of the murderer or other offender, and indeed may even do so, using its own discretion, if the fine *is* paid. In a society such as this one, there is no need to belabour the point that sanctions must be prohibitively heavy. But the Afridi, by and large, meet the demands of their *Pukhtunwali* and adhere to the letter of their law. Informants uniformly mentioned that there are more criminal cases committed or recorded in Peshawar City in two weeks than there are in Afridi land in a whole year! The guns that they all carry thus serve more as preventive medicine than as a cure.

Like all tribal Pukhtuns, the Afridi have Hindu or Sikh clients-in-residence, called *hamsaya*-s, who are not occupational specialists but who run errands for their protectors, carry out commissions for them and the like, and who are totally exempt from *Pukhtunwali* and all that it stands for. As the proverb has it, 'they do not carry guns and exist only to serve us'.[23] Their Afridi protector or *naik* is always a powerful individual, and their houses are always huddled next to his; but should he not be particularly so, then his section assumes the *naik*-ship jointly.

Ahmed has likened Pukhtun Islam in general to the 'muscular Christianity' of the Victorian era and the Afridi are no exception to this: 'a laic, uncomplicated surface reaction to an inherited tradition that is suspicious of dogmas, debates and formalized priesthood'.[24] We need only recall the story, no doubt apocryphal, that the Pukhtuns recount themselves about the *mula* or *pir*, the holy man who went to the Afridi of the Tirah and reprimanded them for not possessing a single saint's shrine or *ziyarat*. The solution made by the Afridi to this problem was to kill the *mula* on the spot and to build over his remains the first such shrine in the region.[25]

In colonial times *mula*-s and *hajji*-s or pilgrims to Mecca could and often did become millennial and charismatic, though ephemeral, leaders of the Pukhtun *jihad* against the British (particularly 1897-8), but since Independence and Partition in 1947 their influence has dwindled to the village-level proportions where it originated and where they participate integrally in the religious aspects of rites of passage (such as birth, circumcision of boys, marriage, and washing and preparation of corpses before burial). There are at least three shrines today in Afridi land of minor importance, and two major mosques, the Friday Congregational Mosque at Bagh in the Tirah, as noted, and the 'Ali Masjid mosque on the bus route through the Khaibar. No non-Afridi has ever seen the former, it would appear, but the latter is an appealing little 'gingerbread' structure in the Mughal architectural tradition (bulging dome and slender minarets with bulging apices), with a green tile roof, located right at the bottom of a Khaibar valley. The mosque is certainly not over a century old, as it was not there in the time of the Second Anglo-Afghan War (1878-81). But lack of antiquity does not necessarily mean lack of attraction. It commemorates a spot where the Caliph 'Ali, the son-in-law of the Prophet, is held to have stopped to pray. Otherwise, it is only in the Khaibar that Afridi villages also have small village mosques. Elsewhere, and especially in the Tirah, everyone prays at home, particularly at night, so as not to have to leave the safety of his own house. The exception is, of course, the Friday noon canonically decreed communal prayer in the mosque at Bagh and the *jirga* meeting which follows it, at which prayers are always said for the success of the task that the *jirga* has undertaken.

* * *

All tribal Pukhtuns have a strong business acumen, which results necessarily from the fact of their very slender ecological resources. As noted, since Independence the transportation industry of Pakistan has been taken over by tribals, and a sizeable chunk of urban real estate in Peshawar is now owned by Afridi, while in recent years there has been much migrant labour to Saudi Arabia and the Gulf Emirates. There is thus a permanent necessity for trade, business, and a laissez faire attitude on the part of the government toward, for instance, smuggling, which is regarded by the Afridi as just one more aspect of business in general. Social change among the Afridi cannot be described as galloping, but there has, however, been a considerable increase in economic opportunities. We end, therefore, with a descriptive account of what has now become a very traditional Afridi business: the rifle factories at Darra Adam Khayl.

These factories are not only most interesting, but they certainly date back well into the last century (perhaps about 1860-70), as the colonial literature is replete with references to them. They are almost entirely owned and operated by the Adam Khayl, and they evidently did not arise in response to any particular urge to combat the British as *mujahidin,* but did so, rather, for the economic reasons just mentioned and also simply because the making of rifles and small arms appealed to Adam Khayl ingenuity. The Adam Khayl gunsmiths deal exclusively in small arms and side arms: rifles, pistols (even including a lethal little variety disguised as a ballpoint pen and labeled 'Made in Etaly' or 'Made in Iran'), shotguns and even stenguns. They do not, however, manufacture any automatic rifles, for the all-manual tools with which they work (hammers, chisels, vises, drills, hand-lathes, etc.) are simply not designed to produce them. The production of automatic weapons may not be beyond the competence of the Adam Khayl specialists, but it is certainly beyond their financial resources, and the various parts of each individual weapon are finished up in the empty lots behind the two to three hundred shops which line both sides of the road.

With respect to the division of labour, five to six men are needed to produce one rifle. One man makes the wooden stock and provides finishing touches and decorations to the other parts; another makes the bolt and trigger unit out of crude iron; a third makes the sight; and a fourth makes the barrel (or body). 'Re-browning', in order to obtain the rich walnut hue of the stock, is then done by a fifth man once the rifle has been assembled, but knowledge of how to do it is a trade secret and there are perhaps only five men up and down the whole street who are able to do the work involved. It only takes three or four days to produce a rifle, as all the necessary parts are available in the bazaar, while only one man is needed to produce a pistol or a stengun; but here again one of the experts must do the 're-browning' job. The shops are generally one-man or at most two-man operations and are by no means necessarily 'family businesses'. Success generally depends on a combination of practice, seniority, and experience.

In 1977 a British-style Lee-Enfield .303, the standard Darra-made rifle, cost a minimum of Rs. 1200 (in that year the currency equivalence was Rs. 9.75 per U.S. dollar), although it is the boast of the Darra gunsmiths that they can copy any rifle presented to them. One elderly informant even said that at one point during World War II the Darra factories were supplying small arms to the British Indian Army during a period of acute shortage (which, if true, is certainly a commentary on Free Private Enterprise and Afridi Industry for the Afridi . . .). The rifles are much in demand, and turnover is quick, but informants either chuckled or groaned when asked a leading question about the extent to which the Darra weapons could compete with standard Pakistan Army issue. In any case, as of July 1980 or possibly earlier, the BBC Overseas Service reported that the whole of the Darra output was being turned over to the *mujahidin,* the freedom fighters in Afghanistan in their incredibly brave struggle to oust the Soviet invaders and to topple the Communist government of Babrak Karmal. In this same connection, a wonderful remark made to the author of these lines in October 1977 by a Kuki Khayl Afridi, who also happened to be a retired Major in the Pakistan Army, to the effect that 'We Are Tribesmen First and Muslims Second' (said while brandishing his own Darra-made pistol) might just possibly, for current purposes, have to be given a priority reversal.

NOTES

1. This article is a recapitulation of a larger work entitled *The Afridi of the Pakistan North-West Frontier: Social Organization and History in an Eastern Pukhtun Tribe—with Comparative Moroccan Berber Window-Dressing.* In the present paper, however, no references are made to the previous fieldwork in Morocco. Field and library research in Peshawar and the Khaibar and Kohat Passes over the autumn and winter of 1977-8, as well as subsequent library and archival research in London at the India Office Library and Records, was carried out with the help of a grant from the Social Science Research Council, New York. In Peshawar, special thanks must be given to Ziyarat Shah, Malik Din Khayl Afridi an Informant Extraordinary, as well as to Muhibb ar-Rahman Kayani, the then Deputy Home Secretary of the North-West Frontier Province, for allowing the author to conduct long and detailed interview sessions in his office.

    Parts of this paper have already appeared as David M. Hart, 'Les Ait 'Atta du Sud-Centro Marocain: Elements d'Analyse Comparative avec les Pukhtuns (Afridi) du Nord-Ouest Pakistanais', in Gellner, Ernest (editor), *Islam, Societe et Communaute Anthropologies du Maghreb,* Les Cahiers du CRESS No. 12, Editions du Centre National de la Recherche Scientifique (C.N.R.S.), Paris and Aix-en-Provence, 1981, pp. 55-70.

2. Barth, Fredrik, 'Pathan Identity and Its Maintenance', in idem, ed., *Ethnic Groups and Boundaries,* Little, Brown, Boston, 1969, pp. 117-34; and in idem *Features of Person and Society in Swat: Collected Essays on Pathans,* Collected Essays of Fredrik Barth, Vol. II, Routledge and Kegan Paul, London, 1981, pp. 103-20.

3. Pakistan Narcotics Control Board, *Opium Smoking in NWFP: A Survey Report,* PNCB, Islamabad, August 1975.

4. The Afridi terminology shows a general but not total conformity with the listing provided by Lorimer and Acheson J.G., *Customary Law of the Main Tribes of the Peshawar District,* Vol. XVII, Government Stationery and Printing, Peshawar, 1934, pp. 1-2.

5.   Ahmed, Akbar S., *Millennium and Charisma Among Pathans*, Routledge and Kegan Paul, London, 1976, pp. 43-4; *Social and Economic Change in the Tribal Areas, 1972-1976*, Oxford University Press, Karachi, 1977, pp. 17, 39 ; and especially *Pukhtun Economy and Society,* Routledge and Kegan Paul, London, 1980, pp. 5-7, 71-7, 91-4, 181-202.

6.   I was even told the story that although in the late fifties on a drive through the Khaibar, no less a personage than the King of Thailand wanted to stop and take pictures of Afridi ladies washing clothes and getting water, he soon desisted when he found the rifles of most of the members of a substantial Zakha Khayl community just off the pass road trained upon him. The presence of the Political Agent was needed in order to extricate him from his predicament.

7.   Ashraf, Khalid, *Tribal People of West Pakistan: A Demographic Survey of a Selected Population*, Publication No. 9, Tribal Area Studies-1, Board of Economic Inquiry, Peshawar University, Peshawar, 1962, p. 55.

8.   Caroe, (Sir) Olaf, *The Pathans, 550 B.C.-A.D. 1957,* Macmillan, London, 1958, pp. 3-24.

9.   Ahmed, op.cit., 1977; and 1980, p. 58.

10. Ridgway, Maj. R.T.I., *Handbook for the Indian Army: Pathans*, Superintendent of Government Printing, Calcutta, 1910, pp. 57-71.

11. Caroe, op.cit., 1958.

12. Ahmed, op.cit., 1980, p. 132.

13. *India Office Records*, L/P&S/10/46, Political and Secret Department, Separate Files, No. 1776, Part 2; NFW: *Zakha Khayl Affairs 1884:* No. 249, Roos-Keppel, PA Khaibar to Willcocks, *Report on Completion of Zakha Khayl Settlement made at Walii*, 28 February 1908. Also ibid., No. b-37, Roos-Keppel to Mullahy, 3 March 1908.

14. Ibid.

15. It would be of interest in this context, to have further details on the exact composition of the Khaibar Rifles at this critical time, especially with respect to proportion of Zakha Khayl sepoys as compared with those from the other clans.

16. *India Office Records,* L/P&S/10/200, Political and Secret Department, Separate Files, No. 46, Part 1: *Afghan and N-W Frontier Diaries (1912-1913)*, pp. 2947, 1912; Source: Lt. Col. G.E. Roos-Keppel, Memorandum of Information received and signed A.H. Grant, Deputy Secretary to Government of India.

17. Molesworth, Lt.-General G.N., *Afghanistan 1919: An Account of Operations in the Third Afghan War*, Asia Publishing House, London, 1962, pp. 99-109.

18. Hart, David M., *Colonel in the Rif*, Emilio Blanco Izaga, editor and translator, 2 Vols., HRAFlex Books, MX3-001, *Ethnography Series*, Human Relations Area Files, Connecticut, New Haven, 1975, pp. I:75, II:328.

19. Howell, Sir Evelyn, *Mizh: A Monography on Government's Relations with the Mashud Tribe,* First Edition, Government of India Press, Simla, 1931; Second Edition, Oxford University Press, Karachi, 1979, p. 96, n. 2. As expressed by Mahsud to the British 'Either blow us all up with cannon or make all eighteen thousand of us *nawabs'*. Howell reckoned this traditional figure to be only two-thirds of the total as of 1929.

20. This refers to 'a fixed date until which all hostilities between warring factions will be suspended. The tribe then ensures the implementation of the *tiga.* There is an interesting theory that this custom derives from a pre-Islamic Rajput practice of

writing an agreement on a stone and placing it at a place selected by the tribe'.
Ahmed, op.cit., 1977, p. 40, citing King, L.W., *Monograph on the Orakzai Country
and Clans*, Punjab Government Press, Lahore, 1900, p. 49.
21.   Ridgway, op.cit., 1910, pp. 50-6.
22.   Ahmed, op.cit., 1977, p. 27; and op.cit., 1980, p. 5.
23.   Ahmed, op.cit., 1980, p.160.
24.   Ibid., p. 168.
25.   Ahmed, op.cit., 1977, p. 50.

2

Hazarawal:
Formation and Structure of District Ethnicity

Akbar S. Ahmed

The creation of Pakistan in 1947 was a consequence of its leaders correctly assessing the political compulsions of Indian Muslims. Pakistan's chronic problems — including the breakaway of Bangladesh in 1971 — are a result of its leaders failing to appreciate its ethnic compulsions. The problem has assumed the form of a paradox for the central government: the greater the need to come to terms with the problems of ethnicity in Pakistan, the greater the tendency to dismiss them with ideological abstractions.[1] This is often done by claiming that the ideology of Pakistan is in danger. Neither the ideology nor the nature of the danger have been successfully defined since 1947. Clearly, ethnic tensions exist in spite of the fact that the majority of the nation belongs to one religion.[2]

The two major approaches to the question of ethnicity may be crudely categorized as 'circumstantialist' and 'primordialist'.[3] The first regards ethnicity as a dependent variable, created in the main by a combination of external interests and strategies, both ecological and political.[4] 'Ethnicity' to social scientists who approach it this way is shown to be essentially a political phenomenon'.[5] To those who adopt the 'primordialist' approach, ethnicity derives from and reflects elemental 'atavistic' loyalties and 'primordial attachments'.[6] Such writers stress that members of ethnic groups give equal attention to past memory and to future strategy. They are concerned with what has been called 'the dynamics of cultural autonomy'.[7] In this paper I explore another expression of ethnicity which may be called 'district ethnicity'.

HAZARA DISTRICT ETHNICITY

The formation of district ethnicity is neither a result of political allian-ces pursuing defined interests (circumstantialist) nor an expression of traditional loyalties (primordialist). District ethnicity is artificially created and fostered as a consequence of externally imposed ad-ministrative arrangements by a powerful central government. When the central authority is colonial, as in this case, its decisions become difficult for the concerned native parties to challenge.

The British acquired the areas constituting Hazara from the Sikhs in the mid-nineteenth century. Under the Sikhs these areas were asso-ciated with and part of their Punjab empire. The British created a sep-arate district to define the areas and called it Hazara.[8] The district was about 8,300 sq. km. and its population in the first *Census* (taken in 1869) was 343,929 (2,007,575 in the *1972 Census*). When the North-West Frontier Province was formed from the Punjab Province in 1901, Hazara was attached to it. There was an ethnic logic to the attachment, as the majority of the people of Hazara claimed Pukhtun origin. How-ever, they were in the process of forgetting their language, Pukhto.[9]

The defining of administrative boundaries laid the foundation for the transformation of local ethnicity. The district was the key ad-ministrative unit in British India.[10] When Hazara became a district, records of ownership, rights, births, deaths, and so on, specifically as-sociated individuals in the area with Hazara District. Four to five generations have come of age in the area the British named Hazara, and the people of Hazara, caught as they are between two large and aggressive cultures, have developed a new identity which they identify as 'Hazarawal', or 'person from Hazara'. This Hazara ethnicity as-sumes an exaggerated identity because it is caught between the two major ethnic groups in the northern half of Pakistan: the Pathans and the Punjabis.

Pathan society is in general a segmentary system based on genealogical charters and possessing a developed tribal code, the *Pukhtunwali*.[11] The tribe reflects egalitarianism in its political be-haviour and economic arrangements. The boundaries of its universe are defined in terms of the lineage and the tribe itself. In contrast, Pun-jabi social structure reflects a more settled and agricultural society.[12] Village boundaries define its universe, which is largely self-sufficient.

Although I refer to two major ethnic zones for the sake of simplicity, there are more extraethnic zones beyond and around Hazara. To the north, in the Gilgit Agency, are people who are neither Pathan nor Punjabi. To the east, there are Kashmiris. Central and South Asia meet in Hazara. Gilgit, which marks the boundary between them, also borders on Hazara at the Babusar Pass, north of the Kaghan valley. Hazara is thus a cultural and geographical 'transition zone' or 'shatter zone'.[13]

The Hazara model is one of ethnicity artificially created by colonial administrative arrangements which incorporate socially and economically distinct groups living in border zones between major cultural systems. It is therefore a system that incorporates the variety to be found in a transitional zone. The system sometimes achieves a successful cultural synthesis, sometimes not; it is in part tribal and in part peasant, remaining in the two worlds but not belonging to either of them. The Hazara model might appear to be unique but in fact it is not. The structural and organizational features of the Hazara model may be recognized in other areas of Pakistan, for example, in the district of Dera Ismail Khan. Conversely, the Derawal ethnicity (between the North-West Frontier Province and the Punjab) may be better understood with reference to the Hazara model.

Figure 2.1: **Ethnic Thrusts into Hazara:**
                Sixteenth to Twentieth Centuries

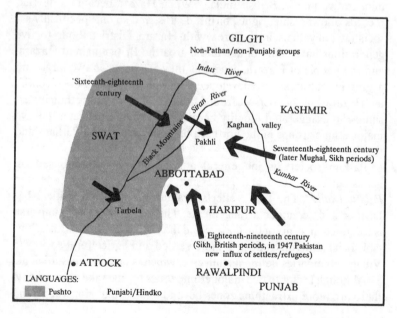

History is embedded in the genealogical charter of the tribes in the Tribal Areas.[14] In Hazara, ethnicity is embedded in the history of the district (Figures 2.1 and 2.2). The history of the areas now constituting Hazara reflects changing ethnic domination based on different religious affiliation. In the Middle Ages, the Turks and, following them, the Mongols, invaded Hazara; then the Mughals ruled Hazara and called it Pakhli Sarkar — a name that survived until the nineteenth century.[15] Swat Pathan tribes, themselves ousted by the Yusufzai Pathans, then invaded north Hazara and laid claim to its forests and valleys. Under Sikh rule, place names such as Haripur, derived from *Hari,* appeared in Hazara. Next the British ruled in Hazara, which explains names like Abbottabad (from Abbott, the first Deputy Commissioner of Hazara District in 1849). In 1947 Hazara became part of Pakistan.

Abbottabad, the headquarters and centre of Hazara, symbolizes ethnic diversity and, to some extent, ethnic accommodation. In terms of my argument, this implies the blurring of primordial ethnic boundaries and the creation of new ones. Numerous non-local settlers, including retired government officials, have bought land and built houses in the valley and live there as Hazarawal. National leaders, too, like Asghar Khan and Qaiyum Khan (both from Kashmir) and Begum Mahmooda Saleem (from the Punjab) have made Hazara their

Figure 2.2: **Ethnic Groups in Mansehra: 1980**

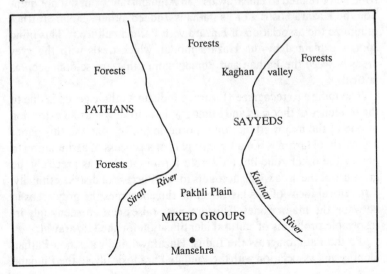

political base and have represented it in Parliament; they are now Hazarawals. For them, their district ethnicity is concrete and complete.

The changing fortunes and geographical limits of Hazara have created a mentality of compromise and accommodation among the people of the district. They are people of the middle way; there can be and are no rebels here. 'They have always been loyal' observes the Mughal Emperor Jahangir[16] of the people of this area. Hazara loyalty to central authority is reflected in modern Pakistani politics. In the sixties, Hazara generally supported the Muslim League headed by President Ayub Khan, a Tarin Pathan from Haripur. After his downfall, many Hazara politicians changed sides in the seventies to join Mr. Bhutto's leftist Pakistan People's Party. Today, by and large, Hazara supports the military government.

Although it was attached to the North-West Frontier Province, Hazara is mentioned only in passing by the standard books on the Pathans and the Frontier.[17] What appears to interest analysts of the Frontier are the famous tribes in the Tribal Areas, such as the Mohmands, Afridis, Wazirs, and Mahsuds, or the Yusufzai of the Peshawar valley. Anthropologists, too, appear to have overlooked Hazara. When he raised the important question of Pathan ethnic boundaries and boundary maintenance in Afghanistan and Pakistan, Barth[18] omitted mention of the Pathan groups of Hazara. He did discuss the Hazara tribe — not related to Hazarawals — in Afghanistan[19] but did not mention the Hazara District or its Pathans. Indeed, other scholars further minimize the association of Hazara with Pathan culture.[20] This blind spot is explained by the Hazara model, which deals with the grey areas *between* the Pathan and Punjabi zones that are seldom seen as critical.

The failure to recognize Hazara as a distinct ethnic group is due to the tendency of theorists and ethnographers to view it as an extension of one of the major ethnic zones bordering it. In contrast, this paper argues that Hazara is not a *stage* or part of a process of assimilation to one or the other zone but a discrete form in itself. It is precisely the greyness of the area which accounts for the success of district ethnicity. The critical focus of this investigation thus becomes the grey areas in between the major zones. This greyness raises certain seemingly irresolvable problems of cultural identification for the Hazarawal.

To the Pathan across the Indus, Hazarawal indicates non-Pathan identity and association with the Punjab. Paradoxically, to the Punjabi,

Hazarawal means a Pathan identity and association with the Frontier. Hazarawals, whether Pathan or not, confront this dilemma when they leave the Hazara Division. 'When we are in the Punjab they call us *"Khan Sahib"* [a Pathan] and when we are in Peshawar they call us "Punjabis". We don't know where we really stand but both groups disown us. Hazarawal is neither Pathan nor Punjabi'. This sentiment was quoted to me by many Hazarawals, including young Awan students as well as powerful Swati Khans.[21] Hazara ethnicity may be frustrating and create ambiguity, but it has its advantages.

The benefits that accrue from the Hazarawal identity are many and varied. Although the foundations for district ethnicity were laid in the middle of the nineteenth century, the concept found its fullest expression after Independence in 1947. The people of Hazara — neither quite Pathan nor quite Punjabi — discovered they could use their situation to advantage. For instance, the Hazarawals in Frontier politics form a natural and distinct group, balancing the extreme Pukhtun nationalists of the National Awami Party (Peshawar and Mardan districts), on the one hand, and the religious party of the southern districts (Bannu and Dera Ismail Khan), on the other. As a result, the Hazarawal lobby has skilfully obtained key positions for members it puts up as compromise candidates, including the chief ministership of the province. The lobby also successfully upgraded Hazara District to Division status in 1973. The upgrading meant a corresponding increase in government employment, educational institutions and projects, and so on. Hazara emerged as the fourth Division of the Frontier province, along with Peshawar, Dera Ismail Khan, and Malakand. The upgrading was seen as a triumph for the Hazara lobby. Recently, a medical college was acquired for Abbottabad as a result of Hazarawal lobbying. The Hazara lobby also keeps a jealous eye on and firm control of its forests. For instance, the Hazarawal lobby pressed for the forest minister's post in government. Hazarawals also apply pressure through political and official networks on those officials disinclined to go along with their demands for illegal cutting of their own timber. Uncooperative forestry officials thus find themselves facing premature transfer, or even retirement.

Hazarawal ethnicity has provided a base for returning individuals, too. Gohar Ayub Khan, the son of President Ayub Khan, returned to Hazara to contest the 1977 elections after a long absence spent making his fortune in Karachi. Rejecting association with any one Hazara group, he appealed to broadbased Hazara ethnicity, both Punjabi and

Pathan. In turn, he was seen as being in a position to benefit Hazara Division through his economic and political connections throughout Pakistan. By winning a seat in the National Assembly against a candidate of Mr. Bhutto's Party, he has emerged as a serious candidate for high office in Pakistan.

Although the expression of Hazara district ethnicity serves to suppress primordial attachments, they may re-emerge in the context of political conflict internal to Hazara, as will be seen later. In Hazara, primordial attachments that are presumed to have faded are activated as a result of circumstantialist factors. The Hazara case thus illustrates an important structural component in the dynamics of ethnicity. As Fortes[22] argues,

> ethnicity is now widely recognized as a 'diacritical' element in intergroup and (at some levels) inter-individual relations in all politically or economically stratified or segmented societies, whether or not they conform to the Furnivallian model of the plural society. Ethnicity or quasi-ethnicity can appear as a 'diacritical marker' of structural divisions even in traditional tribal societies . . . [The diacritical markers are connected] with differential rights of access to scarce resources, be they merely means of subsistence or the goods and services, the legal statuses or mobility opportunities, and so forth, of modern industrial societies.

In the Hazara case, as in modern industrial societies, the right of access to scarce resources lies at the root of the ethnic problem, both in relations of conflict between Hazara and other major ethnic groups as well as in conflict among the groups constituting Hazara.

DIACRITICAL FEATURES IN HAZARA SOCIETY

Beneath its district ethnicity Hazara society remains polyethnic, reflecting what has been termed 'structural pluralism'.[23] For purposes of analysis let me divide the people of Hazara into two broad categories, the 'dominant' and 'dominated' groups. The dominant group includes the traditional leaders of society, the Pathans(from Swat, hence Swatis) and Sayyeds. The dominated group includes the other groups in Hazara, such as Awans, Gujars, Tanaulis, Mughals, and refugees (from India). The dominated group is exclusively non-Pathan, and of these the Awan and Gujar are the most populous and important. They have a famous saying: 'Hazara district is difficult to live in' *(zilla Hazara mushkil guzara)*. Thus, there is a clear ethnic basis for social and economic divisions within Hazara society.

Hazara society has created stereotypes for each group, and the individual is expected to behave accordingly. The stereotypes are sometimes reduced to social caricature: for example, a Swati Pathan must be aggressive, a Sayyed must be gentle, and an Awan or Gujar must 'know his place' (i.e., be humble). Pathans are expected to be headstrong or obstinate in conformity with their belligerent reputation. Gujars are considered the most lowly and have been hitherto 'invisible'.[24]

Although other cultural models offset it, the dominant ideology in Hazara remains that of the Pathans, with its characteristic martial values of bravery and honour, in spite of the recent emergence of primordial ethnicity among the dominated group. Other Hazara groups have until recently accepted the status of the Pathans, in an implicit admission of Pathan hegemony. Recent awareness of separate ethnic identities has not yet created a separate ideological framework for the Awan or Gujars. Both are aware of their own identities as distinct from the Pathan but still tend to identify with Pathan values and ideas. Ethnic consciousness has not yet created ideological distinctiveness. Although Pathans may no longer explicitly dominate Hazara, their ideology remains the pre-eminent cultural framework for the Hazara groups.

As a result of this dominant Pathan ideology, there has been a clear 'Pathanization' or 'Swatiization' process of social mobility at work in Hazara, similar to Sanskritization in India.[25] The Awans, in general conversation, identify themselves as Pathans, freely using Khan to signify Pathan origin after their names, while the richer Gujars often refer to themselves as Awans. Both groups have undeniable origins in the Punjab.

Historically the Pathans have monopolized the forests and the fertile valleys to build a sophisticated system of irrigation for their fields. They pushed the Gujars to the poorer lands on the hilltops where there was no irrigation and where their single crop depended entirely on rainfall. The Gujars perforce remained poor herdsmen.

The spokesmen of Pathan society are the Swati Khans, who often own hundreds of acres of forest lands and used to own thousands. These Khans were often known by the forests they owned, as were the Khans of Tanglai, Giddarpur, and Agror. Poorer Swatis are critical of the bigger local Khans for destroying the forests for their own purposes when in political power. The Khans are seen as selfish and power-hungry.

There appear to be numerous mechanisms in Hazara society for the dominant groups to perpetuate cultural boundaries and maintain exclusivity. Between different groups there are differences in life-style, demographic patterns, household arrangements, cultural values, and even clothes. There is strict endogamy in Hazara. Marriages are ideally contracted within the ethnic group and rarely outside it. The ideal is only now breaking down in individual cases, due to the general economic affluence of the dominated group and the decline of the dominant group.

Language is jealously preserved by Pathan groups as *their* language. Pushto is a key criterion defining Pukhtun ethnicity [26] and therefore is necessary for Pathans to maintain in the face of strong extraethnic influences. But it is significant to note that the younger Swati generations are forgetting Pushto, which creates certain dilemmas and tensions in their society. Although less than 50 per cent of Swatis speak Pushto, there remains a high awareness of the language as a diacritical feature. Only 7 per cent of Sayyeds, who rely on more universalistic features, speak Pushto, and the dominated groups do not speak Pushto at all. Hindko — akin to Punjabi — is spoken by the dominated group. Urdu is commonly understood and spoken throughout Hazara.

There is a clear correlation between genealogical memory and high status. Although junior and less important lineages invariably 'forget' or 'lose' ancestors, senior lineages retain their memory, 'telescoping' unimportant ancestors in the process. While 30 per cent of Swatis and 80 per cent of Sayyeds remembered the names of male ascendants up to four generations back, the figure for the Awans and the Gujars was zero.

There are other figures which correlate status and ethnicity. For instance, there is a correlation between high status and education (Table 2.1). Also, the dominant groups live in better housing than the dominated groups. Figures for the Swatis and Gujars clearly illustrate the point: the highest figure for houses with some cement construction is among the former, 27 per cent, and the lowest among the latter, 7 per cent. Twenty per cent of Sayyed and 12 per cent of Awan houses are cement. The general poverty in the rural areas is underscored by the fact that about 80 per cent of the total population still live in mud houses (Table 2.2). There is also a correlation between high status and land ownership. Swatis own the most land and Gujars the least (Table 2.3).

Thus, ethnicity inside Hazara has a multi-criteria base, which helps to explain the complex social situation in Hazara and the inter-ethnic relationships that prevail. Other factors such as physical characteristics are also important in defining ethnicity underneath the surface similarities of district ethnicity.[27]

Table 2.1: **Education: Secondary School and Above** (Percentages)

	Swatis	Sayyeds	Awans	Gujars
Yes	20	19	10	7
No	80	81	90	93

Table 2.2: **Housing Materials** (Percentages)

	Swatis	Sayyeds	Awans	Gujars
Mud	73	80	88	93
Cement	27	20	12	7

Table 2.3: **Land Ownership** (In acres)

	Swatis	Sayyeds	Awans	Gujars
Irrigated	1	1.8	.1	.1
Unirrigated	8.2	6.4	1.4	.7

But the traditional correlation of ethnicity and status in Hazara is being affected by changing national politics.

ETHNICITY AND THE DEMOCRATIC PROCESS

With democratic politics and adult franchise, benefits such as education are no longer seen as a monopoly of the dominant group. In fact, too rigid a proclamation of ethnicity may be counterproductive for Khans seeking votes from the dominated group. We thus observe a paradoxical trend in Hazara: while certain Swati Khans still maintain language and hospitality as symbols of primordial ethnicity, other Swati

Khans are busy discarding them and emphasizing unity in society based on Hazara district ethnicity. The shift in strategy is largely a response to the emergent and changing politics of Pakistan.

Change in Hazara society is a consequence of three factors: the national elections in 1970, which for the first time made the dominated group aware of its potential strength; the breakup of East Pakistan from Pakistan in 1971, which emphasized the importance of ethnicity in the society; and the labour migration of many members of the dominated group to the Arab States, which opened new sources of income for them and provided them with an escape from the traditional structure. These factors caused interconnected results in Hazara. The traditional model of society, the world view of the dominant group, was no longer accepted as universally valid, and, in consequence, there was a revival and rediscovery of ethnicity in Hazara groups. Many Hazarawals who had successfully completed the Swatiization process were rediscovering their primordial origins. As a result, a 'retribalization' process is apparent.[28] A good example is Sarfaraz Khan of Mansehra, a retired civil servant. When I was posted in Mansehra (1969-70), he called himself 'Sarfaraz Khan Swati' (even on his visiting cards) and was active in the politics of the Swati Pathans. He spoke Pushto and his hospitality was well-known. In 1980 he proclaimed his Awan origin and mobilized Awan voters around himself.

The regrouping around ethnic consciousness assumed a political form and provided a natural base for certain national political parties. For instance, the Pakistan People's Party and its leftist manifesto — and often populist politics — found willing followers among the dominated group. The impact of national and local politics sharpened social cleavages and ended with confrontations at various levels. The traditional order in Hazara was changing (Figure 2.3).

The dominated group awoke to their power in Hazara with the elections of 1970. Unlike the earlier periods, the Khans now went to the houses of the voters, however humble, to canvass. Well-known politicians of Pakistan, like Hanif and his brother Badshah, lords of the Hazara forests and ministers, visited small villages and wooed the dominated group. It was the twilight period of the Swati lords of Hazara. The incidents in the seventies, in which Pathan and Sayyed landlords, in the Siran and Kaghan forests respectively, shot and killed tenants in a desperate bid to turn the clock back, were probably the last of their kind in this area. The Sacha incident in the isolated Siran forests was a straightforward massacre of the dominated group.

The incident in Kaghan in 1974 was more complex and reflects the processes of social and ethnic change in Hazara. It was a consequence of the success of the recently introduced potato crop grown by the dominated group in the Kaghan valley, especially in the Batakundi area. Earlier, the Sayyed landlords had watched with interest the potato experiment among their tenant farmers. Once it was success- ful, they demanded half the crop according to custom. Backed by the Pakistan People's Party, the tenants refused. The Party's leaders came from outside Hazara and encouraged the tenants to stand firm. Encouraged by the national support and attention, the tenants took

Figure 2.3: **Changing Ethnic Status in Hazara**

TRADITIONAL

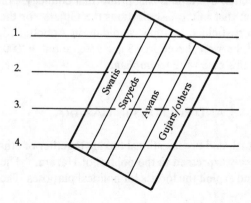

1. Landlords/politicians	Swatis
2. Senior government posts and professions (doctors, lawyers)	Sayyeds
3. Junior government posts (clerical)	Awans
4. Tenants/labourers	Gujars/others

TRANSITIONAL/CONTEMPORARY

1. _____
2. _____
3. _____
4. _____

Swatis / Sayyeds / Awans / Gujars/others

their potatoes directly to the market without paying their landlords any share. The landlords mobilized support and obstructed the tenants in the quarrels that followed. The landlords, who were well armed, gained the upper hand. In one incident 2 tenants were killed, 10 were injured, and 80 received mild injuries. The case was registered and numerous Sayyeds were arrested. Akbar Khan, a prominent Swati lawyer, represented the tenants. After a High Court acquittal, an appeal was made by the tenants and the Sayyed defendants spent six months in jail. However, the case concluded in favour of the Sayyeds.

Although they emerged victorious, the Sayyeds were shaken by the experience: 'We are now *mazloom* (oppressed) and the tenants are *zalim* (oppressor)', they said. The Kaghan incident provided an interesting example of ethnic lines being crossed and class lines being formed. During the entire episode the Swati tenants of Kaghan mobilized the Gujars and led the revolt against the Sayyeds. The incident also illustrates the intrusion of national politics into Hazara and the resultant ambiguity in the concept of district ethnicity in Hazara.

In a changing situation, the classical problem of legitimacy – how men are credited with the right to rule over others – is acute. In 1980 Akbar Khan talked of the forthcoming elections, to be held in the near future, or so it was rumoured. He emphasized his work and service to the community. His political base was in Mansehra town where the population is largely non-Swati. 'We are Hazarawals, not Swatis and Gujars', he stated. He wished to shift the base of leadership from 'ascribed' to 'achieved' status; from politics based on forest wealth – as exemplified by his rival Hanif Khan – to that of talent and public service. In spite of the posture and prognosis of Hazara leaders like Akbar Khan or Gohar Ayub Khan, the politics of Hazara may be heading in an opposite direction by emphasizing primordial ethnicity. For instance, it is significant that in the last elections the Gujars, for the first time in their history, fielded a Gujar candidate in Abbottabad. Although unsuccessful, he won the entire Gujar vote, about 10,000. Primordial loyalties in this case were triumphant.

ETHNICITY, FORESTS, AND POLITICS IN HAZARA

The semantic, conceptual, and organizational linking together of ethnicity and forests is nicely expressed in the politics of Hazara.[29] The big Swati Khans own and exploit the forests for political purposes. The more wealth a man extracts from the forests, the more extensive the networks he establishes and the greater his investment (and success) in politics. Success in politics, in turn, is reinvested into acquiring more forests. It is a cycle of success and corruption. The successful ones are the lords of the forests. But to many in Hazara — like Akbar Khan or Sarfaraz Khan — they are no more than 'thieves of the jungle' (jungle chor).

The relationship between forests and politics is clearly explicated in society. From time to time a landlord obtains an official permit from district forest officials to cut wood from the forest. He may end up cutting ten times the amount allowed on the permit. Stories of rags to riches as a result of cutting timber illegally circulate widely in Hazara. 'In the sixties some notable jungle chors drove old condemned jeeps; now they own Mercedes cars', Akbar Khan complained. There was a recent widely reported case in which a Khan fraudulently bought jungles in Kohistan worth 8,000,000 to 9,000,000 rupees and sold them to Karachi businessmen for enormous gains.

The new and expensive hotels which appeared in Hazara in the iate seventies and early eighties are the visible signs of financial success. The Sarband Hotel is said to have cost 7,000,000 to 8,000,000 rupees and is owned by a forest contractor of the Frontier province. The Zarbat, Gomal, Springfield, and Purush are also owned by forest contractors, one of them a Chief Minister.

The relationship between forests and politicians has made Hazarawals bitter about their politicians. Akbar Khan and Sarfaraz Khan complain: 'There were six ministers and one president (Ayub Khan) from Hazara, yet they did nothing for Hazara'. The bigger the chor, the bigger the politician, and vice versa, they say.

Those who stand to gain most from the wealth of the forests are the loudest in proclaiming Hazara district ethnicity. The Swati Khans traditionally own and claim access to the forests. They argue that the forests belong to Hazara and should be utilized by and for its people only. The owners have invested heavily in larger politics to ensure that their views prevail. On various occasions attempts to nationalize the forests or rationalize cutting have been sabotaged by the bigger Khans. By ensuring minimum administrative interference from outside Hazara Division, the Khans maintain their monopoly over the forests and their political dominance in Hazara. For them, district ethnicity — especially proclaimed outside Hazara — reinforces superior social and economic status inside Hazara. Conversely, for the dominated group, rediscovery of primordial ethnicity involves a reassessment of district ethnicity. They view the Pathans as manipulating district ethnicity to maintain their hold over the forests. The politics of ethnicity in Hazara are thus related to its forest wealth.

The flow between forests, ethnicity, and politics should now be apparent. People of all ethnic groups and economic classes are acutely aware of this flow and connection, and the crucial factor of ethnicity is never far from social or political activity (Figure 2.4).

CONCLUSION

This paper points out that in Hazara society two opposed trends with regard to ethnicity are articulated simultaneously: the formation of Hazara district ethnicity — the Hazarawal — and, underneath it, the survival of deeper primordial ethnicity. For general purposes, interaction *outside* Hazara by Hazarawals is marked by overt signalling of Hazara district ethnicity. However strong the primordial loyalties may be inside Hazara, the notion of Hazara district ethnicity has a momentum of its own. In part artificial, in part real, Hazarawal ethnicity defines the people of Hazara both to themselves and to outsiders.

It is too early to make a final comment on Hazara ethnicity. It is a complex and changing situation allowing large areas of anomaly and ambiguity. Emergence (as among the Awans and Gujar) and submergence (as among the Swatis) of ethnicity may derive from similar reasons — changing political or economic factors. The durability of Hazara ethnicity depends to some degree on the political trends of the country. There are three possible ways in which the situation might be transformed: by general elections where the question of supporting an ethnic candidate or the most suitable Hazarawal candidate is relevant;

Figure 2.4: **Flow between Ethnicity, Forests and Politics**

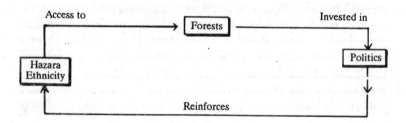

by a political revolution – an unlikely possibility in the near future – in which the dominated group, along with poorer members of the dominant group, challenge the established order through armed confrontation and attempt to overthrow it (ethnic cleavages will generally reinforce economic ones in this case); and finally, a continuation of the present system, Martial Law, where existing structures remain frozen. In the last event, Hazara district ethnicity will continue to be the dominant mode of articulation of regional politics. District ethnicity, I argue, is related to larger political developments in the nation.

NOTES

1. Because ethnicity is such a sensitive topic, traditional 'socio-economic' surveys have collected useful economic data but have ignored the ethnic factors in Hazara. See Hussain, M., *A Socio-Economic Survey of Village Baffa in the Hazara District*, Peshawar Board of Economic Inquiry, NWFP, Pakistan, 1958.

2. This is true of Muslims elsewhere, as in Malaysia. Different religions within national borders may further complicate ethnic problems. Muslims in south Thailand and the southern Philippines – or non-Muslims in the southern Sudan – are examples of this. See Barth, F., 'Pathan Identity and its Maintenance', in *Ethnic Groups and Boundaries: The Social Organization of Cultural Difference*, Barth, F., (editor), Allen and Unwin, 1970; Cohen, A ., *Two-Dimensional Man: An Essay on the Anthropology of Power and Symbolism in Complex Societies*, Routledge and Kegan Paul, London, 1974 (a) and *Urban Ethnicity*, (editor), ASA Monograph No. 12, Tavistock, London, 1974(b); De Vos, B., 'Ethnic Pluralism: Conflict and Accommodation', in *Ethnic Identity: Cultural Continuities and Change*, De Vos, G., and Romanucci-Ross, L., (editors), Mayfield Publishing, Palo Alto, CA, 1975; Geertz, C., *The Interpretation of Cultures*, Basic Books Inc., New York, 1973; Glazer, N., and Moynihan, D.P., (editors), *Beyond the Melting Pot*, MIT Press, Cambridge, 1965 and *Ethnicity: Theory and Experience*, Harvard University Press, Cambridge, 1975; Hsu, F.L.K., (editor), *Kinship and Culture*, Aldine, Chicago, 1971; Keyes, C.F., Introduction in *Ethnic Adaptation and Identity: The Karen on the Thai Frontier with Burma*, Keyes, C.F., (editor), Institute for the Study of Human Issues, Philadelphia, 1979 and *Ethnic Change* (editor), University of Washington Press, Seattle, 1981; Kuper, L., and Smith, M.G., (editors), *Pluralism in Africa*, University of California Press, Berkeley, 1969; Lambert, R.D., Ethnic/Racial Relations in the United States in Comparative Perspective, AAPSS Annals 454, 1981, pp. 189-205; Maybury-Lewis, D.H.P., (editor), *Dialectical Societies*, Harvard University Press, Cambridge, 1979; Nagata, J., (editor), *Pluralism in Malaysia: Myth and Reality*, E.J. Brill, Leiden, 1975; Schermerhorn, R.A., *Comparative Ethnic Relations: A Framework for Theory and Research*, University of Chicago Press, Chicago, 1978; Weiner, M., *Sons of the Soil: Migration and Ethnic Conflict in India*, Princeton University Press, Princeton, 1978; and Young, C., *The Politics of Cultural Pluralism*, University of

Wisconsin Press, Madison, 1979 and *Patterns of Social Conflict, State Class and Ethnicity,* Daedalus 3 (2), 1982, pp. 71-98.

3. Glazer, N., and Moynihan, D.P., (editors), *Ethnicity: Theory and Experience,* Harvard University Press, Cambridge, 1975.

4. Barth, F., 'Pathan Identity and its Maintenance', in *Ethnic Groups and Boundaries: The Social Organization of Cultural Difference,* Barth, F., (editor), Allen and Unwin, London 1970; Caplan L., *Land and Social Change in East Nepal,* University of California Press, Berkeley, 1970; Cohen, A., *Custom and Politics in Urban Africa,* Routledge and Kegan Paul, 1969 and *Urban Ethnicity,* ASA Monograph No. 12, Tavistock, London, 1974(b); Dahya, *et al.,* in Cohen, A., *Two-Dimensional Man: An Essay on the Anthropology of Power and Symbolism in Complex Societies,* Routledge and Kegan Paul, London, 1974(a); Foster, B., Ethnicity and Commerce, *American Ethnologist* 1, 1974, pp. 437-48; Haaland G., 'Economic Determinants in Ethnic Processes', in *Ethnic Groups and Boundaries: The Social Organization of Cultural Difference,* Barth, F., (editor), Allen and Unwin, London, 1970, pp. 58-73; and Leach, E.R., *Political Systems of Highland Burma,* London School of Economics, London, 1954.

5. Cohen, op. cit., 1974(a), p. 15.

6. Geertz, C., (editor), *Old Societies and New States,* Free Press, New York, 1963; and Parkin, D., *The Cultural Definition of Political Response:Lineal Destiny among the Luo,* Academic Press, London, 1978.

7. Parkin, op. cit., 1978.

8. The area was known by the Mughals as Pakhli. Hazara is said to derive from *ming* (a thousand) or *hazar* (the unit of the Mongol Army), used by Taimur's invading forces. But there are other theories: that the name derives from Abisara, a mountain chief who was a contemporary of Alexander, or even from Urag, a district mentioned in the *Mahabharata.*

9. Pukhtuns are called Pathan, and Pukhto is Pushto in Hazara. Both are Anglo-Indian corruptions and neither are used by Pukhtuns themselves.

10. *Gazetteer,* Hazara District (Settlement Census), and Hazara District, Peshawar, Government of Punjab, Lahore, 1883-4 and 1907; Woodruff, P., op. cit., 1965. For extended contemporary case-studies involving district principals in the Tribal Areas, see Ahmed, A.S., *Religion and Politics in Muslim Society: Order and Conflict in Pakistan,* Cambridge University Press, 1983.

11. Ahmed, A.S., *Millennium and Charisma among Pathans: A Critical Essay in Social Anthropology;* Routledge and Kegan Paul, London, 1976 and *Pukhtun Economy and Society: Traditional Structure and Economic Development in a Tribal Society,* Routledge and Kegan Paul, London, 1980; Barth, op. cit., 1970 and 1972; Caroe, O., *The Pathans, 550 B.C.—A.D.1957,* Macmillan, London, 1958; Raverty, H.G., *Notes on Afghanistan and Part of Baluchistan: Geographical and Historical,* Eyre and Spottiswoode, London, 1888; Spain, J.W., *The Pathan Borderland,* Mouton, The Hague, 1963.

12. Ahmed, A.S., *Mansehra: A Journey,* Ferozsons, Pakistan, 1974 and 'Hazara District: Land and Legend', in *Pieces of Green, the Sociology of Change in Pakistan,* Royal Book Co., Karachi, 1977; Ahmad, S., 'Peasant Classes in Pakistan', in *Imperialism and Revolution in South Asia,* Gough K., and Sharma, H.P. (editors), Monthly Review Press, New York, 1973 and *Class and Power in a Punjabi Village,* Monthly Review Press, New York, 1977; Alavi, H., 'Kinship in West Punjab

Villages', *Contributions to Indian Sociology,* (NS) 6, 1972, pp. 1-27 and 'Peasant Classes and Primordial Loyalties', in *Journal of Peasant Studies,* 1973, pp. 23-62; Balneaves, op. cit., 1955; Darling, op. cit., 1925, 1930, and 1934; Eglar, Z., op. cit., 1960; Ibbetson, op. cit., 1883; and Pettigrew, op. cit., 1975.

13. Barth, op. cit., 1953

14. Ahmed, op. cit., 1980.

15. Hugel, C., *Travels in Kashmir and Punjab,* with notes by Major T.B. Jervis, John Petheram, London, 1845.

16. Jahangir, *The Tuzuk-i-Jahangiri,* Beveridge Rogers, (editor), Alexander, R., (translator), Vols. 1-2, Sang-e-Meel Publications, Lahore, 1974, p. 126.

17. Caroe, op. cit., 1958; Elliot, J.G., *The Frontier 1939-1947: The Story of the North-West Frontier of India,* Cassell, London, 1968 ; and Spain, op.cit., 1963.

18. Barth, op. cit., 1970, p. 119, map.

19. Ibid., pp. 125-6.

20. Rittenburg, S.,'Continuities in Borderland Politics', in *Pakistan's Western Borderlands*, Royal Book Company, Karachi, 1979.

21. The matter of Hazara ethnicity is vigorously discussed both in and outside Hazara. At various levels of national politics it is debated whether, for instance, President Ayub Khan, from Hazara, was a Pathan or a Punjabi. The answer becomes relevant when claiming dispensation or apportioning real or imagined grievances by political parties. Ethnically, he was the former, but as he neither spoke Pushto nor lived across the Indus, many Pushto-speaking Pathans consider him the latter.

22. Fortes, M.,'Anthropology in South Africa', *Royal Anthropological Institute Newsletter,* 37, London, 1980, p. 12

23. Smith, M.G.,'Some Developments in the Analytic Framework of Pluralism', in *Pluralism in Africa,* Kuper, L., and Smith, M.G., (editors), University of California Press, Berkeley, 1969, pp. 415-58.

24 Cohen, op. cit., 1974(a).

25. Srinivas, M.N., *Social Change in Modern India,* University of California Press, Berkeley, 1966.

26. Ahmed, op. cit., 1980 ; and Barth, op. cit., 1970.

27. Isaacs, H.R., 'Basic Group Identity: The Idols of the Tribe', in *Ethnicity: Theory and Experience,* Glazer, N., and Moynihan, D.P.,(editors), Harvard University Press, Cambridge, 1975; Horowitz, and Parsons, T., 'Some Theoretical Considerations on the Nature and Trends of Change of Ethnicity', in *Ethnicity: Theory and Experience,* Glazer, N., and Moynihan, D.P., (editors), Harvard University Press, Cambridge, 1975.

28. Cohen, A., *Custom* and *Politics in Urban Africa,* Routledge and Kegan Paul, London, 1969. Another result is that numerous works which I would describe as narcissistic ethnic studies (see my Foreword in Afridi, O.K., *Mahsud Monograph,* Tribal Affairs Research Cell, Peshawar, Pakistan, 1980) have been written by Hazarawals. In such studies, the author writes uncritically and with unrestrained admiration of his own group. For example, Ayub Khan (1967) enlarges on the role of his tribe, the Tarin, in the Hazara struggle against the Sikhs. Hazara histories written in Urdu are plainly narcissistic. Swati history is glorified by the Swati author Samiullah Dhudial in *Swati History, Tarikh-i-Swati.* The author's ascendants die fighting the Sikhs. Sher Bahadur's *Hazara History, Tarikh-i-Hazara* exaggerates his (Pathan) virtues to the detriment of other groups. Turk glory is

recounted by the Turk author Irshad Khan in *Hazara History, Tarikh-i-Hazara;* he traces Turk rule to Sultan Mahmud of Pakhli. The Awans are glorified by Hawari in *Awan History, Tarikh-i-Awan.*

29. It is noteworthy that parliamentary constituencies are divided along the major forest zones providing the base for political and economic strength. For instance, the 5 parliamentary seats for Mansehra are Kaghan, Mansehra, Pakhli, Upper Pakhli, and Tanaul.

3

Leadership Categories and Social Processes in Islam: The Cases of Dir and Swat

Charles Lindholm

It is a recognized fact that there are many versions of Islamic practice and belief; the controversy is how to define these forms and how to judge them. Even more crucial, the role of Islam itself is subject to debate, not only in academic discourse, but in the political arena. This paper contributes to this debate by showing how several Muslim political actors in the North-West Frontier have struggled within and without the indigenous Islamic categories. And also how Islamic institutions, shaped by the realities of Frontier political life, are formative in their own right; not simply as 'ideology', but as structures through which the drama of social life is played out and experienced.

A few general comments about the anthropological-sociological study of Muslim society are in order here. Islam, as we know, is a religion both of orthopraxy and orthodoxy; of action and of learning. In a most insightful article, El-Zein[1] has correlated this dichotomy to the mundane realities of rural and urban life. The urbanite lives in history and is aware of the chaos of contingency, the multiplicity of realities to choose from, the absence of any certainty in the flux of change; the villager, on the other hand, lives in nature and sees continuity and order both in the pattern of the seasons and in the highly personalized structure of his society. The city dweller wishes to capture history and create order through learning, while the tribesman/peasant assumes order and stresses repetition, ritual and the personal intercession of holy men. This opposition is articulated again by Gellner in his well-known contrast between 'doctor and saint'[2] and by many others who have worked in the peripheral areas of the Muslim world.

The two traditions are not necessarily antagonistic to one another. If we consider the urban tradition to be that of the Ulema and the folk tradition to be that of the Sufi, then it is well to remember that in the history of Islam a man could be both scholar and ecstatic. Al-Ghazali is only one example. But today challenges of Westernization and modernization threaten the tradition of urban Islam by transforming the economic and social base upon which it rests. In a defensive response, the scholastics wish to affirm Islam as absolute and unitary, denying the validity of the less articulate (but deeply grounded) traditions of the countryside. Furthermore, the increasing importance of the city and the ever greater power of the state has naturally magnified the religious influence of the centre, while the practices of the periphery have become suspect. Perhaps, as some argue, this process is irreversible, and Islam will assume the monolithic solidity apparently so much desired by many of its spokesmen.

The conquest of folk forms by urban tradition may indeed be inevitable. But, as an anthropologist, I must claim that the success or failure of this movement does not rest only upon the power of argument or upon the supposed truth of the reformer's message. The pattern Islamic institutions will take in the future derives from a complex interaction between local social organization and the religious values exemplified by individual actors. It is not simply a case of universal truth overcoming local heresy. It is more like a discussion between different approaches to Islam. This way of looking at Muslim life is within the realm of orthodox interpretation, since Islam is the most democratic of all major religions, relying on consensus among believers to determine law. The reliance on consensus is essentially anthropological and contextual. What the anthropologist (whether Muslim or non-Muslim) does is simply to reveal what some believers make of their faith. It is for the future to decide which version is most appropriate, but it is the duty of the anthropologist or sociologist to present the version of the people he has studied, so that their reality, which is less scholastic, can also be made a party to the discussion.

The method adopted here is comparative and historical, showing the activities of several political figures over time and explaining some social correlates for what appear to be quite radical shifts in the emphasis on religious institutions and values. The areas chosen for this experiment are Swat and Dir, where I did my fieldwork at various times from 1968 to 1977. Much of the material used in this comparison is from this fieldwork, and is not generally available in the literature.[3] The specific configuration I wish to render intelligible is as follows: Dir has been for generations a secular state, yet it has recently witnessed an impressive movement toward leadership by religious figures; Swat, on the other hand, was founded and ruled by religious charismatics, yet politics there has been increasingly secularized.

Swat is the 'Switzerland of Pakistan', a lush valley nestled in high mountains with good trout streams and spectacular scenery. The royal family, now deposed, have a well-earned reputation for urbanity and sophistication, and Swat itself is perceived as the most 'advanced' of the Frontier regions. Dir, a valley just to the north-west of Swat, is in some respects in marked antithesis to its neighbour. It is dry and harsh, and difficult of access. Dir too had a royal family, also now deposed, but they took pride in their conservativism and isolation; traits shared by the valley as a whole. The two valleys thus offer strong contrasts in some ways, yet they are much alike in others. Both are dominated by Yusufzai Pukhtun, both stress the code of *Pukhtunwali* with its values of revenge, refuge, and the offering of hospitality, both practice rigid purdah, both are populated by strict Sunni Muslims. In other words, not only are the inhabitants of the two valleys cousins genealogically, but also in terms of social life.

The similarity I wish to emphasize here is structural. Both societies understand their social world through the use of a segmentary lineage model. This model, typical of Middle Eastern tribal peoples, bases alliance and antagonism on patrilineal kinship. Kinship determines inheritance of land, so that close male relatives live and work next to one another, and are rivals with one another for the land of their common ancestor. This patterned rivalry extends throughout the two regions, so that individuals oppose neighbours in a ward, wards oppose other wards in a village, and villages oppose one another within a district.[4] This model has been discussed and argued about ad-infinitum, and I will not distract the reader with a restatement of the pros and cons of using it as an interpretive device. I hope, instead, to show by example just what the indigenous model is capable of explaining.

The model is, however, cross-cut and complicated by a dual bloc system of political and marriage alliances, so that each genealogical unit is in fact split in two. The dualistic blocs (*dullah*) have made for many misinterpretations of the Pukhtun social system, with bloc alliances being taken as the foundation of the structure.[5] However, like the dualistic political alliances of other Middle Eastern tribesmen (the most famous being the *liff* of the Berbers), the parties are actually an artifact of lineage rivalries between close male relatives. In daily life, a man's opponent is his most powerful cousin, and he allies with more distant relatives against this cousin on the ancient political axiom that 'the enemy of my enemy is my friend'. Three elements are really involved here: the manipulating political individual, his temporary allies and his temporary opponents. Each person is acting in his own personal interests against his most salient opponents, and will switch sides with alacrity when advantage is perceived. For instance, if one cousin is very successful in his political manoeuvrings, he will find his allied cousins joining his enemies to humble him. This leads to a long-term balance of oppositions.[6] But political alliances do not supercede blood ties, and a man must take revenge if a cousin who is an enemy is killed by a more distant political ally.[7]

Another element worthy of note here is the important role of third party intervention in this structure. Opposing lineages may be incited to war by neighbours who hope to obtain advantages from the violence; while outside groups may also be recruited to help a warring party gain an upper hand in the struggle. But outsiders are also utilized to unite lineages in battle against external aggression, and to mediate between segments engaged in interminable feud. These latter functions are, in fact, the specific duties of the holy lineages and religious charismatics of the valleys. Holding authority by virtue of their conduct and heritage, religious figures have stood symbolically outside the hostility of the segmentary system. The Pukhtun, who will cede authority to no other man, will give way to the word and leadership of one who is an emissary of Allah. As Evans-Pritchard writes, the tribesman's 'need was for some authority lying outside their segmentary lineage system which could compose inter-tribal and sectional disputes and bind the tribes and tribal sections together within an organization and under a common symbol'.[8] This is a need filled by religious practitioners.

Ahmed[9] has seen three ideal types of religious figures in this region: the mullah, the Sufi, and the Sayyid. The contrast is roughly between the learned (who is a servant of the village and officiates at the mosque), the ecstatic charismatic, and the descendant of the Prophet validating authority by reference to genealogy (though Sufis also have genealogical charters). These categories actually weld one into the other. The mullah is rarely very learned, and may become a charismatic leader (as Ahmed documents) and then, perhaps, even dare to claim Sayyid status, while Sayyids, despite their genealogies, may sink to earning their livings by reciting from the Qur'an or become landless labourers, and some may validate their position by following 'Sufi' practices. Sufis are also not so simple to classify. As Trimingham[10] documents, there is an evolution from the charismatic individual to the formation of a school and the institutionalization of a cult. Even within this framework, the positions are not always clear. For instance, the Sanusi described by Evans-Pritchard[11] were an orthodox order, but were seen by the Bedouin as a cult. Nor was the mullah described by Ahmed of one type. Instead, he attempted to move 'up' from the inferior category of mullah/village servant to the exalted role of leader, 'alternating between a secular political programme and a religious-charismatic one'.[12]

Rather than use the triadic model, I would like here to follow the four-stage model offered by Brett[13] who uses movement between learned (Mufti), warrior (Murabit), arbitrator (Marabout), and inspirational leader (Mahdi) to understand Islamic history in North Africa. This model, which focuses on leadership, may allow us to escape from the dilemma of making a strict dichotomy between secular and religious action, and to see the larger pattern. Brett's processual argument, enriched with detail on the interaction between social organization and religious institutions, should help make sense of the apparently counter-intuitive historical movement of Swat and Dir.

In order to understand this movement, we need to look more closely at the historical and environmental context. As mentioned earlier, Swat is richer and far more populous than Dir. 'Swat is soft, Dir is hard', says a local proverb. This difference has a profound effect on the evolution of political hierarchy in the two regions. A further divergence concerns the surrounding political structures. Both Swat and Dir are at the very edges of the Pukhtun world, a world that, like all segmentary lineage systems, tends to expand at the expense of less well organized neighbours.[14] But where the northern frontier of Swat faced the harsh mountains and fierce but impoverished peoples of Kohistan, Dir instead looked toward the wealthy and ancient kingdom of Chitral.

The effect these two factors have had on evolution of leadership in Swat and Dir is profound. Dir, unlike the rest of the mountain Pukhtun tribes, has had a centralized state from the seventeenth century. The Painda Khel lineage, living in the furthest northern regions, managed to decisively defeat Chitral and achieve hegemony throughout Dir, so that Elphinstone, writing in the early nineteenth century, was able to report that Qasim Khan, the head of the Painda Khel, was 'by far the most powerful Khaun among the Eusofzyes . . . . He can imprison, inflict corporal punishment, and even put to death'.[15] Swat, on the other hand, had a more typical Pukhtun system of shallow hierarchies, continually shifting alliances and internal warfare, interrupted only by moments of unity inspired by attempted invasion.

The causes for the variation in political structure lie in the factors cited earlier. Dir, unlike Swat, faced a sophisticated and wealthy kingdom at its northern border. This is a classic situation for the evolution of secondary state systems.[16] In attempting to conquer and subdue Chitral, Dir itself developed centralization; a centralization that was validated by success and by booty. Swat did not have this opportunity for state building. Instead the Swati Pukhtun were fought to a standstill in the mountain lairs of the Kohistani, who had neither booty to take, nor an organization to copy. Dir, then, built up centralized hierarchy through confrontation and through the wealth extorted from Chitral. With its superior organizational and economic capacity, it was able to move south and bring under its sway the relatively sparse population of the rest of the valley and to establish a long-lasting kingdom. The situation in Swat did not permit such a movement. Even a powerful lineage could not move south into the densely populated lowlands. The resistance was simply too massive. A low population density and the proximity of a wealthy state to emulate and exploit were the primary factors in the evolution of Dir into a small but powerful kingdom.

So far, the two areas discussed seemed to bear no relationship with one another. But in fact their relationship is crucial to understanding the further permutations of politics, religion, and leadership in the area. The role of third party intervention in local quarrels has been mentioned earlier. This pattern is pervasive in segmentary systems. As Schomberg writes, 'there have always been two parties in these lawless lands. When one party weakens, it begins to intrigue with some neighbouring ruler, hoping to induce him to come in, occupy the country and enable his supporters to work off their vendettas on their stronger opponents, and so redress the balance of power'.[17] In Swat, it was the Dir Nawab who was so invited. But then, finding the solution worse than the original problem, the Swati Pukhtun would unite on the principle of segmentary solidarity and act 'to repel the common enemy'.[18] This method of 'redressing the balance' apparently functioned fairly well until thrown out of equilibrium by the intervention of the British.

Colonial intervention had important ramifications for the political/religious life of both Dir and Swat. Some of its effects in Swat have already been discussed at length by Ahmed[19] and myself[20] but here I have tried to link the developments in Swat with those in Dir, and bring both under the typologies proposed by Brett.

Continued external pressure, first from the Sikhs and then from the British, pushed the Swatis toward establishing some form of central authority to co-ordinate resistance. The onslaught was envisioned as a threat to Islam, and the leaders who arose came from the class of charismatic religious figures. This pattern is implicit in segmentary society, since the temptation for betrayal is inherent within the social structure, as was evident in the discussion of the role of personal interest and manipulation. The only bond of unity is embodied in the person of a charismatic claiming authority not for himself or his lineage, but as a representative of Allah. In Swat, Abdul Gaffur, a Sufi whose austerities and piety had made him well-known, was tagged by the Pukhtun as the symbolic figure about whom they could rally. In Brett's terms, he was viewed as a Mahdi, one of the 'rightly guided' who provides the faithful with a transcendent order which can subsume lineage rivalries.

After the defeat of the British at Ambela in 1863, Swat no longer suffered under the same threat of invasion, and the image of the Mahdi was no longer appropriate to the situation (nor, indeed, was it an image that Abdul Gaffur seemed happy to adopt). Instead, he slipped into the role Brett calls Marabout, a holy man charged with maintaining social order as a judge and arbitrator whose authority is sanctioned by supposed mystic power. Such persons, function within the fragmented and internally hostile segmentary society as the means for defusing tensions; they cease to have a place when the society becomes centralized and their place is taken by Brett's Muftis. Acting within the 'Maraboutic' framework as judge through the rest of his life, Abdul Gaffur acquired considerable property and prosperity by way of gifts from the beneficiaries of his judgements and from believers anxious to gain grace through their donations. His political authority, however, was negligible as the Pukhtun of Swat returned to their social world of factional struggles and party warfare.

Dir offers an elucidating contrast. The Dir Nawab in his traditional guise is perhaps best characterized as a Murabit in Brett's terms. By distinguishing Murabit and Marabout, Brett is dividing what is seen in North Africa as one and the same . . . . the two terms are actually different spellings of one word. But there is an important shift in emphasis. Where the Marabout is a mediator and keeper of order, the Murabit is a warrior and conqueror 'in the cause of god', a ruler as well as a judge. This is the role characteristic of segmentary leaders in eras of expansion. In such periods when the structure is not threatened, but is instead waxing larger and more powerful, when booty and largesse are available to satisfy the followers, then the temptation to betray is greatly lessened. Religious sanction is nonetheless important for strengthening the hearts of the warriors and justifying the cause, but the central figure is interested primarily in practical matters of war and rule. In Dir, for instance, the Painda Khel lineage held its power by its success in its conquests, but justified itself by claiming descent from a Pukhtun Sufi given mystical rights to rule the valley by his master. The validation of power through legends of this sort is widespread in the Frontier.

Alongside these warrior/ruler figures are men who fall into the Mufti category; the learned who are used to back up the ruler's right to power, to administer his army and court, and to take the place of the dangerously independent 'Marabout' judges and mediators. The famous Shaikh Mali, who organized land redistribution when the Yusufzai first entered the Frontier region, was such a figure: a Sayyid who was administrative second-in-command of the invading army. Similar men were used by the Dir Nawab and, later, by his rival, the Wali of Swat, as advisors, judges, and bureaucrats at the middle level of governmental authority. But such men can also act as centres for resistance, as they may deny the ruler legitimacy, claiming that he has over-stepped the bounds of piety in his use of power.

To return to the historical process, the legitimacy of the Dir Nawab remained unquestioned while his family presided over expansion, but began to crumble when that expansion ceased. In 1888 there was a rebellion in the Jandul region neighbouring Dir which forced the Nawab (Muhammad Sherif Khan) into exile in Swat. At this point, the British again re-entered the picture.

After the debacle at Ambela, the Colonial power had opted for a less costly approach to dominating the tribes by seeking alliances with existing rulers, such as the Dir Nawab and the Mehtar of Chitral. When the Dir Nawab was thrown out of his kingdom the British hoped to avoid direct intervention. But in 1895 the Colonial garrison at Chitral was besieged, forcing the British to act to protect their interests. Regular troops joined the Dir Nawab's tribal army and marched

through Swat towards Dir. Meanwhile, other Colonial troops marched
from Gilgit and defeated the rebel army, driving the leader into exile
in Kabul. Afraid of further uprisings, the British committed themselves to massive support for the Dir Nawab. Large subsidies were
awarded to buy arms and loyalty. Furthermore, the Nawab was given
absolute rule over Jandul and Sind in southern Dir. From being in
retreat and nearly broken, the kingdom of Dir was once again expanding and solid, but only through alliance with the British.

This pact was soon tested. Aided by Dir, the British had set up permanent outposts in Swat. Incensed by this encroachment, Swat rose in
1897 under the charismatic leadership of a Mahdi figure the British
called the Mastan Mullah. Dir was not moved by cries of jihad and supported the British against their old enemies/cousins in Swat. Nearly
4,000 Swatis were killed in this cataclysmic defeat. The 'cause of god'
had taken second place, for the Dir Nawab, to the realities of power.

With British support, and helped by continued party warfare within
Swat, Dir soon invaded Swat once again. And again, as had occurred
before, Swat united behind a religious charismatic to expel the invader.
But casualties were higher than ever, and it seemed that the alliance
between the British and Dir would end with Swat eventually losing its
autonomy. The power of the Dir Nawab (Aurangzeb Khan, who had
succeeded his father), was at its peak, and his victories had only whetted
his appetite for more.

At this point, the Swati lineage leaders met to elect someone to head
the resistance. The man they eventually selected and entitled the Badshah of Swat, was Abdul Wadud, who was the grandson of Abdul Gaffur. Because of this, many looked on him as a Mahdi figure. He utilized
this image to rally the Pukhtun behind him and to once again defeat
Dir. But unlike his grandfather, Abdul Wadud was a veteran of lineage
struggles, and he had fought and killed his two cousins to assert his
authority in his own group. Now that he had gained power in the whole
valley, he was not willing to give it up and settle into being a 'Marabout'
mediator, as had his grandfather. Instead, he stepped into the role of
'Murabit', the conqueror, solidifying his rule by invading Buner, to the
East.

But the politically astute Badshah knew that the possibilities for further conquest were limited, and that his rule could not last without external support. Like the Dir Nawab, he looked to the British, who, on
their part, were glad to see some form of central authority in Swat with
whom they could negotiate. Furthermore, the British were looking for

an alternative to the Dir Nawab, who had not permitted any cultural inroads into Dir. The Badshah, as a shaky newcomer to power, was more than willing to listen to advice from the British, and he quickly built a network of roads and telephones that consolidated his power. But this was not all; he also built Western-style schools and hospitals and installed a system of formal courts. Meanwhile, the only Western innovation permitted in Dir was the use of a veterinarian to tend to the Nawab's kennel.

The relation between the British and the Badshah was a close one, and it was useful for both sides. The British gained a brilliant and modernizing supporter who relied upon them for his continued power, while the Badshah gained a state that was impervious to attack, either from the inside or the outside. Dir was forced to sign a treaty of non-intervention in Swat; a treaty in which Swat was given the lush valley of Shamozai, while Dir was awarded the arid region of Adinzai; a trade-off that perfectly marked the new balance of power in the region.

In Dir, the era of expansion was at an end, and even the conquests gained in the last few years were withdrawn. The warrior ruling house, which had relied on expansion to legitimize its power, was now ravaged by internal splits and antagonisms. Segmentary hostility led to party opposition between close agnates that tore the valley apart for sixty years. After the departure of the British, favouritism was still shown to the Badshah and his family, while Dir was still backward, and still racked by warfare and schism. During this period one of Aurangzeb Khan's grandsons, Shahbuddin, began to gain a following by calling for Islamic reform and strict adherence to the Qur'an. He himself took the role of Imam in the mosque, where he raised an outcry against religious laxity, and exhorted the people against impious rulers, while at the same time proposing himself as the symbol of piety. Simultaneously, he allied himself with the Mishwani, landless migrants from Afghanistan, to whom he became a patron and something of a saviour. Shahbuddin thus moved from the pure assertion of secular leadership in expansionistic war to a more complex transitional position, combining elements from various categories in a volatile brew. To the Mishwani, he was something of a warrior offering them the spoils of conquest, something of a prophet leading them out of oppression to the promised land. To other people of Dir, he appeared as an outraged cleric defending the faith; a position that also moves in the direction of Mahdi exemplar.

As mentioned earlier, the segmentary structure favours charismatic religious leadership in periods of external threat, while an expanding system tends toward secular administrators. In Dir, the threat was actually internal, as stagnation crumbled the power base of the Nawab. But Shahbuddin (aided by his father, Shah Jehan), now attempted to stimulate a siege mentality in order to restore the power of the ruling house, not as Murabits, but as Mahdis. It was claimed that the policies of Pakistan were against Islamic practice. Outsiders who had entered Dir to administer the few hospitals and schools that had been built there were singled out as heathens, and the institutions themselves were called un-Islamic. These allegations did stir up the people, but they also caused problems with Pakistan.

As Shahbuddin stressed prophetic religion in Dir, Swat moved in the opposite direction. The Badshah, far from favouring the rise of religious charismatics, took the precaution of banishing all mendicants and Sufic wanderers from the valley. His own Islamic practice was austere and orthodox, but he carefully denied himself any sacred role and made no claim to fill the holy position held by his grandfather. His sons, meanwhile, were wearing Western suits, learning English, and going to Europe for their holidays. At the same time, he favoured a rationalization of the structure, utilizing men of religious lineage as bureaucrats and administrators, thus replacing the Marabout with the cleric. Working in tandem with the secular British Empire, and presiding over a state expanding in resources if not in territory, his policies were eminently suited to the real situation, just as Shahbuddin's approach suited the reality of Dir. Both men were acting within categories structured by social organization and by indigenous models of leadership.

Shahbuddin's efforts, however, were thwarted by intervention from an enemy he himself had conjured up: the Pakistani state. His elder brother, Kushrow Khan, plotted with Pakistan to overthrow Shahbuddin and Shah Jehan, and in 1960 they were arrested and exiled. Kushrow Khan hoped to emulate the Badshah and construct a modern state, drawing on the resources of Pakistan to buy and hold a following, just as the Badshah had done with the British. But his situation was not analogous. Whereas the Badshah had been elected and was in fact ruling an expanding system, Kushrow Khan was a usurper attempting to stem a tide of religious revivalism in a crumbling state. Having removed his brother from consideration as charismatic leader, Kushrow Khan thought himself secure, forgetting that charismatic figures are more likely to appear not among Princes, but from groups challenging traditional authority. And, indeed, new claimants to leadership in Dir did arise from the religious classes who have historically been the focus for popular discontent: the mullahs and Sufi mediators and mendicants. Furthermore, the Mishwani did not accept Kushrow as his brother's successor. In 1969, resentment against Pakistan and Kushrow Khan erupted into violence; almost all government offices, schools, and hospitals were destroyed in an upsurge of religious fervour. From being the staunchest ally of the British, Dir had become the centre for rebellion against Pakistan.

Swat, in contrast, had evolved from being the most troublesome region to being the most tractable and the most 'advanced'. The Badshah peacefully abdicated in favour of his eldest son, who was entitled the Wali. The Wali increasingly rationalized and modernized the state, while strengthening ties with Pakistan. In fact, Pakistan's President Ayub married two of his daughters into the Swati royal family. In comparison with Dir, internal and external relations in Swat were remarkably amicable.

All of this was not to last. Soon after the rebellion in Dir, the Princely States were completely merged into Pakistan and the rulers were deposed. The reasons for this move are too complex to be discussed here,[21] but the consequences tend to validate the point of view offered in the paper. In Swat, where the state was founded by a man of religious lineage, the trend has been toward greater secularism.[22] In the 1977 elections, the north was dominated by parties led by Khans who said little or nothing about religion. In the south, the Badshah's family split into opposing segments along the lines of party formation traditional in segmentary systems. Neither of the segments, however, professed any great religious fervour.

These trends are continuations of the process outlined earlier. In the era of the Badshah, Swat had extended its influence far beyond the borders of the valley. Expansionist and practical, the Swati royal family utilized the clerical bureaucratic tradition of the Mufti administrators under the rulership of the Badshah, a Murabit warrior. The Badshah himself descended from the charismatic Abdul Gaffur who became a Marabout-like mediator after his task of defense. This heritage helped the Badshah in his climb to power, but it was one he specifically repudiated. It is noteworthy in documenting this process that the shrine of Abdul Gaffur, formerly a major pilgrimage centre, gradually lost its following as the Badshah and his family secularized and gained control over a state that was increasingly rational in structure. The evolution is from a fragmented system under attack, appropriate for the rise of a unifying leader; to one of 'institutionalized dissidence' without central rule, where a mediator-judge finds his niche; to an expansive centralized state, where the warrior holds sway; and finally to a bureaucracy, which needs the literacy and skills of the clerical class.

After the fall of the royal family, the process continued, with the present political leaders competing on the larger ground of Pakistani politics for advantages and favours. Instead of descending back to the welter of local rivalries typical of segmentary systems in stagnation, Swat now sought to assert itself in the new arena for political warriors: the national state. It is , it seems, a nice example of the well-known Weberian progress from charismatic to rational authority.

But Weber saw the movement as irreversible, whereas any student of Islam knows it is not. In Dir, as we have seen, leadership has become less secular and has taken on a highly prophetic tone. In the 1977 elections, Kushrow Khan lost his race to a charismatic Sufi, while the other successful candidate was a Maulana. In contrast to Swat, the people of Dir did not see participation in Pakistan as an opportunity. Instead, it was perceived as a threat. As a result, Dir rose again in 1976 against the Government of Pakistan, which had attempted to intervene in the allocation of wood rights. This further stimulated religious revivalism.

At this point I would like to conclude my excursion into ideal types. The perils of such a venture are many, and I must stress that the categories I have drawn have value not as absolutes, but only as guidelines for understanding cultural complexity. The historical record shows that one man can fill several roles, and that the movement from one to the other is by no means uni-directional, but is contingent upon many factors of time, place, and person. Nonetheless, the categories do help us link structural features with leadership types in the context of religion in a way that helps to make sense of the vicissitudes of Frontier politics. Events since 1977 have been complicated by increased Islamic revivalism in Pakistan itself. In an earlier paper,[23] I claimed that the study of tribal politics can teach us much about the politics of the Middle Eastern state. I leave it to the reader to decide whether this new effort, by connecting structural patterns with a typology of leadership and religion, adds any further strength to that claim.

NOTES

1. El-Zein, A., 'Beyond Ideology and Theology: The Search for the Anthropology of Islam', in Seigel, B. *et al.*, (editors), *Annual Review of Anthropology*, Annual Reviews Inc., Palo Ato, 1977.

2. Gellner, E., *Muslim Society*, Cambridge University Press, Cambridge, 1981.

3. Ahmed, A., *Millennium and Charisma Among Pathans*, Routledge and Kegan Paul, London, 1976; Barth, F., *Political Leadership Among the Swat Pathans*, Athlone, London, 1959; Caroe, O., *The Pathans, 550 B.C.-A.D. 1957*, Macmillan, London, 1965.

4. Lindholm, C., 'The Structure of Violence Among the Swat Pukhtun', *Ethnology*, 1981, 20, pp. 147-56.

5. Barth, op. cit., 1959.

6. Barth, F., 'Segmentary Opposition and the Theory of Games: A Study of Pathan Organization', *Journal of the Royal Anthropological Institute*, 1959, 89, pp. 5-21.

7. Salzman, P., 'Does Complementary Opposition Exist?', *American Anthropologist*, 1978, 63, pp. 322-43.

8. Evans-Pritchard, E., *The Sanusi of Cyrenaica*, Oxford University Press, London, 1949, p. 87.

9. Ahmed, 'Islam and the District Paradigm', in *Contributions to Indian Sociology*, 1983, 17, pp. 155-83.

10. Trimingham, J., *The Sufi Orders of Islam*, Oxford University Press, Oxford, 1971.

11. Evans-Pritchard, op. cit., 1949.

12. Ahmed, op. cit., 1983, p. 160.

13. Brett, M., 'Mufti, Marabout, Murabit and Mahdi: Four Types in the Islamic History of North Africa', *Revue de l' Occident Musulman et de la Mediterrane*, 1980, 29, pp. 5-15.

14. Sahlins, M., 'The Segmentary Lineage, an Organization of Predatory Expansion', *American Anthropologist*, 1961, 63, pp. 322-43.

15. Elphinstone, M., *An Account of the Kingdom of Caubul*, 2 volumes, Longman, London, 1815, reprinted 1972, Oxford University Press, Karachi, Pakistan, Vol. 2, p. 25.

16. Fried, M., 'On the Evolution of Social Stratification and the State', in Diamond, S. (editor), *Culture in History*, Columbia University Press, New York, 1960.

17. Schomberg, R., *Between Oxus and Indus*, Hopkinson, London, 1935, p. 242.

18. Bellew, H., *A General Report on the Yusufzais*, Government Press, 1864, reprinted 1977, Saeed Press, Peshawar, p. 205.

19. Ahmed, op. cit., 1976.

20. Lindholm, C., 'The Segmentary Lineage System: It's Applicability to Pakistan's Political Structure' in Embree, A. (editor) *Pakistan's Western Borderlands*, Carolina Academic Press, Durham, 1977, and *Generosity and Jealousy: The Swat Pukhtun of Northern Pakistan*, Columbia University Press, New York, 1982.

21. Lindholm, C., 'Models of Segmentary Political Action: The Examples of Swat and Dir, NWFP, Pakistan', in Pastner, S. and Flam, L. (editors), *Anthropology in Pakistan: Recent Socio-Cultural and Archaeological Perspectives*, Cornell University Press, Ithaca, 1982.

22. For a detailed account, see Lindholm, C., 'Contemporary Politics in a Tribal Society: Swat District, NWFP, Pakistan', in *Asian Survey*, 1979, 19, pp. 485-505.

23. Lindholm, op. cit., 1977.

4

Frontiers, Boundaries and Frames:
The Marginal Identity of Afghan Refugees

David Busby Edwards

Afghans are less 'fixed' than insinuated into the ethnic geography of south-west Asia, a sort of sociological innuendo woven through larger histories than their own, at once ingratiating and stealthy and, for that, artful.[1]

In a fundamental sense, they are a people in between who partake of but ultimately stand apart from the more distinctive civilizations that have surrounded them and, at one time or another, briefly incorporated them or been incorporated by them.[2]

From its inception, Pakistan has been a place of refuge, and this is no less true today than it was in the late forties when religious refugees *(mohajerin)* from India crossed the border to settle in the newly created *Dar al Islam* of South Asia. At that time, the nascent state had to contend with the resettlement and integration of hundreds of thousands of refugees who had chosen to make Pakistan their home. Now, the problem is one of coping with the several million Afghan refugees who have involuntarily left their homeland in the wake of the Communist takeover of 1978 and subsequent Soviet invasion of 1979. Over the decades since the founding of Pakistan, the Indian *mohajerin* have made a place for themselves within Pakistan society. The Afghans, more recently arrived, have remained in large measure a people apart, a people committed to the belief that they will one day return to their homeland. Until that day arrives, however, the Afghans must be counted as one among the many ethnic groups of Pakistan, for the destiny of Pakistan is fully intertwined with that of the Afghan refugees.

This paper suggests that while the context has radically changed, Afghans have long occupied a marginal niche in the ethnic geography of the Indian subcontinent. Afghan Pakhtuns, who comprise the over-whelming majority of the refugee population, have an especially long association with the Indian subcontinent through nomadism and trade, and we will examine how the ethnic identity which Pakhtuns uphold for themselves reflects this marginal position between more complex social and political systems. Before doing so, however, it is first necessary to consider the concept of 'ethnicity' and the way in which the term is used in relation to tribally-organized social groups.

DEFINITIONS

The Pakhtun heartland between the Hindu Kush Mountains and Indus River valley is a place betwixt and between, and the people who inhabit the region reflect this fact. Unlike many other tribal peoples who have developed uniform social and cultural patterns to exploit single ecological niches, Pakhtuns have demonstrated over time a protean capacity for adapting to diverse environments. In the process, they have also stretched the definitional boundaries of what anthropologists call tribal social organization to the point where it can be questioned whether Pakhtuns can be considered a 'tribal' people at all. Moreover, the sheer diversity of cultural forms which Pakhtuns have adopted opens up the additional question of whether or not Pakhtuns can even be considered a single ethnic group. Before proceeding to this problem of defining the Pakhtuns, however, we must first define our own analytical terms — particularly those of 'ethnicity' and 'tribalism' — and consider the relationship between them.

The concept of 'ethnicity' is of recent vintage, not finding its way into many dictionaries before 1960. Considering this, it is remarkable how quickly the word has gained currency in the popular press no less than the social sciences. Equally remarkable is its resistance to definition. In this regard, a reader of Webster's New Collegiate Dictionary would find 'ethnicity' defined as 'ethnic quality or affiliation'. Thumbing his way backwards to 'ethnic', the first definitions encountered are 'neither Christian nor Jewish: HEATHEN. . . .of or relating to races or large groups of people classed according to common traits and customs'.

Though he has given us no help, we should pity the plight of the poor lexicographer and seek out those who introduced the concept in the first place. Unfortunately, this provides little in the way of enlightenment, for sociologists, who by rights should accept paternity of 'ethnicity', are equally imprecise in their own definitions. Talcott Parsons, for example, admits to the difficulty of pinning down a definition for the word but goes on to write that 'ethnicity is a primary focus of group identity, that is, the organization of plural persons into distinctive groups and, second, of solidarity and the loyalties of individual members to such groups'.[3] The problem with such definitions is that they introduce even more uncertainty than existed in the first place, for in place of one puzzle, we now have a handful with the addition of such terms as 'primary focus', 'solidarity', and 'loyalties'.

As Issacs formulates the term, 'ethnicity' is conceived of as a concept of group identity consisting of 'the ready-made set of endowments and identifications which every individual shares with others from the moment of birth by the chance of the family into which he is born at that given time in that given place.' This set of ascriptive endowments — or 'primordial affinities' — are symbolically represented by each group in the name (s) by which it identifies itself, its myths of origin, shared history, language, religion, and value system.[4]

While providing greater specificity than the preceding definition, this formulation with its list of attributes and others that build on words like 'group', 'membership', and 'boundary' tend to reify a concept that is, in Ronald Cohen's words, 'first and foremost situational'. To get around this problem, he would then define 'ethnicity' as 'a set of descent-based cultural identifiers used to assign persons to groupings that expand and contract in inverse relation to the scale of inclusiveness and exclusiveness of the membership'.[5]

Each of these definitions skirts the fundamental problem posed by the concept of 'ethnicity'. Each attempts to fix a set of nominal characteristics on a phenomenon which does not have the quality of 'thingness' but of relationship and meaning. Even Cohen, who recognizes the reification problem, persists in locating the concept in the markers of identity rather than in the process of definition itself. Instead of denominalizing 'ethnicity', Cohen simply allows for the possibility of shifting boundaries and multiple 'sets of ascriptive loyalties'[6] but does not eliminate the problem that 'ethnicity' continues to be defined as the sum of its interchangeable parts.

In addition to this, Cohen's situational definition raises an entirely new problem, for if ethnicity has this quality of contextuality, if a person's 'ethnic identity' is always relative and situationally located, then what is there that is 'primordial' in ethnic affinity, what is there that binds individuals together and makes them act jointly and believe that they share something fundamental with each other? In contextualizing the concept of 'ethnicity', Cohen ignores the fact that there must be a transpersonal sensibility which invests ascriptive features with meaning and which allows an individual to judge the appropriateness of different loyalties in different contexts.

Given the multitude of attributes available to choose from, there must be a shared ethos which animates certain attributes and not others. Without this nexus of value and meaning, the concept of 'ethnicity' remains unfocused and artificial. It is this nexus, this culture-specific ethos, which allows individuals to invest with meaning what is inherently arbitrary, to make unified and whole attributes that are separate and discrete. If, as Cohen maintains, 'ethnicity' is always situational and relative, there must, at the very least, be a shared conviction on the part of ethnic group members that what binds them is absolute.

PAKHTUN ETHNICITY

One implication that follows from the preceding argument is that any study of ethnicity must give priority to a group's own notions of who they are, for it is through self-definition that ascriptive features become the meaningful indicia of group identity. Before turning to the issue of how Pakhtuns define themselves, however, it is necessary to consider the work of Fredrik Barth who played a pivotal role in developing the study of ethnicity through his work on 'Pathans' (i.e., Pakhtuns) in Swat Kohistan and Baluchistan.

According to Barth, the 'cultural contents of ethnic dichotomies' are of 'two orders':

(i) overt signals or signs – the diacritical features that people look for and exhibit to show identity. . . . , and (ii) basic value orientations: the standards of morality and excellence by which performance is judged.[7]

The 'diacritical features' that Barth mentions as being of central importance to and of necessary association with Pakhtun identity are (1) patrilineal descent; (2) belief in Islam; and (3) the maintenance of Pakhtun customary practices, including, what Barth describes as 'three central institutions', namely provision of hospitality (*melmastia*) according to established forms of exchange; decision-making and dispute settlement through the traditional assembly (*jirga*) system; and the seclusion of females (*purdah*). With regard to the basic Pakhtun value orientation, Barth focuses on the Pakhtun concept of *izzat* ('honour') which 'emphasizes male autonomy and equality, self-expression and aggressiveness'. Together these 'attributes' form a 'native model' that 'provides a Pathan with a self-image, and serves him as a general canon for evaluating behaviour on the part of himself and other Pathans'.[8]

In apparent contradiction to this 'native model', however, Pakhtuns who inhabit areas where there has been greater contact with other ethnic groups and with the state have tended to lose many of the diacritical features of identity mentioned by Barth. Thus, for example, in Baluchistan, on the southern boundary of Pakhtun settlement in Pakistan, Pakhtuns living among the Baluch have become in many cases thoroughly assimilated within the dominant social organization, which 'involves loss of position in the rigid genealogical and territorial segmentary system of Pathans and incorporation through clientage contract into the hierarchical, centralized system of the Baluch'.[9] Similarly, in areas of state and multi-ethnic group contact in Afghanistan, a similar (though perhaps not as dramatic) range of variations is encountered. Schurman, for example, has written that in northern Afghanistan, sedentary Pakhtuns 'tend to lose their language and speak Persian. Fourth generation Herati Afghans [Pakhtuns] are even no longer bi-lingual'.[10]

With regard to Pakhtun ethnicity, the aforementioned examples of Pakhtun assimilation would seem to contradict a basic axiom that has developed out of the study of ethnicity, which is that ethnic identity emerges not in isolation but in a multi-ethnic context. That is to say, a group becomes fully-aware of its own identity and what distinguishes that identity in the interplay of group relations. As Anderson has written, 'ethnic' identities sociologically emerge in situations where people of different traditions and organizations come together or are brought together in contexts set by terms external to themselves. Indeed, it is the emergence of wider community, such as in a territorial state, that creates 'ethnicity' among heretofore disjoined groups which have become components in some encompassing structure'.[11]

The evidence that Barth himself provides, along with the examples cited earlier, would seem to indicate that boundaries are not being maintained in situations of inter-ethnic contact. Thus, Barth does not explain how it can be construed that Pakhtun ethnicity is being maintained in a context such as that of Baluchistan, where Baluch dominance results in 'a flow of personnel from [Pakhtun] groups to Baluch groups, and not vice versa'. Nor does he indicate how 'core'

Pakhtun values are being upheld in a situation in which Pakhtuns are compelled to become clients of Baluch which, 'Judged by [Pakhtun] standards . . . .places a man among the despised failures, subordinates among independent commoners'.[12] To reconcile this contradiction, we need to reconsider, first, how Pakhtuns define themselves and, second, the relationship of this self-definition to the structural context of inter-ethnic relations.

With regard to the first problem, it is necessary to examine the nexus of value that informs the way Pakhtuns define themselves and that invests the quality of the absolute into this self-definition. We must consider, in other words, the cultural ethos that underlies Pakhtun identity and what it means for them to say that they are 'Pakhtuns'. At the risk of over-simplifying the problem, it can be argued that the Pakhtun ethos and the nexus of Pakhtun identity can be located in the concept of *gheyrat* which is usually translated as 'bravery' but which is perhaps more completely realized as 'self-determination' or 'self-definition'.[13] Thus, *gheyrat* is the quality of one who is capable of protecting himself, his rights and his property. A man who possesses *gheyrat* is a man of honour, a man who, while upholding tribal custom, determines his own destiny. A man who possesses *gheyrat* is not defined by others but rather defines himself.

In analysing what makes Pakhtuns different from other groups, it is the notion of self-determination/self-definition. They define themselves as ones who define themselves: the act of defining is itself the definition. As long as a Pakhtun is able to exert a degree of independence and to maintain his personal autonomy of action — which is to say, as long as he can keep from being subsumed within an externally imposed definition, then he can consider himself, in a fundamental sense, a Pakhtun.

The concept of *gheyrat* is the nexus of all that Pakhtuns value, and, in a fundamental sense, it is even more basic than the ideal of honour (*izzat*) since it is the foundation upon which honour is based. In this regard, a man demonstrates his honour in his day-to-day interactions with others, but he demonstrates *gheyrat* in the very conditions of his existence. *Izzat* emerges in action; *gheyrat* emerges ontologically prior to action in the process of self-definition. The two concepts are, of course, integrally related and inseparable in practice, but there is a fundamental reason why *gheyrat* must be given priority over *izzat* even though Pakhtuns themselves contend that one must not only 'speak' Pakhtu but also 'do' Pakhtu.[14] The fundamental issue here is not so much what it means to 'do Pakhtu' but rather what are the conditions under which the ideal can be realized.

In this sense, the ethos of *gheyrat* can be thought of as a unique variant of Frederick Jackson Turner's 'frontier spirit'. Unlike Turner's notion of the American 'frontier spirit', however, which rationalized the development of democracy in the New World as the result of the seemingly infinite space and resources available to the American pioneers, 'the frontier spirit' of the tribes is an adaptation to constraint: to finite space, limited resources, and the constant danger of encroachment and control by the state. Thus, centuries of living on the fringes of empires have taught Pakhtuns how to negotiate the intricacies and interstices of more complex social systems while remaining separate and apart. They have learned, in other words, how to exploit the opportunities provided by a dominant political universe without being swallowed up in it, how to participate in and benefit from the economic wealth of nations without being subsumed by them.

This adaptation to political marginality is best illustrated in the involvement of the Pakhtun, especially the Ghilzai Pakhtun, with British India. As nomads and as traders, in family groupings and individually, Ghilzai annually migrated into the Indian subcontinent. With the consolidation of British rule in the late eighteenth and early nineteenth century, the Ghilzai took advantage of increased security to extend the range of their commercial activities, which included hawking cloth and other articles of clothing, carrying on usury, working in the fields, and labouring in construction gangs, as far afield as Bengal and Burma.

In the process of penetrating the subcontinent, the Pakhtun became fixed in the Indian mind as the very representative of marginal social existence; for the Hindu city-dweller, the Pakhtun traders and moneylenders were like turbaned panthers who wandered through their markets without social constraint or any apparent moral conditioning. As Robinson noted, 'The extent to which they have become part of the winter landscape may be judged from the fact that no Bengali novel or play is considered complete without some reference to the annual visit of the 'Kabuli' to the village. Armed with a heavy bamboo staff often studded with brass, he extorts his dues by threats and even by force; and he will often plant himself on the doorstep, harass the inhabitants, making heavy inroads into their milk and food, and bring them to shame in the eyes of their neighbours until he has at length received payment.'[15]

The Hindu stereotype is augmented by that of the British who, while mocking the Hindu for tolerating such behaviour, were themselves likewise repelled and fascinated by the independent pose of the Pakhtuns in their midsts:

> There is no Powindah [nomad] who does not often wish that he and his family were settled in some such fertile valley as of the Tarnak Rud or Arghandab, with fruit gardens and fields and a house comfortably fortified against his enemies; yet nomadism and unrest are born in him and, were the migration to come to a sudden end, even the camels would stampede. This restlessness in his blood is wedded to a love of gain which is scarcely equalled in any other tribe or people. The prospect of each migration with its unforeseen dangers stirs him with the spirit of adventure; but he is well determined to make India repay him for all its hardships and yield the last rupee. He must take all and give nothing. Poverty and the instinct for self-preservation, which can never be far below consciousness, have made the Powindah what he is — a man, and a hard one. And if some feeling of superiority makes him swagger through the bazars of India, thinking of nothing but his own business, it is scarcely his fault, for he is the tough survival of generations upon generations of the fittest, and he seems to know it.[16]

This quotation refers specifically to the *powindah* nomads who made their migrations into India every autumn, but the sedentary tribes elicited a similar response from those British administrators and officers who worked and fought with them. The nomad, of course, had to be considered especially dangerous and potentially subversive since he was that much less easily categorized or contained; however, sedentary tribesmen were equally adept at upsetting administrative arrangements and evading jurisdictions. Thus, if the nomad somehow managed to survive and prosper on British turf without ever committing himself to the rules of the game, the tribesman on the Frontier proved to be even more difficult to subjugate since he confronted the imperial forces on his own lands, in defence of his home and honour.

Indian and British attitudes towards the Pakhtun traders and tribesmen of the Frontier are not important for our purposes in and of themselves. Such stereotypes naturally tell us as much about the caste-bound prejudices of Hindus and the orderly obsessions of Britons as about Pakhtuns. Nevertheless, such stereotypes do have a certain usefulness beyond their obvious charm as imperial curios. That is to say, they reveal not only how others viewed the Pakhtun but also how the Pakhtun wanted to be viewed. There is, in other words, a degree of reflexivity in such ethnic stereotypes. Pakhtuns have long been aware of the images which others hold of them, and they help to foster these

:mages, both because the rough and feral image accords with their own notion of themselves and because it has been   in their interest to appear to be to others what they appear to be to themselves: a people apart, beyond the pale of urban society and governmental control.

The images which people hold of one another more often than not indicate the nature of ethnic boundaries between those people. In the case of Pakhtuns, they could live and operate in the midst of an alien people so long as they themselves set the terms of their interaction. The relations had to remain partial and transitory, for as soon as the tribesman became fixed in the landscape of social relations then their autonomy became jeopardized by the possibility of incorporation within a larger *structural* system.

In the latter part of the twentieth century, Pakhtun commercial enterprises became somewhat more circumscribed because of border conflicts between Pakistan and Afghanistan. But, the Pakhtuns on both sides of the border have retained their association with trade and transport and continue to dominate the trucking business in both countries. This lasting involvement in trade and trucking is significant because it represents a means by which Pakhtuns in Afghanistan and the North-West Frontier Province have been able to exploit their marginality by operating as middlemen between separate urban centres and cultural systems. In this way, many Pakhtuns have been able to transmute their experience of living on the Frontier between two encroaching and frequently antagonistic state systems into an economic way of life. At the same time, what is particularly attractive to the Pakhtun about trucking as a means of earning a livelihood is that it allows him to maintain his personal autonomy and does not require him to compromise his independence by accepting a subservient position.

PAKHTUN TRIBALISM

The concepts of ethnicity and ethnic identity are theoretical constructs that have emerged in the study of the interactions of groups living in close proximity in complex (and usually urban) societies. The ideal of Pakhtun honour — of what it means to 'do' Pakhtu and therefore to 'be' a Pakhtun — emerges in the structural context of the tribe. The tribe is the framework within which Pakhtun identity is formed and to which it is referred. It is necessary, therefore, to consider in some detail some of the characteristics of tribal structure.

For anthropologists working in the area stretching from North Africa, through the Middle East and south-west Asia, the concept of tribe refers to a specific form of social organization, the generally recognized characteristics of which are the following: patrilineal descent from an eponymous ancestor; the territorial and political division of descent groups according to principles of segmentation and complementary opposition; the replication of the elementary segmental monad at each level of the social structure; and the diffusion of political power at each level of segmentation. Beyond this, tribalism in this region is also characterized generally by certain dynamics or tensions which express the values of the society and which help to generate and maintain the structure over time.

Thus, unlike most other small-scale societies, social organization is not generated through rituals and practices of reciprocal exchange so much as through the possibility of reciprocal violence. It is not the promise of the future gift that binds the tribe but the threat of future conflict. In the case of the Pakhtuns, this basic structural relationship is manifested in the ideal of *tarburwali* (('patrilineal) cousin enmity'), which Ahmed has noted as one of the essential components of Pakhtun tribal structure and ethos. While *tarburwali* specifically refers to the enmity which exists between patrilateral first cousins (i.e., ego's father's brother's son(s)), the term is applied to rivalry between all collateral agnates linked through the patrilineal descent system.

An alternative term which is also frequently encountered and which refers to rivalry between individuals who are not necessarily close kinsmen is *siali*; an individual who competes with another man and who is recognized by others in the tribe or tribal segment as his rival for prestige and influence is said to be his *sial*. Among Afghans, the word *siali* conveys both the notion of equality (only social equals can be *sial*(s) of one another) and of competition.

The structural interplay of equality and competition is the essence of Pakhtun tribal structure, framing and defining social relations within the tribe and in inter-tribal affairs. However, problems arise in the larger sphere of relations: when the tribe must deal with other groups that are not similarly organized or with states. With regard to inter-ethnic contexts on the boundaries of Pakhtun settlement, the problem is again one of how the contact will be framed and defined.

Examining Pakhtun tribal organization in different contexts, we find that those groups which most closely approximate what might be called (from the anthropologists' and natives' points of view) 'the ideal type model' of tribalism are, for the most part, settled in the Tribal Agencies of Pakistan and in areas of Pakhtun settlement along the eastern border of Afghanistan. In Paktia Province, for example, Pakhtuns have maintained a relatively 'pure' tribal structure and uphold tribal custom; territorial distribution is based on genealogical relationship; close kin tend to support each other against more distant kin in conflict situations and in exacting revenge; and status distinctions are minimal and non-hereditary.

In contrast to this situation, Pakhtuns who inhabit areas where there has been greater contact with other ethnic groups and with state institutions have developed very different forms of social organization. The example, mentioned earlier, of Pakhtuns in Baluchistan is one case of tribal Pakhtuns becoming assimilated as clients in an economic system more complex than their own. In Swat, however, on the northern boundary of Pakhtun settlement in Pakistan, the reverse is true; rather than being subordinate, Pakhtuns occupy positions of power and authority in a multi-ethnic, highly stratified society whose economy is based on intensive irrigation agriculture.[17]

Analysing the social organization of Ghilzai Pakhtun tribes inhabiting a large arc of territory in eastern Afghanistan, Anderson has demonstrated the existence of a more continuous variation in social organization reflecting a number of ecological, political, and social factors. Thus, tribes inhabiting the southern portion of the Ghilzai zone of occupation (in the region south of Kelat-i Ghilzai) have been able to maintain greater independence from central government interference as well as the integrity of their territorial homeland. This in turn has allowed them to uphold their self-image as independent tribesmen and to maintain their tribal organization. Ghilzai living to the north in near proximity to Kabul, however, have become more integrated within the administrative and economic networks of the Afghan state, and, consequently, many features of tribalism have been lost. The most important of these features is the patrilineal descent system itself which tends to fragment and dissolve beyond the level of the regularly-interacting lineage segment.

As these various examples indicate, groups tend to maintain the attributes of tribal organization most completely in an inter-tribal environment rather than in close proximity to other (non-tribal) ethnic groups or within an 'encapsulating' state system. At the same time, in different situations in which Pakhtun groups come in contact with other ethnic groups, the structural result of the contact varies: in

Baluchistan, Pakhtun groups become incorporated on the bottom end of the Baluchi social and economic system; in Swat, Pakhtuns largely dominate local-level politics by manipulating ethnic groups on the lower end of the social hierarchy; in urban contexts like Herat and Kabul, they operate as equals with other ethnic groups but, in the process of interaction, tend to adopt the urbanized customs of those around them.

Although the specific results of different kinds of inter-ethnic contact vary, each of these examples would seem to indicate that regardless of whether Pakhtun groups enter an inter-ethnic zone as dominant, subordinate, or equal partners, it is their social organization that inevitably changes. One conclusion which we can draw from this is that tribal social organization is unsustainable in close proximity to other non-tribally-organized groups. Since tribal groups frame relations in the idiom of patrilineal descent and complementary opposition between lineage segments; it provides no mechanism for dealing with outsiders, except such institutions as *melmastia, badragga* (escort through tribal territory), and *nanawati* (asylum), all of which are premised on an absolute distinction between kinsmen and strangers and a spatial division of the world into inside and outside realms.

Multi-ethnic social systems, however, demand more complex distinctions. Individuals must assume a multitude of partial roles which are temporally and contextually defined; relations are based on the notion of a reciprocity of interests, the necessity of compromise and the willingness to accept the incomplete realization of individual objectives in any given interaction. In multi-ethnic systems, hierarchies of individuals and groups emerge, value systems overlap and become contextual; men (and even women) are hired for their labour. In short, what was absolute becomes relative, and in such a world, the holistic structure of tribal relations must give way. Thus, as long as Pakhtuns are dealing with one another in a context in which the conditions of social interaction are pre-determined by the tribal environment, Pakhtun ethnicity can be maintained, but, in complex social settings, the more flexible customs and practices of other groups with longer histories of urbanization and cross-cultural contact tend to hold sway.

ETHNICITY AND TRIBALISM

While it is generally true that ethnic identity emerges in an inter-ethnic environment (i.e., in the competitive interplay of multiple ethnic entities), many of the diacritical features of Pakhtun ethnic identity emerge in the inter-tribal environment. It is here in the context of competition and complementary opposition that Pakhtun most ully realize who they believe themselves to be while in the inter-ethnic environment, identity becomes more murky. Valued institutions are directed towards unintended ends; the complementary opposition of individuals and segments is distorted, and hierarchy emerges from practices that had previously guaranteed equality. In this regard, it is necessary to reconsider the process of inter-ethnic relations and the significance given by Barth to what he calls 'diacritical features' of 'Pathan' identity. It will be recalled that, in addition to patrilineal descent which has already been discussed, Barth cited the Islamic religion as a key feature of identity along with 'three central institutions', namely *melmastia* (hospitality), the *jirga* system (tribal assembly), and *purdah* (female seclusion).

With regard to Barth's use of Islamic faith as a criterion of Pakhtun identity, it is undoubtedly the case that Pakhtuns unanimously consider themselves to be Muslims, and adherence to Islam is thought of as a fundamental attribute of self-identity. Acknowledging this, it is still difficult to conceive of Islam specifically as a feature of 'ethnic' identity since, in areas of Pakhtun concentration, there tend to be few non-Muslims in residence. In most cases, adherence to Islam is simply not a question and cannot serve as a boundary marker between groups. To the contrary, one of the revolutionary effects of Islam in the areas to which it spread was precisely that it acted to break down ethnic boundaries by providing an ideology and set of customary practices which overrode traditional lines of ethnic and kinship division.

Given that few Pakhtun groups come in regular contact with non-Muslims, Islamic identity only becomes an important feature of ethnic identity for them in those situations where they are in contact with non-Sunni Muslims, as is the case with many groups of Ghilzai nomads who spend their summers among the Shi'a Hazara in the central Hazarajat region of Afghanistan. In such instances, however, it is not Pakhtun ethnicity that provides the framework of differentiation so much as sect, which transcends the limits of ethnicity and provides a basis for common identity between, for example, Pakhtuns and Tajiks in opposition to Hazaras.

In the present conflict, Islam again serves as a primary 'diacritical feature' of identity, but its significance is not in marking ethnic boundaries but rather in establishing a universally acceptable basis for group identity in opposition to the infidel Soviets and their Afghan 'puppets'. For the majority of Afghans who oppose the Communist regime, Islam has become the most important of 'primordial affinities' overriding sectarian and ethnic differences and binding in common cause Pakhtuns, Tajiks, Uzbeks, Turkmen (all of whom are predominantly Sunni) and Shi'a Hazara, Qizilbash, and even those Ismailis who oppose the Communist government.

If we consider the 'three central institutions' which Barth describes as being fundamental to the maintenance of Pakhtun identity (i.e., *melmastia*, *jirga*, and *purdah*), we find that they are neither the sole property of Pakhtuns nor equally important to all Pakhtun groups. Further, there is a great deal of variation in how these cultural institutions manifest themselves in different social contexts. With regard to *melmastia*, for example, it is the case that in the tribal context everyone is expected to provide hospitality within the limits of their resources. As one informant from the Zadran tribe of Paktia Province stated in defining the meaning of the word *melmastia*, 'Everywhere you go in Zadran, the people will give you food. If you go to the house of a Khan, he will give as much food as he can afford; if you go to the home of a widow or a shepherd, they will only give you dry bread, but the *jawanmardi* ('generosity') of the Khan and the shepherd are equal. Because everyone gives food according to what they can afford, the dry bread of the shepherd is equal in value to the Khan's meal.'

Emphasizing a different aspect of *melmastia*, one Afghan writer has observed that the main importance of hospitality is to provide a context for association and protection in an insecure social environment. Thus, in defining the Pakhtu word *melma* ('guest'), he noted that the guest 'has specific privileges. In the host's house *melma* is specifically safe. If anyone tries to harm *melma* the *korba* (the host) must treat the offender in exactly the same way he would if he had harmed one of the host's family member (s)....No matter how great a criminal the *melma* is, once he has entered the *korba*'s house, neither the *korba* nor the *melma*'s enemies can harm him.'[18]

In both of these definitions, the practice of hospitality is associated with the interplay of equality and competition that is the basis of tribal social organization and ethos. However, turning to the manner in which *melmastia* is manifested in the context of Swat, we find that a very different institution has evolved. Here, *melmastia* becomes a means by which Khans compete with one another for political power which is a product of a Khan's ability to amass wealth which is then redistributed as food. Those who repeatedly turn up at the Khan's *hujra* ('guesthouse') and accept his 'hospitality' signal their subservient status and their willingness to assume the identity of the Khan's client.

In one sense, of course, it can be argued that even here *melmastia* is functioning according to Barth's model, for the institution can be said to provide a 'diacritical feature' of Pakhtun identity that serves to reinforce the boundary between Pakhtuns, who control most of the wealth and act as hosts, and other ethnic groups, who work for the Pakhtuns and become their clients. Moreover, the essential relationship between equality and competition is also preserved since, as Barth describes it, the ultimate result of this competitive hospitality is a 'zero-sum game' in which political advantages are levelled out over time. Nevertheless, it is clear that a fundamental transformation takes place in the role of the institution of hospitality in the shift from a tribal setting to the multi-ethnic proto-state.

Turning to the institution of the *jirga* as it has developed in Afghanistan, we find a similar kind of transformation but different results. Thus, as the Afghan state has developed, governmental judicial and administrative institutions took over many of the functions of the tribal *jirga*, and few tribes can claim to have retained more than a rudimentary version of the *jirga*, which, in its traditional form, involves an elaborate set of precedents, rules, and protocols that govern all proceedings. At the same time as the *jirga* system lost much of its significance in tribal society, it acquired significance in the context of the nation-state. Thus, the Afghan government adopted the Pakhtun tribal *jirga* as the model for its own national assemblies: the *loya jirga* ('great council' for the constitutional assembly); the *wolesi jirga* ('popular council' for the lower house of the parliament); and the *meshrano jirga* ('council of elders' for the upper house of the parliament). In this way, the government identified its own objectives and structure with those of the tribes in order to gain their support which the government needs to survive.

Examining the third institution cited by Barth, we are again confronted with the problem of determining how and to what extent female seclusion functions as a fundamental aspect of Pakhtun ethnic identity. In this regard, Barth's choice of the word *purdah* to describe the practices associated with female seclusion is itself significant (like his use of 'Pathan' for 'Pakhtun'), for *purdah* is not originally a Pakhtu word and acquires meaning for Pakhtuns most directly as a result of increased contact with outsiders, particularly in multi-ethnic towns and cities. This is not to say that female seclusion does not have intrinsic significance for Pakhtuns, but a basic difference exists between *purdah*, as an institution appropriate to multi-ethnic contexts, and female seclusion as it manifests itself within the tribe. Thus, in tribal villages, women normally do not wear the all-encompassing veil (*burqa*) worn in the cities, nor do they go to extraordinary lengths to hide themselves from view the way city women do. Modesty is certainly expected of them but so too is it expected of men. The precise expectations of either men or women are circumstantially defined and not fixed *a priori*.

In an analytical sense then, it can be said that seclusion functions as one part of a complex set of interactions involving both men and women and exemplifying a situational as well as an absolute logic that is far from unambiguous in its import. As Anderson has described the situation, 'women veil in some situations but not in others, and some women veil in situations where others do not. . . . Women are often unconstrained in interactions where men are most restricted, and there is a sense in which men veil too. Veiling is a variable, not a constant, and no single fact about persons accounts for this variation'.[19]

The significance of veiling therefore depends on the context in which it is found. In one situation, it may mark ethnic boundaries but, in another, status differences between Pakhtuns or divisions between Muslims and non-Muslims. As Anderson notes, 'veiling and seclusion. . . .have more in common with communication than with institutional systems',[20] and this implies that rather than being specifically a 'diacritical feature' of Pakhtun identity, *purdah* might be better viewed as a symbol or cluster of symbols whose meaning is determined contextually and in relation to varying dimensions of identity.

At the same time, it can also be said that underlying the 'communicative' dimension of social interaction there is a core value of Pakhtun identity related to women, but this core value cannot be glossed by the term *purdah*. A more central notion, which reveals the ethical significance of women, is that of *tor* which literally means 'black' and which Ahmed translates as 'female chastity'.[21] Among Pakhtuns, women are thought to be vulnerable, and a man's honour is closely associated with the control which he is able to exercise over his wife and other female relatives. A woman who acts immodestly, particularly one who is even remotely suspected of having an illicit affair with a man, shames herself and her male relatives, becoming symbolically 'black' or impure. The meaning of *tor* here can only be understood in relation to its cognatic opposite — *spin* or 'white', which has the symbolic connotation of 'pure' or 'without fault'. In cases of *tor*, the woman must be killed along with the man with whom she has been or is suspected to have been carrying on the affair. As Ahmed points out, this double killing, which 'alone atones for guilt', is 'the only killing in society that does not invoke the laws of revenge'.[22]

For the present context, what should be noted is that while *purdah* and *tor* refer to similar institutions, they are not isomorphic. Both words convey notions of male honour and female vulnerability, but they have very different connotations and are appropriate to different contexts. In this regard, it can be argued that the practice of *purdah* signals the potential failure of *gheyrat*, for while the value which Pakhtuns place in the concept of *tor* reflects the ethos of self-determination and the importance which is given to male autonomy and control, the practice of *purdah* is a custom that Pakhtuns practice in common with other ethnic groups and that is meaningful not in relation to Pakhtun identity *per se* (i.e., to core Pakhtun values) but to the context in which it arises. In other words, while *tor* has an absolute and independent significance in Pakhtun society, the significance of *purdah* is always relative and dependent upon the variable framework of relations within which it is one among many communicative symbols.

This is not to say that Pakhtuns care nothing for appearances or that their own ideals are not in part an expression of external definitions. Rather, it is simply to state that the primary locus of identity changes in the relocation of a tribal people to an inter-ethnic context. In adopting the practice of *purdah*, Pakhtuns express their adherence to a set of symbolic diacritica which are defined not by themselves but by others. Practising *purdah* thus represents a form of assimilation to a system the co-ordinates of which are determined external to the participants. In this way, what is viewed as absolute in the tribal context (female vulnerability) becomes relative in the inter-ethnic milieu. What begins as a fundamental and immutable notion of 'purity' becomes an arbitrary and highly variable marker of individual status distinctions that is related as much to notions of prestige and propriety as to first principles.

According to Barth, the three 'institutions' of *melmastia*, *jirga*, and *purdah* 'combine to provide [Pakhtuns] with the organizational mechanisms whereby they can realize core Pathan values fairly successfully, given the necessary external circumstances'.[23] In contrast to this, we have argued that in many cases traditional Pakhtun practices have been altered in such a way that they no longer serve to maintain

Pakhtun ethnicity but rather help to break down the boundaries separating Pakhtuns from other ethnic groups. As Barth has formulated the process of boundary maintenance, the common adoption of, for instance, the institution of *purdah* by the various groups in a particular area indicates 'a tendency towards canalization and standardization of interaction and the emergence of boundaries which maintain and generate ethnic diversity within larger, encompassing social systems'.[24]

However, the examples discussed here would seem to point towards a different conclusion, namely that Pakhtun identity tends to fragment in larger social systems. Instead of helping to maintain 'core values', the institutions cited by Barth tend to further the process of incorporation and the diminution of Pakhtun ethnicity. Thus, for example, in viewing the fate of both *melmastia* in Swat and the *jirga* system in Afghanistan, we have to question whether, as Barth states, these institutions provide organizational mechanisms for the realization of core Pakhtun values or if, in the process of becoming involved in larger and more complex social systems, these institutions have become unhitched from the core values with which they are ideally identified. With regard to *purdah*, the question is whether in adapting to an urban milieu, the tribal ethos has not been incorporated into a superficially similar but distinctly different nexus of value in which the tribal concept of honour has been replaced by a more general notion of social propriety.

The essential point here is that whether or not a group demonstrates the diacritical features of Pakhtun identity, their status as Pakhtuns depends upon the perception by themselves and others that the circumstances of their existence live up to the ethos of self-determination. A final example which illustrates this point involves a group encountered during the course of research in a refugee camp near Peshawar, Pakistan. The group refers to itself as a segment of the large Andar branch of the Ghilzai tribe which is centred in the vicinity of Ghazni. The Andar are a well-known Pakhtun tribe, and it would be expected that this affiliation would carry some status for the group, particularly since some members of the group have become relatively wealthy through their ownership of trucks which they managed to smuggle out of Afghanistan and continue to operate as refugees. Further, these same individuals have well-appointed *hujras* where they entertain guests. Their houses are surrounded by high walls, and their women are as careful as any others in maintaining seclusion.

Despite all of this, the group is looked down upon and referred to by every other group as the *kharkaran*, or 'donkey workers', which is the occupation of many men in the group. Though members of the group state that their ancestors voluntarily left the region of Ghazni some decades ago, others assert that they lost their land and were forced to take up their present occupation in the pursuit of which they keep herds of donkeys that are used to carry bricks, sand, and other loads to construction sites on a contract basis. From the perspective of other Pakhtuns, this occupation is doubly demeaning, for it involves donkeys, which are thought of as particularly dumb animals, and the acceptance of a subordinate position as contract workers. Because of this, other Pakhtuns will not even concede this group the status of Pakhtuns, much less as members of a specific tribe. Assertions that they are members of the Andar tribe are thus ridiculed, and this attitude is not changed because of the wealth of some members of the group and their maintenance of Pakhtun customs.

Granted that character slurs are common forms of exchange between members of different tribes, it is not so common to come across a situation in which the very identity of a group as a Pakhtun tribe is denied by others, even though many Pakhtun groups have no better credentials to back up their assertions of tribal descent than the *Andar/kharkaran*. The essential reason for this denial of identity is the perception by other Pakhtuns that in accepting the low-status position of donkey workers, they have abandoned their right to be called Pakhtuns. In becoming defined as an occupational group, they have foresworn their right to self-definition and, in the view of the Pakhtun, can no longer claim to fulfill the ethos of *gheyrat*, whatever other features of identity they do uphold.

In an analytical sense then, we can say that it is in the concept of *gheyrat* that Pakhtun ethnicity intersects with Pakhtun tribalism, for it is this concept of self-determination/self-definition that establishes the normative conditions of social life, the foundation of the relationship between the individual and the collective. *Gheyrat*, with its associated constellation of values and prescriptive norms, both describes who Pakhtuns think themselves to be and lays down the conditions under which this self-description can be realized.

In summarizing the interrelationship between ethnicity and tribalism then, it would seem that the contradiction between the ideal of ethnic identity emerging in a multi-ethnic environment and the reality of Pakhtun ethnicity becoming submerged in this environment comes down to a problem of '*on who's terms?*'. As Anderson noted in a statement previously quoted, '"ethnic" identities sociologically emerge in situations where people of different traditions and organizations come together or are brought together *in contexts set by terms external to themselves*'.[25] The essential and existential foundation of Pakhtun identity, however, is the ideal of self-definition, of setting one's own terms.

Given the structural limitations of the tribal kinship system, this ideal is virtually unrealizable, for, as we have argued, in most multi-ethnic contexts, the limitations of tribal structure entail adaptation of that structure to meet the multi-variant demands of the social environment. Tribalism therefore begins to dissolve and so too does the ethos of personal autonomy and individual directiveness. For Pakhtun ethnic identity to survive, Pakhtuns themselves must set the terms of relationship and control the circumstances within which inter-group contact takes place.

IDENTITY AND FRAME

Turning to the subject of how the Afghan refugees are adapting to prolonged dislocation, several points need to be made related to the preceding discussion. First, given the familiarity of Afghan Pakhtuns with Pakistan, their shared customs and language, and the inherently ambiguous nature of the Frontier itself, the act of leaving Afghanistan must be seen as a logical and natural option for Pakhtuns and one which is largely obscured when we think of these people as 'fleeing' their country. Rather, the act of flight is better termed — to use Hirschman's phrase — as an act of 'exit': that is, an act of strategic retreat in the face of social and political opposition that does not allow for the 'voicing' of dissent.[26]

Because of the cultural ethos of personal autonomy, 'exit' is perhaps a more natural alternative for tribal Pakhtuns than what Hirschman calls 'voice' since 'voicing' dissent implies acceptance of certain shared rules with the politically dominant party (the state) and a willingness to compromise. In other words, 'voice' entails working within a political system, which, given the tribal ethos of self-determination, would entail the abandonment of that which is meaningful in the tribal scheme of things.

In this regard, tribesmen elaborate a set of conceptual contrasts between themselves and their way of life and the state and what it represents. Basic components of this oppositional set, which has been well-analysed by Anderson,[27] include *yaghistan* : *hukumat*; and *atrap*: *shahr*. *Yaghistan* here can be translated as 'land of dissidence' or 'place of unrestraint' and is contrasted with *hukumat* or 'government'. While the term *yaghistan* is used by tribesmen themselves to refer to their tribal homeland (and, concomitantly, their way of life), it would be inaccurate to assume from this that they view their own world as an anarchic one. To the contrary, in areas such as eastern Paktia Province, where tribes hold sway and governmental interference has tended to be minimal, tribal laws are upheld, anti-social behaviour is controlled, and individuals who display self-restraint are respected.

The term *yaghistan* is only meaningful, therefore, in relation to its conceptual opposite — *hukumat* — for the anarchic qualities which the term *yaghistan* describes are only valued in the context of governmental efforts to incorporate and contain the Tribal Areas. This becomes apparent in examining the manner in which tribesmen use the term, for example, in the phrase 'He was born in the year of yaghistan' or 'I came to Peshawar during the time of *yaghistan*.' In the first instance, the informant is indicating that a person was born in the year 1929 when King Amanullah was overthrown; in the second, the point of reference is the year when popular uprisings against the Communist government began in earnest — 1979. In both cases, a word which has a spatial denotation ('the land of dissidence') is given a temporal connotation ('the time of rebellion') to indicate that it was during these periods that the ideal of tribal opposition to governmental encroachment was most perfectly realized.

The other set of contrasting terms — *atrap: shahr* — can be translated as 'countryside: city'. As Anderson has noted, *atrap* 'conveys in Pakhto a notion of room in all directions, lack of differentiation, or continuity, in contrast to the dimensionality, confinement, and partial identities of the 'city' (*shahr*), where the whole man comes apart into specifically located, component roles. *Atrap* is the tribal domain in contrast to the domain of the city, where equality in the Pakhtun sense of 'no difference' dissolves in the face of diversely originated persons engaged in diverse, and all partial, ways'.[28]

Both of these sets of 'cognate distinctions' can be understood in reference to the concept of *gheyrat*, for both reflect the tribal concern for self-determination in relation to the external determinations of city and state. By defining themselves — or, more specifically, their land —

in contrast to the city/state, Pakhtuns set themselves apart from the state, conceptually and politically.

The 'exit' decision in this particular case can therefore be seen as a response which was precedented in tribal custom and which had as its intent the maintenance by the tribes of their traditional position of autonomy and marginality in the face of possible absorption by a state that no longer played by the established rules of tribe/state interaction. Ironically, however, in choosing this option, the Afghan tribesmen did not simply remain what they were; they have also become something else: refugees. That is to say, in seeking to maintain their own self-definitions, they have become defined in entirely new ways. With the introduction into their lives of a large Pakistani refugee bureaucracy, major international agencies such as the United Nations High Commissioner for Refugees (UNHCR) and a myriad swarm of smaller organizations, the simple polarity of tribe and state/*yaghistan* and *hukumat* has become confused and ambiguous. New organizational and conceptual 'frames' have taken on relevance and have had to be negotiated in ways for which there are no precedents in tribal experience.

Here, we are referring to two 'frames' in particular. The first of these is the legal and administrative framework made up of the various national and international refugee organizations providing medical and relief assistance to the Afghans. Within this frame, Afghans are defined as 'political refugees' and are accorded the humanitarian assistance to which they are entitled by international law. The second 'frame' is more ambiguous in its outlines than the first but ultimately perhaps of greater importance with respect to the question of how the refugees will adapt to prolonged dislocation. This is the Islamic frame, according to which the act of flight is defined as *hejrat* ('religious flight or migration') and those who flee are *mohajerin* ('religious exiles').

Considering first the international framework, it should be noted that the notion of 'asylum' is not alien to tribal society. To the contrary, Pakhtuns have their own traditional institution, generally known as *nanawati*, through which individuals who are outsiders in a tribe's territory or who are involved in a dispute can seek the protection of a tribal sponsor. In accepting this responsibility, the sponsor is honourbound to keep the individual out of harm's way even if it entails the loss of his own life. The rules of *nanawati* are carefully articulated in tribal law, and the institution is recognized as an honourable and necessary option which individuals and groups must take to preserve both their own lives and the integrity of the tribe.

At the same time, however, the individual who is granted asylum takes on an ambivalent status which may ultimately result in his having to accept a subordinate position to his sponsor and his sponsor's tribe. For example, if an individual seeks asylum because he has been involved on the losing side of a feud or in some other meritorious endeavour, then he will likely be received as an honoured guest who is entitled to respect. However, in cases where the individual has fled his tribe in a state of disgrace, the individual and his family may be absorbed as clients of the asylum-giver. Thus, the context in which asylum is granted is critical to how the whole interaction is perceived and interpreted in that there is an inherent possibility that the relationship will be defined asymmetrically, such that the one granted asylum loses his status as an autonomous actor.

Viewing the present refugee situation in relation to the tribal institution of asylum, we see that in accepting asylum the Afghans have placed themselves in an inherently tenuous and potentially subordinate position relative to the asylum-giver. In receiving rations on a regular basis, the refugees betray their own notions of the reciprocal nature of exchange relations and, on a conceptual plane at least, place themselves in a dependent position relative to their benefactors. In this way, it could be argued that what we view as an uncomplicated, bureaucratic arrangement for allocating and redistributing resources according to a de-personalized 'humanitarian' ethos can be assimilated in an entirely different fashion within a cultural ethos, that of *gheyrat*, which exalts self-determination, personal independence, the reciprocity of social actions, and the maintenance of symmetrical relations relative to those who are considered peers.

In this respect, one of the principal problems that confronts Pakhtun refugees is that the framework of relief administration and assistance is one that does not fit neatly into their set of binary oppositions. Considering that it is supplying them with needed food, shelter, medical care, and other supplies, the refugee administration cannot be glossed by tribal refugees as an extension of *hukumat* without their admitting at the same time that their oppositional independence (embodied in the concept of *yaghistan*) has been severely compromised. This basic fact presents itself on a daily basis to the refugees who must adapt themselves to an elaborate bureaucratic system that governs the refugees and the refugee camps. This system first requires of every single refugee and every household head that he undergo a lengthy registration procedure before being given any relief supplies or rations. Thereafter, refugees are given identity cards and ration booklets which must be shown when they pick up their monthly allotments of wheat, cooking oil, and other supplies.

The manner in which refugees initially responded to the bureaucratic system of relief administration set up by the Pakistan Government was basically identical to how they have traditionally responded to the Afghan Government and its attempts at control and interference. That is to say, the refugees tried to define the encounter on their own terms so as to limit the points of contact between the group at large and the relief administration. The main issue here was how relief supplies would be distributed. At first, this massive logistical problem was solved, as the majority of refugees wished, by turning over most of the actual distribution to refugee leaders known as *ration maliks*. These individuals would deal with the administration, handle the requisite paperwork, transport supplies to their section of the camp, and distribute rations to household heads.

To a great extent, the *ration maliki* system allowed refugees to equate the camp context with the village administrative system that traditionally existed in Afghanistan. In both situations, the points of contact with the government could be limited and tribal leaders were able to function as the primary representatives of the government to the people. In this respect, the tribe maintained a collective status *vis a vis* the government, and tribal leaders preserved their traditional social position by acting as interlocutors in the dialogue of tribe and state.

As the relief administration enlarged and became better organized, however, they began to change this system in an attempt to limit the autonomy that the refugees enjoyed. Given the nature of the situation, the administration had a number of legitimate reasons for this. Corruption on both sides of the distribution exchange was considered to be prevalent and was difficult to stem without greater accountability than that afforded by the *ration maliki* system. Further, the administration had justifiable reservations about generating a system of what amounted to tacit neglect over a population of several million refugees. In their own tribal agencies, administration was carried out in part through a *maliki* system of tribal representation, and they had reason not to want to extend this same kind of autonomy to the refugees who were difficult enough to control without handing them an administrative *carte blanche*.

Instead of overhauling the *ration maliki* system, the Pakistani refugee administration has simply replaced it with one in which the head of each individual refugee family has to collect his own rations. In so doing, they have severely limited the authority of the *ration maliks* and have split open the collective unity of the individual tribal units. From a bureaucratic point of view, this change in operating procedure has allowed a far more accurate assessment of distribution requirements and perhaps has helped to staunch some of the illicit flow of materials: however, from the tribal perspective, this policy change has individualized a relationship (i.e., that of tribe and state) that had traditionally been approached on a collective basis. As a result, the structural unity of the group has been at least partially exposed to increased fragmentation and assimilation.

A similar problem with regard to the refugee camp administration occurred in early 1984 when the camp commanders were ordered to re-enumerate the refugee camp population in order to eliminate bogus ration cards. As part of this procedure, which, from an administrative perspective, was justified given the existing abuses, the camp commander with his support personnel undertook to inspect each individual family compound so as to count the number of family members present. For the refugees, this was an unacceptable invasion of privacy, an intrusion of the public domain into the restricted universe of domestic relations. It was also another example of how the refugee camp framework forced them to compromise their tribal solidarity and their ethos of autonomy and self-determination.

Viewed from the administrative perspective, on the other hand, accurate enumeration of the refugee population is one element of the structural imperative that governs bureaucratic organizations, which is to seek an ever more precise and minute articulation of segments, greater incorporation and control over disparate elements, and increasing centralization of authority. Ultimately, the conflict over re-enumeration was resolved by the camp commanders accepting compromise arrangements and foregoing inside inspections. Despite this, however, the issue remained a point of contention and a distressing example for the refugees of their own ambiguous position in relation to the camp administrative system.

The problems involved in adapting to the refugee context, however, extend beyond the dilemma of how to establish an autonomous position *vis a vis* the camp administration. In essence, the most important problem is how to adapt to 'being' a refugee, how to maintain traditional definitions of self and society when the day-to-day framework of life is one of benign complacency. In contrast to the Afghan *hukumat*, the refugee administration has no intention of conscripting young men, of raising taxes, or of accomplishing any of the other objectives incumbent upon governments. Rather, the relief organizations want only that the refugees accept their assistance, keep to themselves and complain as little as possible. Nothing else really is asked of them except that they be compliant participants in the fulfilment of the refugee administration's bureaucratic mandate.

The result of this benevolent administration, however, is a gradual acquiescence to clientage, to external definition, a fact which is subtly revealed in the day-to-day conditions of refugee life. Thus, the camps themselves are not markedly different from many villages, especially since the majority of refugees have constructed mud houses to replace their original tents; however, the camps do tend to be much bigger and to have a far greater population density than 'typical' villages. In addition, they differ from villages in that they often have little agricultural land surrounding them. Instead, there are usually only small vegetable plots that seem almost furtive in relation to the vastness of the camp, like flower pots on a fire escape in the city.

Because of this absence of farmland, one of the striking characteristics of the camps is that they seem remote and desolate, cut off from the lifeblood of village life. In the camps, one does not see men dispersing into the fields each morning but, rather, queuing up to receive rations at one of the distribution points or squatting outside the camp commander's tent waiting to make a grievance concerning the number of family members listed in his ration booklet or to take care of some other such problem. Nothing else very dramatic tends to occur in the camps, and the mundane sameness of this scene obscures the fact that a fundamental change is occurring in Pakhtun society. With the re-orientation of economic and social life away from independent subsistence farming towards dependent ration collection, the ethos of self-determination is being subtly undermined. Instead of looking to oneself, to one's kinsmen, and to the land for subsistence and survival, it is now possible and—for some—necessary to look to an external agency for assistance and, in so doing, to abandon the core values of Pakhtun society.

For tribal refugees, the deleterious effects of refugee resettlement can be at least partially overcome in two ways. The first is by maintaining some degree of insulation and independence from the encapsulating framework of the camp and the administrative system. A basic requirement for maintaining an independent stance is that the group itself be large enough to sustain a separate nexus of social activity distinct from other groups. Thus, for example, there must be a sufficient number of families in a group to finance the construction of a mosque and the employment of a mullah. The minimum number of families required to provide the 'critical mass' for a mosque group is generally about 40 to 60 depending in part upon a group's wealth but also reflecting what seems to be an implicit awareness that a mosque is a public space and a small group keeping a mosque to itself is contrary to the role and spirit of the place as it is understood in Islam.

Independence in the camp environment is also achieved by having sources of income other than those provided by the relief agencies. Tribesmen, however, are more constrained in the kinds of employment they will accept than, for example, the aforementioned *Andar/kharkaran*. For tribesmen, this kind of work is shunned as are jobs which involve loss of independence for a sustained period of time or which are categorized as work appropriate to an occupational caste-group (for instance, jewellers, metal-workers, barbers, etc.). Acceptable forms of employment would be those that allow an individual to maintain his *gheyrat*, which is to say his 'self-determinedness'. As has been mentioned, truck driving is included in this category, as is smuggling, which can be classified as the most highly esteemed of professions.

One of the problems encountered by groups in maintaining insularity in the camp setting is how to handle disputes. An unresolved conflict between groups invites intervention by the camp administration, which, for its part, generally prefers to have refugees solve their own problems. Not all groups can do this, however, especially if there is no common tribal relationship between disputing parties, and in such cases, outside involvement is virtually unavoidable.

Certain of the tribal groups have been able to maintain autonomy in this regard. Thus, for example, when disputes arise among the Ahmadzai, they continue to be handled by the traditional *jirga* system, and cases were witnessed in which disputants and elders representing a number of different lineage groups came together from camps located throughout the North-West Frontier Province in order to carry out proceedings according to established precedent. In one particular case involving a dispute over booty captured from the government several years previously, a number of important elders and noted tribal law specialists (known as *marakzan*) came to Peshawar from as far away as Parachinar in order to participate in the *jirga*. The case itself was not considered to be especially significant, and the disputants were not men of great importance. But, because it was a tribal affair and one with potential political repercussions as far as the unity of the Ahmadzai was concerned, men of far greater importance than the disputants themselves came together to solve the problem and to lend the weight of their tribal reputations to the decision reached by the *jirga*.

It has previously been argued that adherence to customary practices such as the *jirga* does not, in and of itself, indicate the perpetuation of ethnic identity by the group in question; what matters most is not whether a given custom is followed but the circumstances and the significance which it is accorded. Given that most disputes of this kind are now turned over — willingly or not — to mullahs and/or to one or another of the provincial judicial committees set up by the various resistance parties, the continuation of the *jirga* system by the Ahmadzai illustrates the vitality of tribal practices and, indirectly, tribal identity, at least for this group.

The second way in which groups maintain autonomy in the camps is by making the system work for them. Tribesmen who are able to exploit the system (legally or illegally) to the advantage of their own group are accorded respect, for it shows both cleverness and independence to do so. A number of disenfranchised *ration maliks* demonstrated this ability when they succeeded in getting schools located in their sections of the camp. Given their experience with schools in Afghanistan and the perception that schools are frequently breeding ground for Communism, there is some ambivalence about schools and education generally among the refugees. However, in the refugee context, the schools have a strongly Islamic orientation, which legitimizes their presence, and they serve as sources of income and patronage since the schools must hire not only teachers (who are often younger tribesmen who completed school in Afghanistan), but also a religious instructor, guards, and those who construct the school building itself.

Similar examples of turning the system to one's own advantage can be seen in two cases in which prominent leaders (*khans*) built *hujras* ('guest-houses') near their homes and then set up small-scale factories on the premises using funds donated by one or another of the international relief agencies promoting income generating schemes. What is

interesting about both of these situations is that while the men sponsoring the factories had succeeded in setting up the factories, they left
the actual management of the enterprises to others. Thus, in one case,
the sponsor got funding to set up a four or five loom carpet factory in
his *hujra*. He thereupon hired an Afghan Turkman living in one of the
other refugee camps to run the factory since he himself knew nothing
about carpets. The Turkman was attempting to train some of the young
Pakhtun boys to weave carpets, but he secretly admitted his scepticism
about the whole arrangement and his view that Pakhtuns were completely unsuited for this kind of work. Nevertheless, from the Pakhtun
point of view, the *khan* was deserving of admiration for his cleverness
in acquiring the funds in the first place and his managing to get others
to work for him, which is far superior to doing the work personally.

Exploiting the system is one of the signs of a true leader in the
Pakhtun view of things. But, there is an inherent risk in this kind of endeavour, and it is not at all difficult for leaders dealing with complex
bureaucracies to find themselves as the exploited rather the exploiters.
This was demonstrated in the *jirgas* that are held periodically on the
occasion of a visit by a foreign dignitary. Initially, it was considered
prestigious to be invited by the camp administrative staff to come to
these functions. Attendance amounted to an implicit recognition of an
individual's status as leader of his group and his qualification to represent the plight of the Afghan people at large to statesmen and
politicians whom, it was believed, were only waiting to hear their stories
of Soviet brutality and their promises of eternal resistance before
ordering their governments to crate up the Kalashnikov machine
guns for delivery to the camps.

Saudi Arabian oil ministers were particularly popular visitors since
it was assumed that they had unlimited funds available to them, much
of which was undoubtedly secreted away in the folds of their robes.
That such notions were not really so curious is evidenced by the fact
that in the early days of the refugee influx into Pakistan, a few wealthy
Arabs and Pakistanis actually drove up to some of the camps and
donated large sums of money to their brother Muslim *mohajerin*.

Over time, however, Afghans began to view these events with considerable ambivalence. While they recognized that some of these dignitaries actually did make substantial donations to both the refugees
and the resistance, they also thought that the *jirgas* were 'show' events
in which Afghans were being asked to act out a script drafted by refugee
administration officials. For Afghan leaders, the question of whether

or not to participate in these events has come to be charged with all of the emotional ambivalence of a classic 'double-bind' situation. Thus, on the one side, they realize that failure to participate in the *jirgas* carries with it a concomitant loss of influence and power since their absence at important events lessens their access to important officials and might be taken badly by the camp commander and his staff. On the other side, the belief that they are being used and that their own *jirga* institution is being controlled by outsiders for their ends creates a contradiction between the actions required of them and their own cultural expectations and standards of behaviour. The result of this contradiction is a sense of confusion and bitterness on the part of the Afghans towards the refugee administration at large which they believe is interfering in their own affairs.

Underlying this 'double-bind' then is a basic disjuncture between the Pakhtun ethos of self-determination and the necessity of adapting to an unprecedented social framework in which they, as refugees, are no longer autonomous actors. The problem for the refugees is exacerbated by the fact that the *jirga* is their own institution and that those dignitaries who attend do so to praise the bravery and resolve of the *mujahideen*, who fight for their homeland and for Islam, and of the *mohajerin*, who have sacrificed their homes to preserve Islam. Such sentiments are important ones for the refugees, but hearing them again and again and in a forum that is their own, but which has been adapted to accommodate the realities of international politics and the imagistic requirements of photo-journalists has created an ambivalence and uncertainty with regard to their own ethical beliefs and customs that had not existed previously.

ISLAM AND IDENTITY

With regard to the role of Islam — the second of the two 'frames' which are shaping the nature of Afghan adaptation to flight and resettlement — it should first be noted that Pakhtuns view themselves unequivocally as Muslims. Acceptance of Islam as the true religion is never questioned by Pakhtuns. They believe in the prophethood of Muhammad and in their ultimate submission to God's will. Obedience to the primary obligations of the religion — for example, the daily performance of prayers (*namaz*), keeping the fast (*roza*) during the month of *Ramazan*, making the pilgrimage to Mecca (*haj*), and giving away a sum of money each year to needy people (*zakat*) — is also praised in theory and practised when possible, particularly by the older members of the society. In addition, many Pakhtuns, especially but not exclusively women, pay regular visits to the shrines of local saints, and a lesser number of individuals are disciples in one of the Sufi orders.

At the same time, however, Pakhtuns do not accord religion or religious leaders a special authority over them. As far as religion is concerned, the tribal attitude is essentially that it is a self-evident part of their identity that cannot be taken away from them and need not be changed. As Ahmed has phrased it, 'Pukhtunness and Muslimness do not have to coalesce, they are within each other, the inferiority of the former is assumed in the latter'. Given this integral and necessary relationship, Pakhtuns assume the implicit right to define what it means to be Muslim just as they alone have the right to define what it means to be a Pakhtun.

One implication of this is that Pakhtuns generally dismiss attempts by outsiders either to alter the way in which they practise religion or to assume a dominant position over them on the basis of religious learning or holiness. Thus, the place given to *mullahs* in tribal society is usually a subordinate one, and when someone from outside the tribe fulfils this role , he is considered to be a client (*hamsaya*) of the tribe who is not thought to be the equal (*sial*) of a tribesman. When the *mullah* comes from within the tribe, he may receive some contributions of grain or meat from other tribesmen in payment for the services which he renders (i.e., in performing at rites of circumcision, marriage, and funeral ceremonies, teaching Qur'an in the mosque, etc.), but his status will still be largely determined on the basis of tribal rather than religious criteria, which is to say, by how he fulfils the ethos of *gheyrat* and *izzat*.

The respect given to Sufi *pirs* by tribesmen does not contradict this argument, for these figures and the centres which they establish tend to be outside of Tribal Areas, frequently on the border between tribal and settled zones or in areas of disputed ownership between two tribes. Their involvement in tribal society therefore has usually been kept at some remove and does not allow them to gain any direct authority over the tribes.

The one exception to this general rule has been when the country at large is threatened by outside invasion. During such periods of *jehad*, religious leaders have taken on the role of ideological propagandists for the cause and occasionally have actually participated in the military operations themselves. In this regard, the figures of Mullah Mushk-i

Alam, who galvanized Afghan resistance during the Second Anglo-Afghan War (1878-9), and the Mullah of Hadda, who initiated a number of border revolts against the British beginning in 1897, loom as particularly important and impressive examples of this kind of leadership. It should be noted, however, that this leadership has always been situational and temporary and represented a means by which disparate tribes could unify in common cause without having to accept one among their number as a superordinate chief. Thus, neither Mullah Mushk-i Alam nor the Mullah of Hadda ever attempted to institutionalize their secular leadership beyond the temporal and ideological context of the *jehad*, and both adopted a position which assumed for themselves the right to ratify and approve the actions of rulers but not to rule themselves.

With the onset of resistance to the Communist government, the popular response followed the traditional pattern in representing the developing conflict as a battle for the preservation of Islam against the scourge of infidelity and atheism. As has happened so many times in the past, Islam became the galvanizing and unifying agent overriding the limited concerns and petty rivalries that normally characterize social life. At the same time, those who fled Afghanistan rather than submit to the government viewed themselves and their actions as sanctioned by the Prophet's own *hejrat* from Mecca to Medina in the face of opposition from the dominant Quraysh tribe. Based on the Prophet's example, many even claimed that there could be no *jehad* until there had been *hejrat;* in other words, one must follow the Prophet's example of fleeing tyranny before taking up arms to overcome that situation.

Not everyone accepts this relationship, but all Afghan refugees certainly do look to the Prophet's *hejrat* as a vital precedent that validates their own choice of exile and gives hope for future vindication. As ones who have made *hejrat*, the refugees are also entitled to the designation of *mohajerin*, which signifies to them and to others that they have sacrificed their homeland and their way of life to defend the faith of Islam.

Where the present situation differs from past conflicts is that a temporary condition has become in essence a permanent one, and the role of Islam has begun to change in the society. The normative assumptions concerning the relationship between Islam and tribe, between 'Pakhtunness' and 'Muslimness', have been altered by the introduction of Islamic institutions, especially the resistance parties and by the very nature of the present crisis and the way in which this crisis has been defined.

The element of this situation which concerns us here is specifically how the evolving role of Islam has affected the refugee population, in particular the cultural identity and social structure of Pakhtun refugees. In this respect, one of the most significant developments, which is without precedent in Afghan experience, is the new status and authority of religious leaders who have come to occupy positions of power in both the resistance parties and the camps and who, in the process, have sometimes relegated traditional leaders to a subservient role . This is the case not only with the well-educated religious scholars and spiritual leaders who direct party affairs. It also includes the more humble representatives of Islam who usually possess but a rudimentary education and who, prior to the beginning of the *jehad*, served as the leaders of prayers (*imam*) in the village mosques of Afghanistan. Where before the village *imam* was held in rather poor esteem, viewed frequently as a client of the tribe, and not infrequently mocked as a ludicrous figure whose pretensions to Islamic scholarship far exceeded his grasp of the basic alphabet , he is now a man to be reckoned with, a man to whom former men of influence pay their respects.

Reflecting this increased status, many of the *imams* of camp mosques have considerable influence, representing members of their mosques before the camp administration and serving on *eslahi,* or 'reform' committees, which have been formed in some of the camps to handle social problems that arise among the refugees. Further, where among the tribal groups, disputes are still resolved through the traditional *jirga* system, some of the more powerful *imams* in the non-tribal mosques have sufficient influence to act as arbiters in disputes involving members of their mosque groups and can effectively intervene on behalf of refugees to gain the assistance of the resistance parties when called on to do so.

The changing balance of power between religion and tribe is symbolically manifested in the relative importance of the mosque (or *jamat*) and the *hujra*. As has been previously discussed, hospitality, or *melmastia*, is an important custom in tribal society, and the activities associated with this custom are centred around the *hujra*. Among tribal Pakhtuns, the *hujra* is the hub of male cultural life. No man can hope to gain social stature and /or political influence without gaining a reputation for hospitality and the practical support of those fellow tribesmen who avail themselves of this hospitality on a regular basis.

In the refugee context, however, most individuals generally have neither the space nor the resources to maintain a fully functioning *hujra*. When guests arrive therefore, they are entertained and fed, but they are said to come less frequently now and are not encouraged to come as often as in the past. In addition, while important rites of passage such as circumcision ceremonies for young boys and marriage engagements continue to be conducted, the food provided and the number of guests invited are far less than in the past. This situation is explained by refugees as being a reflection of their present impoverishment, which is largely the case, but another factor is the relative absence of any political stimulus or rationale for expending limited resources since political influence has shifted from the tribe to the party.

In conjunction with this decline of the *hujra* as a social centre and cultural symbol, the mosque has taken on greater importance as a meeting place and nexus of social identification in the camp environment. Mosques, of course, have always served as places where people could gather to talk about matters religious and secular or just to take a nap, but, in the camps, their centrality in the life of the refugees has greatly increased. Thus, with the relative paucity of *hujras*, mosques have taken on the additional function of being centres for communal hospitality. One advantage of the mosque serving to meet this need is that the obligation to provide food and tea does not fall on any one individual's shoulders. Hospitality is the obligation of the group as a whole, and when a funeral, wedding, or other ceremony occurs, the financial and practical burden of caring for the guests is assumed by the entire mosque group. The event itself usually takes place not in the mosque but in the public space near the mosque — if such exists — or under the *sapar*, a minimal structure often made of branches and straw which provides protection from the sun and serves as a place for men to meet and relax. These make-shift guesthouses belong to the mosque group at large, and members of the group generally take turns in providing tea and meals for visitors so that the financial burden is shared by all.

While this adjustment allows the custom of providing hospitality to continue despite more restricted resources, it also illustrates a significant change in the relative weight of different cultural institutions and illustrates one of the ways in which Islam has assumed a more vital role as a focus for communal identification. Reflecting this, a number of the camp mosques bear 'high profile' religious names, such as *Abu*

Hanifa Jamat or *Qaderia Jamat* (*jamat* being the Pakhtu word for mosque), and are outfitted with expensive loudspeakers, wooden doorways, glass windows, and plumbing systems for ablution. While still relatively humble institutions, these trappings stand out in a setting in which many of the inhabitants are living in tents in reed and thatch compounds. To the refugees, they are clear indications of the relative prestige of different *imams,* for the only way to obtain these accoutrements is influence with one or another of the political parties which provide the necessary funding.

Another such index of prestige is the presence or absence of a *madrassah* next to a mosque. Thus, just as some *ration maliks* have been able to demonstrate their access within the relief administration by securing schools in their areas of the camp, *mullahs* have vied with one another to secure financing for the establishment of *madrassahs* next to their mosques. In contrast to the generally rather humble school structures, however, *madrassahs* are sometimes extensive, multi-room buildings, and the patronage enjoyed by those who control the institutions tends also to be considerably greater.

The changing role and importance of Islamic and tribal values and institutions can be seen in many other substantive and symbolic ways as well. For example, music has always provided a popular diversion for Pakhtuns, but it is hardly ever heard now because of the opposition of religious leaders. In camps, the formerly ubiquitous cassette players are seldom heard now unless they are playing recorded sermons or verses of the Qur'an. This *de facto* ban also applies to the performance of customary songs and dances during wedding celebrations, although interference by religious authorities in this realm of social life tends to be greatly resented by Afghans generally and Pakhtuns in particular.

This resentment was illustrated during the summer of 1983 when an armed confrontation occurred in Parachinar between *mullahs* residing in one of the *mujahideen* camps and a group of nomads who were performing their traditional dances – the *atan* – as part of a wedding ceremony. From the point of view of the *mullahs*, the performance of the *atan* was inappropriate during a time of suffering and religious struggle. For the nomads, and those who supported their action, the interference of the *mullahs* was an unwarranted intrusion of religious authorities into the realm of the tribe and an all-too representative example of what happens when *mullahs* gain too much power.

In addition, this incident dramatizes how 'diacritical features' of ethnic identity—in this case 'Muslimness'—can be separated from core
cultural values. In the refugee context, the political and financial power
wielded by religious authorities has upset the traditional balance of
religion and tribe and has created a disjuncture between fundamental
aspects of their identity. The effect is again to create in the minds of
refugees a 'double-bind' situation as they try to reconcile their established notions of what it means to be a Muslim with the realities of
political power that do not reflect these notions.

In assessing the increasing role of Islam, it is important to note that
not all of these changes are generalized, and they do not affect all of
the refugees equally. Among the Ahmadzai, for instance, tribal structure and customs remain strong. As has been discussed, the *jirga* system continues to function and to provide tribesmen in the refugee
context with an avenue of judicial redress other than that provided by
the resistance parties or by newly-established institutions such as the
eslahi committees which have no traditional basis in society. *Hujras*
also retain their importance with tribal refugees, and those individuals
who are recognized as *khans* maintain separate guesthouses that are
well-appointed and in which norms of hospitality are fully upheld. Further, among tribal groups such as the Ahmadzai, the müllah generally has little more influence than he had in the past, and it is not at all
uncommon to find tribesmen who do not know the name of the *imam*
behind whom they offer their prayers in their camp mosques. Since
few tribesmen chose to attend *madrassahs* in the past to acquire an
Islamic education, most tribes have to hire an *imam* who will often
be known to the congregation of his mosque only by his home area in
Afghanistan (such as *Baghlan mullah* or simply as *mullah saheb*.)

Because of their retention of these central features of cultural identity, however, tribal refugees have become relatively isolated from the
mainstream of political involvement. While non- tribal refugees seek
out the patronage of religious leaders and make the necessary and
sometimes superficial adaptations in their behaviour and expressed
beliefs to appear sufficiently religious to gain acceptance by the parties, tribal refugees reject assimilation or compromise. Thus, in organizing their military activities, they insist on following tribal lines of
organization rather than adopting any non-kinship model supplied by
the parties. In their regulation of social behaviour they uphold their
own precedents and reject out-of-hand attempts to make them con-
form to the dictates of *shar'ia* law, which would entail turning to out-

siders versed in the technicalities of Islamic law rather than to their own legal experts.

In sum then, it can be said that in the refugee context an increasing dichotomization has come about between those who uphold tribal patterns and those who profess primary allegiance to Islam as a practical code of social behaviour. At this point in time, the cultural identity of Pakhtun refugees is essentially hovering between these two poles. In the Tribal Areas of Afghanistan, power and prestige belonged to the man who could demonstrate in his social behaviour the ethos of *gheyrat*. While Islam was respected and upheld as a fundamental component of what it was to be a 'Pakhtun', it played a passive role in social affairs and assumed a self-evident dimension of individual and cultural identity.

In the refugee environment, however, the balance has swung. Political power and leverage are with the various representatives of the fragmented religious establishment, and the ethical ideal which they espouse and look for in others is very different from that of *gheyrat*. This ethos can be characterized in the word *taqwa*, meaning 'piety', and, in contrast to the tribal ideal, it is one that is demonstrated not in self-definition but in 'submission' by which is meant both submission to Islam and the tenets of the faith and, implicitly, submission to the custodians of that faith.

In the refugee context, individuals exhibit *taqwa* by keeping the five daily prayers and the other universally recognized 'pillars' of the religion; however, in a more subtle but equally telling fashion, they demonstrate their conformity to the ideal through other acts and symbols. These include keeping untrimmed beards; wearing the rolled wool cap (*pakol*) that has come to be associated with the *mujahideen* or, if one is a party official, a *karakul* cap; and carrying prayer beads. Party adherents are also careful in their actions and utterances so as not to be judged impious. They are certain to premise statements of conviction on Islamic grounds and tend to steer clear of topics which do not have a clear religious significance or line of argument. Both *gheyrat* and *taqwa* are ideals of personal conduct that express and help to enforce general notions of social propriety. However, in contrast to *gheyrat*, according to which conformity is manifested through self-definition and self-reliance, the ideal of *taqwa* encourages conformity not only with the faith and tenets of Islam, but also to what is believed to be the social and political vehicle of that faith: the party.

In considering the impact of these two frameworks—the humanitarian and the Islamic—we see that both are producing significant changes on the refugee population, and it might even be argued that what is most damaging to traditional Pakhtun society and culture and traditional notions of ethnic identity is not the upheaval of migration but rather the impositions and constraints of resettlement. In this regard, it is likely that the most critical changes in tribal society will be brought about by the conditions of refugee camp resettlement and the increasing influence of the religious framework of ideas and organization. Thus, as camp confinement causes a gradual wearing down of traditional values and institutions, there is also an increase in the importance of religious ideology and institutions. Simultaneously, one sees a widening gulf developing between those who uphold tribal patterns and those who profess primary allegiance to Islam as a practical code of social behaviour. For this reason, it can be stated that the greatest change in the society and cultural identity of Pakhtun refugees is being brought about not because of social dislocation per se but because of contradictions posed by the framing experience of becoming—in multiple senses of the word—refugees.

In conclusion then, it has been argued that in considering the survival of 'ethnic identity' in the refugee context, it is necessary first to understand the cultural ethos around which identity forms and second to contextualize the concept of 'ethnicity' by examining the circumstances within which cultural identity manifests itself. It is not enough to isolate the features of identity; one must also take into consideration the context in which key features operate and the extent to which these features continue to reflect core values of the culture. In the case of the Pakhtun refugees in Pakistan, one of the fundamental problems which they face results from the simple fact that in attempting to uphold their ethos of self-determination, they have placed themselves into multiple and overlapping frameworks within which their identity is defined for them. This is a critical contradiction and one which will continue to affect how the refugees adapt to their status as a marginal ethnic group in Pakistan society.

NOTES

1. Ahmed, A. S., *Pukhtun Economy and Society: Traditional Structure and Economic Development in a Tribal Society*, Routledge and Kegan Paul, London, 1980, p. 68.

2.   Anderson, J.W, *Doing Pakhtu: Social Organization of the Ghilzai Pakhtun*, Ph.D., dissertation, University of North Carolina, Chapel Hill, 1979, p. 18.

3.   Parsons, T., 'Some Theoretical Considerations on the Nature and Trends of Change of Ethnicity', in Moynihan, D.P. and Glazer, N. (editors), *Ethnicity*, Harvard University Press, Cambridge, 1975, p. 53.

4.   Issacs, H.R., 'Basic Group Identity: The Idols of the Tribe', in Moynihan, D.P. and Glazer, N. (editors), *Ethnicity*, Harvard University Press, Cambridge, 1975.

5.   Cohen, R.,'Ethnicity: Problem and Focus in Anthropology', *Annual Review of Anthropology*, 1978, 7, pp. 387-8.

6.   Ibid., p. 387.

7.   Barth, F., 'Introduction', *Ethnic Groups and Boundaries*, Little Brown and Company, Boston, 1969a, p. 14.

8.   Barth, F., 'Pathan Identity and its Maintenance', *Ethnic Groups and Boundaries*, Little Brown and Company, Boston, 1969b, pp. 119-20.

9.   Barth, op. cit., 1969a, p. 22.

10. Schurman, 1962, p. 49.

11. Anderson J.W., 'Introduction and Overview', in *Ethnic Processes and Intergroup Relations in Contemporary Afghanistan*, Occasional Paper No. 15, Afghanistan Council, The Asia Society, New York, 1978, p. 3.

12. Barth, op. cit, 1969, pp. 124-5.

13. Anderson, op. cit., 1979.

14. Barth, op. cit., 1969b, p. 119; and Anderson, op. cit., 1979.

15. Robinson, J.A., *Notes on Nomad Tribes of Eastern Afghanistan*, reprint, 1934 edition, Nisa Traders, Quetta, 1978, p. 28.

16. Ibid., p. 2.

17. Barth, op. cit., 1969.

18. Atayee, 1979, p. 59.

19. Anderson, J.W., 'Khan and Khel: Dialectics of Pakhtun Tribalism', *The Conflict of Tribe and State in Iran and Afghanistan*, Croom Helm, London, 1983.

20. Ibid.

21. Ahmed, op. cit., 1980, p. 202.

22. Ibid , pp. 202 - 3

23. Barth, op. cit., 1969, p. 123.

24. Ibid., p. 18.

25. Anderson, op. cit., 1978, p. 3. The emphasis is mine.

26. Hirschman, A.O., *Exit, Voice and loyalty: responses to decline in firms, organisations, and states,* Cambridge, Mass., 1970.

27. Anderson, op.cit., 1979 and 'Khan and Khel: Dialectics of Pakhtun Tribalism', in *The Conflict of Tribe and State in Iran and Afghanistan,* Croom Helm, London, 1983.

28. Ibid., pp. 25-6.

5

Charismatic Kingship: A Study of State-Formation and Authority in Baltistan
*

Richard M. Emerson

Baltistan offers an unusual opportunity to study traditional and charismatic authority. What appears to have been an ideal typical case of Weberian 'traditional domination' formed and survived for many centuries in Baltistan, not ending completely until 1972 when then President Bhutto annexed the former Balti state of Khapalu. As a result, relative recency makes antiquity accessible to study through oral tradition and the memory of living people; both those people who exercised traditional rule, and those who were subject to that rule.

In addition to the survival of tradition, the analysis of authority and state-formation in Baltistan is important for qualitative reasons. Only recently, the thesis that the state is not found among Tibetan-speaking societies was advanced by Samuel. If this analysis is generally correct, then Balti society becomes important as a clear exception to the general rule. The Balti are Tibetan-speaking people who inhabit the Karakoram mountains in the northern area of Pakistan, formerly organized into small agrarian states. In each of the three regions (Skardu, Shigar and Khapalu), a ruling family and a military class, aided by a distinct group of functionaries, ruled over a peasant population as the sovereign power within a defined territory. While they were small (about 50,000 people in each of the three kingdoms), they clearly met all of the defining features of a state. Thus, if the thesis is correct, then state-formation in Baltistan must have been responsive to factors not

* 'Charismatic Kingship: A Study of State Formation and Authority in Baltistan' was written with the support of the National Endowment for the Humanities and the National Science Foundation. Unfortunately, after submitting the paper, Professor Emerson passed away . But because of its academic value it has been included in the volume although not in its final shape.

found in neighbouring regions. In attempting to locate those factors, this study aims to improve our understanding of state-formation in general, and the foundation of stable central authority, in particular.

Three broad factors relevant to state-formation in Baltistan are discussed: (1) oasis ecology and 'hydraulic society'; (2)alien rule in the internal structure of the state; and (3) warfare between states. Based upon such case material, Weberian concepts of 'legitimate domination' are combined with coalition processes to develop a theory of *authority-validating coalitions*, specifying conditions under which central authority will be confirmed and stabilized.

This study[1] reaches as far back into the history of Baltistan as reasonable inference can carry us, but the major period of interest is from 1500 to 1840, the period of highest political development, ending with the conquest of Baltistan by the Dogra armies of Zorawar Singh. That war, coupled with the British sponsorship of the Jammu-Kashmir state beginning in 1846, ended forever the Balti states of Skardu and Shigar; and began the slow decline of Khapalu into political dependency.

There have been no systematic studies of Balti society for us to build upon. Much of the published material on Baltistan is found in the narrative accounts of travellers.[2] There have been a few scientific expeditions to the region;[3] and Read, a missionary who worked there for some years, published a small Balti grammar.[4] The Reverend A.H. Francke, a missionary-scholar in neighbouring Ladakh, has given us valuable material on Baltistan as well.

The most important published source is a study of history written in 1936 by Maulvi Hashmatullah Khan. He served as *wazir-i-wazarat* (governor) of Ladakh and Baltistan for the Dogra government of Jammu-Kashmir, posted first in Gilgit and then in Leh. He conducted a systematic historical study, travelling extensively in Baltistan for both research and administrative purposes. In addition to records of the ruling families and the oral traditions of the region, Hashmatullah obtained a chronicle in Persian, the *Shagharnama*, written in about A.D. 1700 in the court of Imam Quli Khan, ruler of the Balti state of Shigar. Hashmatullah's historical study draws extensively from that text.[5]

To such published sources I add material from my own conversations with numerous contemporary residents of Baltistan during visits in 1974, 1977, and 1979-80. Most important was a series of visits to the palace of Yabgo Fetah Ali Khan, the last ruler of the state of Khapalu, who still resides there. In the essay I have drawn largely upon Hash-matullah concerning affairs between the Balti states and surrounding regions, while depending largely upon Fetah Ali Khan and other elders of the region for information about the internal structure of the Balti state.[6]

OASIS ECOLOGY: A FOUNDATION FOR STATE-FORMATION

The Boundaries of Baltistan

In the basin of the upper Indus river, Baltistan is the downstream neighbour of Tibetan Buddhist Ladakh and the upstream neighbour of the Shina-speaking Muslim Dards of Gilgit and Chilas. Over mountain passes to the north, the former states of Hunza and Nagar can be reached. Over mountain passes to the north-east, Kashgar and Yarkand are attainable. And on the south side tracks lead into Kashmir.

Balti culture derives originally from Tibet. Their language is proto-Tibetan, making Baltistan the most extreme north-westerly extension of Tibeto-Burman language. Yet they have been Muslims for over five centuries, making Baltistan the most extreme south-easterly extension of Islam into the mountain belt which separates the Indian sub-con-tinent from the rest of Asia. The geographic boundaries of Baltistan coincide exactly with the cultural area defined by the intersection of Tibetan speech and Islamic practice. The Balti people are Muslim-Bhotia.

Baltistan has had contact with all neighbouring regions for several centuries. The contacts have been in the form of trade, military raid, diplomatic ties, and the migration of people. Some local informants now suggest that different parts of Baltistan were settled by migrants from different neighbouring regions, but that is highly unlikely. While there might have been some post-settlement migration of Dard, Turkistani, Kashmiri, and Ladakhi people, they were almost certainly assimilated into an established Tibetan culture now called Balti. This argument was first advanced by Cunningham, followed by A. H. Francke, on linguistic grounds. It has been recently elaborated by P. H. Emerson using linguistic as well as other cultural indicators of the Tibetan background of Balti culture. Francke takes the possible antiquity of Tibetan Baltistan back to Ptolemy,

... who even mentions the notion of *Byltae* (which sounds very much like Balti), of whom he says that they lived in the west of the *Akhassa Regio* (the latter identified as Western Tibet by Cunningham, 1854). . . .

Philological reasons compel us to believe that in the times of Herodotus, . . . an ancient tribe of Tibetan nomads tended their herds on the plains and hills of Western Tibet. Cunningham believes them to have extended as far as Gilgit. . . . They lived in tents of yak-hair, on the produce of numerous herds of yaks, goats and sheep. . . .

The Meaning of 'Balti'

Philology does, indeed, compel belief in the Tibetan origins of Balti culture. But *ecology* leads one to doubt the pastoral-nomadic culture imputed by Francke to the original settlers. Two points suggest that the original Balti were specialists in settled agriculture. The first point is the ecological implication of the meaning of the word *Balti*. The typical Balti dwelling has three levels: a half or fully sunken basement level; a second ground-level set of chambers; with the flat roof of those joined chambers providing a third level. Animals (sheep, goats, yak) are kept at night in the basement level in a room called the *balti*. Thus, in the Balti language, the word *balti* has two referents: the basement chamber where animals are put; and the people who put them there.

When Yabgo Fetah Ali Khan was asked how Baltistan got its name he advanced his own theory. Tibet has three levels: Upper Tibet (the Lhasa district); Middle Tibet (Ladakh), and Little or Lower Tibet (Baltistan). Since the household has three levels, the lower called the Balti, the dwellers of the lower level of Tibet are called Balti and their place Baltistan.

Another theory seems more plausible though no less speculative. Both pastoral and agricultural specialists are found among early Tibetan ethnic groups. One group could have acquired their name from a trait which set them apart: using a subterranean chamber called a *balti* to house animals. Using such a chamber in an otherwise pastoral-nomadic culture implies: (1) a sedentary people; (2) who keep relatively few animals, and (3) who find it necessary to protect those animals (against non-sedentary pastoral neighbours). Such Tibetan farmers could well have been called *Balti-Pa* by pastoral neighbours, meaning 'people who keep animals underground (in a *balti*)'. To the Ladakhi, the Balti have been known as *Balti-Pa*, though with what exact association is not known. Similarly, the Balti refer to Ladakh as *Mar-Yul* (butter country) and to the Ladakhi as *Mar-Pa* (butter people).

Colonization and Oasis ecology

The hypotheses that Baltistan was settled very early by a Tibetan eth
nic group called Balti-Pa, a group specializing in irrigation agriculture,
will be difficult to confirm or refute.[7] But the second reason to doubt
the pastoral-nomadic origins of Balti culture is quite straightforward:
the boundaries of Baltistan, defined linguistically, coincide almost perfectly with a geographic region incapable of supporting pastoralists. By
contrast, the neighbouring regions of Dardistan and Ladakh contain
enough natural grasslands and vegetation to sustain pastoral specialists
alongside agriculturists. The ethnic labels *Brok-Pa, Mar-Pa* and
Balti-Pa reflect the facts of climatic and topographic regions in the
upper Indus basin.

This ecological circumstance in Baltistan is the one which interests
us. It was well described by De Filippi:

> Everybody who has visited the villages of this region speaks of them as oases. . . .
> The country as a whole is arid — it is completely devoid of trees and any expanse of
> grass is rare indeed: while everywhere are immense rocky stretches in which the
> bareness is absolute. . . . The villages, then, are oases in so far as they represent
> islands of vegetation and human habitation . . . isolated from each other and
> wellnigh lost in the midst of barren mountains.

There are no people in Baltistan today living apart from those islands
of intense irrigation agriculture. Clearly, the most fundamental fact
about Balti society is its foundation in oasis ecology. More specifically, had De Filippi described those oases in more detail it would be apparent that Balti society is hydraulic society in the sense put forward
by Wittfogel, though on a small scale. Each oasis has been produced
by irrigation, based on water often transported a great distance through
canals built and maintained by extensive human labour.

The manner in which this land was settled can be inferred with some
confidence from the process of settlement still going on in Baltistan.
It is a colonizing process carried out by corporate villages as the smallest social unit. The process involves six distinguishable phases:

PHASE 1:

Site Selection. A reliable stream from melting snow or glaciers
high above is determined, by village elders or higher regional authority, to be a feasible distance away from a suitable slope of sand,
pebbles or glacial silt. Plans are made by those authorities to develop
the slope. The decision process in site selection is quite complex. For

example, a 'feasible distance' is determined relative to the magnitude of labour-power which the authority can mobilize and the length of time a population can be induced to wait for a return on its labour investment. At the same time, a slope is 'suitable' relative to distance from water, along with numerous other factors. For example, the village of Yugo has, for more than a century, been building terraces for wheat on *a mountain side of bedrock* sloping at 35 degrees. While the slope is entirely bare and solid rock, it is 'suitable' because water is close by, and given careful management, water can bring soil. Wheat is now cultivated in soil placed on constructed stone platforms which are supported on stone pillars, thus transforming the rock wall into a terraced slope. The time and labour invested in this instance has not yet been estimated.

PHASE 2:

Canal Construction. Men from each lineage in the village(s) are organized into work parties to build a canal of stone, wood, and mud to carry water from the source to the slope. The time and labour required will vary. In Hushe village a canal project was completed in the spring of 1980. Approximately fifty men from a village of 500 people worked largely in the early winter and spring season for fourteen years on this canal. The canal is quite short by Baltistan standards.

PHASE 3:

Soil Building. Water is turned onto the unterraced slope, and grass is encouraged by casual seeding and fertilizing (with dung from the *balti*). Animals are allowed to graze (and fertilize) as soon as grass has taken hold, usually after several seasons. Some slopes remain almost permanently in this stage, becoming an irrigated *brok* (pasture) or held for autumn grass harvest for winter fodder. Other slopes pass in a few years into Phase 4.

PHASE 4:

Land Allocation and Terracing. The slope is divided into privately held plots among the set of colonizing lineages. Each lineage then invests labour in construction of terraces and an irrigation network to bring water to each.[8]

PHASE 5:

Planting-Harvesting. Crops of wheat, barley, and millet; turnips, peas, melons, and potatoes are planted and rotated. Fruit trees, especially apricot, are started from seed and, when established, grafts taken from old trees ensure good fruit. Poplar trees are started from cuttings to provide a fast-growing source of wood for building and for fuel.

The duration of Phases 4 and 5 cannot be measured meaningfully in average years. These two phases last until the entire slope is fully cultivated, thus constituting one of the oases described by De Filippi. These mature oases have very sharp boundaries where intense agriculture ends abruptly in rock walls or talus slopes which defy further extension of agriculture (except at Yugo, as described above).

PHASE 6:

Colonizing a New Village. The slope initially selected in phase 1 is typically within a day's walking distance from the village(s) engaged in this colonizing process. If the slope in question is large enough there will come a time when considerations of efficiency in transport and protection of crops will dictate residence on the newly developed land. A ,new village is formed, with kin ties linking back to one or more parent village.

'Hydraulic Society' and Corporate Groups in Baltistan

It is virtually certain that most of the inhabited portions of Baltistan came under cultivation through repetitions of the cycle outlined above. Such colonization is still in motion, and it is a very slow process, measured in human generations. An individual putting work into canal construction today is not likely to live long enough to realize any direct return from it, nor are his immediate offspring assured of such rewards. While grandchildren in his lineage will likely benefit, it is not a benefit which his lineage alone can provide; for colonizing new land typically requires labour in magnitudes far larger than a lineage group can command.

Clearly, the colonization of Baltistan required a level of organization which transcends kin groups. The extended family or lineage as a corporate group appears to be an essential link-pin, being the smallest unit whose integrity spans the two or more generations between labour investment and agricultural return. But lineages are no more than subgroups in the colonizing process involved in Baltistan. The smallest effective group in that process appears to be the *corporate village*.[9] For example, the project observed in Hushe village in 1980, involved construction of a relatively short canal which nevertheless required fourteen years of pooled efforts by 31 lineage groups.[10]

If the ecological argument advanced here is sound, the Balti village should be a more cohesive corporate entity than might be the case either in neighbouring Ladakh or Dardistan. Unfortunately, there are no village ethnographies available for examining this hypothesis directly. Some implications can be tested, however, in census data. We expect to find larger villages in Baltistan; and in particular we expect to find a very low percentage of small villages in Baltistan because of the labour required in the colonizing process. Fortunately, the *Census of India* for 1931 and 1941 obtained, for the first time, quite reliable information on Baltistan, Ladakh, and the Gilgit (Dard) region, *with the village as an enumeration unit*. Table 5.1 clearly confirms our thesis. Very small villages (below 200 people) are rare in Baltistan but very

Table 5.1: **Size of Villages in the Upper Indus Basin, by Ethnicity of Population, in Frequency and Percentage, 1931.**[1]

	Ladakhi (Per cent)	Balti[2] (Per cent)	Dard[3] (Per cent)
1-100	18 (16.7)	18 (9.1)	64 (26.7)
101-200	34 (31.5)	26 (13.2)	55 (22.9)
201-300	15 (13.9)	49 (24.9)	35 (14.6)
301-400	16 (14.8)	17 (8.6)	24 (10.0)
401-500	5 (4.6)	15 (7.6)	16 (6.7)
501-600	7 (6.5)	10 (5.1)	16 (6.7)
601-700	8 (7.4)	13 (6.6)	7 (2.9)
701-800	1 (0.9)	9 (4.6)	8 (3.3)
801-900	1 (0.9)	7 (3.6)	4 (1.7)
901-1000		5 (2.5)	4 (1.7)
1001 +	3 (2.8)	28 (14.3)	
Total	108 (100.0)	197 (100.0)	240 (100.0)

[1] Taken from the *1931 Census of India*.

[2] The Kargil region, reported separately in the Census, is not included because some villages in that region are Ladakhi (Buddhist) while others are Balti (Muslim). The Kargil data shows a pattern midway between the Ladakhi and Balti distributions shown here.

[3] Includes Astor District, Gilgit District and Gilgit Agency including Nagar, Hunza, Punial, Ishkoman, Yasin, Kuh Ghizar. The Dards of Chilas are excluded because they were aggregated in the census report.

common in *both* Dardistan and Ladakh (22.3 per cent, 48.2 per cent, and 49.6 per cent respectively). On the other end of size spectrum, Baltistan has a far larger percentage of villages larger than 1000 (14.3 per cent, 2.8 per cent and 1.7 per cent for Balti, Ladakh, and Dard regions).

The *only* plausible explanation for these differences in village size is the hydraulic mono-culture of Baltistan, compared with the mixed agro-pastoral ecology of its higher and lower altitude neighbours.[11] As is well known hydraulic ecology often produces a higher level of social organization, with authority exercised over larger groupings of people, for example, the *corporate village* as distinct from an acephalous aggregate of lineage groups.

But even the corporate village is too small a social unit to have accomplished most of the colonization now visible in Baltistan. A canal currently under construction involves the joint efforts of Haldi and Balagon villages. The distribution of rights to land and water in this case will require an overseeing authority which spans the villages of a region. Any visitor to Baltistan is sure to notice that many of the existing irrigation systems link numerous village oases into a single hydraulic system. One could infer from this the former existence of hydraulic states in Baltistan. According to Wittfogel

> In a hydraulic setting the need for comprehensive organization is inherent in the comprehensive constructions necessitated by . . . the agrarian order.

Figure 5.1: **Village Size in Baltistan, Ladakh, and Dardistan: 1931**

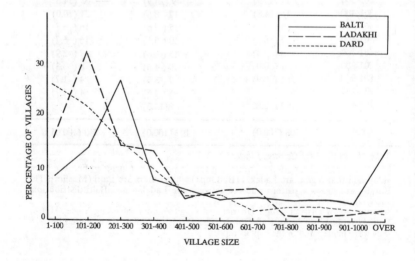

The oasis ecology of Baltistan provides the 'hydraulic setting,' and 'comprehensive constructions' are evident in canal networks which tie clusters of villages together into regional systems.[12] We turn now to the mode of 'comprehensive organization' which might have produced those structures: the Balti States as corporate groups.

ALIEN RULE: HISTORICAL ORIGINS OF THE RULING CLASS

The oasis ecology described earlier is offered as the first factor which fostered state-formation. It is an ecological condition more pronounced in Baltistan than in any of the neighbouring regions. It gives 'selective advantage' to social forms of centralized authority suitable to mobilize and discipline relatively large bodies of human labour. In Baltistan the early origins of such central authority appear to lie in rule imposed from the outside. The Balti themselves are clearly Tibetan in origin, and the ruling class among them are thoroughly Balti. Even so, there is reason to believe that they established rule through conquest, and in so doing formed a more centralized system of authority than is common among Tibetan people.

What are now the three most intensively irrigated regional centres in Baltistan—Skardu, Shigar, and Khapalu—were from very early times foci of political development in the upper Indus basin. Cunningham published genealogies for the ruling families of those three regions. In the period 1900 to 1930, Maulvi Hashmatullah Khan conducted a much more complete study in Baltistan. He published more detailed genealogies of the 'Makpon', 'Amacha', and 'Yabgo' ruling families of Skardu, Shigar, and Khapalu; along with genealogies of cadet lineages ruling in such satellites as Arundo, Parkuta, Khartoksha (the present Kharmang), Tolti, and Karres. Many of the marital ties among the three kingdoms, their satellites, and neighbours (Ladakh, Gilgit, Hunza-Nagar), are also provided by Hashmatullah. He summarizes historical events in Baltistan, based upon (a) family records, (b) oral tradition, and (c) the *Shagharnama*, a chronicle of affairs of state written in the court of Shigar during the rule of Imam Quli Khan about 1700.[13]

Tables 5.2, 5.3, and 5.4 summarize the genealogies published by Hashmatullah. Branching lines have been omitted for reasons of space. The genealogies are likely fairly reliable back to about A.D. 1450.[14] Prior to that period there is no external validation available. The dates in Tables 5.2, 5.3, and 5.4 are all taken from Hashmatullah who used outside historical sources for dating where possible. Where he had no other information to go upon, Hashmatullah assigned 30 years as an assumed average period of reign, and arrived at the earliest dates in the tables on that basis.[15] But external historical documents from Tibet and China make it clear Balti powers were involved in the affairs of Turkistan prior to A.D. 750. Thus, the genealogies do not reach as far back as they might.

The early portions of these three genealogies are interesting here because they suggest possible alien rule at an early time. As Cunningham wrote about the rulers of Shigar (Table 5.3), 'the title of Tham,

Table 5.2: **The 'Maqpoon' Ruling Lineage of Skardu**

1. Ibrahim (Maqpoon)	1190-1220
2. Astak Sange	
3. Zak Sange	
4. Brok Sange	
5. Sek Sange	
6. Tam Gori Tham	
7. Sa Gori Tham	
8. Kho Khor Sange	
9. Ghota Cho Sange (Entrance of Islam)	1437-1464
10. Behram Cho	1464-1490
11. Bokha	1490-1515
12. Sher Shah; son of 11	1515-1540
13. Ali Khan; son of 12	1540-1565
14. Ghazi Mir;	1565-1595
15. Ali Sher Khan (Anchan)	1595-1633
16. Abdal Khan; son of 15	1633-1634
17. Adam Khan; son of 15 (Gained through Delhi; ruled through regents)	1635-1660
18. Shah Murad; grandson of 15; son-in-law of 17	1660-1680
19. (Sher Khan; brother of 18; Usurped from Muhammad Rafi; son of 18)	1680-1710
20. Muhammad Rafi Khan; son of 18	1710-1745
21. Sultan Murad; son of 20	1745-1780
(Annexed to Shigar by Azam Khan, of Shigar)	1780-1785
22. Muhammad Zafar Khan; son of 21	1785-1787
23. Ali Sher Khan 2nd; son of 22	1787-1800
24. Ahmed Shah; son of 23	1800-1840
25. (Muhammad Shah; son of 24; first of line of Jagirdars under direct Dogra rule)	1840-1947

or King, borne by the earlier princes, proves that the family must be connected with the Dards of Hunza-Nagar, whose chiefs bear the same title at present'.[16] Regarding Skardu, Hashmatullah suggests that 'local folk songs, customs, rites, and archaeological findings' suggest that in ancient times 'persons entered from the side of Gilgit'. He lists the names of persons said to have 'initiated the population' in various regions around Skardu. Among them, one (Shakar Gyalpo) rose dominant, but having only a daughter, her husband (an 'able and

Table 5.3: **The 'Amacha' Ruling Lineage of Shigar**

1. Cha Tham	1140-1170
2. Bolgo Tham	
3. Yolgo Tham	
4. Ramoon	
5. Baker Din	
6. Ram	
7. Razi Tham	
8. Azi Tham	
9. Tanzan Tham	
10. Gori Tham	
11. Ghazi Tham (Ghazi Mir)	1440-1470
Entrance of Islam	1470-1490
12. Ali Mir	1490-1520
13. Gazri	1520-1535
14. Abdullah Khan	
15. Haider Khan	1535-1633
16. Hamid Khan	No Details
17. Rozi Khan	Available
18. Sultan Khan	
19. Muhammad Khan	
20. Hasan Khan (In exile; Shigar ruled by Abdal Khan, Skardu)	1633-1634
21. Hissam Quli Khan	
22. Imam Quli Khan	1634-1705
23. Azam Khan, and Wali, guardian during minority of 24.	1705-1784
24. Suleman Khan	1784-1787
25. Ali Khan; son of 22, younger half brother of 23	1787-1789
26. Hussain Khan	1789-1790
27. (Wars of succession among three sons with various alliances to Khapalu and Skardu)	1790-1819
28. (Haider Khan under guardianship of Skardu)	1819-1840
29. (Imam Quli Khan, son of 28; first of a line of Jagirdars under direct Dogra rule)	1842-1947

Table 5.4: **The 'Yabgo' Ruling Lineage of Khapalu**

1. Gori Tham	
2. Baig Manthal (First Yabgo; Built fort at Haldi)	Ca. 850 A.D.
3. Tekum Baig	
4. Mehmood Mazd Qali	
5. Sultan Mehd Ghazali	
6. Malik Ghoshali	
7. Malik Shah	
8. Junaid Shah	
9. Haider Karrar	
10. Malik Mir	
11. Jor Khane	
12. Alam Malik	
13. Rustam Malik	
14. Malik Mir	
15. Malik Jabbar	
16. Mehdi Mir	
17. Jaleel Baig	
18. Rustam Baig	
19. Tallab Khan	
20. Muqeem Khan	
21. Shah Azam Khan (Entrance of Islam)	1420-1450
22. Nur Ghazi	
23. Alamgir Ghazi	
24. Asi Ghazi	
25. Yabgu Barat Khan	
26. Yabgu Seemday	
27. Yabgu Bardalday	
28. Yabgu Malik Bal	
29. Yabgu Azrad	
30. Yabgu Begam	1485-1494
31. Yabgu Behram (son of 30)	1494-
31. Yabgu Korkor (brother of 31)	-1550
32. Yabgu Sekum (son of 31)	1550-1590
33. Yabgu Ibrahim Khan (3rd son of 32; Saling Khar*)	1590-1605
34. Yabgu Sher Ghazi (son of 33) (Saling Khar)	1605-1620
35. Yabgu Rahim Khan (son of 34) (Saling Khar)	1620-1630
36. Yabgu Hatim Khan (son of 35; Saling and Khapalu)**	1630-1690
37. Yabgu Dalba Khan (son of 36)	1690-1725
38. Yabgu Mohammad Ali Khan (son of 37)	1725-1760
39. Yabgu Yahya Khan (son of 38)	1760-1810
40. Yabgu Mahmood Shaw (Mehdi Ali Khan; son of 39)	1810-1820
41. (Pulchang Karim, Governor for Ahmed Shaw, Skardu)	1820-1840
42. Yabgu Daulat Ali Khan (son of 39)	1840-1860
43. Yabgu Mohammad Ali Khan 2nd (son of 42)	1860-1880
44. Yabgu Hatim Khan 2nd (son of 43)	1880-1890
45. Yabgu Nasir Ali Khan (Ali Sher Khan, Regent 1890-1900)	1900-1944
46. Yabgu Fetah Ali Khan (son of 45)	1944-

intelligent' man from Kashmir) became heir to the throne. He was the Ibrahim from whom the line in Table 5.2 descends, according to speculations reported by Hashmatullah.

But at a time much earlier than the genealogies suggest an incipient state of Skardu was prominent in the political affairs of Chinese Turkistan. Tibetan documents describing the early part of the eighth century have Isvara-varman, king of Skar-rdo, along with the king of Khotan, killed in battle in the 'Gold Country' (Hunza-Nagar region); the new kings of Skar-rdo and Khotan were described as enemies; and the Skar-rdo king was defeated (*in* Skar-rdo) by the king of Khotan. The Chinese histories of that period report similar involvement:

> The Tibetans having attained suzerainty over Gilgit, the imperial general Kao Sien-chih, second in command to the governor of Kucha, crossed the Pamirs in 747 and came down into Gilgit by the Baroghil Pass[17] and imprisoned the Tibetan vassal king. In 749 the *yabghu* of Tokharistan — that is, the Turkic Buddhist ruler of Kundus — sought the aid of the empire against a petty mountain chief (an ally of the Tibetans) who was cutting communications between Gilgit and Kashmir. Kao Sien-chih crossed the Pamirs once more with a Chinese expeditionary force, and again drove off the Tibetan partisans (750). (Grousset).

The 'Tibetan partisans' in this case could only have been Balti.

This quotation has been included partly because it makes reference to the Turkic Buddhist rulers of Kundus, carrying the title or office of *yabghu*. This brings us to the third Balti state, Khapalu, and the genealogy in Table 5.4. The genealogies published by Cunningham have *Yagu* as the name of the ruling lineage in Khapalu. The last and still living ruler in the line, Yabgo Fetah Ali Khan, pronounces the name *Yabgo*. He claims that his family came from Turkistan 'too long ago to give a date'. The following local legend about the origin of the Khapalu kingdom obtained by Hashmatullah in about 1910 are still told in the area.

Among several petty chiefs in the Khapalu area, Gori Tham became prominent. During his time, Yabgo Beg Mantal came by way of Kundus valley and built a fort at village Halti. Because of his cruelty and cunning he came to be called 'y-Chan-Pho-ckho' (literally translated, 'big snow-leopard man' or 'predatory giant'). He gained suzerainty over the Khapalu region from his fort at Halti.[18] When Gori Tham failed to produce a male child, and attempted to pass his authority to the son of his low-born paramour, Beg Mantal took excuse to arrest and execute Gori Tham, and annex his region.

That is the legendary origin, in condensed form, of the Yabgo lineage in Khapalu. In a publisher's note appended to Hashmatullah's text it is speculated that the Khapalu ruling family might have come from Tokharistan where *yabghu* was a title for ruler (see Grousset quotation earlier). That the name should remain recognizably intact for many centuries, and through transfer across languages seems improbable. But there is interesting support in place-names and geography. The Kundus valley referred to as Beg Mantal's route of entry is one of the valleys in the Khapalu kingdom, said to have been colonized by people from a place called Kundus. Local informants today, including Yabgo Fetah Ali Khan, do not appear to know that another Kundus was the political centre of Tokharistan. Further, local residents say that a mountain pass (the Sin-La) once led from Kundus valley to Kashgar, but glaciers make it impassable in modern times. In fact, the pass is still passable, and it gives access to all of Chinese Turkistan, including Kundus. To my knowledge no previous observer has been aware of this parallel tie between Khapalu and Tokharistan, involving both the Yabghu family name and Kundus as a place name.

The evidence for an early (eighth century) tie between Turkistan and the rulers of all three Balti states is strong enough to lead F.W. Thomas to write:

> Baltistan was not a Tibetan country. Hence during the period A.D. 696-741 its rulers, apprehending attack, thrice dispatched missions to the Chinese Court.
>
> . . .whatever the original ethnical difference between Hunza on the one hand and Nagar and the Baltistan on the other, it seems likely that the Baltistan dynasty was of Huna origin.[19]

I must agree with Francke that the peasant population of Baltistan is of early Tibetan origin. If Thomas is also correct, and I think he is, then from at least A.D. 750 onward, a Tibetan peasantry was under foreign rule in Baltistan.The Tibetan peasantry would have been Pon, the pre-Buddhist religion of Tibet; and the rulers would have been Buddhist. Future archaeological study of the Satpara waterworks which gave irrigation to Skardu in some early age, and iconographic study of Buddhist culture associated with that hydrology would prove very informative.[20]

For our purpose here, the importance of conquest and foreign rule adds an additional dimension to the state forming process. In addition to the oasis ecology and colonization process described earlier, we have reason to suspect a factor no longer seen in Baltistan:the use of forced labour in the settlement process; in a two-tiered social structure. The labour used in early colonization was almost certainly a combination of (a) Balti peasants indigenous to the local region; and (b) slaves obtained as prisoners of war, or through trade.[21] Thus, Balti society might have been three-tiered in an early era: Turkistani ruling class; Balti peasantry; and slaves most of whom were likely Dards. There is a small class of landless dependents in the current population of Baltistan which might descend from slaves, but this is speculative.

INTERNAL STRUCTURE OF THE KHAPALU STATE

Having given some historical and ecological reasons to suspect that alien rule was a factor in Balti state-formation, the next step must be an analysis of how alien rule was incorporated into the structure of those states. This task is undertaken in two parts:

1. a description of the interial structure of one of the states; followed by
2. a theoretical interpretation of the sources of 'legitimacy' of the ruling class in that state.

The descriptive material is presented in this section. The question of legitimacy taken here to be an integral aspect of state-formation is taken up later.

All three Balti states perished in whole or in part between 1840 and 1850, leaving behind no written record of their internal structure.[22] Khapalu, however, died out through slower stages, leaving its oral traditions relatively more available for study today. I wish to describe the state as it was prior to 1840, before the process of decay commenced. My information comes from repeated conversations with Yabgo Fetah Ali Khan (the last name in Table 5.4), Munchi YahYah, the last Wazir of Khapalu, and numerous villagers. Since the information has been filtered through 140 years of declining statehood, the history of the decay of the Khapalu state is summarized in a note.[23]

Ruler, Ruling Family, and Ruling Class

The word Yabgo is used today as the name of the male lineage of ruling family. Whether or not it derives from an ancient title in Tokharistan, it is not a title in Baltistan. The title of the ruler of a Balti state is Cho; a title used at least as far back as A.D.1532 (see Mirza Haider's discussion of this title, used in Khapalu at the time of his visit). It is the Balti equivalent of King; for there was one and only one Cho in Khapalu at a given time. The Cho and his household and court were located in the main fort/palace, on the summit of a mountain overlooking the main oasis of Khapalu.[24]

The state was divided into regions, each having a subsidiary for⁺ (Khar) to protect regional granaries. Such peripheral political centres included at various times: Saling; Halti; Karku; Thale; Karas; Chorbat; and at an early time, Nubra. The number varied somewhat from one century to another, as the boundaries of the state changed through warfare, growth or atrophy. I have found no proper Balti title for the regional authority in these places, other than Kharpon (herd of the fort). In modern times—beginning with British Dogra suzerainty in 1846—they have been called Raja. Thus, Yabgo Fetah Ali Khan, identifying himself to me as Cho, now refers to the Raja of Karas. But the Balti title of Kharpon, which might have been used in earlier times, has more administrative connotation than does the Indian appellation Raja, (more research is needed on this matter).

The Kharpons, as I will call them, usually carried the lineage name of Yabgo. While seldom used to refer to persons other than the line of rulers in the Khapalu centre (Table 5.4), it can be used properly by persons descending from that line on both parent's sides.[25] Thus, the Raja or Kharpon of Karas was a Yabgo descended from Behram Cho (Table 5.4). For a more complete genealogy of the branching lines of Yabgo see Hàshmatullah's narrative. It appears from those records and from current informants, that the Yabgo name was carried only by persons whose mother (as well as father) was a member of the Yabgo line. Thus, the name marks true Khapalu nobility. But an important thing to note, in terms of the organization of the state, is that most Kharpons appear to have been Yabgo.[26] If the Yabgo family line derives from Turkistan, as suggested above, then the line has followed customs which (a) preserve its genealogical integrity, and (b) control both central and peripheral foci of power as an 'alien' ruling elite.

Far more numerous in the Khapalu population than the ruling family of Yabgo, is what can best be called the ruling class of Kha-Cho ('brothers of the Cho'). Yabgo is a royal sub-set within this class. Kha-Cho are the male descendants of the brothers of the Cho. Thus, in a given generation, the class will include the ruler's real brothers (if any), his paternal uncles and male cousins of 1st, 2nd... nth order. The title of Kha-Cho is used if patrilineal kin-ties to Cho are claimed and acknowledged, no matter how great the 'kin-distance'. A non-Yabgo mother does preclude a son being Kha-Cho; and lineage ties back to Cho do not appear to require documentation. Thus, it is a much larger category than Yabgo.

Most important, however, is the unambiguous functional definition of Kha-Cho: they were a warrior class, serving as commanders of groups of soldiers of size 10, 100, 1000. Informants who today refer back to this decimal ranking of Kha-Cho are not able to describe the system clearly (it went out of use a century or more ago), but it is likely a variant or vestige of the well-known Central Asian mode of military organization.[27] It could have come to Baltistan directly from Turkistan at an early time; or it (more likely) could have entered as late as A.D. 1600-1700 from Mughal Kashmir.

The Kha-Cho of high rank were generals; close relatives of the Cho (brothers, sons or close cousins), located at the court. If not part of Cho's household, they had income in kind from lands (Cho-pi-tsa; Cho's land) tenants. The Kha-Cho landlords share in such share-cropping is reported to have been, 'in early times,' one-half, two-fifths, and one-fifth from three grades of land, assessed on a fixed evaluation of expected annual yield. Kha-Cho of low rank and distant kin-ties to the Cho resided out in the villages, again on Cho-pi-tsa worked by tenants. Thus, the entire class of Kha-Cho was sustained on royal lands. While rights to produce from parcels of such land were retained in the family through inheritance, the land was in principle under management by the Cho on behalf of Allah.[28] The British Land Settlement (1903 in Khapalu) converted these Jagir-like rights to produce into ownership of the land.

The Kha-Cho class was apparently a 'standing army' or officer corp. They were trained in the martial arts of war. They engaged in regular polo contests; that sport most likely having its origins in Baltistan. It is today a royal sport in the region, very well suited to develop and display keen horsemanship. As a standing officer corp, they mobilized in time of war an army of peasant soldiers. The state claimed the right to mobilize one male member from each peasant household, to serve as a soldier under Kha-Cho command when need arose.

Revenue

In addition to revenue shares derived from Cho-pi-tsa, land revenue as high as 1/5 was collected by Cho from all other lands, both agricultural and pastoral. Again, the conception that Cho was managing what belongs only to Allah was applicable, making the revenue payment a form of rent in exchange for the use of another's property. 'Spang-mar,' for example, was a payment in butter (*mar*) made by a village in return for the grass (*spang*) the village grazed animals upon. All payments were made in kind until well into this century. The village headman (Trampa) delivered the wheat, butter, etc., directly to the Cho or to a regional Kharpon. If the latter, the Kharpon retained a fraction which varied, up to one half of the revenue. I hesitate to describe the revenue rights regional authorities as 'jagirs' granted by the Cho until more re-search is done on the topic. We likely will never know the details of the traditional revenue system.

Pha-Cho: The Class of Ministers and Functionaries

The Kha-Cho class has lost its Kshatria-like status and function in Bal-tistan, yet any visitor to that region today will meet people who are ad-miringly called Kha-Cho so-and-so. Such descendants of the military ruling class are now found as jeep-drivers, school teachers, small peasants or large land owners; all proudly identified with an honoured past and kinship with the Cho.

In sharp contrast, there is a class of people who were once impor-tant, but in a way people now prefer not to remember: the Pha-Cho.

The Queen-mother in Baltistan did not nurse her son, the Prince-to-become-Cho. Custom ruled that a woman-dependent in the royal household should serve as wet-nurse. Her husband was typically the minister in the court; and they and their offspring were called Pha-Cho. Thus, the prince was raised side-by-side with the son of his own 'milk-mother'; a person who might one day serve him as minister; and side-by-side a girl daughter of his milk-mother to his own children. These two families in the court formed parallel lineages, one compris-ing the ruling Kha-Cho; the other defining the serving Pha-Cho.

Very little is known about the functions performed by Pha-Cho. I have found only two references in the literature to their existence. Drew comments that the Balti 'Wazir class intermarry among them-selves,' and in Hashmatullah's passages taken from the *Shagharnama* notes an instance when a Pha-Cho girl from Khapalu married into the royal family of Skardu. All that I can say about the Pha-Cho, there-fore, comes from informants who in every instance preferred to change the subject. Out in the villages, people reacted to persons identified as

Pha-Cho with contempt and a little fear. Informants at the village-level have Pha-Cho once serving 'like police' or overseers, while Kha-Cho are remembered as protectors and much admired to this day. In the royal household and court, the Pha-Cho class ranged from high administrative office down to menial servants such as stable hands. In all likelihood, much of administration of the state was carried out by Pha-Cho as intermediaries between Cho and Kha-Cho, on the one hand, and the peasant corporate villages on the other.

Islam in Khapalu

The history of the entry of Islam warrants lengthy study in its own right. I will provide here only a brief description of its place in the structure of the kingdom. More attention is desirable for two reasons:

1. Khapalu might be unique as possibly the only place where the Persian Sufi order known as Nurbakhshi is still practised; and
2. As traditional state authority has withered, the religious sector appears to be gaining even more importance.

The religion of Khapalu was almost certainly pre-Buddhist Tibetan Pon when the first Sufi teachers entered from Kashmir (c. 1450).[29] The rulers of all three Balti states became their patrons; and mosques and Khanqahs were constructed; and to this day their descendant line of Nurbakhshi Sayyids conduct religious practice in virtually every region of Khapalu.[30]

It is apparent that in early times Sayyids and mosques were beneficiaries of royal patronage or grants, but I do not know how the major mosques and religious centres have been sustained in recent times. At the village level, however, the village as a total community provides land for its Maulvi, labour and material for construction of the mosque and the Maulvi's home, and labour for the maintenance of the Mosque. Most of the village-level Maulvi's are born and educated in the Sayyid lineage, and take wives from that lineage. As a result, the village Maulvi and his family are seldom natives of the village they reside in and serve. They come, instead, from such centres of religious influence as Tagas; Sermo, Khapalu proper; Karas; etc.

THE FUNCTIONS OF STATE:
JUSTICE, WELFARE, AND WAR

Judicial Process in Khapalu

Cho was required by custom to make himself personally accessible to individuals from all social and regional sections of the Kingdom. In a regular Durbar-like public forum, publicly heard complaints were resolved at once, unless (1) the issue involved points of religious law, in which case the matter was delegated[31] to the Sayyids for study; or if (2) the Cho felt need for (or was advised to obtain) the results of a fact-finding-commission known as *Ul-sum-mi-Trampa* (a panel of three village head-men or Trampa) in which case a decision was postponed to allow an inquiry by that panel.

Yabgo Fetah Ali Khan, in his conversations with me, attached great importance to this institution. The Trampa were commoners who held hereditary status as village headmen. Thus, they were independent of both the ruling Kha-Cho and Pha-Cho classes.[32] The panel of three Trampas was selected in the public Durbar, specifically to inquire into the case at hand. While their findings were advisory to Cho, it was most uncommon for Cho to rule against them. The *Ul-sum-mi-Trampa* was involved only in non-religious civil disputes, such as petitions regarding revenue, *ress* (labour for the state, see later), public works or civil crime.

Welfare and Public Works

In a state based upon subsistence villages, each one well organized as a corporate unit, care for the impoverished, the aged or the infirm is typically handled inside the village. So it is in Khapalu. Even so, a largely symbolic institution in Khapalu expressed in principle a state responsibility. It was defined by firm custom that the Cho would care for 120 orphans to be reared in his royal household.

Far more important was state involvement in the colonization of land and other public works such as 'road' building, flood control, and famine relief. Much of the Cho-pi-tsa (Cho or state lands) derived from Cho's claimed share of land developed through projects conceived and supervised by central authority. Some rulers in Table 5.4 are remembered more than others for an active role in developing and populating new regions. The state provided co-ordinating authority in such colonizing projects. It did not subsidize them. (See earlier on the colonizing process.) They are not truly 'public' works.

In true public works, the state mobilized labour through an institution called *ress* (turn-taking). Peasants were required by custom to 'take their turn' in working for the state, when called upon by an appropriate authority to do so. A principle of equity in providing such labour is embodied in its name.[33] *Ress* operated at all levels in Balti society. In small villages today, *nur-ress* (taking turns as shepherd of village flocks — *nur*) and *cha-ress* (serving — tea cha — to the community after juma services in the mosque) are among many examples of turn-taking supervised by village Trampa. Further research will likely show special forms of *ress* operating up through intermediate levels of authority to Cho.[33] At that state level *ress* labour was mobilized and paid a daily allowance of grain from the central or regional stores, for road construction and repair, flood protection work (building dikes and canals), etc.

In times of famine, relief was provided directly from state stores. Most notably, seed grain was distributed from state stores after famine, and in normal times as well as under some development circumstances (in which case, subsequent revenue would return such 'loans' to the state stores). As a result of this practice, land units and revenue value assessments were commonly expressed as so many seed the amount of seed grain required to produce a crop from that land unit. (A villager in Hushe, asked in 1980 how much tax he paid on the land he worked, answered 'two seed'). These traditions make it clear that, at least in time of stress, the state had a custodial role in managing the grain surplus of the community.

Warfare: The Protective Function of the State

Warfare and military-political alliances — the 'foreign affairs' of the Balti states are treated analytically in the next section. Here I will draw upon oral tradition and ceremony to describe warfare as an internally defined protective function of the state.[34]

For some centuries, it is said, an important state festival occurred in Khapalu on a 36 year interval. The last time the festival occurred was in 1940.[35] The occasion before that was witnessed by Duncan in 1904, and the next previous occasion was witnessed by Raja Spindia in 1868. He and Duncan compared notes about it. That such a long time interval should pass between these ceremonial occasions testifies both to the importance and to the 'traditionalism' of the festival. The festival was organized around the following 'story' according to Yabgo Fetah Ali Khan.

Long ago the Khapalu Cho and his army were away on a military mission. In the mountains south of Khapalu, members of a peasant clan detected the approach of a large band of warriors planning to attack the Khapalu fort. Knowing that the fort was poorly guarded, the head of the peasant clan organized his clan into an ambush and killed all of the 'soldiers from the south' thus saving the Khapalu area from plunder. Upon return from his own military, the Cho was delighted with the clan's achievement and asked the clan head what he would like done in return. The clan leader said: 'I have done what Cho should do Therefore, I should wear your clothes and ride your horse'. The Cho called all the people of Khapalu together, and honoured the clan leader by placing his own robes upon him, and presenting him the personal horse of the Cho. Every 36 years this ceremony was repeated in a festival of several days, culminating in the ceremonial installation of a 'substitute Cho' from that very clan.

I asked why this ceremony is repeated every 36 years. Answer: just as the Cho's authority passes to his own son, so the authority and honour of the 'temporary cho' should pass to a son in that clan. This was done every 36 years because that is the span of one generation. (It is also a convenient multiple of twelve. The Balti group years into dozens for measuring age.)

This legend might be interpreted to contain a number of themes expressing various aspects of rulership in Khapalu. Self evident implications include: (1) protection of villages and accumulated surplus, as a responsibility of the Cho; (2) the transmission of that responsibility through inheritance; and (3) the right to rule (to claim the office of Cho being based upon the exercise of that responsibility. But there are additional features of this legend that are interesting for analytic reasons: (4) vulnerability is portrayed, the Kingdom being attacked from one side while the Cho is off doing military work on another side: and (5) the potential for fragmentation, the military function being performable by lesser leaders. To ceremonially honour the clan leader as a 'Cho' was a necessary act to preserve the authority of that office. Failure to do so would allow peasants to be their own protectors.

The potential for fragmentation is a simple structural implication examined further later. The vulnerability I point to in this legend is, I believe, more than happenstance – it is a theme in the folklore of Bal-

tistan. In the next section I will attempt to develop a theoretical analysis of the 'legitimacy' of concise rule, making important use of that theme. The theory will also address the conditions under which such states will or will not fragment.

CHARISMATIC KINGSHIP: A THEORY OF LEGITIMATE COERCION

Centre versus Periphery

The factors in state-formation in Baltistan identified so far fall short of a satisfactory account. A summary of the points made above will make their inadequacy apparent.

1. The ecological circumstance in Baltistan, as compared with its immediate neighbours, favours the formation of relatively large corporate groups with authority capable of mobilizing and maintaining relatively large hydraulic projects.
2. Domination by a military class (possibly of alien origin) over a peasant population provided such authority in each of three territories.
3. In addition to mobilizing and maintaining hydraulic projects, that military ruling class provided protection for those hydraulic investments and the surplus produced by them.
4. Within that ruling class there was an institution of central authority called Cho, exercising control over lesser regional authorities called Kharpon or Kha-Cho.

As an account of state-formation in Baltistan the argument breaks down at point 4. The central authority or sovereignty described in point 4 is usually taken as a defining feature of the 'state'. Therefore, point 4 might support a premise of this study to the effect that Skardu while back from K_i to C (as portrayed in Figure 5.2) by *duty* comes both a portion of the revenue and military support. Between K_i and T_j, the responsibility to protect and the duty to provide soldiers and wheat (revenue) are 'exchanged'. To so describe the flow of benefits as operating within definitions of 'rights', 'duties' and 'responsibilities' is to assert that transactions among the actors was institutionalized; and the institution described in this case is centralized at location C.

However, the resources which flowed among groups inhabiting the Khapalu region can be described in noninstitutional terms; and the structure so described need not be unicentric at C. If socially prescribed rights and duties are removed from the description, the network can be described in terms of the flow of three essential resources: (1) land revenue; (2) military manpower; and (3) military-administrative leadership. Any point in the network where these three 'factors of production' come together is a potential power centre. At such points in the network an actor will have some measure of coercive capacity to retract revenue, and some military capacity to protect the source and substance of that revenue. The network portrayed in Figure 5.2 contains four such foci of potential power. Hence, viewed in terms of basic resources, the network in Figure 5.2 (and the state of Khapalu which it represents) could have remained a cluster of smaller regional centres; or having formed around a single centre as Khapalu did, could have fragmented into a mere cluster of undisciplined contending chiefs. Shigar and Khapalu were Balti states; but it does not advance our understanding of the state-forming process, either in Baltistan or in general. Thus, we come to our final question: what factors produced centralized authority in Baltistan?

This question can be sharpened a bit by portraying the internal structure of Khapalu state as an 'exchange network' involving the flow of major resources among major classes of 'corporate actors' who comprise the state.

In the schematic diagram shown in Figure 5.2, each letter represents a corporate social group with an internal structure which the

Figure 5.2: **Schematic Representation of Khapalu State as a Centralized Exchange Structure**

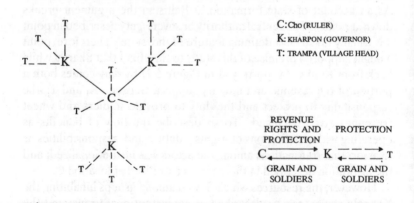

diagram does not show. Thus, C is the household and court of the Cho; K_i is the household, court and Castle-Fort of a given regional Kharpon; and T_j is an agricultural village under the hereditary headship of a given Trampa. These letters can be understood either as persons acting with authority on behalf of (managing the resources of) their respective groups, or the letters may be understood to stand for the groups in question. Either way, the lines represent relationships of negotiated mutual benefit or exchange between groups (and therefore between persons as members of those groups).[36]

The valuable resources which flow along the lines in this simplified diagram can be variously described. One way to describe them is in terms of culturally defined rights and duties among the actors involved. For example, from C to K_i goes the right to collect and retain revenue (from T_j)

The almost cyclic rise of central power and subsequent fragmentation into lesser regional foci of power is a familiar theme in the politics of traditional agrarian empires and kingdoms. The potential for such fragmentation in the state of Khapalu is implicit in the 36 year festival described above. Yet, the main message conveyed in that ceremony is the institutionalized pre-eminence of the Cho as the central source of military protection.

The Theoretical Issue

The conditions which give rise to and sustain such institutions of central authority as the Balti Cho must be included as central factors in the study of state-formation. In studying the Balti state or – perhaps any other historical study of state-formation – this task is more a problem of theory than one of fact. One could argue, for example, that the central power enjoyed by the Mughal rulers in India and by the Tokagawa dynasty in Japan was based in both cases upon a policy of reclaiming and redistributing land grants to the military nobility. This argument is theoretically sound; but on the side of historical fact, it can be no more than plausible. Equally theoretical is the notion that a central policy of separating the military from the administrative functions on the periphery helped to maintain centralized Mughal power. It has also been observed (by Saran and many others) that the Mughal policy of reassigning governors and *Mansabdars* to different regions preserved the central power of the Mughal Court. Again, the observation is theoretical. That the policy was in effect is all that history tells us.

Unfortunately, in the case of Khapalu we cannot fall back upon the implicit theories behind the above efforts to explain centralized power. There is no historical indication [37] that the jagir-like grants from Cho to Kha-cho (making the latter a Kharpon) were retractable; no evidence exists that regional Pha-Cho were separated from region courts and centrally controlled; and we know that regional reassignments of Kharpon by Cho were *not* made in any systematic-strategic way.

Thus, in the case of Khapalu, we are forced to fashion a fresh theoretical account for the emergence of the institution of a central sovereign power, under essentially 'feudal' conditions of potential dissolution of power into the hands of rival members of a ruling class. Such theoretical efforts regarding a given case – the Balti state in this instance have more general value than cogent interpretation of one case; they provide the conceptual framework for comparative analysis and generalization across many 'cases.'

Coalition Theory and 'Legitimate Coercion'

The historical 'facts' regarding the Balti states are few and tenuous. They consist of oral and ceremonial traditions regarding Khapalu; and the history of warfare (both among those states, and between Balti and non-Balti powers) as reported by Hashmatullah. The following paragraphs attempt to organize those materials into theoretically cogent themes, drawing upon empirical detail to illustrate points in a theoretical analysis. Few if any of the theoretical notions advanced are original. I draw up existing concepts in three areas: (1) coalition formation, as found largely in the work of Gamson and Riker, (2) forms and sources of 'legitimate domination' taken from Max Weber; and contemporary economic theory regarding public goods, taken from Mancur Olsen.[38]

'Legitimate Domination.' The two descriptions of relations portrayed in Figure 5.2, one in terms of rights and duties, the other in terms of resources provided, correspond directly with Weber's distinction between *Herrschaft* (domination) and *Macht* (power), respectively. As he points out, power in a general sense involves 'market-like' negotiations of interest in which one complies with another's will because of benefits received protection in exchange for revenue; military support in exchange for control of sub-region; etc. The process is one of bargaining and negotiation, and power is the potential to gain preferred outcomes through that process . By contrast, domination involves a relationship of acknowledged superiority-inferiority between 'status unequal'. The process in commands and the right to issue them, and compliance based upon duty rather than benefit. In the pure case of domination (*Herrschaft*) there is no negotiation. Unlike power, Weberian domination is not based upon the market phenomenon of control over desired commodities. As he put it:

> No precise conception of domination could be built up upon the basis of (exchange); and this statement holds true for all relations of exchange, including those of intangibles.

For Weber, true domination can be based on coercive force, but even then it must be contained with a framework of 'legitimacy,' derived from *tradition*, *charisma* or *rational-bureaucratic organization*. Clearly , in Weberian terms our problem is to specify the conditions (in Khapalu) which brought about the conversion of power based upon resources into legitimate domination expressed in the right of the Cho to rule.

Weber's genius for separating analytically pure types or principles is very useful here in helping to define the problem. Having separated 'power' from 'domination,' I must now insist that they not be fully separated even in analysis, when the analysis is operating at a macroscopic level. More specifically, I will advance as a principle the assertion that collectively defined rights and duties are themselves subject to negotiation over time; and such negotiations are based in the 'marketplace' of power. This important point needs a concrete illustration. When Sher Khan (19 in Table 5.2) was ruling in Skardu he sent a message to Quli Khan of Shigar which he meant to be a 'command' that Quli Khan join forces with him in an attack upon Gilgit. Quli Khan preferred to interpret this as a request which he politely turned down for stated reasons. Sher Khan did without him, and successfully looted Gilgit. Feeling strong upon his return he attempted to chastise Quli Khan for his insubordination. The response of Quli Khan was a very non-polite assertion of his sovereignty and that of the state of Shigar under his rule . Thanks to coalitions around him, he prevailed in his assertion. This episode was one of many in the process of Skardu's loss of eminence gained earlier under the charismatic warriorship of Ali Sher Khan *Anchan* ('the Great').

I view the above episode as an example of the power/ negotiation process whereby institutionalized domination and the right to rule is gained or lost.[39] Had Quli Khan engaged in the Gilgit operation he would have gained a little booty while granting to Sher Khan a reinforced claim to domination in Weber's full meaning of the term. Thus, while the micro-level relation between a ruler and one subordinate might involve compliance through'duty' to 'legitimately' issued commands, with little or no benefit obtained by the subordinate through negotiation processes, at a macro-collective level those very 'rights' are subject to negotiations backed by coalitions . When such macro-negotiations reach equilibrium we may refer to the resulting system of 'contracts' as an institutionalized exchange structure.

In an attempt to understand such 'macro-negotiations' resulting in centralized domination, I turn to coalition theory.

Minimum Resource Theory. Gamson, Riker and others have developed a very useful concept known as the minimal winning coalition. Imagine, for example, a legislature in which a known proportion, x, of the votes will 'control a decision.'Assume that certain legislators control the votes of certain others , and let the number of votes one person controls be the amount of resources that person can contribute to any potential voting coalition. Assume, further that winning coalitions obtain some finite political spoils to be divided among coalition members. Who, among all of the legislators, will form a coalition?

If the distribution of resources is known, then a list can be made of all potentially winning coalitions. One of these will form. Which one? The set of winning coalition can be reduced to a much smaller sub-set of minimal winning coalitions. If $x = 51$ per cent then the coalition(s) containing exactly 51 per cent of the total votes when resources are pooled is preferred (more likely to occur) over all larger winning combinations. Reason: the 'Pareto Optimizing' process of excluding redundant members with whom spoils would have to be shared.

Coalition formation, in this branch of theory, is a resource mobilizing process in which sufficient but not excessive resources are gathered together around a task (or'decision'). The basic concepts can be carried out of simple legislative arenas into much more complex contexts, such as raising an army to attack a fort with hidden treasure inside.

Uncertain Outcomes and the Leadership Role. In analyzing more complex situations, the basic principle of minimum resources must not be abandoned . Rather, it should be elaborated taking important complexities into account.

Attacking a fort is also a simple problem, as we shall see, yet it has important features not confronted in legislative voting. The payoff for victory (amount of booty) may be an unknown, subject to various assessments. This fact renders uncertain the size of the army beyond which a given potential recruit will decide that the potential benefit is less than the likely costs. Thus, subjective probability and 'expected utility' theory [40] are essential to an expanded theory of coalition formation.

But more important than the uncertain size of the prize hidden in the fort, is the indefinite number of soldiers required to conquer it. That is, x is an unknown subject to various assessments. Furthermore, it is itself likely to be a function of the quality of leadership the coalition is forming around. The leader of an assault upon our figurative fort must be able to convince would-be followers that there is treasure inside (and should they win, he had better have been correct!); and if he is to build a career as a charismatic warlord, he must acquire a knack for knowing when to stop mobilizing, turn away would be followers, and attack with a minimal but adequate force — a force whose adequacy depends upon his leadership.

Thus, Gamson's coalition theory can easily enrich Weber's discussions of charisma, give us a first handle on coalition processes and conditions leading to one form of legitimate domination. In Figure 5.3, the relevant principles are summarized.The curve portraying the likelihood of success is hypothetical in particulars, but it is most definitely 'S' shaped. In the'zone of redundance' a successful warrior will gain little or no charismatic reputation; his followers will gain little benefit; and only a Sancho Panza will pledge loyalty (grant dominance) to him. Any warrior who mobilizes followers for successful combat in the zone of uncertainty will be hounoured as a military genius or viewed as the instrument of some super-natural purpose. Leaders who launch attacks in the zone of futility either die or loose all but their most bonded followers.

Predatory and Protective Coalitions. Any effort to mobilize military resources is considered here to be an instance of coalition formation.[41] Surveying all of the information we have about the history of Balti states, most of it pertains to coalitions so defined; and virtually every one of them can be classified easily into one of two types: predatory, which we have implicitly examined above; and protective. The distinction is self-evident; yet as always, the boundary between them is blurred. Offense is said to be the best defence, a principle which the

Balti rulers obviously understood. The distinction,therefore, is based on the judgement (by the historian) as to whether or not territory and established resources are being *preserved* or *expanded* as the major motive in the mobilizing of resources.

For example, the valley of Kharmading was populated by ethnic Baltis dwelling outside the young state of Skardu, on the side of the Dard territory of Chilas. After a history of plunder by increasingly aggressive Chilasi, they sought the protection of Skardu. The ruler of Skardu at the time not only accepted the request: he also made contact with other regions of the Dard frontier far removed from Chilas, and convinced them of a similar need. He built forts in and took over direct administration of those formerly independent areas. While the Skardu Cho likely had expansion of territory as a motive, what he offered those who joined him was protection of what they already had. I consider the case an instance of protective coalition. Most other instances are more self-evident. Vigne,the first westerner to contact a Balti Cho, met Cho Ahmed Shah leading troops (in that same Kharmading area) on a mission to intercept Chilasi raiders and recover the women and animals they were carrying off from a village under his protection. The mission was trivial and easily effected. On a larger scale, the Khapalu Cho had to mobilize (in different century) military resistance against a combined attack by Skardu and Shigar. His protec-

Figure 5.3: **Probability of Coalition Success as a Function of Resources Mobilized**

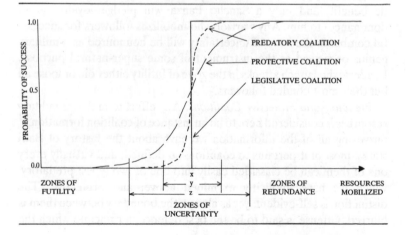

tive coalition failed, and at great cost to the peasants whose standing crops were destroyed to prevent use by the Khapalu armies and the ruling class alike, a Skardu Kharpon was installed in Khapalu. Five years later he—the Skardu Kharpon—and military attachments were overthrown by a 'revolutionary coalition.'

But the descriptive difference between protective and predatory coalitions is trivial. The important differences are analytic. First, where predatory coalitions have specific targets chosen by the leader, protective coalitions—the defensive mobilization of the state itself—has an unspecified or ambiguous enemy of unknown strength. Indeed, the enemies requiring protective mobilization in Baltistan came in an historical series of opponents, large and small. Some were small plundering bands hitting only a few villages. Others were large enemies seeking territorial annexation. Others were large armies seeking widespread plunder (the most dangerous, by far). On one such occasion in 1532, the Khapalu Cho, with forces mobilized, met an army too big to handle. His tactic was to 'welcome' and 'join' the invading army in an attack deeper into Baltistan. The state of Shigar was sacked. (See *Tarikh-i Rashidi* for the account.)

Based upon this difference between predatory and protective coalitions, I suggest in Figure 5.3 that the zone of uncertainty is broader in the latter; and the role of leadership is therefore far more important and demanding in the protective context. Thus, while 'charisma' is usually discussed in the context of predation; there is as much or more basis—in theory—for charismatic leadership to form in the protective arena. I will use the term *Charismatic Kingship*, taken in its parts from Weber, to describe the 'routinized charisma' of the ruling office—of Cho in the Khapalu case. But for this to be more than a descriptive label, the 'routinizing process' must be subjected to analysis.

Public Goods and the Right to Coerce. The first step in that direction comes in with the second distinguishing feature of protective coalitions: protection is a classic example of a public good. In this respect, protection differs sharply from predation. The recruit in a predatory process is mobilized on the basis of a private good: his share of the booty, obtained if and only if he takes part and the coalition wins. By contrast, in the protective context every person whose resources are being mobilized (a Khapalu household facing a demand for grain or soldiering duty) has an incentive to hide, to 'free ride' as Olsen calls it; for if the coalition wins, *all* persons living with the protective sphere will gain protection; whether or not they play their part. Therefore, by Olsen's

'Logic of Collective Action,' large protective coalitions will not occur unless participation can be coerced. The potential contributor, who would want the protection the coalition would provide, would not contribute to it unless he could trust the state (the leader) to require contributions from other recipients of protection. Thus, the fundamental insight arrived at is that a citizen will agree to contribute only if he and others are forced to contribute. Thomas Hobbes' problem of order and the social contract are directly addressed by the logic of public goods in protective coalitions.

The territory aspect of state is also deducible from that logic. Protection must be provided only to those who can be (coercively) taxed.

The Marginal Utility of Defence Budgets. Having established the basis for legitimate coercion, we must now locate the limits of legitimacy, for the 'right' to rule can be withheld or withdrawn, despite the logic of protection as a public good. A first step in locating the limits of legitimate coercion is presented in Figure 5.4.

Recall the S curve presented in Figure 5.3. Calculated directly from it is the bell-curve in Figure 5.4, showing *marginal benefit* from added resource mobilization. This curve necessarily diminished toward zero as the likelihood of success in Figure 5.3 approaches 1.0. Imposed upon that benefit curve is a family of *marginal cost* curves which, as microeconomic theory stipulates, will increase from zero by some exponential function toward a point where a peasant is driven to starvation, or

Figure 5.4: **Marginal Benefit and Cost of Protective Resources Mobilized.**

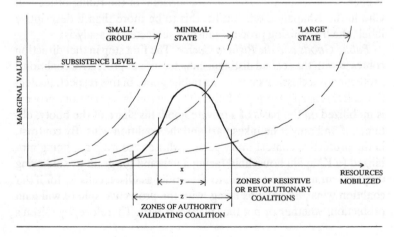

nobleman to revolt. Note: in a more refined statement, separate cost curves could be advanced for peasants and for nobility—T and K in Figure 5.2—and principles could be advanced regarding which class absorbs the greater cost under given conditions. Such additional elaboration is postponed to a later paper.

If the resource base of an agrarian social group, at a given time, includes a fixed amount of land of a given productive potential and a specific population size, then the group can be classified in size relative to the strength of potential predators. Cost curves can then be advanced with some confidence for groups of varying size, as shown in Figure 5.4. Since the cost curve for the hypothetical small group does not intersect the marginal benefit curve, that group is too small to form a viable state, and must find protection within some larger coalition. Our interest, then, lies in the 'medium' and 'large' sized groups.

Resistance versus Authority Validating Coalitions. In order to interpret the points of intersection of the benefit and cost curves in Figure 5.4, we must return to the concepts of public goods and free riding. When the two curves intersect for a given group, there is a range of resource mobilization, shown as y and z in Figure 4, for which benefits outweigh costs for the citizen. But since the benefit is a public good, that same citizen will, if he is 'rational', attempt to withhold revenue or avoid the military *ress* (turn taking service as a soldier in Khapalu). Therefore, the logic of public goods not only requires coercion, it requires state monitoring as well. (We are familiar with the logic of the spiralling costs of monitoring—who will watch the watcher—which has been advanced to support the argument that a moral consensus is an essential condition for organized society.)

Monitoring by the state can also take on the legitimacy accorded to coercion. But most important, 'legitimate' coercion and monitoring will bring the citizenry into the monitoring process—people will police each other under specified conditions. The conditions are presented in Figure 5.4; and the process of self-policing occurs in what I will call an authority validating coalition.

The important feature of the bell curve in Figure 5.4, is that it displays the benefit to ego from having other people comply with a ruler's demands for revenue and soldiers. While each is inclined to free-ride, each is inclined to support the state against other free-riders. The strength of that support for the state is shown in the marginal benefit curve. Thus, we come to two more types of political coalition. In the most simple three-person case, involving a ruler and two subjects, if one subject resists an increase in revenue demand by the ruler, the other subject will do one of three things:

1. remain inactive;
2. side with the subject, forming thereby a resistance coalition;
3. side with the ruler, forming there by an authority validating coalition.

The intersection of curves in Figure 5.4 are predictions concerning the likehood of these two coalition processes. In the zone of futility, a subject has no incentive to support either the ruler or his fellow subject. He will hide his resources and seek a stronger leader who will use them for effective protection. When the cost curve intersects the benefit curve, the subject has incentive to join the ruler in an authority validating coalition against free-riding fellow-subjects. When the cost curve rises and again intersects the benefit curve, the zone of redundance becomes a zone of increasing likely resistance coalitions.

The Predatory State. Levi has developed the notion, in some detail, that rulers will attempt to maximize the resources they control. 'Rulers as persons or as governments are predatory'. If she is correct, then, rulers will attempt to move the state as far to the right side in Figure 5.4 as they can. If the zone of redundance is entered, the consequences will be quite predictable: (1) free-riding will increase: (2) monitoring costs will increase as authority validation gives way to collaborative resistance; and (3) most important, the state is likely to fragment into smaller, more cohesive regions, each providing more spartan protection in the zone of uncertainty. If Levi is correct, once in the zone of redundance, the ruler will (4) launch predatory attacks abroad, spending state resources not on (public) protection but on (private) booty. The result will be increased resistance and more likely fragmentation.

If rulers are by nature predatory and therefore prone to mobilize maximum resources: and if over-mobilization has the long-term destructive consequences listed above, then states in institutionalized equilibrium should have some institutional mechanism through which resistive coalitions can put a check on over-mobilization. In Khapalu the institutions of public Durbar and *Ul-sum-mi-Trampa* appear to be well suited both to authority validation and to collaborative resistance in disputes between state and subject.

The dynamics based on Figure 5.4 make the state which is of minimal size relative to the strength of its enemies an equilibrium condition for viable, institutionalized, central authority. Larger structures are prone to fragment back into this size category, as both history and theory suggest.

I will conclude by advancing an hypothesis: given that margin benefits exceed costs (in Figure 5.4), the probability of an authority validating coalition will increase as cost increases. If this hypothesis is sound, it implies unusually high cohesion in support of the rulers of small states, fighting problematic protective wars; a condition which could give rise to Charismatic Kingship.

Charismatic Kingship in Khapalu

The argument above has built the basis for understanding the origins of institutionalized central authority, exemplified by the Khapalu Cho. But among the forms of authority advanced by Weber, why should *Charisma* be invoked? Rational-legal authority is ruled out on the organizational grounds presented in connection with Figure 5.2. The Cho and all Kha-Cho and Kharpon in Khapalu were all functional equivalents to one another as warriors. But if the 'Zone of Uncertainty' characterized Khapalu's historic condition, then a central warrior among warriors was essential.

On the other hand Weberian 'traditional' authority, the other alternative in the classic trio, is a form of authority quite vacant of analytic substance. To say that a ruler is granted compliance because compliance has always been granted, leaves a lot unsaid.

If more is to be said about 'traditional' authority, based upon this study of state-formation in Khapalu, it would be this: traditional authority is routinized military charisma. The state so organized might be called a Charismatic Kingship. In such a state, it does not follow that each ruler will enjoy personal charisma. Rather, his office (the Cho of Khapalu) will place charismatic criteria of excellence upon him.

The folk-lore of Khapalu contains survival of those charismatic criteria, and they are imbedded in portrayals of the 'zone of uncertainty' which, in the above theory, generates such charismatic rule. I will describe briefly two items: a dance; and a long epic poem — the *Kesar Saga*.

A dance performed frequently by peasants, is a complex sword dance by seven (some say eleven) men. After watching a very impressive display, its story was explained. The Cho and many Kha-cho were taken to Ladakh as prisoners of war, where they were required to dance to entertain the gathering of Makpon (military elite). The clever Cho explained that their dance is a sword dance—they must have the swords during the dance. The rhythms of the dance take the dancers out in a wide circle, then into the centre; out; and in; out and in. With each wide circle out, the Ladakhi nobles grow more accustomed to an armed Balti near them; with each movement in, Cho gives an unread assignment to one Kha-Cho, until a full attack has been planned. The dance ends in the slaughter of captors by captives.

The Kaser Epic is an early pre-Buddhist Tibetan saga about King Kaser, a legendary ruler with magical powers to transform himself, and to fool as well as subdue almost any enemy. Yet, a repeating theme in his exploits, is for some enemy to capture his castle and carry off his wife, while he is dealing with some other enemy, forcing him to recapture his wife and subdue her captor—which, of course, he does. He has the magical powers of a charismatic warrior/ruler, yet he always is forced to use them in see-saw wars. And despite his powers, he needs loyal followers; he mobilizes all of the resources available for war.

To recite this saga requires over twelve hours of memorized verse, song, and dance. It has been transmitted from special teacher to selected pupil in many Balti peasant villages, from pre-Islamic times at least five centuries ago. It is a pagan art form, not sanctioned by (at least contemporary) Muslim clerics in Baltistan. Yet it has survived. The Balti version, recorded in 1980, has not been translated. A.H. Francke gives the following translation from the Ladakhi version. Kaser, king of Ling, is speaking:

Thou host of the heavens, come to the fight,
And Wangpo Gyabyhin be at thy head!
Thou host of the earth, come to the fight,
And Mother Shyabdun be at thy head!
Thou host of the waters, come to the fight,
And Water-king Ljogpo be at thy head!
At the head of the heroes of Ling, Palle must stride;
At the head of the women of Ling, Astag must ride!
At the head of the Lamas of Ling, Tsegu must ride;
At the head of the Mons of Ling, Penag must stride!
At the head of the smiths of Ling, Karog shall ride;
At the head of the Bhedas of Ling, Kangrings shall stride!
You boys who know how to use the sling, go to the war;
You girls who know how to use the spindle, go to the war!
Whoever can provide for himself, let him do so;
Whoever cannot, let him be provided for at the castle of Ling!
Whoever has a horse of his own, let him bring it;
Whoever has none, let him get one at the castle of Ling!
March off then towards the land of Hor,
And the king shall march in front of you all!

CONCLUSION: THE FORMATION OF
FEUDAL STATEHOOD

The dual purpose of this study has been (a) to introduce the interested reader to the history of a society about which little has been written, and (b) to examine the process of state-formation in that society in the hope that the Balti state might yield insights into the more general nature of centralized authority in South Asia. The latter objective has been pursued through theoretical study of a single case; yet, because it is theoretical the principles developed are at least potentially applicable across a broad class of cases. It is well to conclude, therefore, by identifying more specifically the class of societies or states which the Balti state might typify; and summarize the main theoretical points which might apply across that class.

The Balti states were typical of what might be called, with due caution, feudal agrarian states. The essential defining features of such a state are portrayed in Figure 5.2. The state is organized as an 'exchange network' with a branching 'tree' structure. It has at least three social levels, from a single centre through one or more intermediary positions, to the most peripheral (peasant village) level. The network is held together by the exchange of specified basic resources: protection provided by military leadership flows from the centre outward; in return for land revenue and military manpower flowing from the periphery inward. Functions other than protection are centrally provided (for example, the management and financing of public works and land development), and they might even be essential conditions for the formation and continuation of the state. In Baltistan, regional authority transcending many villages was certainly essential in land development. But such state functions are not offered as defining features of the feudal state. It is clear that in Baltistan, at least, the central authority of Cho was institutionally legitimized around the provision of military protection.

Land revenue and military manpower, combined to provide protection, are the three 'factors of production' in the feudal state. But more important are two structural features. First, any location in the structure of the state where those three resources co-exist *is* a position of potential power. In Baltistan, the Kharpon was a military commander who was also managing (with the aid of subordinate Pha-Cho) both revenue collection and troop mobilization in a region. Therefore, each region was a potential locus of power. The feudal state is defined here as a structure having multiple foci of potential power. Social systems having institutions such as fiefdoms (in feudal Europe) or *mansabs* (in Mughal India) meet this defining structural feature of a feudal state.

The second structural feature is institutionalized central power which overrides regional positions of potential power. Thus, a feudal state is one which forms around a central sovereign ruler, despite a specific structural potential for fragmentation into lesser quasi-sovereign regions. The theoretical analysis advanced in this paper is an attempt to specify the conditions and reasons for fragmentation *versus* centralization of state authority in such feudal states, drawing heavily upon principles of coalition formation.

Without repeating the analysis above, this summary will identify the three general points which appear to be most important. First, a feudal state is produced by war against predatory enemies too large for sub-regions to handle. Central power gains legitimacy to the extent that its power remains minimally adequate for defense of the state. If it grows beyond this minimal size (relative to enemy states) it is increasingly likely to fragment into smaller, minimally adequate units. Thus feudal states form as 'Charismatic Kingships' around rulers expected to provided the genius required to prevail in war, despite the vulnerability of such a minimal state. Such states will of logical necessity be found in sets of two or more enemy states; each being predator to and defender against the other; each stimulating demand for the protection the other provides its population. This is a 'solution' to the Hobbsian problem of order.

Second, states and their rulers are likely to be by nature predatory, prone that is to mobilize as much power as is possible. The major internal counter-force against this exploitive tendency is found, theoretically, in the logic of protection as a public good. That concept helps to identify conditions under which authority validating coalitions on the one hand, or resistive and potentially revolutionary coalitions on the other hand, will prevail. Institutions which bring those coalitions into the process of rule *(Ul-sum-mi-Trampa* in Khapalu) might provide 'feed-back' which prevents the expansion of the state in redundant levels of mobilized power, thus preserving legitimate rule in feudal states in the absence of intermittent war.

The third and final point can be stated as a conclusion: state-formation can be explained on the basis of rational self-interest alone, without invoking moral solidarity as an essential social ingredient. This conclusion is interesting primarily because it contrasts with a well-known argument advanced by Durkheim and by recent social theorists as well.

Durkheim anticipated the dilemma now identified as the 'free-rider problem'. More recently, Collins has explicitly integrated that concept into the analysis, and has fully re-affirmed Durkheim's classic conclusion: The participants in a mutually rational or self-interested contract will, if they are rational, attempt to cheat (free-ride) on the contract. Therefore, there must be a non-contractual moral solidarity behind contracts, for otherwise there could be no social order at all. The state as a coercive enforcer does not alter the argument; for the state must monitor the individual, and who will monitor the monitors? At the bottom some moral bond must exist.

The reasoning developed in this paper does not need such a primal moral bond as a starting condition. The concept of an authority validating coalition is also based on the free-rider problem, but it 'solves' that problem in a rationally motivated coalition process. A person rationally motivated to free ride would be irrational if he tolerated other's free-riding. Thus, he will (rationally) coalesce a leader to locate and punish other free-riders. A son who would like to take his father's throne, will coalesce with father against the brother who tries to take it. A peasant who wishes not to give up grain to the king, will side with the king in collecting grain from another peasant under certain conditions.

The major strength of the theory advanced in this paper is that it specifies the conditions under which such authority validating coalitions should occur (see Figure 5.4). They are the same conditions which generate a form of authority termed as *Charismatic Kingship*.

NOTES

1. Within the limits of space, descriptive material on Balti society is brought into this presentation. The purpose, however, is to illustrate or document some point of possible analytic importance. More complete description of Balti society must be left to future writing and research. For a first step in ethnographic work, see Pat Emerson (1982).

2. The first westerner to enter Baltistan was Vigne in 1835. Having spent considerable time as the guest of Ahmed Shah, the last ruler of the sovereign state of Skardu, his narrative is very useful. He was followed by Thompson (1852) whose observations are also useful, and by Drew (1875), the first visitor whose observations qualify as scholarly. After the British assumed effective control of the administration of Jammu-Kashmir in 1885, British travellers exploring the edges of their empire visited Baltistan in growing numbers, some to hunt Skeen (Ibex) or L-Chan (snow leopard), others to learn about strange lands. Some of the latter have given us interesting accounts (Jane Duncan, 1906; Martin Conway, 1894; Fosco Maraini, 1959).

3. Most important was the 1913-14 scientific expedition led by Filipo De Filippi (1932), for it included some ethnographic research by Giotto Dainelli.
4. On the Balti language, my source is Pat H. Emerson, who has been studying the language, along with informants in Baltistan.
5. I have found no other reference to the *Shagharnama* and I do not know the present location of the text used by Hashmatullah.
6. Much of the work reported was made possible by support from the National Endowment for the Humanities, carried out in London, and in Pakistan with the permission of the Tourism Division, while assembling material for a forthcoming guide to Baltistan.
7. Modern Tibetan practices of animal husbandry in agricultural communities, and the contemporary Tibetan vocabulary surrounding those practices, have not been studied. Furthermore, both the practice of keeping animals in such a chamber, and the word used to refer to that chamber have had ample time to change. See Pat Emerson, 1982, for further analysis of the problem.
8. If a Balti ruler (Cho) or member of the ruling nobility (Kha-Cho) was instrumental in sponsoring, authorizing or overseeing and protecting the colonizing project, some portion of the land was designated Cho-pi-tsa (land owned by the Cho or Kha-Cho). Such lands were normally cultivated by tenant farmers. It is very likely that in early times slaves obtained through warfare were employed in the colonizing process. Local tradition has it that certain villages were originally settled in that way, examples being Satpara, near Skardu, and Hushe in the Khapalu region. The women of Satpara are still Shina-speaking Dards who might well descend from women taken in war by the Skardu Cho some centuries back. The men of Satpara warrant attention also, but the topic is beyond the scope of this paper. See below for more material on Cho and Kha-Cho, the ruling nobility of Baltistan.
9. There are instances of colonizing activity which failed or were aborted at one stage or another in the cycle. One effort sponsored out of Hushe village early in this century was abandoned in Phase 4 because it was too small. A set of intermarrying families started the project on a sub-village level, only to be forced to abandon it for want of sufficient labour power. The case underscores my claim that the *village* is the smallest ecologically viable group in Baltistan. Why, in this case, the project was abandoned rather than enlarging the colonizing group relates in part to the kinstructure internal to the Balti village. See Pat Emerson, 1982.
10. Such projects require leadership. The Balti village has a *Trampa* (a hereditary headman) and typically a Muslim maulvi, both of whom enjoy considerable authority in village affairs. Again, see Pat Emerson (1982).
11. It is possible that the census data in Table 5.1 reflect the *size of the smallest revenue-collecting authority*, as much as literal village size, due to the possible use of revenue authorities in obtaining census data.
12. Carraseo (1959) describes Western Tibetan irrigation agriculture as follows:

> In most of Tibet agriculture is of an intensive type. Irrigation, manuring, and some crop rotation keep the best lands in almost continuous production. Irrigation works, however, are relatively smallscale. The great rivers, such as the Indus or the Tsangpo, are not controlled by any major works ... Many irrigated areas tap the water of the lesser courses flowing into the great rivers and occupy a limited amount of land where the small river opens into the main valley ....

On mountain slopes fields are terraced. Dams are built across small mountain torrents . . . Long canals carry water to the fields, and it is taken across ravines by means of conduits of hollow logs (Carraseo, 1959:7-8).

This description of Tibet and Ladakh would fit Dardistan and Baltistan equally well.

But the relative *scale* of hydraulic construction cannot be described with available evidence. The *only* known instance of pond irrigation in all of Tibet is described by Ekvall and Downs (1964) and attributed to a Sakya ruler in 1905-1930. In Baltistan the one impressive case is a very large lake formed by a dam near Satpara built some time prior to A.D. 1633 (see below). This relatively ancient hydraulic system at Satpara warrants careful study by experts. Meanwhile, for us its existence suggests a more advanced form of hydraulic society in Tibetan-speaking Baltistan than is found in any region of Tibet proper.

13. I have seen no other reference to the *Shagharnama*, and the present location of the text used by Hashmatullah is not known to me. It is possibly in the possession of his family, and it might be the only copy in existence.

14. Islam entered all three Balti states at approximately that date.

15. Hashmatullah does not always make his dating sources clear. Having not attempted to validate his dates, I refrain from building any argument which depends upon them. The plunder of Shigar in A.D. 1532 reported by Mirza Haider in the *Tarikh-i-Rashidi* (1973:422) is the earliest date I rely upon. It fixes the period for the rulers (12), (14) and (31) in Tables 2,3 and 4 respectively.

16. F.W. Thomas (1935) shares this view ' . . . it is, we can see, no accident that the little state of Si-sgar, north of Skar-rdo, the valley of which was starting-point, or terminus of both [Hunza-Nagar and Chinese Turkestan], has retained in a title (*tham*) . . . of its early chiefs traces of connection with those two regions.' According to the *Shagharnama*, quoted extensively by Hashmatullah, the Shigar (Si-sgar) state had diplomatic ties with Chinese Turkistan and trade over the Mustag Pass, in some unspecified early time. I am willing to venture that family line in Shigar known as *Amacha* (Table 5.3) derives from the title *Amacas* granted by the Chinese government to the kings of Khotan. See F.W. Thomas (1935:Rt. 2:191) for a discussion of this title.

17. By this route, the force would have come directly through the Hunza-Nager region.

18. A few remnants of a very old fort at Haldi called locally *Kharmung Khar* – 'fort of many forts'–can still be seen, on a promontory commanding the confluence of the Saltoro and Hushe rivers.

19. Huna being a Turkic group from which, he suggests, Hanza might derive its name.

20. Hashmatullah attributes the hydrology works of Satpara-Skardu to Ali Sher Khan (1595-1633),the ruler who brought Skardu to its peak of power, as do all contemporary informants. But I doubt this for two reasons; (a) the Buddhist sculpture obviously predates Ali Sher Khan by a century or more, and it appears to be associated with the hydrology (Duncan, 1906: 305); and (b) the stonework in the dam and related structures is unlike and far more refined than anything else in Baltistan. Furthermore, one apparently old dam used as a simple building block, large stone fashioned to form a shluss-gate in some *earlier* dam. Local informants suggest that Ali Sher Khan used engineers from the court of Akbar. This is possible if the Buddhist sculpture is not associated with the irrigation.

Otherwise, Kashmiri construction during the time of Lalitaditya (A.D. 724-761) would account for both sculpture and irrigation works. Note that Lalitaditya was in friendly contact with Chinese Turkistan through Gilgit when a force from the latter entered Skardu (750) to put down Tibetan disruptions along that route.

Regarding Buddhist sculpture, the best account to date is found in Duncan (1906), but careful study has not been undertaken. A Tibetan inscription, partially preserved, is possibly more recent than the deep-relief sculpture. There is reference to a Buddhist temple in Skar-rdo in A.D. 804 (Francke, 1926: 193), but whether Tibetan or Kashmiri in origin is not known; and its relation to irrigation works is unknown. Interesting observations by Thompson (1852) of 'ruins, showing large blocks of well-hewn stone, fragments of marble fountains, and some solid walls supporting terraces which appear at one time to have been gardens, alone remain to show the former magnificence of the place,' (p. 218), give some basis to a local theory of a former 'Mughal Garden' at Skardu. The terrace walls mentioned by Thompson are still there and, like the dam at Satpara, they contain large stones which in my opinion were carefully fashioned for use in some earlier structure. Whatever that structure was, it was almost certainly tied to the hydraulic works at Satpara.

In summary, a little bit of careful archaeology will uncover a lot of history in Skardu. It appears very likely to me that the hydrological structures were pre-Islamic, and non-Tibetan. Initial construction during the period of Lalitaditya or even Ashoka is within reason.

21. There was considerable demand for slaves, for the state of Hunza is said (F.W. Thomas, 1935) to have served as a marketing point. Local legends in Baltistan have some villages being founded in whole or part by prisoners of war. Satpara is one such village, said to have been Dards taken prisoner from Chilas. On Baltis taken off to slavery elsewhere, see below.

22. As is typically the case, court scribes or chroniclers did not trouble themselves to record the profane practices which a late-twentieth century social scientist would now like to know about. The *Shagharnama*, for example, tells us virtually nothing about the administrative structure of the Shigar state. Inferences which might be drawn from it are not made by Hashmatullah. The records of the ruling family of Skardu are said to have been destroyed (Vigne, 1835), and those of Khapalu are said (by Yabgo Fetah Ali Khan) to have been acquired by Hashmatullah from Ali Sher Khan, Regent of Khapalu during the minority of his (Fetah Ali's) father. Efforts by Fetah Ali to recover his family's records did not succeed.

23. Six years before the British 'sold' Kashmir to Gulab Singh (the Dogra Rajput of Jammu), his armies had conquered Ladakh under the command of Zorawar Singh. From Ladakh in 1840, Zorawar Singh was in position for the conquest of Baltistan, at a time when Ahmed Shah, the ruler of Skardu, was enjoying considerable strength. Ahmed Shah, however, had two problems at that time: (1) he had recently won a war against Khapalu, and was holding precarious control over that restive Balti state; and (2) having favoured his younger son, had angered an ambitious eldest son. The son sought the help of Zorawar Singh in attaining his 'rightful' rule of Skardu, and the armies of Khapalu conspired to join Zorawar Singh. Skardu was defeated; Ahmed Shah was carried off as prisoner, while his eldest was put on charge as governor on behalf of Gulab Singh; and Khapalu was freed from Skardu, but rendered a subordinate ally of Zorawar Singh. Zorawar

marched away (as the Khapalu leaders no doubt assumed he would. This was not the first time that Khapalu made use of strong but temporary invasions of Baltistan. See Mirza Haider, *Tarikh-i-Rashidi*). Zorawar was killed in an attempt to gain Lhasa, and Khapalu regained full independence as the only Balti state to benefit from the 1840 Dogra conquest of Baltistan.

But the independence regained in 1840 was soon lost forever. When the British granted Gulab Singh the right to rule the new state of Jammu-Kashmir, he went at once to the military task of securing that right. In Baltistan the former states of Skardu and Shigar were totally annexed. Khapalu was attacked, and its ruler at the time (Yabgo Danlat Ali Khan) was taken as prisoner to Srinagar where he was held eight years. Negotiations during that time led to his release and return to Khapalu, to govern that area under the explicit suzerainty of the Maharaja of Jammu-Kashmir.

24. The reduced status of Khapalu was given symbolic expression in a dramatic way: the mountain top Palace-Fort which had symbolized central authority in Khapalu for over three centuries, was forcibly *dismantled* and reassembled at the *base* of the same mountain. In exchange for the right to maintain traditional local rule, Khapalu relinquished all claim to sovereignty through submission to this architectural act in c. 1850. For the next fifty years an annual tribute of ten talons of gold reconfirmed the subordinate status of Khapalu. In addition, Khapalu was expected to provide military support to the central Jammu-Kashmir government when needed. The last military involvement by Khapalu was a contingent of 400 soldiers to aid in the British-Dogra conquest of Hunza-Nagar in 1895.

The peasants of the Khapalu region, as compared with Skardu and Shigar, gained significant benefits from this 'semi-sovereign' condition. Their *ruler* had become their *patron* in dealing with the Dogra regime in Kashmir. In this role, four successive Yabgos (42 through 45 in Table 5.4) negotiated 'preferred' status for the residents of the region, *which exempted them from begar labour*. As a result, the Khapalu peasantry was spared from the most oppressive measures of Dogra rule: the use of forced labour to supply the Gilgit garrison, between 1880 and 1900. (See Lawrence, 1967:411-14).

The final period in the decay of Khapalu Authority came in 1900-03 with the British Land Settlement. The revenue records of the former state were taken over by the (British) assessment officers of Jammu-Kashmir. While traditional rights to land use were confirmed, along with the 1/5 assessment from the high grade lands, that assessment was henceforth divided so that one-tenth of the assessed value was paid to the Dogra government agent in Skardu. This payment was made in rupees, representing the first major step toward a monetized economy in Khapalu.

25. The endogamous marriage preference of the Yabgo family is *not* to be attributed solely to the preservation of royal lineage, for this marriage preference is also pronounced at the village level among Balti peasants, where it appears to function as a property-preserving pattern, in a society governed by Islamic laws of inheritance.

26. If Yabgo dominated Kharpon positions it was through the result of political process rather than culturally defined status right. There is an oral tradition referring back to land grants made by early Cho to adventurers from abroad (for example, Dardistan) who then colonized those regions of Khapalu. Saltoro valley

is said to have been colonized by a Chilasi called Palday under a grant from Beg Mantar, then ruling at Halti. This makes geographical sense.

27. See Barfield (1981) on this decimal mode as early as 200 B.C. on the northern frontier of China; and see Aziz on this system among the Mughals in India. This Khapalu case, if it does link to that tradition, has dropped the 'horse rank'. The Balti armies were foot-soldiers except for the mounted officers or Kha-Cho.

28. This is the way informants describe rights to land prior to the British settlement of 1900-1903. It is a common Islamic conception based in the Qu'ran. (See, for example, H.K.Sherwani, 1942.)

29. The Sufi missionary Sayyid Ali Hamadani, accompanied by seven hundred more Sayyids, left Persia to escape Timur and entered Kashmir in 1372 A.D. Local Balti legend has it that Sayyid Hamadani himself visited Baltistan and converted the entire region. (Scattered across Baltistan, but notably in Khapalu, are ancient wooden mosques, more properly, Sufi-style *Khanqah*, on the same rather unique architectural style of the Shah Hamadan Mosque in Srinagar.) In 1492 Mir Shams-ud-Din Iraqi, a disciple of Sayyid Muhammad Nurbakhsh, established himself and the Nurbakhshi Sufi sect in Kashmir, and loosing favour, was driven into Baltistan. Local custom has it that when the Mir arrived in Baltistan the way for his teaching had been paved by former teachers. The facts will probably never be known. If Hashmatullah's dates for the Balti rulers who first embraced Islam are approximately correct dates, then Mir Shams-ud-Din was not the first Sufi teacher in Baltistan.

30. There are some villages under traditional Sunni and Shia leadership, but Nurbakhshi (which is now itself very close to Shia) is the most prevalent in the Khapalu region.

31. Yabgo Fetah Ali Khan used the word delegated, explaining that the authority was considered to lie with Cho. But matters having to do with, for example, marriage and inheritance required technical study by the Muslim clerics of the kingdom.

32. In relatively recent times the Dogra Maharaja of Kashmir obtained a ruling through the Council of Regency granting to Rajas the power to appoint village headmen. Applied to the former state of Khapalu, this presumably undermined the traditional independence of the *Trampa* and the importance of the *Ul-sum-mi-Trampa* in the affairs of Khapalu prior to Dogra suzerainty.

33. The institution of *ress* is of early Tibetan origin, being practised in Ladakh under the same name. It corresponds with the Kashmiri *begar* which evolved into corrupt forced labour.

34. Oral tradition records an episode when crops were destroyed in Saltoro valley. While the Cho was away on a visit to a neighbouring state, a group of peasants broke into the regional grainery without the Kharpon's approval and carried off measured amounts of grain. The Kharpon sent a messenger to Cho asking if he should obtain the arrest of the peasants involved. The Cho's return message said no: Having taken a measured amount, they took only what was theirs by right. Whether or not the tale derives from an historical event is less important than the fact that it is told. It defines for the state a custodial role in managing the grain surplus of the community.

35. The festival would have occurred in 1976 according to schedule, but Khapalu was annexed and Yabgo Fetah Ali Khan was placed on small government pension in 1972.

36. The idea that *groups* negotiate with each other through persons acting as agents is not an unfamiliar or troublesome notion. The internal relations of power and coalition formation among members place important constraints upon, or give added impetus to, the bargaining power of the agent. Such internal affairs involve the separation of function between Kha-Cho and Pha-Cho (military and administrative, respectively), but in the schematic diagram of Figure 5.2, the simplifying assumption is made, that those functions are integrated in the structure of the court, fort or village represented in the singular as C, K and T.

37. We *do* have an oral tradition which clearly separated Kha-Cho from Pha-Cho, and treats both as having hereditary claim to their respective positions. This could plausibly provide central control over divided functions on the periphery, but evidence is not sufficient on this point to allow us to attribute the centralized structure of Khapalu to this single structural hypothesis.

38. I must acknowledge three current efforts in theory construction which are highly relevant to the ideas presented below. They are Marget Levi's work on 'A Predatory Theory of Rule' (1981); Michael Hechter's research on group solidarity (1981); and a study by Lorne Tipperman on factors aiding the persistence of dynasties (1981). It is possible that my observations, below, will become elaborations on a special case of Levi's more general treatment.

39. Throughout the very long history of Yabgo rule in Khapalu, no subordinate region is known to have advanced a serious claim to independence from the Cho of Khapalu. Why should the Khapalu Cho have been so stable?

40. For a broad summary of utility theory, and an effort to include it in macro-sociological processes, see Blalock and Wilkens (1979).

41. Mobilization for non-military ends such as canal construction projects are not included in this formulation because they lack a strategic (i.e., human) opponent.

42. Space will not allow a full comparison of strategic problems faced by protective *versus* predatory leaders. For the protective ruler, matters are made especially complex by the fact that an enemy with intent to annex can be 'welcomed as a friend' by local peasants or nobility if the leader's revenue assessments have been excessive; yet if assessments have been smaller, the ruler might be unable to mount a protective effort at an effective level.

6

Shrines, Succession and Sources of Moral Authority in the Punjab

David Gilmartin

One of the most persistent problems within the Islamic tradition has been the definition, in both theological and institutional terms, of the proper relationship between religious and political authority. The tension between political and religious authority has reappeared over and over again in different guises, and yet has repeatedly eluded an effective solution. In its roots,the problem may be one that is inherent in Islam itself, for the Islamic tradition tells its followers that religion and politics, the inner life and the social life, should be united. In practical terms, however, the political world of Muslim society, particularly at the village level, has at best been only partially defined by Islam. One answer to this dilemma has been the evolution in the Indo-Pak subcontinent of institutions which, though not providing fundamental solutions to the inherent contradictions in Islam, have traditionally provided the hinges at which the popular political organization of the mass of Indian Muslims and the system of the Qur'an have met. This paper focuses on the evolution of the authority wielded in recent times through one such institution, the rural *dargah*, which has traditionally presented a form of Islam accessible to the great mass of the rural Muslim population.

The emphasis will not be specifically on the *adab* of the religious leaders associated with these *dargahs*, though that would no doubt be a rewarding study, but rather on the more general question as to how in the modern period the changing political system in which these shrines have been embedded has affected expectations about the character of the religious leadership which these shrines should provide. Two shrines in particular will provide the material—two of the most important Chishti *dargahs* of west Punjab—the shrine of Baba Farid Ganj-i Shakar at Pakpattan and the shrine of Khwajah Suleman at Taunsa Sharif on the Indus. Using evidence primarily from a few cases in the British courts, I hope to suggest that a study of the changing character of the moral authority of the religious leaders at these shrines may help to unlock larger questions concerning the relationship between Islamic ideals for social organization and the popular political organization of Muslim Indo-Pakistan.

The shrine of Baba Farid is a natural focus for a study of rural shrines in the Punjab, for it stands at the head of the Punjab's rural *dargahs*, the oldest and the most venerable. As Richard Eaton has shown, the development of the shrine provides almost a classic case-study of the close relationship between ecology and political structure on the one hand and the organization of religious authority on the other. Dependent largely on the support of gradually settling nomads in the *bar* country between the Sutlej and the Ravi rivers, the shrine at Pakpattan served from an early date as a bridge between the religious system of the localities and the wider world of Islam. Though the system of popular devotionalism which developed at the shrine had little relationship to the Qur'anic tradition, the continued presence of the spirit of Baba Farid himself provided both an intermediary vehicle for access to divine favour, and a link to the community of Islam. The recognition of Baba Farid as a great Sufi saint within the Sunni tradition was visibly confirmed at the shrine by the official recognition given by the Delhi court, and by the magnificent tombs constructed by the Sultans on the site. Political recognition from an early date underlay the shrine's popular recognition as an important spiritual centre, and subsequently the role of the shrine as an intermediary religious focus within Islam was inextricably tied to its place within the larger political system. Just as the spirit of Baba Farid was at the hinge between the belief systems of the marginally Islamized tribes and the Qur'anic tradition, the shrines' ritual also symbolized its intermediary position between the local political systems of the tribes and the larger Muslim empire. As Eaton shows, this was embodied in the very terminology used to describe the organization and functioning of the shrine, terminology which was drawn from the functioning of the Muslim court.[1]

The central figure of religious authority at the shrine was the *sajjada nashin*, whose hereditary succession to the *gaddi* had been established from an early date. The precise character of the *sajjada nashin*'s authority is not easy to define, however, because his authority derived from his simultaneous participation in more than one system of values. As a descendant of Baba Farid he was the inheritor of the saint's *baraka*, which placed him in a line of direct access to the moral authority deriving from the saint's proximity to God. Such access to higher spiritual authority was critical to the *sajjada nashin*'s influence, and the concern of many of the early *sajjada nashins* with the religious values Baba Farid had expressed was indicated by the continued Sufi teaching at the shrine. The successful exercise of the popular authority of the *sajjada nashin*, however, also depended on his ability to operate effectively in a localized political network. In sharp contrast with the ideal of religious leadership which Baba Farid himself had exemplified, according to which moral authority was acquired by moving outside the world of normal political relations in order to gain closer access to God, the religious influence of the *sajjada nashin* derived from the very fact that he was able to operate within such an everyday political world.

The character of the influence of *sajjada nashins* in the centuries after Baba Farid was defined by the nature of the local religious system which had developed around the shrine. The religious authority of the shrine was not centralized under the *sajjada nashin*'s control, but was dispersed among the entire Chishti *baradari*, the descendants of Baba Farid in the districts surrounding the shrine. These descendants were sometimes the *sajjada nashins* of other small shrines in the area, the tombs of many of Baba Farid's more pious descendants,[2] and they were sometimes substantial landowners or village officials.[3] All shared, however, in the moral authority that derived from Baba Farid's own sanctity and in the access to divine favour which this gave them, and all were able as *pirs* to offer this access to others. 'All the descendants of Baba Farid', said one witness with only slight exaggeration, 'do the business of *Piri Muridi*'.[4] By the nineteenth and twentieth centuries, the *sajjada nashin* of the shrine presided over a system of authority which paralleled the local systems of authority headed by the tribal chiefs and landowners. As Pamela Price has shown for another part of the subcontinent, such systems were themselves normally based on the control of the movement of resources in a framework in which power itself was not concentrated, but diffuse.[5] Ironically therefore, though the moral authority of the shrine derived from a single source, the exercise of such authority depended largely on the *sajjada nashin*'s political management of a system of which the shrine was at the centre.

The success of a *sajjada nashin* depended on his ability to increase the resources which came into the shrine, both from the state and from the devotees, and to distribute those resources at the shrine itself and among the *baradari* so that the number of adherents would be increased and the prestige of the *dargah* maintained.[6]

The precise religious expectations of the *sajjada nashin* himself in these circumstances seem to have been somewhat ambiguous and to have been closely tied to the political context. Though in the early days the piety and the spiritual reputation of the *sajjada nashin* were certainly important in maintaining the reputation of the shrine at court and thus enhancing its prestige, subsequent changes in the political roles of the *sajjada nashins* appear to have affected the exercise of their religious authority. The interrelationship of the political context with the character of the religious leadership offered by the *sajjada nashin* at Pakpattan was perhaps most clearly demonstrated by the situation during the years of Mughal decline, when the Diwans of Pakpattan asserted their political independence of the Mughals and battled with neighbouring Rajas and with the Sikhs to defend their own petty kingdom. Though far more extensive research would be necessary to verify this, important changes in the style of religious leadership of the *sajjada nashins* seem to date to this time. From the time of the sixteenth Diwan, the Pakpattan *sajjada nashins*, as local tradition had it, 'were inclined to make conquests, to maintain armies and to build forts. They themselves stopped giving spiritual education and employed Maulvis, Imams, Khatib, and Mubalighs for the purpose'.[7] Though it can be doubted whether this was a completely new element at this time, we can speculate on the general political pressures which may have led to this development. With the growing divorce of the local political system of the shrine from the larger Muslim empire, there seems to have been a concomitant tendency toward functional specialization between the making of *murids*, which the *sajjada nashins* continued to do, and the provision of religious instruction and the leading of the prayers — functions which symbolized the inclusion of the *sajjada nashin* and his followers in the larger Muslim community. With the *sajjada nashin* himself no longer serving an intermediary political role in a larger Muslim empire, but instead concentrating his attention on his local political leadership in mobilizing his *murids* for battle, the religious functions linking the shrine to the Qur'anic tradition were more appropriately assigned by the *sajjada nashin* to subordinate religious specialists. This did not mean that the shrine had ceased to be a crucial link between the local traditions and the greater tradition of Islam, but that the type of religious leadership provided by the *sajjada nashin* had changed with the changing character of his political position.

The importance of the political context on the types of religious leadership provided at such rural shrines can be seen even more clearly in the development during this same period of the second shrine in our discussion, the shrine at Taunsa. Though more recent in origin, the shrine at Taunsa served a similar role as a focus for local religious authority. In terms of local circumstances, the development of the shrine at Taunsa followed closely the pattern at Pakpattan,for the shrine, which developed on the west bank of the Indus in the late eighteenth and nineteenth centuries, drew much of its support from an area in which largely nomadic Baloch and Pathan tribes had come under increasing political pressures and were, particularly after the middle of the nineteenth century, gradually settling.[8] The larger political milieu in which the shrine developed however, contrasted sharply with the pre-Mughal situation in which the shrine at Pakpattan had emerged. The religious impulse which inspired the establishment of Khwajah Suleman's *khanqah* at Taunsa had originated during the eighteenth century at Delhi in a period of declining Muslim political authority. In contrast with the strictly spiritual concerns of Baba Farid, therefore, Khwajah Suleman drew his inspiration from a tradition which was in its origins preoccupied with a concern for popular religious reform as a religious answer to the decline of Muslim power. Religious reformers of Delhi, of whom Shah Walliullah was the most famous, had increasingly emphasized during the eighteenth and nineteenth centuries the importance of education and popular organization of Muslims according to Qur'anic ideals in order to compensate for the collapse of the authority of the Mughals. The immediate spiritual mentors of Khwajah Suleman were not direct disciples of Shah Waliullah, but they were nevertheless strongly influenced by these same reformist concerns. Shah Fakhruddin of Delhi and his most important *khalifa*, Khwajah Nur Muhammad Maharvi, had sought in the eighteenth century to spread this reforming spirit through a revitalization of the Chishti order, seeking to reach the still partially Islamicized and politically semi- independent tribes. Khwajah Nur Muhammad had, accordingly, established a *khanqah* north of Bahawalpur near the frontier of settled society, and his *khalifa*,

Khwajah Suleman had established his own Taunsa *khanqah* 150 miles further west.[9] Set among the tribes of western Punjab, this *khanqah* and the subsequent shrine had as a result displayed many of the same institutional features which had characterized the shrine at Pakpattan, but due to its intellectual antecedents in the reforming tradition at Delhi these were overlaid by a strong emphasis on religious education and popular reform.

Ironically, the *khanqah* of Khwajah Suleman thus emerged as a centre of reforming rural religious leadership only a short time after the Diwans of Pakpattan had begun to withdraw completely from an active, educating religious role. At the same time that the Diwans were abandoning their role as religious instructors, Khwajah Suleman of Taunsa was emphasizing more strongly than ever the instruction of his disciples in the *Shariat*, a task in which he was accompanied at one time by as many as fifty of his *khalifas* at the Taunsa *khanqah*.[10] This was not merely a return to the 'other-worldly' religious style of Baba Farid, for particularly under Khwajah Suleman's successor, Khwajah Allah Bakhsh, the authority of the *sajjada nashin* at Taunsa was to become as firmly embedded in its own local political milieu as was that of the Diwans of Pakpattan. Rather, the style of religious leadership at Taunsa represented an alternative religious answer to a general crisis in the nature of rural religious authority which had followed the collapse of the Muslim state. With the establishment of colonial rule, the religious relationship between the locality and the world of Islam could no longer be effectively defined in the nineteenth century, whether at Taunsa or Pakpattan, by the political relationship between the local leaders and an imperial state. Changes in the character of religious leadership at both shrines can best be seen, therefore, as part of a wider search in a new political context for new bases of authority — not, ultimately for a new source of moral authority, for that could not change, but for new standards of religious leadership in the new political context. I will now look at one manifestation of the changing character of religious leadership at this time — disputes over religious succession. Such disputes represented only one limited aspect of the more general problem, but they highlighted in a particularly accessible way the changing principles under an alien regime on which the authority of these *sajjada nashins* was based, and the new religious pressures which they faced.

SUCCESSION AND MORAL AUTHORITY:
THE CASE OF PAKPATTAN

The nineteenth and twentieth century battles over the succession at Pakpattan were particularly significant as they indicated the principles on which the authority of the *sajjada nashins* had come to rest. As a dispute between the grandson and the uncle of the late *sajjada nashin* demonstrated in the 1880s, succession at the shrine was at that time subject to several traditional constraints which pointed to the origins of the moral authority which the *sajjada nashins* claimed to exercise. First, though the succession had normally been hereditary, the validity of the appointment of a successor by the old *sajjada nashin*, even when his eldest son, depended on his receipt of a revelation from 'the spirit of Baba Farid-ud-din'.[11] In practical fact, the question of such a revelation does not seem to have seriously impeded the old *sajjada nashin*'s free right of appointment, but the appeal to such a revelation, no matter whom the successor, indicated clearly the continuing centrality of Baba Farid as the source of the *sajjada nashin*'s moral authority. It was Baba Farid himself who, in effect, with his direct access to God, decided who would occupy his worldly seat of authority. This constraint on the succession was balanced, however, by a strong appeal to the right of the general body of *murids*, and more specifically of the Chishti *baradari*, to approve the decision. The basis for this claim lay partly in the common interest of all members of the *baradari* in the shrine, as all shared in the sanctity of which Baba Farid was the source, but it also pointed to the strong political element in the authority which the *sajjada nashin* exercised. Though his authority derived ultimately from Baba Farid's own close association with God, the exercise of his authority was by no means absolute, but depended also on the consent of those who participated in the religious system at the shrine. Without such consent the very basis for his religious authority would be compromised. The key to the authority of the *sajjada nashin* thus lay in the traditional balance between these contrasting elements – elements which reflected the simultaneous links of the system to the Islamic moral order and to the political systems of the countryside.

As the succession crisis of the 1880's demonstrated, the very presence of the British courts tended to upset this balance. The existence of a higher court of appeal for deciding the succession was not in itself a challenge to the moral authority of the shrine, for the grounding of the shrine within a larger political system clearly implied its traditional subordination to higher political authority in such matters. Rather, it was the disjunction between the religious and the political elements in the *sajjada nashin*'s authority which such an appeal to the British implied. As representative of the sovereign political authority, the role of the British courts, in spite of their adversary format, came very close, by and large, to the traditional mediatory role of the sovereign in the localities — a role reflected in the courts' strong legal emphasis on the reaching of a settlement based on the customs of the locality. The decision of the courts was thus well-suited to the preservation of the legitimate political authority of the *sajjada nashin* as an intermediary between the locality and the empire, and to the preservation under the British of the local customs which nurtured the shrine. But the decision was nevertheless rendered in a context which isolated it from the value system of Islam, a situation which was emphasized by the way the court weighed the contrasting customs affecting the shrine's succession. Though the courts tried to assess, for example, the customary political claims of the *murids* and of the Chishti *baradari* in determining the succession, they found it far more difficult to assess the legal significance of the religious claims of Baba Farid. As a prominent Muslim lawyer put it, 'it is not in the province of a civil Court to decide whether a particular *Sajjada Nashin* has received a revelation from the founder'.[12] The court could in fact weigh whether or not such a revelation had been communicated by the old *sajjada nashin* to his followers, but even at that, the emphasis normally fell not on the religious significance of such a revelation, but on the immediate political pressures involved in its communication.[13] The result was, therefore, that in practical fact the moral authority deriving directly from Baba Farid, and thus indirectly from God, became largely irrelevant to the succession of the *sajjada nashin*, as it was interpreted by the sovereign political authority. It was the custom associated with the *sajjada nashin*'s political leadership in the local context which in official eyes solely determined his right to succeed.

This, of course, did not mean that the *sajjada nashin* was denied the authority that derived in the eyes of his *murids* from his descent from Baba Farid. Though the official *sajjada nashin* changed three times during the course of litigation as the District Court, the Chief Court of Punjab, and the Privy Council each in turn reversed the other and installed a new *sajjada nashin*, there is no evidence that the popular following of the shrine was significantly affected.[14] For most of the shrine's rural followers who sought out the *sajjada nashin* for mediation, it does not seem to have mattered precisely what sort of man the *sajjada nashin* was, or whether he had been named in a confirmed revelation, so long as he was a descendant of Baba Farid and carried out the necessary rituals. As one witness declared, 'I am a follower of the *Gaddi nashin*, whosoever may be occupying it'.[15] But the increasing dissociation of the *sajjada nashin* from the value system of Qur'anic Islam nevertheless deeply affected the shrine's traditional position as a hinge between the culture of the locality and the larger Muslim community. Perhaps the most striking demonstration of this was the character of the new *sajjada nashin* himself. Diwan Said Muhammad, who had ultimately emerged successfully from the court challenges of the late nineteenth century, was not himself a learned religious man or a Sufi teacher. As the salaried *khatib* of the Jama Masjid at the Pakpattan *dargah* declared, though the Diwan continued to make *murids*, he was not a religious teacher; he 'used to get information about religion from me'.[16] What was emerging as increasingly significant under the British therefore was that neither the *sajjada nashin*'s personal teaching and example, nor the structural position of the shrine, could provide any longer the religious system of the shrine with a firm place in the tradition of Islam. In the wake of the shrine's encounter with the British courts, the growing separation of the shrine's political place in the empire from its religious place within the value system of Qur'anic Islam was becoming increasingly clear.

This situation naturally produced criticism of the role of the *sajjada nashin* from those outside the local rural context who were concerned with the definition of general standards of religious leadership and authority for the Muslim community. The most pointed religious criticism in the twentieth century came from *ulama* in the reformist tradition, who had long been sensitive to the lack of a central Muslim political authority and had, as a result, offered a view of Islamic authority which was defined not in political but in idealist terms. These *ulama* were critical not only of the lack of religious guidance offered by *sajjada nashins* such as the Diwan of Pakpattan, but also of the very nature of the mediation in such local systems, which aimed toward the linking of the local Muslims to the values of Islam through the interposition of the *sajjada nashins* and the shrines rather than through the dissemination of Islamic standards of personal behaviour. For them such a mediatory solution had become under the alien British regime meaningless.[17] A more practical approach to reform, however, came from the Chishti *pirs* in the reformist line which had included the *pir* of Taunsa, who recognized the continuing vitality, even under the British, of the local Muslim political systems which had long nurtured the religious authority of the shrines. These *pirs*, unlike the reformist *ulama*, did not underestimate the significance of the political context in which the shrine's religious leadership was exercised, but offered instead new standards of religious commitment in the local context for the *sajjada nashins* themselves. Pir Mehr Ali Shah of Golra, for example, who was one of the more reform-minded of the new Chishti *pirs*, recognized clearly the continuing importance of the political component in the local religious authority of the Diwans of Pakpattan, even under the British. Demonstrating his own awareness of the significance of a symbolic political model for the organization of authority at the *dargah*, Mehr Ali Shah observed that he personally reserved for the *darbar* of an important *sahib-i sajjada* like the Diwan of Pakpattan the respectable behaviour (*adab*) which others reserved solely for worldly (i.e., Government) officers.[18] In spite of his own refusal, like many of the *ulama*, to associate politically with the British, therefore, he recognized the political responsibilities which the Diwan's political position required him to fulfill. Though Mehr Ali Shah himself refused an invitation to attend the Delhi Darbar of 1911, for example, on the grounds that for him to attend would be an insult to Islam, he admitted that it was nevertheless proper for the Diwan Sahib to attend, as the Diwan — in addition to being a *pir* — also claimed status as a *jagirdar* dating back to the days of Islamic government.[19] The main problem in defining new standards for the exercise of the religious authority of the *sajjada nashin* was, therefore, to reconcile reformist standards with the maintenance of the *sajjada nashin's* political position — to restore, in effect, the balance between the authority he could claim in a system of Islamic values and that which derived from his role in the local political context.

The pressures for reform and the political problems such reform entailed, however, were indicated most clearly in the wake of another succession crisis at the Pakpattan shrine in the 1930s which exposed once again the bases of the moral authority of the *sajjada nashin* of the shrine of Baba Farid to public scrutiny. This case, which erupted on the death of Diwan Said Muhammad in 1934, was in many ways similar to the case of the 1880s and'90s, for the issues revolved around the traditional clash of the old Diwan's right of appointment with the right of the *baradari* 'to approve or reject any nomination made by the last holder and in the last resort itself to select a successor'.[20] But the case also brought to the forefront the problem of defining the *sajjada nashin*'s suitability for religious leadership in reformist terms – in terms independent of the rights of either Baba Farid or the *baradari*. This issue was called into question particularly by the claims put forward by one side in the case for the succession of the old Diwan's minor son, Ghulam Qutabuddin, who was only 11 years old at the time of the Diwan's death. To bolster its own claim, the opposing side in the case argued that the succession of a minor to the Pakpattan *gaddi* was not compatible with the important position of religious leadership the Diwan would have to fill for it was 'utterly inconsistent with Mahomedan law'.[21] This argument by no means indicated an acceptance by the *baradari* of Muslim law as the touchstone for the moral authority of the *sajjada nashin*, for the lawyers in the case themselves admitted that the local customs of the shrine had always outweighed the Muslim law with regard to the establishment of succession. But the introduction of this consideration into the case nevertheless pointed toward the recognition of standards outside the customary religious system of the shrine – standards which tied the shrine to the ideals of the community as a whole. Though such standards hardly preoccupied the competing parties, the implications of an awareness of these standards for the type of leadership which could be expected of the *sajjada nashin* were indicated clearly by at least one witness in the case, a village *lambardar* and a *murid* of the *gaddi*, who had been exposed to religious influences outside the local system while studying for a year in a *madrasa* at Kasur. The succession of a minor to the *gaddi* would be inappropriate, he thought, because a minor could not possibly perform the duties which a *sajjada nashin* should be expected to perform. Not only would a minor as yet lack religious education, but, equally important, a minor could not meet the standards of religious leadership which the Islamic tradition required; 'a minor cannot', he noted, 'lead in prayers . . .'.[22]

Though the succession of Ghulam Qutabuddin to the *gaddi* was subsequently confirmed by the court, the concern with the kind of leadership which could be expected from a minor *sajjada nashin* by no means disappeared. On the contrary, the education and training of the young Diwan and the management of the shrine during the Diwan's minority subsequently became the subjects of intense public debate – a debate precipitated by a British move to take the estate of the shrine under the Court of Wards and to educate the *sajjada nashin* themselves. Perhaps as nothing else could have, this British move galvanized local concern for the protection of the religious authority of the *sajjada nashin*, for it dramatized, even within the local context, the dissociation between the shrine's position in the political world and its place in the world of religion. The underlying motive of the British was only to preserve their traditional political relationship with the shrine by making special arrangements for the management of the estate during the Diwan's minority and by training the *sajjada nashin* in such a way as to ensure that the exercise of his authority continued to fit effectively into the British political system. The direct takeover of the administration of the shrine, however, highlighted as never before the strength of the shrine's political ties to the alien British Government, and thus called into question even for many at the local level the effective religious functioning of the *sajjada nashin*. As a petition from the *sajjada nashin* of one of the subordinate Chishti shrines near Pakpattan indicated, the takeover of the shrine by the Court of Wards was seen as political interference in the functioning of the shrine — a challenge which represented a direct threat to the Diwan's authority to perform the shrine's religious rituals.[23] The Anjuman Islamia, Montgomery, put the issue even more bluntly: the British takeover would, it declared, 'seriously undermine [the] diwan's position and [the] status of [the] *gaddi*'. This would, it implied, undercut the authority of the *sajjada nashin* even within the local network; 'income from religious sources', it warned, 'will dwindle' . . .[24]

The most open concern with defining new standards of moral authority, however, was prompted by the British plan to send the young *sajjada nashin* to the Aitchison Chiefs College in Lahore for his education. For the reformist Chishti *pirs* this marked the crux of the issue, for though they had accepted the importance of the *sajjada nashin*'s political position within the British system, his education at Aitchison College would signal his absorption into the British value system as well. As a very result of his political position, they had come to see an increasing emphasis on his religious education in the values of Islam as absolutely essential to the continued maintenance of his moral authority. Even before the old Diwan's death therefore, these religious leaders had strongly criticized an attempt by the old Diwan himself to send his son to Aitchison, an attack which had soon forced the Diwan to withdraw the youngster from the school.[25] Now that Ghulam Qutabuddin had succeeded to the *gaddi* it was even more critical that he be trained in a proper way so as to maintain the links of the *sajjada nashin* to the moral values of Qur'anic Islam. As the mother of the young Diwan Sahib reported to the Governor in 1936, the proposal to send the boy to Aitchison was being 'hotly opposed by the *Sajjada Nashins* of Ajmer, Delhi, Mangrol, Piran Kalyar, Golra Sharif, Taunsa Sharif, Bassi Sharif, Hansi, Upana, and Khwajah Hasan Nizami of the Dargah of Khwajah Nizamuddin Aulia, Delhi, etc.'. 'They still persist', she emphasized, 'in maintaining that the *sajjada nashin* should be a Darwesh and he has no need of receiving the education which is imparted to the sons of rich families'.[26] As an answer to the dilemmas in the sources of the authority of the *sajjada nashin*, these *pirs* thus looked finally to a new emphasis on religious education, as an essential element in the definition of the moral authority the *sajjada nashin* wielded.

THE CASE OF TAUNSA: RAIS AND DARWESH

In practical fact, of course, the balance between religious education for a *sajjada nashin* and the ability to operate effectively within the rural political milieu in British Punjab was not an easy one to maintain or to define. The practical dilemmas in the development of such a model for the behaviour of a *sajjada nashin* under the British was demonstrated in the twentieth century by a series of disputes over the succession to the *gaddi* of the shrine at Taunsa. Though the *sajjada nashins* who succeeded Khwajah Suleman generally continued his emphasis on religious education and even built new schools at the shrine, they became increasingly susceptible in the twentieth century to the same sorts of local political pressures which affected the shrine at Pakpattan. The shrine at Taunsa had not by the turn of the century developed either a distinct Chishti *baradari* or a complex set of succession customs such as existed at Pakpattan, but the shrine had nevertheless under the leadership of Khwajah Suleman's grandson, Khwajah Allah Bakhsh, developed strong ties into the local political networks of southwest Punjab. It was, in fact, precisely Khwajah Allah Bakhsh's ability to expand the social and political influence of the shrine which had earned him a reputation among many as 'an even greater saint' than Khwajah Suleman.[27] Working astutely to develop strategic political alliances, Khwajah Allah Bakhsh was able to attract the contributions needed to build an impressive group of buildings at the shrine. As at Pakpattan centuries earlier, such outward display and political recognition proved critical in creating and in providing a validation for the shrine's growing popular religious influence. As a court deposition related in describing this process, 'Allah Bakhsh appears to have been a very businesslike as well as a very saintly man. . . . ,' a combination which accounted for his particular influence.

> . . . During his lifetime the mosque and the family tomb became places to which pilgrims resorted in considerable numbers, particularly on the occasion of the *urs* or fair held on the anniversary of Khwajah Suleman's death. With the offerings made to him by these pilgrims, with the contributions from the Nawab [of Bahawalpur] and other neighbours, and with the money made in agriculture and in trade which he started, and also with the estate of his sons hereinafter mentioned, he built all or nearly all the buildings at Taunsa . . .[28]

Khwajah Allah Bakhsh himself appears to have been able to effectively balance his roles as a religious teacher and as an increasingly important local magnate, at least so long as he was alive. But the tension between these roles, even at a shrine like Taunsa which had developed initially with a strong reformist impulse, became evident in disputes over the succession after his death. The basic cause of the succession disputes at Taunsa were the marriage connections which had been established by Khwajah Allah Bakhsh in order to bolster the social and political position of his family. Khwajah Allah Bakhsh, who was himself by caste a Pathan, took as his third wife the daughter of Ghulam Qadir Khan Khakwani of Multan District, who was one of the wealthiest and largest Pathan landowners of south-west Punjab. This marriage, which was no doubt calculated to improve his social status and to bring land into his family, succeeded admirably, for Ghulam Qadir Khan fixed 300 squares of land in Multan District on the heirs of Khwajah Allah Bakhsh by his daughter. The result was that Khwajah Allah Bakhsh's son by this marriage, Mian Mahmud, emerged as a wealthy landed proprietor, who himself contracted several socially and politically strategic marriages with leading Pathan families of Dera Ismail Khan.

It was Mian Mahmud's growing political connections which laid the groundwork for the eruption of a protracted conflict over succession at the shrine. In spite of his rising social position, Mian Mahmud was not the oldest son, and consequently at the death of Khwajah Allah Bakhsh, it was not the well-connected Mian Mahmud, but rather the more saintly but less wealthy Mian Muhammad Musa who succeeded to the *gaddi*. Mian Mahmud's social and political position, however, had placed him at the centre of a group of influential and wealthy religious followers, which made his influence at the shrine undeniable even in the face of Mian Muhammad Musa's official succession. The succession thus produced immediate tension, which was initially mediated by a council of *tumandars* or Baloch tribal chiefs, and later by local *maulvi*.[29] With the death of Mian Muhammad Musa in 1906, however, the dispute broke into the open when opposing groups favouring the succession of Mian Muhammad Musa's son, Mian Hamid on the one hand, and Mian Mahmud on the other held rival *dastarbandi* ceremonies. Though the British Deputy Commissioner officially recognized Mian Hamid's claim, Mian Mahmud secured the intervention of Diwan Said Muhammad of Pakpattan who arrived in Taunsa and ceremonially placed 'the sacred relics' indicating succession to the *gaddi* on Mian Mahmud's head.[30] To gain full religious control of the shrine it was ultimately Mian Hamid who had to sue, claiming that Mian Mahmud was infringing his prerogatives and performing religious rituals at the shrine which were by right the responsibility of the *sajjada nashin*.[31]

The case between Mian Hamid and Mian Mahmud dramatized on the surface at least the tension between the opposing styles of religious leadership expected of a *sajjada nashin* at a politically influential *dargah*. As John Maynard observed when he visited the shrine in 1911, the two *pirs* represented markedly different styles of leadership. Mian Hamid's style of leadership seemed to be closer to that of a *darwesh*; he was a generally reclusive religious man who avoided contact with British Government officers. Mian Mahmud, on the other hand, was a frequent visitor at Government offices who cultivated his political contacts. 'I recollect nothing', Maynard stated, '[except] that this older gentleman's [Mian Mahmud's] manner and dress differed markedly from those of the younger gentleman [Mian Hamid] whom I understood to be the *sajjada nashin*. The older gentleman appeared to be a man of the world, a *rais*. I should say the younger had a very retiring and modest appearance'.[32] The course of the conflict indicated, however, that there was no easy answer to the reconciliation of these styles. Though Mian Hamid eventually emerged successful from the courts and had his rights confirmed, this represented by no means a vindication of his style of religious leadership, nor did it win him the religious support of those important local leaders who had social and political ties to Mian Mahmud. As the largest landowner of the Baloch Kasrani tribe declared, 'by Government order the plaintiff [Mian Hamid] is *sajjada nashin*, in eyes of Musalmans [the] defendant. . . .'[33] Though the nature of the political influence at Taunsa was somewhat different from that at Pakpattan, the succession conflicts at Taunsa nevertheless indicated as much as those at Pakpattan, the critical importance of the political milieu in affecting the expectations for the *sajjada nashin*'s authority. In the end, this proved to be as true for Mian Hamid as for Mian Mahmud. Though the importance of religious education and teaching remained for the *sajjada nashins* at Taunsa an ideal which they pushed for the Diwan of Pakpattan—in fact such an ideal had little integral relationship to the character of their influence in the locality.

The tensions between the political and the religious elements in the authority of the *sajjada nashins* were indicative of wider cultural tensions in India under colonial rule. The attempt to work toward a general model for the exercise of authority by *sajjada nashins* reflected a concern, a concern implicit it would seem in the very concept of *adab*, to define standards for social interaction which at the same time expressed the commitment of Muslim society to a larger Islamic moral order and which provided Muslims with an effective programme for dealing with the social and political world in which they lived. The intrinsic problems in such an effort, however, had grown considerably in the context of colonial rule. Since the fall of the Mughals, and particularly under the British, the *sajjada nashins* of Punjab lived in an increasingly culturally fragmented world—a world which lacked the political framework to bind together the diverse cultural systems of the localities and to express, at least in symbolic terms, the commitment of all to the moral order of Islam. As a result, the practical meaning of a commitment to the Muslim community had become increasingly unclear.

In spite of the collapse of the Muslim state, however, Muslim reformers in India had worked hard in the period of British domination to develop standards for Muslim communal solidarity based not on the political framework provided by the state, but on the dissemination of ideal standards of behaviour and conduct. To restore the unity and wholeness of Muslim society they had emphasized a commitment to religious education and to the spread of Qur'anic standards of behaviour among religious leaders and the common people alike. The root answer to Muslim problems thus lay, in reformist eyes, in the spread of knowledge as a basis for direct individual commitment to an Islamic moral order—a moral order which would itself provide the basis for Muslim political solidarity. Islam would, in the confusing colonial world of British India, no longer need to be adapted by symbol and ritual to the political order; it would rather, as a moral force, itself begin to shape the political order.

This view provided an idealist answer to the long-standing tension between political and religious authority, a tension which had helped to shape the peculiar forms of authority associated with the Sufi shrines. But the reformist emphasis on education could not alone transform the nature of religious authority in Punjab, particularly so long as the structure of tribal and landed authority in the rural localities remained basically unchanged. The attempt to define individual standards of behaviour on the basis of Qur'anic Islam served, to a large degree, only to isolate reformers from the main political currents in rural society, where the majority of illiterate Muslims remained deeply rooted, even in the twentieth century, in the cultural systems of the localities. Though the pressures of foreign rule brought increasing tension to the exercise of moral authority at the shrines, the very structure of Punjabi society, a structure which the British themselves had helped to maintain, prevented any easy answers to the dilemmas rural Muslim religious leaders faced.

NOTES

1. Eaton, Richard M., 'The Shrine of Baba Farid in Pakpattan, Multan Suba', Paper presented at the Association for Asian Studies, Los Angeles, April 1979, p. 17.
2. How many such subordinate shrines existed is impossible to say, but religious leaders associated with several testified at the Pakpattan succession case in the 1930s. Lahore High Court, [LHC]. Regular First Appeal No 93 of 1939; Dewan Ghulam Rasul *versus* Ghulam Qutabuddin. Evidence, Vol. II, pp. 66-9, 122-4, 167-8. There were also shrines to *khalifas* of the *sajjada nashins* at Pakpattan, who were not themselves part of the Chishti *baradari*; for example, Evidence, Vol. II, pp. 199-200. I'd like to thank Dick Eaton for letting me use his copies of these evidence volumes.
3. In the 1890s the Chishtis owned 9 per cent of all the land in Pakpattan tehsil. Fagan, P. J., *Final Report of the Revision of Settlement of the Montgomery District, 1892-99*, Civil and Military Gazette Press, Lahore, 1899, p. 25. Large landowners and village officials showed up among the Chishtis who gave evidence at the 1930s trial.
4. Statement of Shaikh Din Mohammad Din, Zaildar of Daliana. LHC . . .Appeal No. 93 of 1939, Evidence, Vol. II, p. 28.
5. Price, Pamela, 'Raja-dharma in Ramnad: Land, Litigation and Largess', Paper presented to SSRC Conference on Intermediate Political Linkages, Berkeley. March 1978.
6. Perhaps the most obvious outward parallel between the display of authority by the *sajjada nashin* and by local chiefs was in the maintenance of a *langar* or free

kitchen. The constant hospitality symbolized by a *langar* was important for the maintenance of the authority of many Punjab chiefs. Similarly the maintenance of a *langar* was critical for the status of a *sajjada nashin*. As Mian Mahmud of Taunsa said, ' a *sajjada nashin* may or may not keep a *langar*, as far as I have seen a *sajjada nashin* who keeps a *langar* is considered greater than one who does not'. Deposition of the plaintiff. Privy Council [PC] Appeal No. 118 of 1921; Khwajah Muhammad Hamid *versus* Mian Mahmud and others. Evidence, Vol. II, pp. 31-41.

7. Evidence of Mohammad Husain, Qureshi, age 37, zamindar of Pakpattan. LHC . . .Appeal No. 93, of 1939, Evidence , Vol. II, p. 278.

8. The character of the following of the Taunsa shrine requires considerably more research. But it appears that the influence of the shrine, which is in the Indus riverine, rose markedly at the same time that the influence of the shrine of Sakhi Sarwar, which is located at the base of the hills, was gradually declining in the late nineteenth century. The shift may be explained by a decline in the nomadic movement of the Baloch to the hills and increased agricultural settlement in the river plain. This, however, is at the moment speculation. The work of Emily Hodges may help to illuminate this.

9. The careers of Shah Fakhruddin of Delhi, Khwajah Nur Muhammad Maharvi and Khwajah Suleman of Taunsa are all traced in Khaliq Ahmad Nizami, *Tarikh-i Mashaikh-i Chisht*, Maktabahyi Arifin, Karachi, 1975, pp. 460-560, 608-66.

10. Khaliq Ahmad Nizami, *Tarikh-i Mashaikh-i Chisht,* pp. 620-2.

11. Report of PC Appeal, 1894; Sayad Muhammad *versus* Fatteh Muhammad and others. *Indian Law Reports,* Calcutta Series, Vol. XXII, p. 328.

12. The quote comes from a later case, but the Court faced the same problem in the 1890s. Report of LHC . . .Appeal No. 93 of 1939; Diwan Ghulam Rasul *versus* Ghulam Qutabuddin. *All India Reporter* [AIR], Lahore, 1942, p. 144. The lawyer quoted is Sir Wazir Hasan.

13. The problem the courts had with the issue is indicated by their tendency to judge the question of the legitimacy of the *sajjada nashin*'s appointment according to legal standards of 'undue influence'. If the old Diwan could be shown, in other words, not to be in possession of sufficient faculties to rationally decide the issue, and was accordingly influenced to make an appointment without recognizing the consequences, then the appointment could, the courts argued, be thrown out. This was in fact precisely the line taken by the Chief Court of Punjab in rejecting the old Diwan's appointment of Said Muhammad, though this decision was later reversed. Obviously this left little room for a legal consideration of the receipt of a revelation from Baba Farid. If, for example, the Diwan was shown not to be of legally sound mind, then could a revelation from Baba Farid himself be thrown out as 'undue influence?' *Indian Law Reports*, Calcutta Series, Vol. XXII, p. 329.

14. The popular following of the shrine is, of course, hard to judge. But P. J. Fagan, writing in 1898 just after the succession dispute, noticed no decline in the shrine's popularity, and estimated the yearly attendance at the *urs* between 50 and 70 thousand. Fagan, P.J., *Gazetteer of Montgomery District, 1898-99*, pp. 237-9. (Reprinted in *Punjab Past and Present*)

15. Evidence of Pir Khan, Wattu, age 62. LHC . . .First Appeal No. 93 of 1939, Evidence, Vol. I, p. 138.

16. Evidence of Maulvi Abdul Haq, Qureshi Chiraghi, Khatib, Jame Masjid and head Qazi, Pakpattan. LHC . . .Appeal No. 93 of 1939, Evidence, Vol. II, p. 213.

17. The rejection of the religious authority of these *sajjada nashins* as a result of their political associations under the British was perhaps most eloquently expressed by Muhammad Iqbal. In his poem, 'To the Punjab Pirs'; Iqbal contrasted his craving of 'the saints' gift, other-worldliness', with what one could actually expect to get from *sajjada nashins* in twentieth century Punjab:'God's people have no portion in that country/ Where lordly tassel sprouts from monkish cap;/That cap bred passionate faith, this tassel breeds/Passion for playing pander to Government'. Kiernan, V. G. (translator), *Poems from Iqbal*, John Murray, London, 1955, p. 58.

18. Maulana Faiz Ahmad Faiz, *Mehr-i Munir*, Syed Ghulam Mohyuddin, Golra, 1973, p. 291.

19. Ibid., p.283.

20. Diwan Ghulan Rasul *versus* Ghulam Qutab-ud-Din, *AIR*, Lahore, 1942, p. 143.

21. Ibid., p. 144.

22. Evidence of Qamar Din, Bhatti Rajput, age 62, cultivator and lambardar. LHC . . .Appeal No. 93 of 1939, Evidence, Vol. II, p. 38.

23. Petition from a number of followers of Baba Farid, submitted through Pir Muhammad Badar Din, *sajjada nashin* of Opana, Tehsil Muktsar, Ferozepore, n.d. Punjab Board of Revenue, File 601/1/24/1.

24. Telegram, Anjuman Islamia, Montgomery to Revenue Member, Punjab, 19 October 1936. Punjab Board of Revenue, Ibid.

25. Details reported to be in *Munadi*, Delhi, May 1935. Punjab Board of Revenue, Ibid.

26. Petition, the mother of Diwan Qutabuddin to Government, 2 November 1936. Punjab Board of Revenue, Ibid.

27. Report of Punjab Chief Court, First Civil Appeal No. 452 of 1913; Khwajah Mahmud *versus* Khwajah Muhammad Hamid and others. *Indian Cases*, Vol. XXXVIII, 1917, pp. 387-8.

28. Summary of Respondent's Case, background on Khwajah Allah Bakhsh. PC Appeal No. 118 of 1921; Khwajah Muhammad Hamid *versus* Mian Mahmud and others. Vol. III, pt. 2, p.3.

29. Khwajah Mahmud *versus* Khwajah Muhammad Hamid and others. *Indian Cases*, Vol. XXXVIII, 1917, p. 388.

30. Letter, H.A. Carson (DC Dera Ghazi Khan) to Mian Mahmud, 22 February 1906. PC Appeal No. 118 of 1921; Vol. III (Documents), p. 156.

31. Khwajah Mahmud *versus* Khwajah Muhammad Hamid and others. *Indian Cases*, Vol. XXXVIII, 1917, p. 389-90.

32. Evidence of H. J. Maynard. PC Appeal No. 118 of 1921, Vol. I.

33. Evidence of Sultan Muhammad Khan, Kasrani. PC Appeal No. 118 of 1921; Khwajah Muhammad Hamid *versus* Mian Mahmud and others. Evidence, Vol. II, pp. 74-5.

7

The Politics of Sufism:
Redefining the Saints of Pakistan

Katherine Ewing

Sufi *pirs*[1] and shrines are a central but controversial part of the religious organization of Pakistan, as they are in many countries of the Muslim world.[2] Leaders of Pakistan have found that the organizational structure of the shrines, traditionally maintained by hereditary living *pirs*, is a force that hampers their efforts to control the political and social organization of the country. Leaders of other Muslim countries, such as Turkey and Saudi Arabia, have in the past also decided, for various reasons, that the conceptual and organizational structures of Sufism and the shrines were incompatible with their political and religious goals.[3] In both Turkey and Saudi Arabia, the solution was to suppress the shrines. In Pakistan, the secular government of the military leader Ayub Khan (in power from 1958 to 1969) established a different policy toward the shrines, which his successors Zulfikar Ali Bhutto (the 'Islamic Socialist' prime minister from 1971 to 1977) and General Zia-ul-Haq have continued essentially unchanged. Through the vehicle of a newly founded Department of Auqaf,[4] these leaders maintained a policy toward the shrines that was consistent with their ideologies and goals. Because their approach was not as dramatic as the suppression of the shrines, scholars have ignored their strategies for dealing with the shrines, and the saints and their followers.

Ayub Khan was concerned with building a strong central government, which would give him the power to pursue modernization and development. Traditionally, political leadership in Pakistan rested on the shaky foundation of cultural and linguistic diversity. Ayub sought to impose a nationally oriented bureaucratic administration that would overcome existing regional ties and disruptive political parties. This strong central government would be reinforced by the bond of Islam and by rapid economic growth.[5] Part of his strategy was to educate the rural population in the democratic process, so that they could intelligently elect their representatives. Some of Ayub's strategies were common to other modernizing countries, such as those concerning education and the provision of services through a national government.[6] Unique to Pakistan was his effort to change the significance of the shrines and of the saints attached to them. He also used the shrines directly as a vehicle for modernization.

Bhutto's strategy was to eliminate the middlemen who were the backbone of Ayub's economic and political organization. He nationalized many industries and appealed directly to the ordinary citizen. As the head of the People's Party and successor to Ayub's fallen regime, he was acutely aware of the power of mass protest. He tried to be a charismatic leader, whom everyone would look up to as the supreme benefactor,[7] and he used the shrines to carry out this policy. Instead of using the shrine festivals to teach villagers modern agricultural techniques, for instance, he emphasized governmental participation in the rituals themselves.

˙ General Zia-ul-Haq has pursued a policy of 'Islamization', contrasting his regime with what he has called the secularism and corruption of previous administrations. His ideological slogan, especially in the early days of his administration, has been *Nizam-i-Mustafa* (the system of the Prophet). He periodically asserts that he is working to set up an Islamic political structure in preparation for elections, though even religious leaders who supported him in the past have become impatient because of his failure to keep his promise (Fazlur Rahman, personal communication). They have found it difficult to attack him, however, because he is promoting an Islamic order.[8] As part of his implementation of an Islamic system of government, laws were passed that decree Islamic punishment for crimes and ban the sale of liquor. Zia-ul-Haq has moved to diminish Western influences, including a push toward the use of Urdu instead of English in government administration and the enforcement of a traditional dress code in schools and colleges. His government has tightened control over local religious institutions and leadership. For instance, governmental administration and enforcement of *zakat* (contributions for charity as dictated by the Qur'an) were announced in early 1979 and hailed as a way of extending proper Islam to the masses. The government is planning to appoint *imams* (leaders of mosques) in rural mosques; the Auqaf Department will pay their salaries and therefore retain direct control over them. Government supporters have suggested that living *pirs* be licensed and taxed by the Auqaf Department.[9]

Despite differences in the policies and goals of Ayub Khan, Bhutto, and Zia-ul-Haq, the three governments have administered the shrines in similar ways. Each has drawn on basic aspects of Sufi doctrine, emphasizing especially the activities of the early saints. Each administration has defined the symbols of the shrines somewhat differently to fit in with its particular goals. Many of these shifts in meaning, however, have been in the same general direction. These new meanings have not, of course, emerged from nothing, but rather have been based on doctrines of the Sufi tradition. Each identified the supporting doctrines as 'pure' Sufism and claimed they were compatible with the socio-political structure he was trying to construct.

Since the creation of Pakistan in 1947, there has been a continual struggle to define the Islamic state. This struggle has been reflected in the prolonged disagreement over self-definition that became manifest after the loss of Bangladesh in 1971. One central issue has been the place of Islamic law in the judicial system and the related issue of the religious status of the legislator. In the broadest terms, leaders of most political groups agree on the idea of a 'Muslim democracy' but differ sharply when it comes to precise definition.

The notion of Muslim democracy is compatible with the Islamic idea of a religious community in which the *'ulama* (plural of *'alim*, scholar of Islamic law), who are more knowledgeable about Islamic law, are the most qualified to make decisions for the benefit of the community. In Pakistan, some *'ulama* have been struggling for direct political control, in the name of the creation of a true Islamic state. In the period of Muslim rule in India, the relationship between the *'ulama* as interpreters of Islamic law and the holders of political power had been worked out so that the Muslim sultan's administration could deviate from Islamic law as long as its supremacy was acknowledged and the potential for the evolution of society toward a more perfect embodiment of Islam was possible.[10] With the establishment of British supremacy in India, the *'ulama* took various positions toward the new rulers, but, since the British did not interfere with the *'ulama*'s authority to enforce Islamic law within the Muslim community, most *'ulama*'s accommodated themselves to British rule during the nineteenth century.[11] But the threat to the authority of the *'ulama* presented by such leaders as Sir Sayyid Ahmad Khan and the development of political parties in early twentith-century India provided the stimulus for many *'ulama* to organize politically. Although they took various positions on the questions of independence and the formation of a separate nation for Muslims once Pakistan was formed, some *'ulama* and religious leaders, such as Maulana Maududi, a self-educated fundamentalist and head of the Jama'at-i-Islami, hoped to control the direction of the new government themselves.

The governments of Ayub Khan and Bhutto, though different in fundamental ways, both wanted to avoid direct participation of the *'ulama* in politics; yet they also wanted to identify their governments with Islam. They both chose to steer a course between the opposing religious camps of the politically active *'ulama* on the one hand and the traditional *Sajjada-nashins*, the hereditary *pirs* who were tied to traditional land-owning interests, on the other. They considered both sides to be incompatible with their goal of developing Pakistan into a modern nation state. From the perspective of these political leaders, the *pirs* threatened a literal return to Islamic law which the secularists believed to be unsuited to the modern world. The hereditary *'ulama*, on the other hand, were too closely linked, both ideologically and materially, with the hierarchically organized system of land tenure and political control that had been maintained by the British.

Though the hereditary *pirs* were embedded in this political structure from which they derived much of their present power and authority, their authority as *pirs* ultimately derived from the Sufi tradition. Their ancestors, with whose shrines they were associated, were Sufis. In the Sufi tradition, political leadership is clearly separated from spiritual authority. The secular governments of Ayub Khan and Bhutto chose to identify themselves with the doctrines of Sufism in order to create for themselves a link with religious authority. The Sufi was the symbol these secularists chose to represent their position and to legitimate their position as leaders of a Muslim democracy. They strove to enhance the shrines and the Sufi origins of these shrines for the glorification of Islam and Pakistan. At the same time they sought to strip the hereditary *pirs* of their traditional functions.

The ideology of Zia-ul-Haq's government has involved a shift toward a policy of Islamization. He has therefore felt less need to identify this government with Sufism than formerly. In fact, the language of Sufism and references to mysticism are less evident in newspapers and magazines than they were during Bhutto's time. There has been a more direct participation of the *'ulama* in govenment, as evidenced by the institution in 1978 of a Shariat Bench at each High Court, the function of which is to declare a law invalid if it violates the Qur'an and Sunnah.[12] Maulana Maududi (d. 1979) was also influential when Zia first came to power. Unlike many 'ulama, Maududi was vehemently opposed to the idea of pirs and the shrines, rejected the traditional Sufi-disciple relationship, and denied the Sufi distinction between exoteric and esoteric understanding, thus denying any difference between Sufism and shariat (Islamic law).

The government has not adopted Maududi's anti-shrine policy, but it has attempted to minimize the distinction between Sufism and shariat. In defining Sufism and the significance of the saints, Zia's administration has emphasized the idea that the original saints were themselves 'ulama, trained religious scholars who followed the shariat.[13] The two main schools of 'ulama in Pakistan today are the Barelvis and Deobandis. The 'ulama who organized Deoband, a theological school founded in India in the late nineteenth century for the training of 'ulama, took a reformist position in an effort to revitalize the Islamic tradition in India after the Muslims had lost their political ascendancy to the British. They attacked the hereditary saints associated with the shrines for being ignorant of both the tradition of the shariat and of Sufism. They sought to combine the roles of pir and 'alim, espousing a doctrine according to which each individual was to look to a single 'alim as his definitive guide to religious law.[14] This 'alim would also serve as the individual's pir, overseeing his spiritual development. The Barelvis, who united into a school of thought in opposition to reformists, such as the Deobandis[15] advocate the perpetuation of popular traditions and customs surrounding Sufism and the shrines, including the role of the hereditary pir. The present government, taking an essentially reformist position, stresses the synthesis of Sufi and 'alim in its definition of the saint, while denying the legitimacy of the hereditary pir. The government also asserts that a similar role can be played in today's society by religious leaders who are well educated in government-supported institutions.

THE PLACE OF SHRINES IN
TRADITIONAL WORLD VIEW AND POLITICS

According to traditional, especially rural, cosmology, God is the remote, All-Powerful Ruler, inaccessible to the common man. The Prophet Muhammad was the channel of the final direct revelation of

God's Will to man. He presented man with the tenets of Islam, which are embodied in the Qur'an. This point of contact between God and man is symbolized spatially by the Ka'aba at Mecca, the point from which the rest of the Muslim world radiates. Once in a lifetime the Muslim is obliged, if possible, to go on pilgrimage to this sacred centre of the world.

Though, according to Islamic doctrine, there can be no more prophets, the world and human society still require spiritual guides and guardians. For this purpose, God had chosen *walis* ('friends' of God) and assigned each a specific territory of the world to watch over. In a theory that has evolved from the thirteenth century, these *walis* commonly known in Pakistan as *pirs*, are organized in a hierarchy of authority. At the top is the *qutb* ('pole' or 'axis'), who is responsible for the smooth operation of the entire world. According to many traditional believers, the *qutb* is 'Abdu'l-Qadir al-Gilani of Baghdad (d. A.D. 1166), founder of the Qadiri Order of Sufis, whose spiritual realm is said to extend from Istanbul to Delhi.[16] In the Punjab, celebrations are held in honour of him every month. This is in contrast to rituals at the shrines of other saints, who are honoured once a year. Founders of the other Sufi orders are also considered to be of wide influence, which is not limited by any political or cultural border.

The saints of Pakistan in contrast, are identified with the areas in which their shrines are situated. In rural areas many tribes are associated traditionally with a particular saint, who is thought to have originally converted that tribe to Islam. The tribe usually retains memory of the conversion as a focus for maintaining the traditional tie with the shrine. Most Jat and Rajput groups who moved into the Punjab and became Muslim in the medieval period claim to have been converted either by Baba Farid (d. 1265) of Pakpattan or by Baha al-Haqq Zakaria (d. 1262) of Multan.[17] The original conversion did not usually occur as a mass movement, but rather in the form of a political move, in which the tribal leader went to the *khanqah* (Sufi centre) of the saint and accepted conversion in the name of the saint.[18] Even today allegiance to these traditional saints is not a matter of individual choice. A man is the follower of a certain saint because this is the saint of his tribe. The tie is political as well as spiritual.[19] This traditional relationship is not limited to those tribes who consider themselves to have been converted to Islam by the saint to whose shrine they are attached. In other cases, the relationship rests on tales of miracles, which the saint performed for a member of the tribe. The hagiographies of the saints abound with such miracles, which affirm the blessing and spiritual power of the saint.

The original allegiance ceremony (*bai'at*) is reproduced each generation in a hereditary relationship. When the founding saint died, he passed on his office to his son or other descendant in a turban-tying ceremony that identified the son as *sajjada-nashin* (literally, 'he who sits on the prayer rug'). Each *sajjada-nashin* takes on the spiritual responsibilities of the saint *vis-a-vis* his followers, as well as the caretaking responsibilities of the maintenance of the shrine. This traditional relationship is reinforced by an economic one: the *sajjada-nashin* annually makes a circuit of the tribes and villages traditionally tied to the shrine to collect contributions, known as *nazar*. This circuit further reinforces the association of a shrine with a particular territory over which it has direct influence.

The prime spiritual responsibility of a *sajjada-nashin* to his followers is to act as a mediator between them and God. The original saint brought his followers closer to God by means of his spiritual blessing. He is the channel through which communication with God flows. At his death his tomb becomes a source of blessing, but he is personally 'hidden' and thus relatively inaccessible to the common man, who must contact him through his living representative, the *sajjada-nashin*. The *sajjada-nashins* are thus hereditary *pirs*.

Access to God for the common man is through a lengthy chain of authority: from the *sajjada-nashin*, to the original saint, to 'Abdu'l-Qadir al-Gilani (or in many cases to the founder of the Sufi Order to which the saint belonged, if that was not 'Abdu'l-Qadir al-Gilani), to the Prophet, who has direct access to God. This spiritual chain of authority is reinforced by heredity: only a *Sayyid* (descendant of the Prophet) can be a real *pir*. This authority is symbolized by spiritual blessing, which has flowed from God to his Prophet Muhammad and then eastward with the saints. Others can come into contact with this blessing and benefit from it, but they cannot transmit it, because blessing cannot flow through their impure or undeveloped souls. Since the members of a tribe cannot themselves transmit blessing to their descendants, they maintain contact with the source through which blessing originally flowed to them. This source of blessing is the saint with whom they are spiritually connected through the allegiance ceremony of *bai'at*.

The position of the individual in the tribe and in the cosmological scheme is replicated in the traditional socio-political structure. Individuals are expected to act according to the wishes of the family and *baradari* in most spheres of activity, including marriage, occupation, and choice of saint. Their relationship to the government is mediated by tribal leaders or powerful landlords, just as their relationship to God is mediated by saints.[20]

The religious and political structures, however, have never been merely separate but parallel structures. The original saints were representatives not only of God but of a remote Muslim ruler. The Muslim rulers, realizing the political importance of the saints, tried to bring the *sajjada-nashins* under their control by granting them large properties and contributing to the building of the shrines.[21] Saints, since they controlled access to God, had an enormous influence over their followers and could use it for political purposes. Government support of the shrines was one way of ensuring the legitimacy of the ruler among the population.

Pir Pagaro in Sind is an extreme example of how powerful a force a *pir* and his followers can be. The Pir Pagaro has traditionally had a large following in Sind and surrounding areas. Among the disciples of the *pir* are the Hurs, who are willing to lay down their lives for him. The Hurs staged two rebellions against the British, in the 1890s and again in the 1940s. Pir Sabghatullah Shah was the Pir Pagaro during the second rebellion. The British saw him as a threat to their administration and executed him in 1943. They educated his son in England with the intention of having him become a successor who would keep the Hurs in order.[22]

The British continued the policy of their Muslim predecessors with respect to the shrines, making further grants to influential *pirs*. They saw the *pirs* primarily in terms of their economic power and treated them in essentially the same way that they treated landlords and tribal leaders. Their policy was to try to maintain the traditional social structure intact, securing the loyalty of the *pirs*, landlords, and chiefs by reinforcing their economic positions and educating them in the British tradition.[23] Their treatment of Pir Pagaro was an instance of this policy. In effect, the British merely took over the role of remote ruler from the Muslims and Sikhs before them.

There were some changes that occurred in the Punjab with respect to the shrines in the eighteenth and nineteenth centuries, during the decline of the Muslims and the rise of the British. At that time there was an influx of Chishti Sufis from the Delhi area. These Sufis preached a reformed religious doctrine and by this means supplanted some of the older shrines in the territories where they settled. According to Gilmartin, this 'Chishti revival' did not represent an attempt to change the organizational structure of religion in the Punjab, but merely infused it with new religious content.[24]

Despite the religious reform movements and political upheavals that occurred in the Punjab in the nineteenth and first half of the twentieth centuries, the basic socio-political infrastructure of the area did not fundamentally change. The *'ulama* had developed independent organizations,[25] and, once Pakistan was created, they hoped to control the direction of the new country themselves, thus adding an additional element to the political scene, but the landowners and *pirs* continue to be major political forces with which any politician who wants to remain in power must still contend.

REDEFINITION OF THE *PIR*

The ideology of modern Pakistan is founded on the idea of democracy, of direct participation in government. Muhammad Iqbal was one of the most important thinkers in generating this ideology for Pakistan. In his effort to synthesize what he perceived as the best of European social thought and government administration with the ideals and laws of Islam, he stressed the notion of 'Muslim democracy' as the political ideal of Islam. [26] Throughout Pakistan's history a tension has existed between the traditional political, economic, and religious structure, which had been reinforced by British administrative policy, and this Islamic, democratic, socialist ideology around which many members of the Muslim League rallied. The pre Partition Punjab Provincial Muslim League, for example, had Socialist, even Communist leanings, and declared that there should be nationalization of key industries and a ceiling placed on landholdings. According to Khalid bin Sayeed:

> Jinnah himself had thundered against the exploitation of the common people by landlords and capitalists . . . But the realities of Muslim politics forced even a domineering personality like Jinnah to work within the existing powerful social forces like the landowners and the new industrial magnates. Jinnah knew that the Muslim masses were too ignorant to be fully aware of their interests and too content to follow their pirs and landlords.[27]

By the time Bhutto came to power in 1971, this tension still had not been resolved. Bhutto had tried to avoid the support of large landowners and *pirs* when constituting the Pakistan Peoples' Party. The ideology of Bhutto's regime was based on the theme of Islamic socialism. He labelled himself the 'Quaid-i-Awam' (Leader of the People), a title that was strongly reminiscent of the Quaid-i-Azam, Muhammad Ali Jinnah, Founder of Pakistan, but that stressed Bhutto's overriding ideological concern with the common man. By the 1977 elections, however, he had fallen back on the landowners and their political influence:

> PPP tickets have gone to old feudal families of Multan Division for garnering votes. The return to influence of families like the Leghari, Mazari, Qureshi, Gilani, Dasti, Daultana, Khichhi, etc. marks a reversal of the political process to the old pattern after a break of seven years, when the PPP had routed them throughout Multan Division.[28]

The role of the *pirs* in the election process was explicit:

> In Khusab Tehsil, particularly, the landlords' hold has been strengthened by the 'pirs.' . . . Another important factor in this constituency [Shahpur Tehsil] will be the role of the Pir Sahib of Sial Sharif, who has a large following in the districts of Sargodha and Jhang. At present both contenders are claiming the Pir Sahib's support but this has yet to be confirmed by the gaddi ['seat' of the *pir*].[29]

Though, as these passages demonstrate, the traditional landlords and *pirs* are still at the heart of the political structure, administrative and legislative machinery for changing the political structure of the country has been set up over the years. The approach to removing landlords as mediators between the people and the government has been through a series of land-reform acts, the idea being that by divesting the landlords of economic power over the population, the landlords would also lose control over their votes. The hope was also, more directly, that dividing up the land would be politically popular. When land was allocated to peasants,

> each grantee was given an official certificate that clearly stated that these benefits had been conferred on him because Zulfikar Ali Bhutto, as chairman of the Pakistan People's Party and as Prime Minister of Pakistan, had fulfilled the promises that he had made to the peasants of Pakistan.[30]

Nevertheless, such land-reform measures were not effective in seriously altering the position of landlords, because many found ways of evading the legal ceilings on land ownership, ways that were permitted because Bhutto did not want to lose their political support.[31] Even if this had been an effective strategy for altering the political and economic structure of the country, such a policy by itself could not have affected the *pirs*, either as holders of *waqf* properties (religious endowments, which could be vast), or as religious and political mediators who supported the traditional economic and social structure.

With respect to *pirs*, Ayub Khan initiated a new administrative policy in 1959, a policy that was continued and extended by Bhutto. The West Pakistan Waqf Properties Ordinance of 1959 *(All Pakistan Legal Decisions* 1959) gave the govenment the power to take direct control over and to manage shrines, mosques, and other properties dedicated to religious purposes. The act was superseded by the West Pakistan Waqf Properties Ordinance of 1961 (Government of West Pakistan 1961-62) and, under Bhutto's regime, by the Auqaf (Federal Control) Act of 1976 *(All Pakistan Legal Decisions,* 1976), each of which further extended the authority of the Auqaf Department. The 1959 Ordinance was promulgated less than one year after Ayub's *coup d'etat,* while he was intent on reforming what was considered to be a corrupt administration. The Auqaf acts were intended to undercut the political power of both the hereditary *pir* families (the *sajjada-nashins*) and the *'ulama*.

Land reform acts were efforts to remove the landlord from his position as economic mediator and thus to remove him as a political mediator as well. The power of the *pir* as a political mediator, however, is difficult to eliminate as long as he retains the role of religious mediator. Only by changing the religious significance of the *pir* and the world view of his followers could any real political reorganization be effective. Thus the removal of *waqf* land from the control of the sajjada-nashins was equivalent to the breaking up of the lands of major landlords, but one more step was required: the religious hold of the *sajjada-nashin* also needed to be broken.

The governments of Ayub and Bhutto, perhaps wisely, did not choose to do this by abolishing shrines and *pirs* entirely. They did not ban them, as Ataturk had done in Turkey in order to advance the cause of secularism. Nor did they destroy them, as was done in Saudi Arabia for the almost opposite reason of returning to a more fundamentalist interpretation of Islam.

One of the main sources of inspiration for how to deal with the problem of *pirs* and shrines was undoubtedly the thought of Muhammad Iqbal. Iqbal, who inspired much of the ideology for Pakistan, criticized the spiritual role of the *pir* in the lives of Indian Muslims, calling the doctrines that generated the institution of *piri-muridi (pirs* and their followers) 'Persian mysticism'.[32] At the root of this 'Persian mysticism', Iqbal saw the distinction between esoteric and exoteric knowledge: 'Thus Muslim democracy', he wrote, 'was gradually displaced and enslaved by a sort of Spiritual Aristocracy pretending to claim knowledge and power not open to the average Muslim'.[33] In his opinion, this claim of limited access to secret doctrine was the source of both the status of the *pir* and the thralldom of the people.[34]

But Iqbal did not associate this brand of mysticism with all forms of Sufism. On the contrary, his own poetry was inspired by the Sufis. He felt, for instance,that the philosophy of his major poem, *Asrar-i-Khudi* [*The Secrets of the Self* (1972)], had developed directly from the experience and speculation of old Muslim Sufis and thinkers.[35] The doctrine Iqbal presented in *Asrar-i-Khudi* connects his interpretation of Sufism with the political action necessary to create a new Muslim community. The orientation he advocated eventually led to the creation of Pakistan.

After the death of Iqbal in 1938 and the creation of Pakistan, his son Javid Iqbal tried to translate the ideas of his father into concrete policy measures. In his book *Ideology of Pakistan*, originally published in 1959, Javid Iqbal offered his advice with regard to the creation of a ministry of Auqaf. He suggested that this ministry should take possession of and administer all religious endowments *(auqaf)* in Pakistan.[36] He quoted his father's negative views on the mysticism that 'enervated the people and kept them steeped in all kinds of superstition' and concluded:

The establishment of such a Ministry on the lines suggested above is the only remedy for the paralyzing influence of the Mullah and the Pir over the rural and urban masses of Islam. Unless and until the Mullah and the Pir are excluded from our religious life, there is no likelihood of the successful dissemination of enlightenment, liberalism and a meaningful and vital Faith among the people of Pakistan.[37]

Javid Iqbal's book was enthusiastically received by Ayub Khan who declared that he was also thinking along the same lines after having read the book with great interest.[38] The first Auqaf Ordinance was passed in 1959, shortly after the publication of this book.

The Ayub government thus adopted Javid Iqbal's suggestion. Its strategy was to develop a new ideology with respect to the saints and shrines – a twofold strategy. On the one hand, the Auqaf Department had to demonstrate that it could maintain the shrines as well as, if not better than, the *sajjada-nashins*. But this task alone was not adequate, because to most people the *sajjada-nashins* are not mere caretakers of the shrines. They are seen to possess blessing in their own right and thus to wield spiritual power over their followers directly. From the perspective of the follower, failure to follow the wishes of the *sajjada-nashin* in any sphere of activity was thought to have serious consequences. The government therefore had to demonstrate simultaneously that the *sajjada-nashin* was superfluous in both his religious and his caretaking functions.

Historically, the importance of the shrines derives directly from the Sufi tradition, because most *pirs* were originally respected as Sufi masters and teachers. As the tradition has developed in South Asia, however, and in somewhat different ways in other parts of the Muslim world as well, there has been a partial split between Sufism as rigorous spiritual discipline transmitted from spiritual teacher to qualified disciple on the one hand, and *'piri-muridi'* as the term is usually used, rather pejoratively in Pakistan today, to mean the blind devotion of the lay follower *(murid)* to a *pir*, whom he expects to act as a spiritual mediator for him. Such *pirs* are exemplified by the traditional *sajjada-nashins*.

As part of the direct assault on the traditional meaning of *pir*, which gives him almost magical power, the Auqaf Department stressed the aspect of Sufism that Iqbal had drawn on and himself embodied: the original Sufi as poet and social reformer. The government published pamphlets describing several of the major Sufi poets of Pakistan .[39] These pamphlets were published on the occasion of the annual *'urs* celebrations at the major shrines. They describe in detail the historical context of each saint, his individuality in appearance, and his social and political action. In sharp contrast to traditional hagiographies, they do not give accounts of the miracles performed by the saint. Rather, they stress pious actions of the saint, actions within the capacity of the ordinary man.

The contrast that the government made between the saint and the *sajjada-nashin* is explicit in the following passage taken from a pamphlet about the shrine of Sachal Sarmast:

> The region of Sind has been under the influence of Syeds and Pirs due to the hold of mysticism over the simple and straightforward masses of the area. Sachal Sarmast, like his elderly contemporary Shah Abdul Latif of Bhit, also belonged to one of the most influential and dominant Pir families, and the shape of things in Sind would have been different had both these saintly poets indulged in the type of life which the people of their class usually lead.

> The personal life and character of Sachal was exemplary for he had not only studied various voluminous books on religion and philosophy but his mind was so open because of his spiritual experience in the pursuit of Truth, that he gave up all legacies, and stood for a very noble cause to foster unity among human beings without any consideration of caste, creed, and geographical factors.[40]

In addition to mentioning the corruption of the traditional *pir* families, this passage stresses that Sachal Sarmast was a *pir*, and yet he was not a *pir* in the traditional, degenerate sense. The universalist message is presented. The mention of 'caste, creed, and geographical factors' is particularly important because it is precisely on these factors that the authority of the traditional *pir* usually rested. Many castes or tribes were associated with specific shrines. The local influence of each shrine was clearly defined by the *sajjada-nashin* and other descendants, who would make regular circuits of their territories in order to collect contributions from followers.

The governments of both Ayub Khan and Bhutto drew parallels between the social goals and reformist activities of the saints and those of the government. 'Caste, creed, and geographical factors' were considered to be major sources of disruption in the effort to build Pakistan as a nation. By attributing such concerns to the founders of Islam in Pakistan, a universalist and nationalist orientation acquires historical depth. This striving for historical continuity is particularly evident in the following passage from a *Pakistan Times* article about the saint Data Ganj Bakhsh. The article traces the idea of Islamic socialism, Bhutto's key phrase in summarizing his general policy, back to this major saint: 'He [Data Ganj Bakhsh] preached egalitarianism and visualized a classless society based on the concept of *Musawat-i-Muhammadi* which Allama Iqbal and Quaid-i-Azam later termed as 'Islamic Socialism'.[41]

In outlining the philosophical orientation of the Sufi saints, the government pamphlets emphasized that the saints described adhered to the philosophical doctrine of *wahdat al-wujud* (unity of being), which was first expounded by Ibn 'Arabi (A.D. 1165-1240) and which was vehemently denounced by some Muslim thinkers. Although later philosophers have accommodated to the doctrine and made it less controversial by carefully distinguishing it from pantheism, these pamphlets do not hesitate to label it pantheistic, apparently not pejoratively. Such a doctrine is congruent with the cosmological system that the government was trying to project. If these saints were pantheists, believing that God is immanent in all things, then there is no need, according to their own doctrine, for any mediator between God and man. It can be inferred that the role and reponsibility of the individual in such a system is analogous to the role he is expected to play in a Muslim democracy as an informed, voting citizen participating directly in the government: the government is 'immanent' in its citizens.

The pamphlets also discussed conversion, but its significance was shifted away from emphasis on the conversion of some tribes by a particular saint toward the idea of the saints as a collective body who worked together to convert Pakistan as a nation to Islam. In the story of Four Friends, for example, four important early Sufis were supposed to have worked together: 'Under these conditions these Four Companions travelled thousands of miles to preach and propagate the message of Islam and to exemplify the godly way. They radiated their message to the lands and peoples of the Punjab, Sind, and Baluchistan'.[42]

In keeping with this change in emphasis was the effort to make some shrines and 'urs celebrations (marking the anniversary of the death of a saint) national rather than regional affairs. For example, in 1974 the Federal Minister for Information and Broadcasting, Auqaf and Haj, inaugurated the 'urs of Madho Lal Hussain in Lahore. In his speech he said that this 'urs was the second largest in the country after that of Hazrat Data Ganj Bakhsh and that in years to come it would not only remain a mela (fair) of the Punjab but would also become a mela on the all-Pakistan level.[43] In 1959 the 'urs of Shah Abdul Latif of Bhitshah in Sind received extensive newspaper coverage in the Punjab.[44] President Ayub Khan, a national figure, inaugurated the cultural festivities associated with the 'urs. An academic conference attended by poets and writers from various parts of the country was also held.[45]

In addition to pamphlets, books, and newspaper articles presenting the perspective on the saints that the government wished to popularize, the Auqaf Department used other strategies more immediately visible to the common man. Under Ayub Khan, the Auqaf Department concentrated on shifting the focus of activities at the shrines away from those that directly involved the sajjada-nashin. The goal was to make the shrines centres of more general social welfare by building hospitals, schools, and other facilities for poor and rural people. The hospitals are, in a sense, in direct competition with the sajjada-nashins, who claim as one of their spiritual powers the ability to cure their followers by writing amulets for them. Though many see the two approaches as complementary, access to a hospital provides a hitherto unavailable alternative to many rural people. Activities such as an agricultural and industrial exhibition and a horse and cattle show were scheduled at 'urs celebrations.[46] An emphasis on these scientific and technological activities was consistent with Ayub Khan's overall approach to religious ideology, as revealed in his speeches:

> I humbly request that whenever in any public or private functions and ceremonies any passages from the Holy Qur'an are recited, they should invariably be translated into the language of the audience, followed by a clear and lucid interpretation of the mode and application to the life and conditions of today. Representative institutions like the various tiers of the basic democracies, corporations, municipal committees, etc., can play a valuable part in this mission.[47]

> I feel that during the early period of Islam the rationalists and the religious divines were not so wide apart as they are today.
>   Science has made tremendous progress . . .on the other hand, religious thought has lost its original dynamism and is bogged down in a quagmire of stagnation. Actually there is no conflict between science and religion.[48]

To encourage a scholarly rather than what was regarded as a superstitious approach to the shrines and Sufism, research centres and libraries were set up at or planned for several major shrines, including those of Khawaja Ghulam Farid,[49] Shah Abdul Latif, Bullhe Shah in Kasur, and Lal Shahbaz Qalandar. The Auqaf Department itself undertook to publish and to support the publication of religious books that were expected to become the nucleus of small libraries at various mosques and shrines.[50] This emphasis on the educational potential of the shrines had been urged by Javid Iqbal.[51]

In addition to developing the shrine areas as centres of social welfare, the Auqaf Department also makes improvements on the shrines themselves, thus demonstrating that the government can satisfactorily fulfill the caretaking functions of the *sajjada-nashins*. The policy of the Auqaf Department has been to concentrate its attention and resources on a limited number of shrines with a large following and to let the rest gradually diminish in importance. At several of these important shrines, the government has made major, highly visible repairs and improvements, greater than those that the hereditary *pir* family would have been willing to undertake. The government has taken care to stress that, in supporting and maintaining the shrines, it is also following the tradition of other Muslim rulers.

In an Auqaf pamphlet written in the Ayub era, the author summarized the history of the construction and development of the shrine of Lal Shahbaz Qalandar. In this summary, the Auqaf Department is the last of a series of Muslim rulers who have made major repairs and additions to the shrine.[52] There follows a detailed account of improvements and expenditures made by Auqaf on the shrine. Guest houses and other facilities for the comfort of pilgrims were an important part of the development plans for this and other shrines. Such improvements are immediately visible to the large number of people who visit the shrines and thus were intended to dispose them favourably toward the government control of the shrines. They also served as concrete evidence that the government, in displacing the *sajjada-nashins*, was not out to destroy the shrines themselves.

The replacement of the *sajjada-nashins* by the government was also symbolized ritually. Especially in Bhutto's time, the government played an active role in ritual proceedings at the shrines. Under Ayub Khan, participation in the *'urs* by government officials was generally limited to the literary and social-welfare activities scheduled to occur in conjunction with the *'urs*. When, for example, Ayub Khan attended the *'urs* of Shah Abdul Latif in 1959, he did not perform the *chaddar* (sheet)-laying ceremony himself. But the policy of Bhutto was to promote direct participation in *'urs* by government officials, perhaps because in his religious ideology Bhutto placed less emphasis than Ayub Khan did on the rationalization of Islam. Bhutto also wished to project an image of himself as personally involved in the activities of the common man, including shrine activities. In 1972 the Sind Department of Public Relations published a book entitled: *The Poet of the People: A Miscellany of Articles to Commemorate the 220th Anniversary of Shah Abdul Latif of Bhit*.[54] It includes a speech given by Bhutto ten years earlier when he personally performed a ceremony at the shrine. The title of the book is reminiscent of Bhutto's self-designation as 'leader of the people' and suggests that he wished to be seen in a position analogous to that of the saints, who were in touch with the common man.

During the Bhutto era, the central ceremonies of the *'urs* were performed by high government officials, and their activities were publicized in the newspapers and often filmed on television. At most shrines, the *'urs* includes a washing of the grave and the laying of a new *chaddar* to cover the grave for the following year. Traditionally, the central ceremonies of the *'urs* are performed by the *sajjada-nashin*. When an *'urs* at a small shrine is announced in the newspaper, for example, it is usually mentioned that the *chaddar*-laying ceremony will be performed by the *sajjada-nashin*. Under Bhutto, however, government officials performed the ceremony at most of the major shrines, and this ceremony was the main part of the *'urs* to be publicized. The following account from the *Pakistan Times*[55] is typical:

> The 932nd annual *urs* of Data Ganj Bakhsh Hazrat Ali Hujweri is commencing in Lahore on Monday. Chief Minister Sadiq Hussain Qureshi will inaugurate the three-day celebrations by laying a *'chaddar'* at 9 p.m. The Auqaf Department has made special arrangements to celebrate the *'urs* in a befitting manner.

The announcement for the 1974 *'urs* of Data Ganj Bakhsh laid particular stress on the participation of government officials. Ten sessions of speeches on the life and works of the saint were conducted, various sessions being presided over by the Chief Justice of Pakistan, Chief Justice of the Lahore High Court, and three other High Court Justices.[56]

During General Zia-ul-Haq's administration, there has been considerably less overt promotion of the *'urs* celebrations and activities at the shrines than there had been in Bhutto's time. Clearly, the government has not needed to demonstrate its ties to Islam through its support of shrine activities, since it is pushing so heavily a programme of Islamization. The *Pakistan Times* used to include articles announcing and describing the *'urs* celebrations of many saints, for example, Shah Abdul Latif and *Mela* Chiraghan, that now receive no mention at all.

Nevertheless, there has not been a disavowal of the saints and shrines, as might perhaps have been expected from an administration so overtly concerned with reinstating the original Islamic social order that prevailed at the time of the Prophet Muhammad. Emphasis has instead been placed on the saints as models of the pious Muslim, as devout men who observed all the laws of Islam. Because of their piety, they impressed the population and spread Islam throughout South Asia. This is clearly a continuation of the efforts at redefinition that occurred under Ayub and Bhutto.

The policy of turning the shrines into multifunctional religious and social welfare centres administered by the Auqaf Department, which began under Ayub, has continued under Zia-ul-Haq. Shortly before the *'urs* of Data Ganj Bakhsh in January 1980, the provincial minister of Auqaf announced that the hospital associated with the shrine was to be expanded. He also announced plans to begin construction of a new mosque at the shrine, which was to be the second largest in the city.[57]

Current policy concerning the definition of the proper role of the saints and shrines has been explicitly stated by Mian Hayat Bakhsh, the Punjab provincial advisor for Auqaf. In 1980 he conducted a seminar in conjunction with the 'urs of Data Ganj Bakhsh, the one Lahore shrine that continues to receive extensive publicity. According to him, the 'urs was meant to invite devotees to make self-appraisals and to determine whether their actions were in accordance with the teachings of Islam and the Islamic mystics. The 'seats of the saints' were training centres where people were 'transformed into noble human beings.'[58]

Though continuing most of the Auqaf policies of previous administrations, the government of Zia-ul-Haq has created a subtle shift of emphasis in defining the meaning of the saints. Articles describing the lives of the saints now regularly list key writings and sayings of the saint, which the ordinary man can take to heart and try to follow. The sole *Pakistan Times* article announcing the 1979 *urs* of Baba Farid (who formerly received much more extensive coverage in the newspapers) included a list of fourteen of his sayings, which emphasized piety and obedience and made no reference to esoteric practices or understanding.[59] Associated with this emphasis on the writings and sayings of the saints is a stress on the fact that the saints themselves were educated scholars, that is, *'ulama*. A 1980 article about the mission of the saint Data Ganj Bakhsh highlights the attributes of the old saints that are now being emphasized:

> Missionaries of today have much to learn from the old pioneers, particularly in the acquisition of proper, methodical education. Those pioneers were not miracle mongers but educated luminaries well versed in the physical sciences and the dialects of the people they worked amongst. Today no missionary who does not have a perfect command over their languages can hope to succeed. . . He will also have to be proficient in some of the sciences or a recognized scholar of some such subject as philosophy or geography or history or the indispensable economics. Character and devotion to prayers are of prime importance but the mundane arts and sciences must keep pace with the pursuits of the spirit. Above all, the masses must not be neglected. Mission work should be done intensively among them, for it is the common man that controls the destiny of nations.[60]

This emphasis on the education of missionaries suggests that the early Sufi saints are being equated with those who are presently being trained to serve as *imams* in local villages. The emphasis seems to be on minimizing the distinction between the saints and the *'ulama*, Sufism and *shariat*. A 1980 article, *'Ulema* and Saints of Sialkot', suggests the same thing. The two saints focused on are also *'ulama*.[61]

The recent promotion of Sufism in Pakistan has not been restricted solely to the level of political formulation of ideology. There appears to be a general resurgence of interest both in the Sufi tradition and in living Sufi *pirs* (not usually *sajjada-nashins*) as representatives of that tradition. Evidence of the former lies in the book bazaars, where recent reprints of older Sufi works in English, Urdu, and Persian, as well as newer works on the subject, abound. Some of these are government-sponsored publications, but many are put out by private publishers.

Faith in living *pirs* is widespread, not only among the rural and less-educated, but at all levels of society. Educated followers concentrate on the Sufi aspects of the relationship, describing it in a manner fairly consistent with the image of the Sufi that the government is trying to project. In Ayub Khan's time, Pir Dewal Sharif acquired a wide following in the army. According to Fazlur Rahman, who was the director of the government-sponsored Islamic Research Institute at the time, Pir Dewal Sharif extended his influence over many army officials and high civil servants and even won Ayub's favour (personal communication). In 1976-7, when the primary research for this study was conducted, several justices of the Lahore High Court were devout followers of various *pirs* and were intensely interested in Sufism. This was also true of army generals, police officials, a former chief minister of the Punjab, authors, businessmen, and other members of the Western-educated elite of Pakistan. Thus, many government servants who publicly participated in the rituals at the shrines were in fact practitioners of Sufism themselves.[62]

THE CREATION OF A NEW SHRINE

One living *pir* who had a number of influential followers, including at least one High Court Justice and a government minister under Bhutto, was Sufi Barakat Ali of Dar al-Ahsan, near Lyallpur in the Punjab. Sufi Barakat Ali was regarded as a living representative of the Sufi saints whose shrines are now so imporatant in Pakistan. He embodied precisely those qualities and actions that the government pamphlets attribute to Lal Shahbaz Qalandar, Sachal Sarmast, and the other major saints of Pakistan.

One of the main activities in which Sufi Barakat Ali was engaged at the time of this research was the conversion to Islam of a poor tribe living in the Lyallpur area. According to Sufi Barakat Ali and several of his followers, this tribe had no religion before Sufi Barakat Ali 'spread the light of Islam' among them. He provided them with food and clothing, and he was particularly concerned with educating their children. At a ceremony held at Sufi Barakat Ali's *khanqah* on the Prophet's birthday in 1977, about fifty of these children between the ages of six and eight were obliged to get up one by one before a large crowd and recite into a microphone the verses of the Qur'an they had learned. Sufi Barakat Ali's involvement in conversion explicitly linked him to the sufis of old whose most important activity in historical terms was according to the government perspective, the conversion of the area now called Pakistan to Islam.

The *khanqah* of Sufi Barakat Ali resembles a major shrine, except that, when I visited the *khanqah*, there was no grave. It possesses all facilities for social welfare that the government is building at the major shrines: a hospital, school (*madrasa*), mosque, and library. Since there was no grave, no shrine, Sufi Barakat Ali was the major source of *barakat* at the *khanqah*.[63] He is a living representative of the Sufi saint tradition, yet he is totally independent of the *sajjada-nashin* pattern. When he dies and a shrine is built, the architecture will be as impressive as that of any other shrine in Pakistan, regardless of how elaborate the grave itself is, because it will be surrounded by the mosque, library, *minar* (hospital), and school already in existence. An original mosque of humble clay and mud embodies the history and simple beginnings of the *khanqah* and in years to come will add to the emotional impact of Sufi Barakat Ali's accomplishments as a saint.

The presence of a living representative of the Sufi tradition who possesses all attributes of the original Sufi *pirs* further reinforces the position that the *pirs* were not mysterious, magical figures of the mystical past who can now be reached only through intermediaries in the form of *sajjada-nashins*, but were instead pious, yet ordinary, men. They performed for their era what living saints can do today for ours. This living *pir*, however, does not have the landed base that successors of the original *pirs* have traditionally had. By identifying such individuals with the original *pirs*, government leaders are in a position to downplay the importance of the hereditary landed religious leaders.

CONCLUSION

The Sufi ideology that was formulated by the government of Ayub Khan during the course of the establishment of the Auqaf Department represented a new, relatively coherent world view intended to replace the traditional cosmology, which prevailed among much of the population. The traditional cosmology, which placed the common man in a position where God was inaccessible except through spiritual mediators, was congruent with the traditional social, political , and economic structure. Similarly, the new cosmology was congruent with the social and political goals of the government. This cosmology is grounded in certain aspects of Sufi doctrine. In this model God is not absolutely transcendant, but is immanent in his creation. Any man, if he is pious and receives the proper training, can achieve the goal of the Sufi, closeness to God. The Sufi poets and saints whose shrines are venerated were pious, educated men who achieved this goal and now serve as examples for others to follow. The political ideologies of Ayub and Bhutto rested on the principles of democracy and socialism, which require for their successful implementation an educated, voting population. The relationship between the government and the people is, ideally, interactive; the Sufi model of the relationship between God and man is also interactive: the religious experience of God is open to anyone. Perhaps it is also because of this congruence with the Western-influenced goals of a secular government, which stressed the autonomy of the individual, that Sufism, which highlights an awareness of the individual's inner experience, has become so popular among many of the educated elite of Pakistan.

Despite the Islamic reformism of General Zia-ul-Haq's government, some basic goals, such as educating the people, eliminating the political mediators that have traditionally come between the people and the central government, and creating a national rather than a local orientation, have remained the same since Ayub's time. Sufism and the saints continue to be defined in a way congruent with these goals.

There has also been a shift in emphasis, however. In the effort to build a new political process and goverment, a central organizing symbol has been the Muslim community (*ummat*) united by obedience to God and His Laws (*shariat*). Zia himself seems to think that the highest political principle is obedience to a truly Muslim ruler. The retention of a system of political parties and democracy is not necessarily compatible with such a system,[64] because the highest value is not the will of the People but rather the will of God. In keeping with this shift in ideology and goals is a change of emphasis in the definition of Sufism and the saints. Instead of the traditional Sufi concern with the course of spiritual development of the individual, which includes esoteric understanding for the spiritually advanced, the stress is on conformity to *shariat*, which is in turn expected to lead to spiritual growth within the community. Thus, the Sufi is seen primarily as an *'alim*, whose main function is to educate and guide his followers in the proper application and understanding of Islamic law.

NOTES

1. In Pakistan *pir* is the general term for spiritual guide, holyman, and wielder of spiritual power and blessing. Its original meaning in Persian is 'old man' or 'respected elder'.

2. Trimingham, J. Spencer, *The Sufi Orders in Islam*, Oxford University Press, London, 1971.

3. Smith, Wilfred Cantwell, *Islam in Modern History*, Princeton University Press, Princeton, 1957, pp. 56, 198-9.

4. *Waqf* (plural *auqaf*) is a property that has been dedicated for religious purposes.

5. Sayeed, Khalid bin, *Politics in Pakistan*, Praeger, New York, 1980, pp. 54-5.

6. Deutsch, Karl W., *Nationalism and Social Communication*, Massachusetts, Cambridge, 1966; and Kerr, Clark, *Industrialism and Industrial Man*, Harvard University Press, Cambridge, 1960.

7. Sayeed, op cit., 1980, p. 94.

8. Cohen, Stephen P., and Marvin G. Weinbaum, 'Pakistan in 1981: Staying On', *Asian Survey*, 1982, 22, No. 2, p. 137.

9. Chaudry, M. Iqbal, *Pakistani Society: A Sociological Perspective*, fourth edition, Aziz Publishers, Lahore, 1980, p. 166.

10. Hardy, Peter, *Partners in Freedom and True Muslims: The Political Thought of Some Muslim Scholars in British India, 1912-1947*, Scandinavian Institute of Asian Studies, Monograph Series, 1971, No. 5, pp. 18-19.

11. Ibid., p. 20.

12. Munir, Muhammad, *From Jinnah to Zia*, Second edition, Vanguard Books, Lahore, 1980, p. 141.

13. This effort to minimize the distinction between the saints and the *'ulama*, Sufism and *Shari'at*, is not new to South Asian Islam or to Islam in general. Efforts at synthesis have been made since the ninth century A.D. As a result of the thought of al-Ghazzali (A.D. 1058-1111), Sufism was accepted by many *'ulama*, but through the centuries, the tension between adherence to the *Shari'at* and the popular beliefs and practices that have been identified with Sufism has remained.

14. Metcalf, Barbara, *Islamic Revival in India: Deoband 1860-1900*, Princeton University Press, Princeton, 1982.

15. Ibid.

16. Schimmel, Annemarie, *Mystical Dimensions of Islam*, University of North Carolina Press, Chapel Hill, 1975, p. 248.

17. Eaton, Richard M., 'The Political and Religious Authority of the Shrine of Baba Farid', in *Moral Conduct and Authority: The Place of Adab in South Asian Islam*, Metcalf, Barbara D., (editor), University of California Press, Berkeley, 1982.

18. Gilmartin, David, 'Religious Leadership and The Pakistan Movement in the Punjab', *Modern Asian Studies, 13*, July 1979, pp. 485-517.

19. I found this to be true in my own conversations with many Punjabi Muslims, especially among those from rural areas and from *baradaris* (tribes) strongly attached to a particular shrine. The pattern appears to be different, however, in Lahore, an urban area, where many people chose a *pir* on their own initiative. Often this *pir* would not be a *sajjada-nishin* attached to a major shrine.

20. Gilmartin, op.cit., 1979.

21. Eaton, Richard M., *Sufis of Bijapur*, Princeton University Press, Princeton, 1978.

22. Lambrick, H.T. (translator and editor), *The Terrorist*, Ernest Benn, founder, 1972.

23. Gilmartin, op.cit., 1979.

24. Ibid.

25. Metcalf, op.cit., 1982.

26. Iqbal, Muhammad, 'Islam as a Moral and Political Ideal', in *Thoughts and Reflections of Iqbal*, 1964 b, pp.51, 52. (Essay originally published in *Hindustan Review*, 20, 1909.)

27. Sayeed, Khalid bin, Pakistan: *The Formative Phase* 1857-1948, Second edition, Oxford University Press, London, 1968, pp. 209, 210.

28. *Viewpoint*, Lahore, 1977, 'Inner Feuds lessen PNA Chances: Multan, Sargodha', Vol. 2, No. 27. p. 11.

29. Ibid., p. 12.

30. Sayeed, op.cit., 1980, p. 93.

31. Ibid., p. 92

32. For a discussion of the changes in Sufism that Iqbal criticized, see Trimingham, op.cit., 1971. Trimingham labels these changes the development of the *ta'ife* (organization) stage of Sufism, which developed between the thirteenth and fifteenth centuries. At that time there was transition from a teacher-pupil relationship at the core of Sufism to the veneration of the shaikh and his tomb.

33. Iqbal, Muhammad, 'Islam and Mysticism', in *Thoughts and Reflections of Iqbal*, Syed Abdul Vahid (editor), Sh. Muhammad Ashraf, Lahore, 1964 a, p. 81.

34. Ibid., p. 82.

35. Iqbal, Muhammad, 'Letter to Dr. Nicholson', in *Thoughts and Reflections of Iqbal*, 1946 c, p. 101.

36. Iqbal, Javid, *Ideology of Pakistan*, second edition, Ferozsons, Karachi, 1971, p. 57

37. Ibid., p. 58.

38. Letter from Ayub Khan to J. Iqbal, 11 July 1959, in ibid., p. 170.

39. Khalid, K.B. (editor), *Asar-i-Latif*, Directorate of Information, Government of West Pakistan, 1967 and *Sachal Sarmast*, Department of Public Relations, Government of Sind, Karachi, 1971; *Qalandar Lal Shahbaz*, Sind directorate of Public Relations Karachi, 1971; and *Qalandar Lal Shahbaz*, Sind Information Department, Karachi, n.d.

40. Khalid, op.cit., 1971, p.14.

41. Shibli, A.R., 'Crusade against Social Injustice: Data Gunj Bakhsh', *Pakistan Times*, 15 March 1974.

42. Sind Information Department, n.d., p. 17.

43. Pakistan Times, ' Kindle Hearts with Divine Splendour: Madho Lal's urs Begins', Lahore, 31 March 1947 a.

44. *Pakistan Times*, 'Governor's Address to Adabi Conference at Bhitshah, 22 August 1959 b.

45. *Pakistan Times*, 'Shah Latif 'Urs' Begins at Bhitshah Today', 20 August 1959 a.

46. Sind Directorate of Public Relations, op.cit., 1971, p. 24.
47. Message to the nation on the occasion of Eid-uz-Zuha, 26 May 1961. Reproduced in Jafri, Rais Ahmed, *Ayub: Soldier and Statesman, Speeches and Statements (1958-65) of Field Marshal Muhammad Ayub Khan, President of Pakistan*. Muhammad Ali Academy, Lahore, 1966, p. 85.
48. Speech delivered on the occasion of the foundation-stone laying ceremony of the Jamia Taleemat-i-Islamia, Karachi, 3 September 1962. Reproduced in ibid., p. 129.
49. *Pakistan Times*, 'Fareed Academy to be Set up', Lahore 11 June 1969.
50. Khaliq, M.A., *Auqaf Report*, Produced for the Auqaf Department, Government of West Pakistan, Hyderabad, 1969, p. 46.
51. Iqbal, op. cit., 1971.
52. Sind Information Department, n.d., p. 22.
53. Pakistan Times 'Shah Latif Urs Begins at Bhitshah Today', Lahore 20 August 1959 a.
54. Khalid, K.B. *The Poet of the People: A Miscellany of Articles to Commemorate the 220 th Anniversary of Shah Abdul Latif of Bhit*. Department of Public Relations, Government of Sind, Karachi, 1972.
55. *Pakistan Times*, 'C.M. to Open Data's 'Urs', Lahore, 7 February 1977.
56. *Pakistan Times*, 'Data Ganj Bakhsh Urs on 13th', 10 March 1974.
57. *Pakistan Times*, 'Details of Data's Urs Arrangements', Lahore, 6 January, 1980.
58. *Pakistan Times*, 'Data's Services to Islam Commemorated', 29 December 1980.
59. Amin, Sheikh Parviz, 'Baba Farid Shakar Ganj', *Pakistan Times*, 26 November 1979, p. 4.
60. *Pakistan Times*, 'Thousands Visit Data's Shrine', Lahore, 29 December 1980.
61. Sabri, Ehsan Qureshi, 'Ulema and Saints of Sialkot', *Pakistan Times*, 17 December 1980.
62. Fazlur Rahman (personal communication) attributes the resurgence of interest in sufism to the fact that many people are disillusioned with the idea of an Islamic state and need something to clutch at in a time of rapid social change. He claims that even some members of the Jama'at-i-Islami, the fundamentalist-oriented political party that is unqualifiedly opposed to shrines and *Pirs*, have said that the solution to Pakistan's spiritual problems lies in Sufism.
63. Richard Kurin (personal communication) reports that, since I last visited the *khanqah*, Sufi Barakat Ali's wife has died and that her tomb has become a focus of ritual activity and a source of blessing.

8

The Shrine and Lunger of Golra Sharif

Hafeezur Rehman Chaudhry

Sufism embraces those tendencies in Islam that aim at direct communication between God and man. Mysticism is a particular method of approach to reality (*haqiqat*) that makes use of intuitive, emotional, and spiritual faculties that are generally dormant and latent unless called into play through training under guidance of a Sufi or *murshid* to a circle of his pupils or *murids*. In the thirteenth century the Sufi circle acquired an institutional foundation and the means of maintaining continuity over time.[1] Through private endowments Sufis acquired their own hospices in which they lived and held their gatherings.

A number of Sufi saints (*murshids*) who later came to be called Pirs, propagated Islam in the subcontinent since the death of Prophet Muhammad (peace be upon him) and acquired fame and recognition for their sanctity and benevolence.

The popular form of Sufism that emerged after the 15th century remains the basic model for the social organization of Sufi tombs which continue to remain the foci of worship and pilgrimage to both the Muslims and the Hindus of the subcontinent. Each tomb has a community of Pirzadas living nearby whose descent from the saint gives them a claim to organize religious activities around the tomb, maintenance of a *piri-muridi* relationship with a band of followers, the *murids,* who follow their teachings blindly, and providing a wide variety of social and medical counselling such as for family tensions, business problems, and chronic illness. Barrenness among women, of course, is the staple of the *piri-muridi* relationships. At the shrine of Nizamuddin Auliya, members of Pirzada families practised *piri-muridi* in small cubicles surrounding the saint's tomb. However, it seems that clients first come to a local Pir with a specific problem for remedy and remunerate accordingly. Patronization of the Pir is subject to satisfactory results leading to a more generalized pattern of reciprocity established between the two.

A more exclusive and spiritual relationship exists between a Pir and a *Murid*, suggests Mayer.[2] Moreover, acceptance of a Pir as one's *Murshid* implies an allegiance to that Pir for life which is often renewed in the next generation.

Shrines are visited in case of need, or for a moment of spiritual intimacy with the deceased saint who is believed to be always alive and active.[3] Moinuddin Chishti's mausoleum in Ajmer, India, is an outstanding example of this veneration. Muhammad Tughlaq and Sher Shah Suri were amongst its regular visitors. So was Akbar who went several times on foot to Ajmer while his son Jahangir wrote an account of its '*Urs*' or memorial celebrations.

Very little has been written about this widespread form of patronage in Pakistan. However, the shrines in Pakistan are major social institutions that command the loyalties and adherence of a large section of the Pakistan society and perform wide-ranging tasks from the religious to the economic.

To cater to the functional needs of the society the shrines have developed complex institutional set-ups distinctively characteristic to their role in the life and culture of Pakistan. At the top is the resident Pir or manager supported by a number of essential functionaries. The success and reputation of shrines are closely dependent on the selection and training of personnel for their respective roles, which in turn affect their output and how best they can carry out the tasks entrusted to them. A sort of network of affiliation exists with other shrines extending to even the geographically remote areas of Pakistan bringing together people in a common interest despite the diversity of their individual backgrounds. The shrines have not only important historical connections but also co-operative economic and visiting arrangements as well. The network includes the followers or *murids* attached to individual shrines representing a cross-section of Pakistan society. Thus shrines function as linking institutions, serving unity in diversity. As such the shrines possess capabilities of positively contributing to the integrity and unity of Pakistan society.

Saints of Pakistan are identified with the areas in which their shrines are situated. In rural areas many tribes are associated traditionally with a particular saint, who is believed to have originally converted that tribe to Islam. The tribe usually retains memory of the conversion as a focus for maintaining the traditional tie with the shrine. Most Jat and Rajput groups who moved in to the Punjab and became Muslim in the medieval period claim to have been converted either by Baba Farid of Pakpattan or by Baha-ul-Haqq Zakkaria of Multan.[4]

This paper describes the conceptual framework of mysticism and the historical development and continuity of the shrine of Golra Sharif in Punjab, Pakistan.

Shrines such as Golra Sharif represent a long tradition of Muslim theological and proselytizing activity in South Asia. The rituals, doctrines, and mode of operation of these institutions attract a vast majority of the population of this ethnically diverse country. Many of them have also developed a highly aggressive entrepreneurial orientation, that has occasionally brought them into conflict with the state. This orientation has been quite successful in amassing immense wealth and power in some shrines. This success and prominence, therefore, is due in part to their long historical association with Islam in South Asia and also to the entrepreneurial and organizational skill of their leaders.

CONCEPTUAL FRAMEWORK OF MYSTICISM

The primary Islamic belief is that Allah is All-Powerful, and Hazrat Muhammad (PBUH) is his chosen prophet to whom God revealed the Holy Qur'an — the first channel of communication presenting the Muslims with a prescribed way of life. The second channel of communication are saints or Pirs who act as spiritual guides and guardians. The Saints are the chosen Sufis or Aulias (Friends of God) who by virtue of a lifetime of devotion and spiritual attributes have acquired sainthood.

The role of the Sufis and Saints in the spread of Islam in the South Asian region is universally acknowledged: 'In India, Sufis rather than the Ulema were the religious inspiration of the Muslim intelligentsia and the masses.[5] 'Sufis were responsible more than any other religious or cultural group, for the conversion of masses of Hindus to Islam'.[6]

The *Encyclopaedia Britannica* acknowledges this fact thus:

The main contribution of the Sufi orders is their missionary activity. Sufism has helped to shape large parts of Muslim society. The missionary activities of the Sufis have enlarged the fold of the faithful. The importance of Sufism for spiritual education, and inculcation in the faithful of the virtues of trust in God, piety, faith in God's love, and veneration of the Prophet (PBUH) cannot be over-rated.[7]

These selfless men of God often travelled thousands of miles on foot or by primitive transport for the spread of Islam to remote, alien, and in many cases hostile lands, simply for the love and welfare of humanity. These Sufis and Walis migrated from places such as Arabia, the Middle East, Iran, and Central Asia. By their personal example of morality, piety and other worldliness, they invariably attracted a large and devoted following which resulted in mass conversion. People from far off places thronged to have a glimpse and to receive blessings in their needs and sufferings. These Saints usually gathered some bright disciples around them, who helped in the further propagation of Islam. The foundation of each Sufi order is based on the relationship of the master and the disciple: *Murshid* (religious guide) and *Murid* (aspirant). The early Sufis were more concerned with experience than theory. They taught their Murids how to work effectively and this was called Tariqa. A Tariqa is a practical method to guide a seeker by training him in a definite way of thought, feeling, and action leading through a succession of *Maqamat* (stages) to the ultimate reality.

The eleventh century saw the development of the *khanaqahi* system which provided temporary resting places for wandering Sufis. These *khanaqahs* played a decisive role in the Islamization of border lands and non-Arab regions in Central Asia and North Africa. By the twelfth century many *khanaqahs* had become rich and flourishing establishments. From the beginning of the thirteenth century certain *khanaqahs* became the centres of Tariqas. This happened when a centre or circle became focused on one Murshid and his particular way of teaching. Each Tariqa was in turn handed down through a continuous chain of *silsilas*. There are many *silsilas* but four have had considerable influence in the Indo-Pakistan subcontinent. The Chishtiya *silsila* had a widespread impact on the people of the subcontinent — the emphasis here is on this particular *silsila*.

CHISHTIYA SILSILA

From the thirteenth century onwards Central Asian Sufis had been migrating southwards into India. Moinuddin Chishti of Sijistan (A.D. 1236) finally settled at Ajmer, capital of a powerful Hindu State. The Chishtiya *silsila* won widespread popularity under him and his successor Qutubuddin Bakhtiyar Kaki (A.D. 1235) to become eventually the leading Tariqa in the Indo-Pak subcontinent.

Khawaja Moinuddin Chishti of Ajmer, the pioneer of the Chishtiya *silsila*, links with Khawaja Abu Ishaq Sami after seven generations. Like other Sufi orders, the specialized methodologies of the Chishtiya *silsila* soon became crystallized into a simplified love for music, an emotional arousal equated with spiritual experience. People from every strata of society flocked to him to attend the music session called *sama*. The Sufis committed themselves to the spiritual welfare of the people parallel to the political governments exercised by the Sultans and Amirs. These Sufis divided the State into regions and appointed Walis (Saints) for the propagation of Islam and as a counter measure to the anti-state activities of the Sultans.

Hazrat Moinuddin assigned the territory of Delhi to his disciple Bakhtiyar Kaki who initiated several *Khalifas* moving in different directions for the spread of Islam. After his death the *Khalifas* maintained their *khanaqahs* as independent institutions in which succession became hereditary.

In India the *khanaqahs* were regarded as focal points of Islamic centres for holiness, fervour, ascetic exercises, and Sufi training. Thus *khanaqahs* sprung up around a pious figure and associated itself with a particular Tariqa, method of discipline, and exercises. On the death of King Feroz Tughlaq, his son Muhammad Ibn Tughlaq came to the throne. From then on (A.D. 1325-57) Sufism showed a sharp decline, perhaps because he attempted to make the Sufis work under his guidance. It went against Sufi traditions to work under supervision of rulers, hence they refused to obey his orders, though some were compelled to work. This caused restlessness among the Sufis (Shaikhs) and they moved into different directions of the subcontinent to establish independent *khanaqahs*. At about this time the central power of Delhi was declining and independent governments came up in the provinces of Gujrat, Jampur, Dekan, Bengal, and Maloh. Nasiruddin Muhammad Charagh Dehlvi (A.D. 651/1356) successor to the great Shaikh Nizamuddin Auliya chose to establish independent *khanaqahs* in these provinces for the propagation of the *silsila*. These independent centres began to spread the *silsila* in accordance with the Tariqa and sayings of Moinuddin Chishti. And the Chishtiya *silsila* spread in different parts of the subcontinent.

Hazrat Fariduddin Masuad popularly known as Ganj-i-Shakar (A.H.1175-1265) is regarded to have been in the forefront of the spread of the Chishtiya *silsila* in West Punjab (now eastern-central Pakistan) as a distinct school of mystical ascription. The leading propagationists of this *silsila* were Noor Muhammad Maharvi (A.H. 1143-1205 tomb in Maher Sharif, District Bahawalnagar) and Khawaja Sulaman Townswi, disciple of Noor Muhammad Khawaja Sulaman Townswi (A.H. 1183-1267).

In Pakistan, the chief propagandist of the Chishtiya *Silsila* is Pir Mehr Ali Shah (A.H. 1275-1356) whose Mazar is located at Golra Sharif, in District Rawalpindi. The ancestors of Pir Mehr Ali Shah hailed from Sadora, District Ambala (India) and settled in Golra Sharif in the seventeenth century A.D. His *Nasab* (genealogy) links with Hazrat Abdul Qadir Jillani after 25 generations and with Hazrat Imam Hussain after the 36th link. *Hasban* he links with the family of Hazrat Moinuddin Chishti after 18 generations. His early religious education was arranged by his parents and elders under carefully selected and eminent local teachers. Later, he himself sought good teachers in the remote parts of the subcontinent and travelled to other schools to complete his education.

Pir Mehr Ali Shah was a competent *Faqih* (jurist). The quality of his proficiency as a jurist may be assessed from the extensive library he maintained and references that appear in his legal texts. The precise number of books which can be classified as Islamic *Tafseer*, *Fiqh*, are not known but there are indications that his library was one of the best stocked.

A more satisfactory evaluation of Pir Mehr Ali's background in jurisprudence comes from the legal texts he wrote. From these it is obvious that he was a widely read scholar. His style was clear and precise if not always highly sophisticated. His writings are an indication of his versatility in *Hanafi Fiqh* and other *fiqhs*. His knowledge of *Hadith* and *Tafseer* was widely accepted. Quranic references appear throughout his correspondence and there is no doubt that in addition to having memorized the Qur'an, he had memorized many *Hadith*. Pir Mehr Ali wrote several books on different aspects of Islam. These books were written in the Persian language and were subsequently translated into Urdu. His writings include:

a) *Tahki-ka-Tul Haq* (1897). This book is a rejoinder to a book that contains material against Islamic ideology.

b) *Shamsul Hidayat* (1900). This book was written against the preachings of Mirza Ghulam Ahmed Qadyani, the founder of the Ahmadya sect.

c) *Saife Chishtai* (1902) is also against the Qadyani movement.

d) *Ala-e-Kalma Tulah Al-Fatuhatus Samdia* and *Tasfia Mabain Sunni aur Shia* are other learned treatises.

A comprehensive analysis of Pir Mehr Ali's legal writings cannot be attempted here, but something can be said about the themes upon which those writings concentrated. The best documentation on Pir Mehr Ali's juridical activities comes from a consideration of his correspondence and his legal opinions (*Fatwa*). In *Fatwa* one often finds reference to the Qur'an or *Hadith* in his recommendation to the individuals and tribes.

Pir Mehr Ali was a distinguished and accomplished Sufi (Mystic) in an area in which training in Islamic Science was held in high esteem. He developed a policy of political neutrality from which flowed much of his influence as an arbiter in political affairs. He was beneficial to the clients of the area and the immediate neighbourhood who consulted and associated with him in terms of social, economic, political, and religious advantages. They were known as *Talibs* (students of religion) and *Mutawasaleen* (persons receiving training). The politico-economic effects of their presence in his Majlis accounted in part for Pir Mehr Ali's reputation as a generous patron and of his tribe as a place of sanctuary. Pir Mehr Ali is also well known for his involvement and leadership of many movements dealing with the cause of Muslims in general , and Islam, in particular. He launched a powerful movement against Qadyanis (who do not believe in the finality of prophethood of Hazrat Muhammad, (PBUH)) and, for this purpose, he wrote several books and arranged *Manazaras* (public discussions) with the leaders of the Qadyani movement.

Following World War I when the Ottoman Empire was broken and the Caliphate of Islam was abolished he joined in the Khilafat Movement and aided the Turkish Muslims in the battles at Tripoli and in the Balkan Peninsula with men, material, and money. The leaders of the Khilafat Movement consulted him and sought his guidance on many occasions. When the British Government tried to woo him on its side and offered the bait of a *jagir* covering 400 acres of land, he refused its acceptance and continued his support for the movement. Pir Mehr Ali was thus a great Mujahid (Crusader) for the cause of Islam. His continuous struggle for the cause of religion earned him about a million followers in the subcontinent.

Pir Mehr Ali died in 1937 after a prolonged illness of five years. He was buried in Golra and his tomb became the foci of pilgrimage for his followers. The village Golra came to be called Golra Sharif (Sharif, the noble). It is believed that during his lifetime he performed miracles. Several stories of his spiritual power are narrated by his followers and those who visit his Mazar during the annual congregation, the *Urs*.

Pir Mehr Ali left behind one son and three daughters. In accordance with the rules of succession his son Ghulam Mohiyuddin succeeded him and carried the line of descent. He extended the already established school, Madrassa Ghausia and arranged the publication of his father's writing. He died in 1974 and left behind two sons and one daughter. His elder son Ghulam Moinuddin is at present the *Sajjada Nasheen* (successor). His younger brother Abdul Haq Shah assists him in organizing the shrine establishment.

BACKGROUND OF THE VILLAGE AND LUNGER

The shrine or *Mazar* of Pir Mehr Ali Shah is located at Golra Sharif 20 km north-west of Rawalpindi in the province of the Punjab in Pakistan. It is situated at the base of the Margalla hills, a steep range which marks the beginning of the ascent to the Khyber Pass to the west and the Karakorums and the Hindu Kush to the north. The name Golra Sharif pertains to both the shrine and its attached village of approximately 400 households. No definite historical records exist which could document the founding of the village, but numerous accounts of its origin are offered by village residents as well as functionaries of the shrine compound. Oft repeated is that of Shahbuddin who settled nearly 300 years ago near Sargodha and had visited the area now occupied by the shrine on a hunting expedition. The dogs used in his hunt, however, were intimidated by the rabbits who faced the dogs and refused to flee. Shahbuddin attributed this power of the rabbits to some supernatural quality in the water and so he relocated his family from Sargodha beside the stream where the shrine is now located. Another account is that when the ancestors of Pir Mehr Ali settled in Golra, most of the local population was Hindu. Though Muslims were the possessors of land, but the system of interest was such that they were subordinate to the Hindus. Trade and commerce were exclusively in the hands of the Hindus. Muslims were constantly pitched in battles and internal quarrels and strifes handed down from generations. On account of their quarrelsome nature this place was called 'Golra'! Whatever the reason for the name of the village, documentary evidence of its existence is found in the revenue papers of the seventeenth century located in government offices in Rawalpindi. Lexicographically, the term means the 'land of illiterate people' in Persian. In the times of Raja Ranjeet Singh the tribes of Golra came to the present site in the caravan of Syedoan Muhammad from the hills of Soan Sikariser. Since the region remained under the control of the Hindus for several years it was devoid of Muslim spiritual education. In the times of the British Raj it assumed significance as a recruiting ground for sepoys for the British Army. It was in these circumstances, that Pir Mehr Ali undertook construction of mosques in which he started teaching the Shariah. He established a library and arranged a *lunger* (free distribution of sacred food) and lodging for visitors.

It has been historically inferred that *lunger* started in the time of Alp Arsalan, 49 Hijri (A.D. 1038) at the mausoleum of Imam Abu Hanifa in Baghdad. *Lunger* was at its zenith in the renowned period of Abdul Qadir Jillani, A.H. 529 (A.D.1106), the founder of the Qadiryia Silsila, popularly known as Ghausal Azam. Students from all over the world were educated at *Madressa-e-Ghausia* and a large number assembled to hear his teachings. The *Lunger* termed *Lunger-e-Ghausia* or the *Lunger* of Ghausal Azam (Abdul Qadir Jillani) was revived after a lapse of 870 years. Hundreds of followers continued the *lunger*. Similarly Pir Mehr Ali Shah followed in the traditions of his great grandfather by starting a *lunger* at Golra Sharif in 1903.

Anniversaries of Sufis, called *Urs Sharif*, are celebrated here. At the time of the *Urs* thousands of visitors are distributed food from the *lunger*. Hundreds of disciples offer themselves for services at the Mazar Sharif leaving their business, home, and hearth behind. Thus each visitor contributes towards the *Urs* celebrations according to his ability. An average of 1200 people visit the Mazar daily and take their meals from the lunger — the cause of its fame being sound administration, morality, and discipline.

INTERNAL ORGANIZATION OF
THE LUNGER AND THE SHRINE

The shrine of Golra Sharif has a large administrative network in order to perform the numerous activities associated with it. One of the most powerful individuals is the cashier or *Khazanchi* of the shrine. The current incumbent is a former officer of the Land Revenue Department of the Government of Punjab appointed by the Pir as general treasurer

Figure 8.1: **Golra Sharif**
Internal Organization of the Shrine

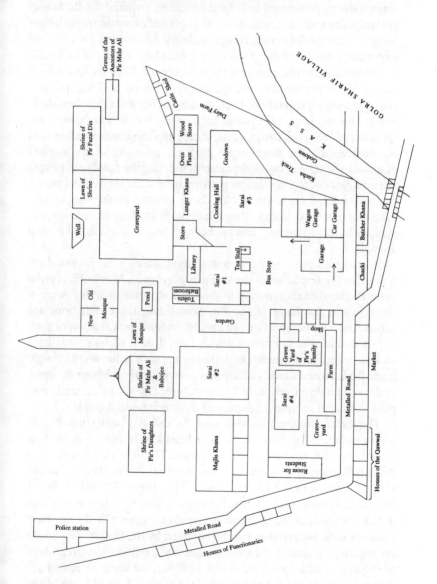

and overseer of property and income as well as the custodian of the numerous personal gifts received by the Pir. He directly supervises the shrine's stores, particularly bulk food purchases required for the *lunger*. He maintains extensive accounts of receipts and expenditures in ledger books. Financial data concerning the shrine, however, is a secret — an important function of the cashier being guarding secrecy of its funds.

Subordinate to the cashier is the storekeeper. With his four subordinates, he supervises the storage and distribution of flour, pepper, salt, ghee, sugar, vegetables, beef, onions, garlic, and other foodstuffs needed for the *lunger*. He is also responsible for the purchase or acquisition of firewood, cattle, goats, sheep, and chickens as well as feed for the livestock. The storekeeper prepares estimates of the number of meals to be served, usually by closely observing the number of people attending *qawwalli*, the musical performance at the shrine, and passes this information on to the cooks. There are two cooks who, in turn, have their own assistants in the shrine's large kitchen. In addition, the staff includes a butcher, several bakers, and individuals who tend animals.

It is important to note that not all food, animals, or firewood required for the operation of the shrine is purchased. Much of it is given to the shrine as donations by individuals who are *murids*, or followers of the religious teachings of the Pir. Sometimes, these donations are substantial — money, portion of a harvest, animals such as a cow or goat, or donated labour. Groups of *murids* from distant villages sometimes make a collective presentation to the shrine, such as firewood brought from distant forest lands, or they may contribute their labour to repair and maintain shrine property. The *murids* represent a substantial, non-paid, source of volunteer labour and donated material goods.

The shrine also contains what might be called a 'professional' staff. These include a librarian, teachers, and resident scholars — all of them are permanent appointees of the shrine. The librarian maintains a small collection of religious books to be used by the students in the shrine *madressa* or the Islamic school. The current librarian is fluent in Arabic, Persian, and Urdu as the books in the collection are written in these languages. Students in the *madressa* generally do not have books of their own so they may be supplied by the library. The books are regarded as sacred and are consequently handled with a great show of respect. In addition to the books, however, the librarian has an additional duty related to the history of the shrine. A small room of the library stores many of the utensils and items of clothing used by the founder, Pir Mehr Ali Shah. These relics are kept sealed in the room but at the time of the *Urs*, and other specified occasions, the room is opened and *murids* are allowed to view the contents.

Four teachers are responsible for instruction in the *madressa* or the Islamic school. The school provides religious education and students are attracted to it from all over Pakistan, especially Azad Kashmir, Hazara division, and Multan. In 1983 during the time of research, there were about 40 resident students in the school. Subjects taught include the Qur'an, Islamic law and the teachings of the saint and subsequent Pirs. One of the teachers also functions as an arbiter, settling personal, family, and village disputes on the basis of Islamic principles. He also functions as the historian of the shrine and has written a book on the founding Pir as well as published the latter's collected speeches. He is a permanent appointee of the shrine.

The shrine also has a resident director for agriculture. He is a member of a prominent Rawalpindi family and retired from a high position in the Department of Agriculture. He is responsible for the crops produced on the shrine lands. He not only acquires the seed but also uses his extensive knowledge of improved varieties of plants to experiment in order to increase agricultural output. He uses his good ties with government agricultural officials to further these aims. He also supervises the large number of villagers who come from neighbouring areas to harvest wheat, corn, rice, and other crops on the shrine lands. This labour is donated although a token payment of 1/20 of the harvest is given to the labourers. They contribute substantially to the 1500 maunds (1,245,000 pounds) of wheat required each year for the *lunger*. It is also understood that the labourers earn religious merit for this work. The agricultural director also sells a portion of the crop in the local market.

Finally, there is an electrician and several mechanics permanently attached to the shrine as paid employees. They maintain the machinery and plant of the shrine and, because of their reputation as skilled workers are much in demand for repair work in the surrounding villages. They also work alongside the artisans who are hired for construction and decorative work on the shrine buildings and the mosque.

Another religious functionary of the shrine is the *mujaver*, an elderly man who sits in a corner of the shrine and distributes *taweez* to those who request one. The *taweez* is a small metal case into which is inserted a strip of paper containing a verse from the Qur'an. The *taweez* is believed to have protective as well as curative powers and those who request them secretly whisper the nature of their problem into the ear of the *mujaver*. Typically, the *taweez* is worn around the neck on a string or necklace, preferably black, and the *mujaver* maintains a large supply of metal boxes and previously prepared religious inscriptions in a basket at his side. Supplicants are expected to give cash donations for their *taweez* without which it may lack its special power. The *mujaver* has two assistants to help distribute the *taweez* as well as control access of those seeking them.

Qawwalli is the spiritual music with singing in the shrine and has long been associated with the Chishtiya School of Islamic thought. It was begun by Pir Moinuddin Chishti Ajmeri in 565 Hijra as a method of attracting converts from among the Hindu community. As a recruitment technique, it was strikingly successful and soon became an established feature of many shrines although, in the beginning and even at present, there are many Muslims who regard *qawwalli* as un-Islamic. At Golra Sharif, *qawwalli* is one of the central features of the shrine and is regarded as a principal method of teaching Islamic ideas. It functions in the place of speeches or preaching about Islam.

The *Qawwal* of the shrine comprises of two brothers and two of their kinsmen, all of whom are well-known musicians. They have been permanently appointed since 1950 and competitive groups are not permitted on the shrine grounds. Their instruments include a *tabla*, *sitar*, and a harmonium. One musician claps his hands. Whenever the Pir travels, which is frequently, he is accompanied by the *Qawwal* as their performance is an essential part of his religious presentations.

THE CEREMONIAL CALENDAR

The ceremonial activities of the shrine are conducted on a daily, weekly, monthly and annual basis. Daily rituals begin with the *Azan*, the call to prayer, chanted five times each day by the *Muazan* of the mosque. The first call is one hour before sunrise during which residents and pilgrims of the shrine gather at the mosque. After sunrise, breakfast is taken and the Pir is available for consultation with any of his followers until ten in the morning. This is followed by the gathering of the pilgrims in the assembly hall for *qawwalli*. Men and women are separated and all participants sit in a carefully arranged hierarchy with those highest in position (including the educated, landlords, politically important, and the wealthy) in the front ranks of the gathering.

Women stand or sit in a verandah-like area behind and to one side of the men. The participants sit in a large U shape with the Pir, sometimes his brother, and the *Qawwal* near the top of the U, facing the congregation. The ceremony begins with a lengthy period of uninterrupted *qawwalli* music, during which the Pir sits and opens letters and telegrams brought to him by the shrine's own mail and telegraph office. At regular intervals, the Pir offers a rupee note to the *qawwalli* players and, at this signal, large numbers of participants crowd forward to offer rupees of their own. This is done repeatedly four or five times during each *qawwalli* presentation, the money being collected in a large blanket on the floor and, finally, rolled into a bundle and carried away by the *Qawwals*. At the end of the *qawwalli*, approximately noon time, the Pir offers prayers, and verses from the Qur'an are read. This ends the morning ceremony and again the pilgrims gather around the Pir to offer money, kiss his hands, or to receive the touch of his breath which is considered a special blessing. The men visit the Pir in this informal way first and, when they have left, women are admitted for an audience. Women often present a thread, grains of wheat or a glass of water to the Pir. He blows on these objects infusing in them curative power, and these are then carried away by their grateful owners. At this time, women are also allowed to become *murids* or spiritual followers of the Pir. The Pir does not touch women directly but rather holds one end of a short piece of cloth, the women holding the other. The Pir then recites a series of short prayers. This act signifies his acceptance of the women into the company of his spiritual followers.

There is another call to prayer in the mosque following lunch for all the pilgrims. The shrine itself is closed during prayers so that all attention and interest is focussed on the mosque. After prayers, the shrine is again opened and people read and recite the Qur'an. Prayers are again offered in the mosque at five o'clock in the afternoon, at sunset, and about 9 o'clock in the evening. After prayer, the faithful return to the shrine for further prayers. Pilgrims sleep in the rooms (*sarai*) provided for that purpose, on the flat roofs and on the lawn in front of the mosque in the summer.

Jumma (Friday) prayers are the most significant weekly event. Friday is the weekend holiday and large crowds gather at the shrine from the villages as well as the metropolitan centres of Rawalpindi and Islamabad. Prayers are offered in the mosque and there is usually preaching and recitation from the Qur'an. After prayer, the Pir sits inside the mosque and meets his followers. Money is often offered to the

Pir for which his followers earn religious merit. Each month a small
religious festival or *Urs* called *gyarhween sharif* is held to honour Pir
Sheikh Abdul Qadir Jillani. Speeches are made in his honour and
people from the village of Golra Sharif prepare a special rice dish made
with milk and distribute it amongst neighbours and the poor.

There is a series of annual ceremonies intended to honour famous
personalities associated with Islam and the shrine. Each ceremony is
a major or a minor *Urs* — fifty-three in all. The most important are
those honouring the birth of the Prophet Muhammad and the annual
Urs for Sheikh Abdul Qadir Jillani, Pir Mayudin Babojee, son of Pir
Mehr Ali Shah; and Pir Nazaruddin Shah, father of Pir Mehr Ali
Shah. The annual Urs of Abdul Qadir Jillani is held from 9 to 11 Rabi-
us-Sani (the third month of the Islamic Calendar). With a million participants it is the biggest *Urs* of the year; all villagers arrive at the shrine
and participate in the event. Conspicuous among the participants are
the people of Hazara, Azad Kashmir and Multan.

CONCLUSION

The study of Golra Sharif, the home village of the shrine of Pir Mehr
Ali Shah and his family members, has been conducted to examine the
functions of sacred shrines in relation to the life of the associated communities. Such shrines are found all over the country and are
known to have a large following.

The spiritual system of the shrine at Golra Sharif owes its origin to
and is drawn from the Sufi order of Islam. Affiliation with the system
is dependent upon the practice of *Bay'at*, according to which a person
accepts the Pir as an intermediary between himself and the supreme
being, the ultimate truth and reality. Such a person is called 'Murid'.
He submits completely to the dictates of the Pir for attaining spiritual
guidance and becomes his 'Murid' after going through a formal ritual.
Once the *Bay'at* is performed the 'Murid' enters into the fraternity of
which all the followers of the Pir are members. The Murids of the same
Pir are known as 'Pir Bhai' a fictive kinship term indicating sibling
relationship.

The operation of the shrine activities and its increasing popularity
among the people can be explained in terms of satisfactory fulfilment
of the religious, psychological, social, economic, and political needs of
the followers. The largest number of followers are those who seek
financial security and material prosperity either through the Pir or by

acquiring membership of the fraternity. Next in line are those who suffer from various ailments and seek cure through healing methods.

Thus the shrine which is apparently a religious institution seems to perform multiple functions for its followers. It provides a social network in which participating individuals achieve their objectives by using selectively and manipulating carefully the relationship created among them by their spiritual affiliation to the sacred shrine.

NOTES

1. Hodgson, Marshal, *The Venture of Islam*, Vols. I and II, University of Chicago Press, Chicago, 1975.
2. Mayer, Adrian C., 'Pir and Murshid: An aspect of Religious Leadership in West Pakistan', *Middle Eastern Studies,* London, 1967.
3. Schimmel, Annemarie, *Islam in the Indian Sub-continent,* E.J. Brill/Leiden-Koln, 1980.
4. Ewing, Katherine, 'The Politics of Sufism', *Journal of Asian Studies,* Vol. XIII, No.2. *Journal of Asian Studies.*
5. Ahmed, Aziz, *An Intellectual History of Islam in India,* Edinburgh University Press, Edinburgh, 1969, p. 3.
6. Ibid, p. 44.
7. Encyclopaedia Brittanica, Vol. 9, 1974, pp. 947-948.

GLOSSARY

Murshid	Religious guide.
Murid	Follower of a spiritual guide.
Piri-Muridi	The relationship between spiritual guide and disciple.
Nasab	Relationship to a family; genealogical relationship with spiritual guide.
Hasab	Spiritual linkage by following a traditionally accepted way of teaching.
Hanafi Fiqh	Islamic Jurisprudence presented by the first Imam Abu Hanifa which is widespread in Turkey and Pakistan.
Hadith	Tradition from the Prophet containing his remarks in a given situation.
Tafseer	Interpretation of the Qur'an.
Fatwa	Formal legal opinion pronounced by a lawyer (Mufti) trained in Sharia Law to a problem put up before him either by a Qazi or a private person. Usually dealing with personal status law.
Madressa-e-Ghausia	Religious School at Shrine associated with the name of Shaikh Abdul Qadir Jillani alias Ghausal-Azam.
Sajjada Nasheen	The successor of the Pir.
Carvan	Group.
Lunger	Free distribution of sacred food at Shrine.
Lunger-e-Ghausia	Free distribution of sacred food at Shrine in the name of Shah Abdul Qadir Jillani alias Ghaus al-Azam.
Urs Sharif	Celebration of Saint's death anniversary.
Qawwali	Spiritual song set to music by professional singers.
Mujaver	An important functionary who looks after the shrine and distributes *taveez*.
Taweez (Tawedh)	Amulet, containing verses of the Qur'an or other pious prescriptions.
Qawwal	Professional singers at Shrines/Melas etc.
Azan	Call for Prayer.
Muazan	The person who calls the prayer five times a day.
Bay'at	Pledge of allegiance of a *Murid* to his Master by grasping his hand.

9

Urban Growth and Political Change at the Local Level: The Case of Faisalabad City, 1947-75

Mohammad Waseem

Faisalabad district was profoundly affected by the political turmoil which accompanied the Partition of the Indo-Pak subcontinent. One third of its population migrated to India in 1947, while it attracted a large number of incoming Muslim refugees. The subsequent economic and demographic changes brought about new tensions in various sectors of the society, leading to new group alignments. This process saw a radical transformation in the nature and scope of the government's administrative machinery as it involved itself increasingly both with the management of economic growth and the containment of its disruptive effects on the district's social and political order. These changes were even more significant in the urban sector, especially in Faisalabad city, thereby giving it an enormous lead over the rest of the district. In common bureaucratic parlance, Faisalabad came to be called an 'urban' district, to distinguish it from the 'rural' districts like Attock and Mianwali. The 'urban' character of the district lay in the predominant role of trade and industry in the economic and administrative fields, even though it contained a more productive cropping pattern and a more progressive peasantry than the so-called rural districts. Here, an attempt has been made to analyse the political consequences of rapid urban growth in Faisalabad city.

PATTERN OF GROWTH

In demographic terms, Faisalabad city grew by 156.2 per cent between 1941 and 1951, as compared with a 54 per cent increase in the overall district population.[1] Throughout the fifties, the rate of growth of the urban population in the district was 8 times that of the rural population, with an even higher rate in Faisalabad city proper. This phenomenal expansion of Faisalabad and other towns continued in the sixties.

At the heart of urban growth lay rapid industrial progress of Faisalabad city. In 1947, it had only one industrial unit, the Lyallpur Cotton Mills, which had an installed capacity of 55,752 spindles and 1,114 looms, with an investment of Rs. 232 lakh; in addition there were 63 small manufacturing units.[2] After the establishment of the Kohinoor and Crescent Textile Mills in 1950 by the Sehgals and the Chiniotis respectively, a host of textile and other industrial units emerged, till by the mid-sixties Faisalabad became the most industrialized city of Pakistan after Karachi. Although textiles remained at the core of industrial expansion, other investment areas included beverages, fertilizers, vegetable ghee, jute mills, sugar mills, plywood and baggasse board, pharmaceuticals, agricultural machinery, and re-rolling and textile machinery. A total of more than 3000 industrial units accounted for 20 per cent of the total built-up area in the city and employed 75 per cent of its total urban work-force of 65,000 in 1965.[3]

The relatively advanced agrarian structure of Faisalabad played a crucial role in its industrialization. Thus, local production of cotton provided a firm base for the cotton textile industry. The presence of cotton ginning factories and the elaborate agricultural marketing structures greatly facilitated the supply of raw cotton for spinning and weaving. Similarly the extensive railroad network linking the countryside with Faisalabad city led to the emergence of markets for manufactured

Table 9.1 : **Population Growth of Faisalabad District**

Population	1951	1951-61 Percentage	1961	1961-72 Percentage	1972
Faisalabad District	2,152,863	24.7	2,683,838	58	4,241,785
Faisalabad Rural	1,869,824	12.88	2,110,757	51.1	3,188,769
Faisalabad Urban	283,039	102.47	573,081	83.74	1,053,016
Faisalabad City	179,144	137.37	425,248	93.61	823,343

Source: *Population Census of Pakistan, 1972,* Lyallpur District, Islamabad, 1977, pp. 16-17.

goods of the local industry. In this way, the city drew upon the relatively developed economic infrastructure of the district from pre-Independence days.

As large-scale manufacturing sector took giant strides in Faisalabad city, small-scale industry also expanded on its fringes, partially dependently and independently. In two decades, there emerged about two and a half thousand small industrial units, employing 14,000 workers. The power-loom industry took the lion's share; it produced towels, bed sheets, and coarse cloth in general and its small 'factories' were strewn all around the residential colonies. Hosiery has been the main cottage industry, usually located within the residential quarters. Many petty merchants, especially Sheikhs, operate at this level, as do a few artisans, transport workers and recent migrants from the country-side who have managed to accumulate a small amount of capital. These people have a more direct experience of labour in their day-to-day production cycle than the large-scale manufacturer, the average number of workers being as little as five. They are even more ruthlessly committed to containment of labour militancy than the latter. In the framework of local politics they represent religious extremes within rightist parties.

It is interesting to note how the forces of market and state have shaped the spatial structure of the city. Faisalabad, which is often called the Manchester of Pakistan because of its textile industry, also followed the latter's concentric zoning pattern of horizontal expansion. Its central business district, with eight *bazaars* meeting at the famous Clock Tower — girdled all around by the Circular Road — housed major whole sale markets and about 50 percent of the shops in the city.[4] This pattern can be compared with that of mid-nineteenth century Manchester as described by Engels. Manchester's central commercial centre was half a mile long on each side. Over time it was abandoned by the original residents. The 'money aristocracy' passed through its thoroughfares without seeing misery prevalent on both sides.[5] In Faisalabad also, the half-mile square business district bustles with a hectic business activity which tends to spill over to the adjoining areas on all sides. Because of extreme geographical proximity all the important business firms keep a direct and often personal link with each other and with the retail buyers and sellers of manufactured goods. The Clock Tower area has, therefore, over time approximated the situation of a perfect market.

The residential colonies which grew up all around the eight *bazaars* after Independence, have followed a crude stratification pattern. The

Model Town, Gulberg, and Jinnah Colony, in its vicinity, and People's Colony and Batala Colony at a distance, were built by the private sector, although planned and 'developed' by the Government. Further away, the latter constructed some residential quarters for low-income refugee families in Ghulam Muhammad Abad, Samanabad and D type colony. Industrial land-use developed along link-roads — Sheikhupura, Samundari, Jhang, and Sargodha—within a five mile radius of the Clock Tower. Around these factories large concentrations of hotels and huts emerged, called *kachi abadis*. Here the industrial workers formed the nucleus around which various groups of the self-employed and unemployed gathered. The haphazard character of the industrial location was reflected through the expansion of *kachi abadis* in different parts of the city.

THE REFUGEES

Faisalabad city's growth drew essentially upon the entrepreneurial activity of certain trading communities, which also brought about a spatially stratified society in the locality. Among the various factors responsible for Faisalabad's emergence as an industrial city, the exchange of population in 1947 played an important role. Sixty-three per cent of Faisalabad's population migrated to India leaving behind a considerable gap in trade, banking, and agro-based industry.[6] Subsequently, the huge influx of refugees drastically changed the demographic composition of the city. They included a veritable cross-section of the small trading communities from the East Punjab towns of Jullundar and Amritsar—Kashmiris, Khojas, Gaubas, and Pirachas. Most of them were previously shopkeepers, skin and hide merchants, wholesalers, contractors and depot-holders. Certain self-employed artisan families from the agricultural castes of Ludhiana and Batala also settled in Faisalabad; many of them were Arains who, as market-gardeners, had gained experience of urban business and thus managed to establish workshops and foundries. Finally, the two big industrial houses of Sehgals and Chiniotis, though originally from West Punjab, came from Delhi and Calcutta respectively where they were mainly engaged in export trade. Together, they initiated a remarkable entrepreneurial activity in Faisalabad.

Others among the refugees from East Punjab included (a) such petty bourgeois sections as retailers, commission agents, teachers, and 'para-professionals'; (b) the urban poor—day-labourers, transport workers, and the unemployed; and (c) poor peasants. Among the last category, many failed to get agricultural land allotted to them and thus 'preferred to stay on in the city to get free from the yoke of Chaudharis once and for all'.[7] They formed the vanguard of recruitment to what later became the formidable working class population of the city. In this way both the employers and employees of the emergent industrial sector were engrafted on the city from outside. Within four years, the refugees accounted for 83 per cent of Faisalabad's population (Table 9.2). Later, however, when business activity expanded and attracted a large number of people from within the district and the country at large, their ratio in the local population went down, even though their absolute numbers continued increasing.

A crucial factor in Faisalabad's industrial development was the refugee entrepreneurs' close links with the government which was committed to a policy of rapid industrialization based on favourable monetary and fiscal measures. Initially, the Urdu-speaking refugee leadership of the Muslim League provided economic incentives mainly to the trading communities from Bombay, who helped industrialize Karachi in the immediate post-Independence years. Later, however, the rise to power of such East Punjabi financial bureaucrats as Ghulam Muhammad and Chaudhry Muhammad Ali gave considerable advantage to their co-ethnics in the West Punjab towns and cities. In addition, the centre's need to have a political constituency in the Punjab, especially as the spectre of general elections loomed large, ensured a rising share for the Punjabis in the country's expanding industrial wealth. Therefore, Faisalabad was the prime candidate for industrial expansion, not least because it contained a large number of refugee entrepreneurs.

Table 9.2: **Refugees in Faisalabad City**

	1951	1961	1972
Number	148,564	264,001	367,653
Percentage of Total	83	62	47

Source: Calculated from *Census of India, 1941,* Table V, pp. 36-7; *Population Census of Pakistan 1961*, Part IV, Table 10, p. 147; *Population Census of Pakistan, 1972,* Vol. II, Part 1, Table 12, pp. 136-7; and The World Bank, *Pakistan Economic Developments and Prospects,* Report No. 20, 3328-PAK, 1981, Table III, 1, p. 69.

DEVELOPMENT ADMINISTRATION

All along the government spearheaded Faisalabad city's march towards economic progress. This led to institutional proliferation on an enormous scale. Three main areas of administrative activity can be outlined. First, the government took up general promotional activities like transport surveys and analysis of the civilian labour force mainly through its established office of the provincial Directorate of Industries in Faisalabad. This office issued licences and controlled the overall industrial and financial activity. Other institutions followed—Chief Controller of Imports and Exports, Trading Corporation of Pakistan, Industrial Development Finance Corporation, Export Promotion Bureau, Investment Promotion Bureau, Registrar Joint Stock Companies, and the like. The long-winded procedural work involved in dealing with these offices gave them enormous powers of selective patronage and extraction of bribes. In addition, the lower staff, which was often recruited from Faisalabad itself, became a formidable channel for articulation and advancement of commercial interests because of the pre-existing *biradri* loyalties and/or clientele structures. The state machinery, therefore, stratified the emergent society of Faisalabad according to the capacity of each individual or group to articulate its interests through the available channels.

The second area revolved around the government's fiscal measures and charges for various public services like railways, telecommunications, and electric and gas supply for the industrial sector. Here, corruption was less endemic but where it occurred it was on a larger scale than in the promotional agencies, because it involved avoiding direct payments to the government. Such a situation encouraged toutism in and around the departmental offices, and thus established an 'invisible' relationship between industrialists and government officials. However, unlike the promotional institutions which thrived on the state's role as a provider of the implements of capitalist production, the regulatory agencies also exercised coercive power against private capital.

As against these two functions which related essentially to the management of capital, the third was concerned with the management of labour. The district labour department under a joint director was responsible for implementation of the labour laws. Being directly involved with this important factor of production the labour department officials developed a vested interest in the perpetuation of industrial conflict. Most of them were on the pay roll of industrialists, along with their counterparts from the Police and Excise Departments. An over-all commitment to the status quo characterized their political role in Faisalabad city. Sometimes they even encouraged the 'outsiders' in the trade union movement to mobilize labour on certain issues or estab-lish rival unions, so as to increase the price of their services to the mill-owners.[8] Overall, they enjoyed a central position in the web of labour relations in which the industrialists, trade unions, individual workers, police, magistrates, legal practitioners and Labour Court officials all became involved in various capacities. On the one hand, the official in-volvement in labour relations has deterred labour from outgrowing its own class position economically and ideologically through the legal and procedural structures of the state, and on the other served the entrepreneurial class by saving it from the rigid application of laws.

RISE OF THE CAPITALIST CLASS

Local power structure underwent internal changes as combined forces of the administration and the merchant/industrialist class promoted economic progress. There were no big landlord families in Faisalabad to challenge the emergent bourgeoisie. In fact, the local zamindars al-ready had a strong tradition of participating in commercial transac-tions; they dealt with traders in cash crops in market towns, those running processing industries like ginning factories and flour mills, and the government's food procurement agencies. A few active lawyer-zamindars were no match for the enormously resourceful in-dustrialists; they were thus soon marginalized in the city's politics. The massive influx of refugees had already destroyed whatever entrenched power blocks existed from pre-Independence days. All these factors helped base the power structure of Faisalabad on the new industrial wealth of the emergent entrepreneurial class.

With the establishment of industrial units in the city, several dis-tribution agencies for their products started emerging in the eight central bazaars around the Clock Towers. This gave the millowners tremendous power of patronage as they could pick and choose the dealers of their products. Among them were many of the new allottee (refugee) zamindars, especially from the Arain *biradri*. However, a majority of them belonged to the refugee commercial *biradris*, collec-tively called Sheikhs, including Gaubas, Khojas, Chawalas, and Pirachas. Many of them migrated twice, first settling elsewhere in the

Punjab and later shifting to Faisalabad, once economic activity gained momentum there. They increasingly dealt in processed raw materials for industry and other implements of production. By the early sixties, many had already started their own auxiliary/small scale industries. They thus played second fiddle to the big industrial houses for whom they performed various functions on both the input and the output scales of the production cycle, leading to new patron-client relations between them. In the elitist mode of operation of parliamentary politics in the fifties, such patronage structures opened the way for the politically ambitious Sehgals to control the leading figures of the locality as they operated from the platform of, first, the Muslim League and, later, the Republican Party.

At the more direct level of appointments for various jobs in the industry, patron-client relationships were more individualistic and were geared essentially to a trade-off between the authority of a public office and the job offer from the management of mills for the kith and kin of the respective holders of this authority. The millowners thus managed to create a whole group of clients among the officials of various departments, members of central and provincial legislatures, political workers, employees, and trade union leaders of their mills.[9] As these patronage structures were underlined by carefully thought-out transactional relationships they were couched strictly in the dynamics of capital and represented the obliging powers of the state in terms of cash economy. The employment-creating industrial progress, therefore, became a new political resource in Faisalabad, which subjected all other social groups and classes to the domineering role of the bourgeoisie. Its practice of outright bribery bound the interests of individual government officials to itself. Individuals in various government departments, District Boards, Municipality, and District and Labour Courts came to be known as the henchmen of either the Sehgals or the Chiniotis. These bilateral patron-client relationships kept the wheels of capitalist economy moving through the jungle of administrative procedures.

The local industrialists made a bid to control the political organs of the state in the 1951 elections of the Punjab Assembly. Their greatest strength in terms of electoral politics lay in the fact that they commanded the votes of their fast expanding workforce. In the prevalent conditions of job insecurity and lack of any organizational base for trade union activity, the latter readily 'sold' their votes and took part in bogus voting in thousands. The industrialist group financed the campaign of the Muslim League candidates, Mir Abdul Qayum and Sheikh Mahboob Ellahi, who eventually won the elections. Apart from providing huge funds to them, the millowners used their workforce for bogus voting on an enormous scale. Thus, the former was mainly 'supported' by the Lyallpur Cotton Mills workers while the latter won on the strength of the Kohinoor Textile Mills' workers.[10] The near-serf position of industrial workers, who were still small in number and largely unorganized made them behave like urban counterparts of tenants. A virtual absence of class consciousness characterized their political behaviour and made them objects of their employers' will, despite cases of individual dissent here and there.

This new pattern of worker-use became even more pronounced in the Municipal Elections of 1956. The Municipal Committee had been given first-class status in 1949. In 1951, however, it was superseded, and it remained so until the first post-Independence elections in January 1956 — 21 years after the last elections. The elections were marred by large-scale bogus voting of scandalous proportions. All tactics which had been employed in the Sargodha District Board elections in 1953, as stated in the *Laghari Report*, were used unabashedly. Thousands of workers personated as genuine voters, many of them more than once at the same polling station; out of them 528 persons were arrested from whom the police recovered mill attendance cards which showed them on duty.[11] Both active and passive connivance of the district administration was starkly obvious. Many presiding officers, in fact, facilitated the whole process of personation by giving the *goondas* of the Sehgals free access to the electoral rolls inside the polling station; from these they got the numbers of the uncast votes, on the basis of which bogus voters were sent in.[12] Even those who could not give their (impersonated) father's names were allowed to vote.[13] Some boxes contained more ballot papers than the number shown on the electoral lists.[14] When the results came out, the Sehgal group won a clear majority, and their henchman Sheikh Bashir Ahmed became the President of the Faisalabad Municipal Committee.

There followed a country-wide furore over the election malpractices. The District Bar Association of Faisalabad passed a resolution demanding an enquiry into the matter. Dr. Khan Sahib, the Republican Party Chief Minister of West Pakistan, first conceded the holding of an enquiry but then balked over the whole issue. He could ill-afford to lose the support of the industrialists who were the patrons of many of his own Party's MPA's and who had direct links with the top bureaucracy, including Iskandar Mirza. The shift of the focus of the industrialists' support from the Muslim League to the Republican Party had already followed the ascendancy to power of the latter, both in the centre and the province.

After the imposition of Martial Law in 1958, the intermediary role of politicians was eliminated. The unabashed bureaucratic rule that followed tended to disregard the zamindars. In its pursuits of economic development along the lines of import-substituting industrialization, the bureaucracy favoured and helped the entrepreneurial groups, both big and small. While the Sehgals and Chiniotis saw a special rise in their status, the emergent commercial middle class, including the cloth wholesalers, yarn merchants, transporters, exporters and importers from the central bazaars, provided an economic base for developmental activity. In due course, the orthodox sections of petty bourgeoisie, retailers, foremen and overseers of various industrial units, petty officers of different public or commercial institutions, and the ulema emerged as the ideological supporters of the bourgeoisie and the commercial middle class.

These two classes together formed the core of right-wing political activity in Faisalabad. They were dispersed in different political parties according to *biradri* ties, patron-client relations and individual ideological predilections. In the early fifties, the Muslim League enjoyed a firm support base in the city. Its local leaders were 'public men' of little importance in provincial politics, who had no weight in the city's power structure either. Its MPA, Mir Abdul Qayum, for example, belonged to the District Bar and had no urban or rural property to boast of. During the Martial Law years of the Ayub regime, those on the right of centre thrived on the greatly expanded entrepreneurial activity and developed a big stake in the 'stability' of the government. Consequently, a majority of them supported the Convention Muslim League in the 1965 elections for the President and the National and Provincial Assemblies.

Chaudhary Muhammad Ali, the leader of the Nizam-e-Islam Party, mobilized considerable support among the Arain *biradri* of Faisalabad city. But, the local Muslim League stalwart, Zahid Sarfraz, gradually won a stronger constituency among both the Arains and assorted sections of the Sheikhs, even though in electoral terms he turned out to be an all-time loser. Among religious parties, the orthodox ulema of the JUI enjoyed the support of the 'business' refugees from Doaba Bist Jullundar, who had a long tradition of pro-Deoband, pro-Ahrar-e-

Islam political and religious activities. The JUP was more popular among the 'liberal' petty bourgeois sections from Amritsar. The JI's support was thinly spread over a spectrum of the middle class professionals and students as well as the lower sections of the salariat. Overall, their ideological battles over the Islamic nature of Pakistan's constitution dominated their political activity, which was characterized by hostility to such demands as provincial autonomy, labour reforms, and holding of general elections. After the 1965 Indo-Pakistan War, economic recession hit the city very hard. Criticism of bureaucracy became the rallying ground against the Ayub regime. This crisis saw the local base of the state itself shifting away from the industrial-commercial class.

In opposition to this alignment of rightist forces in Faisalabad city, a 'liberal-progressive' stratum existed among certain sections almost from the beginning. The great onrush of East Punjabi urban refugee entrepreneurs had alienated a section of local zamindars, especially the abadkars, who were increasingly marginalized in the framework of local politics. A new contradiction emerged between zamindars and non-zamindars, which sometimes took the form of a class conflict, as the former tried to create a support base in the trade union movement of Faisalabad city. Among them were included persons like Habibullah Saadi, an ex-Khaksar Leader, whose vision of Islamic egalitarianism impelled them to publicly support the cause of industrial labour, and offer refuge to certain trade union activists under persecution by the police at the behest of millowners. Other forms of help included public criticism of the employers' ruthless tactics, use of *biradri* links in the government departments of Labour, Police and Magistracy to redress the workers' grievances as well as provision of funds for the dismissed workers and their organizational activity in general.

After the 1958 *coup*, the zamindars rapidly declined in social importance as the new regime committed itself to support the industrialists whole-heartedly. In the emergent set-up of power politics, the latter clearly outcompeted the former and sought to ride over the state machinery. We can look at one such example in which the local power wielding groups and institutions competed with each other, providing a clue to the new alignment of forces in Faisalabad. The Sehgals bought 48 squares of agricultural land and built a model farm on it, using the most modern technology. They behaved like feudal lords of yore, harrassing the neighbourhood and coercing others into compulsory deals with them. In one such dispute about purchase of land, .

one Hakim Dilbar Rana sided with their opponents.[15] The Sehgals tried to put pressure on him, and threatened to freeze his account in their bank – the United Bank. However, Hakim went ahead with delivering evidence against them in court. He was murdered soon after, allegedly by a gang of the Sehgals' *goondas*, led by one Faiz Gundawala. Subsequently, there were attempts to hush up the matter by the press and the judiciary. One journalist, Mahi, who tried to cover the case in his paper *Kohistan* was assaulted. It was widely rumoured that Justice Yaqub Ali of the Punjab High Court had specially 'ordered' the newspapers not to publish the Sehgal name in this regard.

On the other hand, the kinsmen of the late Hakim Rana approached General Bakhtiar Rana, the Deputy Martial Law Administrator to help his *biradri* fellows against the Sehgals. At the local level, many journalists, trade union leaders, and lawyers organized a resistance movement and demanded full press coverage of the case in the papers. Finally, the *Nawa-e-Waqt* and *Imroze* obliged. On the other hand, the SP had his own personal grievances against the Sehgals.The day before President Ayub, who was touring Faisalabad, was to dine at the Sehgals, the SP's men 'managed' to arrest Saeed Sehgal while he was armed, thus pre-empting pressure either from the DC, or higher police officers. The scandal was so big that Ayub had to cancel his dinner. In this episode we can outline a pattern of interaction between local forces along four distinct lines:(i) class conflict between the 'capitalist' farmers and medium farmers, (ii) *biradri* links, especially with those in authority, who are then put under pressure to deliver goods to their less-privileged compatriots in the *biradri* at large,(iii) patronage structures, established between the entrepreneurial elite and local bureaucracy, and (iv) potential autonomy of the state as reflected in the SP's initiative, apparently in pursuit of establishing the rule of law.

EMERGENCE OF INDUSTRIAL LABOUR

While in 1941 agricultural and industrial workers accounted for 35.7 per cent and 7.4 per cent of the city's workforce respectively; in 1961 the corresponding figures were 12.5 per cent and 49.8 per cent,[16] an almost seven-fold increase in the proportion of industrial workers in Faisalabad's total workforce. If we take into account the phenomenal population growth in the two decades, the real increase was almost forty-fold. That factor brought about a qualitative change. Previously, there were only a few mills, and the management had an all-pervasive hold over the workers. By the sixties, workers in all the mills were in regular contact with one another and with the 'outsiders' — political party workers and other sympathetic elements among lawyers, journalists, and landowners as well as with the Labour Department itself, thereby learning the rules of the game. The workers became conscious that they had a common cause and that some ways and means existed to fight for it.

The industrial workforce of Faisalabad has been internally divided along the lines of a) area of origin and b) residential pattern, giving birth to shifting patterns of alignment within the labour movement. As for the area of origin, the workers fell into three main categories: the Indian refugees, the up-country migrants, and the natives of Faisalabad district. Initially, an absolute majority of the workers in Lyallpur Cotton Mills consisted of the Urdu-speaking refugees from India. In the sixties, however, the non-migrant workers already accounted for 30 to 40 per cent of the mills' workforce.[17] The early predominance of refugee workers was responsible for a certain organizational maturity and pragmatism in trade union activity, mainly because these workers had longer experience in this field in and around Delhi from pre-Independence days.

The workers from the northern districts of the Punjab have suffered from the added pressures of continuing family obligations back home. They brought with them attitudes of passive hostility against the landlord oppression, which were engrafted on their new relations with the millowners. On the other hand, workers from the surrounding villages have been less militant; in many cases they own or cultivate a small piece of land, rear livestock, and are engaged in cottage industry. Inflation and job insecurity are, therefore, pressing comparatively less on them than on the migrants. This internal division of Faisalabad's labour community, however, assumes a meaningful character only when seen in the overall context of opportunities of interaction within the local workforce.

While the area of origin plays a significant part in the organization of labour politics, its importance diminishes with every day that passes. On the other hand, the workers' residential pattern has a decisive impact on their day-to-day understanding of their own class position, emerging leadership patterns, and organizational capacity. As noted earlier, nearly one-third of the labour force commutes daily from the surrounding villages within a radius of 10 miles around Faisalabad.

Although less militant than certain other groups, the commuter workforce played a very significant role in spreading class consciousness in the countryside in the sixties. Therefore, their long-term political role has been decisively mobilist. In contrast, those who find accommodation in the mills' residential quarters generally suffer from an acute sense of insecurity derived from the risk of being evicted. Their combative strength, therefore, has been much lower as their contact with other social groups remains minimal.

Finally, it is the slum dwellers who have been the real backbone of labour militancy in Faisalabad. The slum areas, popularly called *kachi abadis* are clusters of hovels and huts which were constructed by the inmates themselves on state land near various factories. The biggest among them is the *Kachi-Basti* (Factory area) outside the Lyallpur Cotton Mills. It is a low-lying area, with nearly a hundred ponds of dirty water, heaps of filth, and no drainage system. Electricity and Sui gas are almost unknown. Water comes from the community hand pumps. Many of the inmates keep buffaloes and cows within the living quarters, which usually consist of one or two rooms only. The same situation obtains in other *kachi abadis* — Haji Abad, Akbar Abad, Mustafa Abad, Mai-di-Jhuggi, Bole-di-Jhuggi, Negehban Pura, Jhung Road, Ghulam Muhammad Abad and various other places around the city. The government tried to impose a slum clearance and resettlement policy from time to time and allotted plots to some of the residents in other places but nothing worked. Some of the security mechanisms in the *kachi abadis*, characterized by primary ties of language, caste, *biradri* or area of origin, kept the residents firmly rooted in their respective communities. Other considerations like proximity to the place of work also militated against moving elsewhere. Although the industrial workers constitute a majority here, these *kachi abadis* include elements from all occupations — artisans, retailers, mechanics, *hakims, mullahs*, midwives, students, teachers, beggars, domestic servants, vendors, and a large army of the unemployed. The internal differentiation of these mini-societies is characterized by the existence of community leaders who usually have permanent jobs in some government office or industrial/commercial concern. Among them are creditors, rentiers, *dadagirs* (urban counterparts of *rassagirs*), shopkeepers, and 'penny capitalists' with investments in transport, or residential/shop sites. Many ex-employees/'outsiders' residing in these slums forged a link between trade unionism and the larger working class movement in the late sixties.

The emergent labour force of Faisalabad was thus divided along various lines related to areas of origin, residential pattern, and to a lesser extent, *biradri* loyalties. In the Nishat Mills, for example, the conflict between local and non-local workers played the leading role. Among the predominantly non-local workers of the Crescent Mills, the main groupings emerged on the basis of the area of origin, variously called the Jhelum *biradri*, the Pindi *biradri*, the Mianwali *biradri* etc. In the Kohinoor Mills, it was the Arain/Rajput controversy which underlay the politics of trade unionism for a long time.[18] The workers from various *kachi abadis* developed their own factions, which muddled with industrial relations inside many factories. Together, these primordial ties kept labour activity pinned down to sectarian conflicts. While generally class consciousness increased among the workers, their political organization still followed traditional patterns.

The task of political articulation of Faisalabad's working class problems has been carried out essentially by the 'outsiders'.[19] Many outsiders have had their political links with the NAP and later the Mazdoor Kisan Party (MKP) and the Pakistan Socialist Party (PSP). Their revolutionism and strike-orientation often isolated them from the ongoing pragmatic struggle of the workers. Also at the ideological level their 'scientific socialism' proved too pedantic and apparently 'atheistic'. Increasingly, however, the younger generation of 'outsiders' was influenced by the post-Partition political culture of Pakistan, laden with the spirit of Islam and nationalism. Many of them were previously the progressive minded workers of the opposition parties. Islamic Socialism, therefore, became the *raison d'etre* of the new left in the city represented by 'outsiders' such as Mukhtar Rana.

Our findings upto now point to various factors responsible for Faisalabad's phenomenal industrial growth—its relatively advanced agricultural infrastructure, absence of big landlords, influx of refugee entrepreneurs, and the government's commitment to a policy of rapid industrialization. These factors brought fundamental changes in the structure of local politics. On the one hand, the loci of power shifted from the rural to the urban sector in two senses: the emergent industrial-commercial class introduced a new political resource into the locality in the form of its patronage powers based on industrial wealth, and the district administration drew its strength increasingly from the management of the urban economy. On the other hand, the role of industrial labour changed from being a mere object of the employer's will in the early fifties to playing a central part in the politics of the late sixties, especially through the increasing rural-urban linkages. This brought forth a new political stratum which was to lead the working-class population of Faisalabad in its confrontation with the bourgeoisie through the turbulent years of anti-Ayub movement and the 1970 elections.

PROFILE OF TRADE UNION POLITICS

The strikes in the Punjab textile industry in 1963 and the West Pakistan Railway strike in 1967 expanded the organizational links between the trade union leaders from many cities, especially from Karachi, Hyderabad, Lahore, Faisalabad, and Multan. Some trade union leaders had to change their area of operation from one region to the other — when Mukhtar Rana was banished from Karachi for his trade union activities, he landed in Faisalabad.[20] He first opened a bookshop in Bhawana Bazaar, but later started a People's Academy in which regular classes were held and seminars were given on the organizational techniques of a broad-based workers' movement. Many students from the Government and Municipal Colleges, who were usually members of the only progressive student organization, the National Students Federation (NSF) with its links with the NAP, attended the Academy, as did various labour leaders, artisans, small shopkeepers, and lower employees from the public transport sector and various government services. The new Academy thus became a conduit for transfer of ideas about a revolutionary reform in the system from the urban to rural sector via the migrant labour.

The veteran trade union leader, Saleh Niazi, also came from outside Faisalabad.[21] Previously he had been active in the northern towns of Mianwali, Bakkar, Liaquatabad, Laiya, and Sargodha. He settled in Faisalabad in the early sixties and soon became the central figure in local politics of industrial relations. His continued leadership in unions of different industries at different places made him the conduit of inter-regional trade union activity. In addition to leading several trade unions in the Faisalabad mills he became President of such big labour federations as the Pakistan Road Transport Workers Federation at Lahore, Punjab Textile Workers Federations at Faisalabad, Mazdoor Ittehad Committee in the Sargodha region, and the Pakistan (Bus) Transport Workers Union at Lahore.[22] Thus trade union activity developed and expanded territorial and inter-industrial organization linkages focused around central figures like Saleh Niazi. By the late sixties, these linkages were already assuming a political character in a sense of disgust with the prevalent form of class relations.[23] The anti-Ayub movement brought in many 'outsiders' who were not so ideologically oriented as their predecessors from the Communist Party and the splinter groups of the NAP. They showed considerable skill in organizing mass rallies of workers as well as the lumpen-proletariat comprising the recent full/part-time rural migrants to press for their demands.

The new labour leadership of Faisalabad can be divided into three categories. The first category consisted of trade unionists like Saleh Niazi, who had a peasant background. They developed leadership qualities in their respective communities through exposure to the outside world in the form of education, army service and/or some petty business enterprise like oil or concrete supply contracts. Despite their relatively unsophisticated manner, this leadership enjoyed the enduring confidence of their followers within the framework of industrial relations, mainly because of sharing their class origins. However, like Mirza Ibrahim, Bashir Bakhtiar, and other veteran labour leaders of the Punjab, Niazi was denied a leadership role in the wider political context. This dichotomy between factory politics and the general politics of the locality remains a feature of trade unionism in Faisalabad to this day, preventing the possibility of the emergence of an autonomous base for industrial labour in the political system.

The second category of professional trade unionists was represented by the rapidly emerging labour leader Sabiha Shakeel.[24] An overall commitment to moral and legal fairness has characterized her leadership. She is based in the largely Urdu-speaking workforce of the Lyallpur Cotton Mills. The emphasis is placed on the skilful use of labour courts and other legal provisions for securing the recruitment of labour strictly on merit, and struggling for workers' rights. She favours imposing strict discipline on the labour itself.[25] While Sabiha's leadership enjoyed the qualified support of the labour department, certain industrialists and some rightist political parties, her followers, in fact, supported the PPP in the 1970 elections, as the campaign gradually took a class line. Thus Sabiha's leadership was not fully accepted outside the framework of trade unionism. It was the third category of trade unionists — the group of intellectuals like Mukhtar Rana, who provided political leadership to the working class movement. They discarded the use of scientific socialism as their ideological platform and called for a new approach to the labour problem grounded in indigenous culture.[26] Their biggest asset was their link with the PPP which provided them with a certain legitimacy in the wider context of provincial and national politics. Locally, they had contacts with the non-industrial workforce as well as the non-working population through their work in the *kachi abadis*. They worked outside the narrow framework of trade unionism.

THE 1970 ELECTIONS
AND PPP'S ASCENDANCY TO POWER

In the next phase of political transformation in Faisalabad, the election campaign played a crucial role. The PPP's campaign not only differed sharply from its rivals on the right, it also competed with such parties as the Pakistan Socialist Party, which were far less pragmatic in their approach to current problems. For example, Rao Mahroze Akhtar and Chaudhry Fateh Muhammad, the President and Secretary General respectively of the latter's sister-organization, the (W) Pakistan Kisan Committee, addressed a meeting in Toba Tek Singh, where they announced their struggle against 'monopoly capitalism' and 'feudalism'.[27] By contrast, the PPP chairman of Faisalabad invited the Governor of Punjab to visit the looms and see the plight of the slum dwellers in the city.[28]

In the elections, the PPP won all the National and Provincial Assembly seats in the district. Some of the factors responsible for this pattern of voting were the PPP's 'externality' for the local power structure. In other words the industrial workers took the great risk of annoying the millowners only because the PPP leader, along with his all-encompassing movement, seemed to be capable of riding the powerful machinery of the government and turning it in their favour. In this process, the provision for secret ballot helped them vote according to their own choice in a moment of fearless encounter with the powers that be. Also, their capacity for 'independent' voting was helped by the fact that the industrial workers from more than a hundred mills came into contact with each other and with the large section of middle and poor peasants. Together they opted out of the orbit of influence of bourgeoisie and rich farmers, largely because of the mobilizing force of the PPP.

In the ensuing struggle for power between Yahya, Mujib, and Bhutto in March 1971, Bhutto felt the need for a 'show' of force. It was decided in a conference of the PPP's MNAs and MPAs that if Bhutto's negotiations with the other two parties did not show positive results, the mills should be taken over by the workers.[29] The only organized pro-PPP labour force existed in Faisalabad. Following Bhutto's signal from Dacca the Faisalabad workers staged an abrupt take-over of the mills. In the subsequent round-up more than a thousand workers were interned. Later, when Bhutto visited them in jail, he publicly denied any involvement in the whole affair, alienating a large section of workers in the city.[30] Their defiant mood kept the sentiment of revolt simmering almost from the moment the elections were over. As the PPP's chances of taking over power in a united Pakistan looked remote, throughout the year 1971 the persecution of labour increased at the hands of local bureaucracy and millowners who were out to take revenge. During this process, the PPP high command could not provide any protection to its political cadres/labour leaders in Faisalabad. However, soon after the PPP Government was installed, the organized labour of Faisalabad tried to assert their position in a direct encounter with the millowners, and indirectly with the government machinery. Instead of remaining a passive support base for the regime, the workers demanded fulfilment of the election promises. They chose to demonstrate their power in individual cases of *gherao* — encirclement of the mill-management till it agreed to certain conditions under duress. Such 'extremism' was not to be tolerated by the new regime.[31] Mukhtar Rana, the celebrated labour leader and PPP MNA, was arrested and later unseated from the National Assembly. In the following by-election for his seat, his supporters mustered considerable strength behind his sister against the PPP's official nominee, Afzal Randhawa, who finally won the seat. The earlier labour solidarity was completely shattered in the wake of this new militancy, matched by the strong-handed measures of the regime. As the PPP's nationalization scheme left the whole textile sector untouched (which was predominant in Faisalabad), local labour did not experience any structural change in industrial relations, as against the situation in Karachi. The government, however, worked hard at the trade-union level. The local MNAs, MPAs and party office-holders became actively involved in industrial relations. In the Crescent Textile Mills, the PPP leader Nargis Naeem and the PPP MNA Afzal Randhawa were successfully sponsored by the millowners in the election for the presidentship of the Collective Bargaining Agent (CBA) union.[32] Such readiness to become politically involved distinguished the PPP regime from the earlier periods.

From 1972 onwards, the city of Faisalabad presented a tense political situation. On the one hand the labour unrest had, in theory at least, assumed a definite political character. On the other, a combination of the government's policies of outright suppression of militant labour leadership and readiness to play the political game of mass mobilization and recruitment contained this militancy within the framework of industrial relations. In sum, the general mobilization of the masses in Faisalabad city from 1968 to 1975, created a citizenry which was alive to the larger political context of local issues and had the potential of waging a struggle in pursuit of their aims. But, within three years, the PPP regime had managed to adjust the political system of Pakistan to the new pressures, through an elaborate system of political bargaining.

In the post-Independence period, Faisalabad city experienced rapid industrial growth. The existing social and economic infrastructure attracted large capital input, especially from the refugee trading families. The emergence of large-scale manufacturing industry was accompanied by the influx of migrant workers from the surrounding countryside and the northern districts of Punjab. The majority of them settled in the *kachi abadis* on high-rent land in and around the centre of the city. Such squalor in the midst of prosperity became a constant source of worker militancy and a fast-spreading sense of class solidarity among the city's working class population. In this situation, the PPP functioned as an outside force producing a certain 'freeing' effect on the political consciousness of workers. Thus in two decades of economic development, the predominantly vertical organizational pattern of social and political institutions—based on primordial ties of caste, language and region—changed into a broad-based horizontal alignment of forces manifested through the emergence of class consciousness, which was in turn catalyzed by secondary institutions such as parties and labour unions.

NOTES

1. *Population Census of India, 1941*, Delhi, 1942-6, pp. 36-7, 42-4, and *Population Census of Pakistan, 1972*, Karachi, 1977, pp. 16-17.
2. *Pakistan District Gazetteers: Faisalabad District*, PDGFD, 1980, p. 128-9.
3. Faisalabad Labour Office Department, Survey Report, quoted in Bokhari, M.H., *Lyallpur: A Study in Urban Geography*, Ph.D. Thesis, London University, 1968, p. 103.
4. Ibid., p. 90.
5. Engels, quoted in Harvey, D., *Social Justice and the City*, London, 1973, pp. 132-3.

6. Out of Faisalabad's population of 69,930 in 1941, Hindus and Sikhs accounted for 43,793, all of whom migrated to India in 1947. *Population Census of India 1941*, op. cit., 1942-6, pp. 36-7.

7. Interview with Mr. Shamim Ahmed Khan, ex MPA of the PPP.

8. Interview with trade union leader, Saleh Niazi.

9. Interview with trade union leader, Mukhtar Rana.

10. Ibid.

11. Memorandum presented to the Honourable Chief Minister of West Pakistan by the Citizens of Lyallpur, April 1956, p. 3.

12. Ibid., p. 2.

13. Ibid., p. 4.

14. Ibid., p. 4.

15. Interview with Mukhtar Rana.

16. Bokhari, op.cit., 1968, p. 174.

17. Interview with Mrs. Sabiha Shakeel, leading trade unionist of Lyallpur Cotton Mills.

18. Information gathered from various trade union leaders and workers during my stay in Faisalabad.

19. The outsider is social worker-cum-intellectual-cum-philanthropist. On the one hand, he helps the labour through its 'legal' battles against the government which is perceived as the super-backer of the industrial management and on the other, brings his own wider intellectual approach, rooted in his original party line, and thus tries to bend the essentially pragmatic struggle of labour towards the attainment of political goals. Thus, while in the short run he could establish his credentials with the trade unions through his help in matters of dealing with complex state machinery, in the long run his class-based idealism and wider political affiliations contrasted with the narrower and more mundane ends of the working class as a whole.

20. Mukhtar Rana, a refugee from Hoshiarpur, started his career as a political worker of the Khaksar Tehrik. He was a lecturer in Municipal College, Faisalabad in 1961, when he left for Karachi, to return after a few years as an established trade unionist. He trained workers, students, and activists from *kachi abadis* in the art of political agitation. Presently he is living in England.

21. Saleh Niazi, an ex-army man, belongs to Mianwali District. During the Second World War, he spent some time with Sobhash Chandra Bose's Azad Hindustan Fauj. On return he started supplying concrete to a PIDC sponsored building project of a fertilizer factory in the early fifties. Later he organized the factory workers unions there. Other unions from the nearby towns also sought his leadership and so his name 'travelled' to Faisalabad, where he finally settled. He is based in the Crescent Textile Mills.

22. From pre-Independence days, it had been geared towards forming federations of unions. They are first formed independent of individual trade-unions at the plant level and then invite the latter to join their ranks. These federations behave as 'reserve' banks of potential strikers for bargaining with the management. In an event of strike, individual unions seek the support of the federation which tries to 'guide' them in preparing action plans, negotiates with the government authorities in case of arrest of their members and in this way spreads a consciousness of the common worker 'cause' across the country.

23. Interview with Saleh Niazi.
24. Sabiha Shakeel, an Urdu-speaking Muhajir, is the leading trade unionist of Lyallpur Cotton Mills. In the late sixties she attended Mukhtar Rana's Academy. She joined the Tehrik-e-Istiqlal in 1972 and rose to be its Vice-President. She is a moralist in politics and a professionalist in trade unionism. She was ousted from the Tehrik, when she joined President Zia's Majlis-e-Shoora. She fought and lost elections for the National Assembly in March 1985.
25. Interview with Sabiha Shakeel.
26. Interview with Mukhtar Rana.
27. *The Pakistan Times*, Lahore, 2 January 1970.
28. *The Pakistan Times*, Lahore, 3 January 1970.
29. Interview with Mukhtar Rana.
30. Ibid.
31. For a detailed description of the labour militancy in this period, see Shaheed, Z. A., 'Role of the Government in the Development of the Labour Movement', in Gardezi H. and Rashid J. (Editors), *Pakistan: The Roots of Dictatorship*, London, 1983, pp. 281-3.
32. A union acquired the status of Collective Bargaining Agent after winning more votes than any other union in the elections.

10

The Structure of Blessedness at a Muslim Shrine in Sind

Richard Kurin

In Pakistan and Muslim South Asia the shrines (*mazar, dargah*) of saints (*pir, murshid*) have been particularly important in the propagation of Islam. Previous ethnographic studies have generally concentrated upon the varied functions of such shrines. A popular view enunciated by Arnold[1] is that shrines serve as specialized loci within which the particular and relatively mundane problems of visitors may be alleviated. For example, one such typical problem is illness, and as Pfleiderer[2] illustrates in the case of Mira Data Dargah in Gujerat, the shrine may provide for varied curative and therapeutic routines. Other functions are also to be noted. Shrines encourage social participation; they provide entertainment in the form of devotional music and song (*qawwali*); they are educational; they allow for a redistribution of money, food, goods and services among living saints, followers, pilgrims, *faqirs*, vendors, and beggars. And as control over such activities may become an issue, as for example in the case of the Dargah Sharif of Nizamuddin Auliya, the shrine may also function as an arena of competition, with public ceremonial providing the means for the expression of status rivalries.[3]

A shrine and the actions surrounding it may also be viewed in a broader societal context. Shrines may enable the formation of new social groups through the establishment of spiritual brotherhood.[4] Eaton[5] investigating the constituencies of saints (for example, Baba Farid Ganj-i-Shakar) finds that shrines, such as that at Pakpattan, may serve as regional centres of moral authority, exercising legitimacy over inter-ethnic and intra-societal relationships. Studies oriented toward historical socio-political issues have revealed how shrine management has expressed governmental policy – for example, those of the Delhi Sultanate and British Colonial Government in the Punjab,[6] – and how actions at shrines constitute and encode relationships between political and religious authorities (for example, Government of Pakistan officials at the shrine of Data Ganj Baksh).[7] Shrines may serve all these functions in one or another circumstance. Yet in addition to viewing shrines in terms of the fulfilment of personal desires or the expression of socio-political dynamics, it would appear to be of more fundamental importance to consider the actions undertaken at shrines in their own right. While such actions may be performative, and while they may indeed have functions and be correlated with other issues, such actions themselves have a meaningful structure which requires ethnographic investigation.

Three general strategies exist for pursuing such an investigation. The first is to treat the actions of those at a shrine as irrational and superstitious; to assume or 'conclude' that shrine participants are fooling themselves with notions of misplaced causality. This analytic strategy is often adopted by 'rational' Muslims such as Maududi,[8] Thanvi,[9] and 'faithful' as well as 'positivistic' Europeans, for example, O'Brien,[10] concerned about the wrongful interpretation of a reality they take to be true, given and accessible. A second strategy is to formulate explanations of shrine behaviour in terms of Euro-American action systems. That is, the actions at a shrine may be represented in terms of 'faith', 'worship', 'deification', 'icons', 'psychosomatic curing', 'social legitimation', and so on. The units and relationships posited for efficacy of action, as well as the definition of action itself remain Euro-American. As Geertz[11] argues, this leaves us on the outside of our own analysis, telling us more about how twentieth century scientific-humanism approaches the religious than about those who experience it. A third strategy, that adopted here, is to proceed along lines suggested by Turner's[12] analyses of Ndembu rituals, by seeking the exegetical in systems of interpretation used by the actors themselves, and positional and relational messages in the context delimited and enriched by such interpretations. A recent analysis of Hindu pilgrimages in south India by Marriott and Moreno[13] well illustrates how an indigenous conceptual scheme may be utilized as a framework for understanding social-action in its own non-Euro-American terms. Following such an approach, this study seeks to understand intersubjective recurrent action associated with the shrine of Abdullah Shah

Ghazi in Karachi in terms utilized by those involved in the performance of such actions.

THE SHRINE

The tomb of Abdullah Shah Ghazi is the centre of a shrine complex located in the Clifton section of Karachi. The tomb rests upon a huge boulder overlooking the Arabian Sea. Presently housed in a multi-storeyed concrete building painted a bright green, the shrine is visible for miles around and serves as a popular local landmark. While centred around the grave of Abdullah Shah Ghazi, the present complex includes graveyards of his supposed followers, a *bazaar* for religious offerings, ablution facilities (*ghusalkhanah*), eating stalls, a mosque, a dispensary, a large kitchen, an outdoor courtyard for devotional music and song, and makeshift huts for itinerant wanderers. On most Thursdays, in the estimate of shrine attendants, 10 to 25,000 people make their way to the tomb and take part in some or all of the activities associated with the complex. The shrine draws supplicants, dervishes, beggars, itinerants, vendors, and the curious. Most seem to come from Karachi itself, but sizeable numbers journey from interior Sind and Punjab, and some come from as far away as Afghanistan and distant tribal territories.

The central focus of activity is the grave of Abdullah Shah Ghazi. The grave itself is quite simple and usually hidden under mountains of flowers and cloths laid upon it by supplicants. According to a locally published genealogy[14] of the Prophet Muhammad, Abdullah Shah is a Sayyed, a son of Abdullah Mahaz, the son of Hasan Masni who was the son of Hasan and paternal grandson of Ali. Abdullah Shah became a Ghazi when martyred in the cause of Islam in A.H.151.There are many stories circulating in Karachi concerning the power of the saint. Abdullah Shah is said to have been able to make milk flow from a rock; he could fly; he had the ability to move things just by his will. It is generally assumed that the source of his powers rests in the blessedness (*barkat*) he received from Allah because of his exemplary characteristics — piety, honesty, obedience, and submission to God.

TO BE BLESSED

People coming to the shrine do so for a variety of explicitly stated reasons. Some may come to cure an illness, others to secure the birth of a child, others to exorcise a demon (*jinn*), obtain satisfactory grades in school, or secure financial success. Still others may come because of some vow (*manat*) which had as a condition their visitation of the shrine. And others may come because they like or enjoy being at the shrine. Common to all stated reasons is the idea that being at the shrine can lead to the satisfaction of some personal lack or unresolved condition. It is from partaking of the saint's blessedness that satisfaction can be achieved—that wholeness may be gained or regained.

Blessedness is commonly conceived of as a transcendent spiritual (*ruhani*) quality originating from Allah. Blessedness may become substantiated, or imbued within material objects or human beings in the form of *tabarak*. All things in the world may, in some contexts, be regarded as blessed since they were created by Allah. Food and children, for example, may be commonly spoken of as being imbued with blessedness. Blessedness is regarded as beneficial to humans and particularly cooling in its effect. Blessedness is said to cool or satisfy desires, to control the animal nature (*nafs*), and to give peace and tranquillity to its recipients. Blessedness emanates from Allah, who alone creates it, and flows in a one-way direction to human beings. It flows constantly and continuously—it is identified with the spirit (*ruh*) of all humans at all times and available to all through various types of actions. Some human beings, such as saints, are extraordinarily receptive to this flow. These humans have the ability to channel and direct this flow to allow for the concentration and dispersal of blessedness .[15]

Most commonly, persons coming to the shrine do so with some type of offering (*nazarana*). It is the offering which may serve as a vehicle through which supplicants may partake of the saint's blessedness and open themselves to the flow of divine spirituality and its personalized substantiation.[16] The reception of blessedness depends upon several features. First, the saint must indeed constitute a conduit for the flow of blessedness from Allah. Second, the supplicant must undertake the proper actions and make the correct offerings so as to become a receptacle for blessedness. Third, blessedness, as a spiritual entity must be focused through the saint and transformed or substantiated so as to be capable of incorporation by the supplicant.

THE SAINT AS THE CONDUIT OF BLESSEDNESS

According to the devotees (*malang*) at the shrine of Abdullah Shah, the saint is not dead. Rather, he lives in spirit form behind a curtain (*purdah*). Only those who serve the saint deeply and truly can see beyond the curtain and glimpse this existence. Most people cannot. To the saint, however, is ascribed the ability to see all within the purview of his spiritual sight (*nazar*). This form of sight is an active way of seeing, wherein the spirit of the seer is conveyed to and, depending upon circumstances, possibly absorbed by the seen. Using a Western metaphor, rather than conceiving of sight as the reception of light waves from an object, spiritual sight is more like radar – directing light to an object, perhaps having some of that light absorbed, and then receiving the image of that object as revealed by the returning light.

In the case of Abdullah Shah Ghazi, the saint's light (*nur*) – commonly equated with spirit and blessedness – radiates to all who come to the shrine.[17] All those at the shrine are bathed in this light as they come within the spiritual gaze of the saint. This gaze focuses the blessedness flowing from Allah through the saint to those supplicants prepared to receive it. Because of this, the shrine is a place of power, a locus of actions and objects within which concentrated blessedness may be dispersed.[18]

VEHICLES AND RECEPTACLES OF BLESSEDNESS

Offerings serve as vehicles and persons as receptacles of blessedness dispersed through the saint. Offerings may take many forms – the most common being flowers or garlands of flowers, usually rose, marigold, and jasmine. Other items used as offerings are thin cloths (*chaddar*), simple hard white sweets (*batasha*) and incense (*agarbhatti*). Money, oil, copies of the Qur'an, and food (for example, lamb, rice) may also be brought as offerings, although they seem less common than flowers and sweets. Articles brought as offerings are regarded as pure things (*pak chiz*). Impure (*napak*) articles are regarded as inadequate vehicles, blocking the transfer of blessedness.

Human actions such as praying (beseechment [*dua*], memoriam [*fatiha*]), petitioning (*mangna*), chanting (*zikr*) and kissing or caressing the grave may constitute vehicles or means by which the blessedness of Abdullah Shah is conveyed. Even sitting or sleeping in the presence of the grave may provide a means for such transfer. For the devotees who inhabit the building of the shrine, such tasks as cleaning and washing the tomb area are regarded as an offering (of service, *khidmat*). In such cases, all those actions done in the name of Allah or the saint may be an offering if done with a clean or clear heart (*saf dil*)

Such actions are thought to make one an able receptacle of blessed-ness. Actions performed for devious purposes or with an impure heart block the flow of blessedness to the person.

Supplicants coming to the shrine may become pure or clear so as to receive the blessedness of the saint by undertaking ablutions (*wuzu, ghusal*) either at home or at shrine facilities. Some supplicants may not undertake such ablutions, regarding cleanliness of heart as sufficient and not subject to obstruction by material substances (i.e., bodily fluids, excrement, etc.).In either case, resultant states may be thought of as opening the person, or clearing a channel through which blessedness may flow.

Supplicants may purchase various offerings at the shrine, or bring them from home. Flowers, sweets, and cloth sheets (green, pink, etc.) are prominently displayed in the *bazaar* enclosed within the gate of the shrine and may be purchased before entering the tomb proper. Before ascending the long and steep staircase leading up to the grave of Ab-dullah Shah, supplicants remove their shoes, and by the time they reach the top, cover their heads. At the top of the stairs they may either proceed directly through an antechamber to the coffin of the saint, or they may visit with devotees ensconced in a side chamber they share with several graves of the saint's followers, a parrot, and a makeshift kitchen. In the antechamber between the saint's coffin room and the devotees' chamber is a green contribution box (from the Government's Auqaf Department), an oil holder, and a container of sweets, all over-seen by a shrine attendant.

Women as well as men may enter the tomb and come in contact with the coffin.[19] In the tomb, offerings of flowers or garlands are either placed directly upon the coffin of Abdullah Shah, or given to an atten-dant for such a purpose. Repeatedly through the evening the huge volume of flowers is pressed and flattened in layers delineated by of-fered cloth. Supplicants may offer a prayer (*fatiha*) typically done in the memory of the deceased. Less formal prayers (*dua*) may also be offered, and often include a request for desired action. If a supplicant has brought a Qur'an as an offering it is placed in a wall alcove near the coffin. Some supplicants remain in the room praying, chanting, and meditating in various poses of standing, sitting or reclining for hours; others may quickly leave.

Supplicants typically touch, kiss, and caress the coffin. Many eat flower petals previously placed on the coffin. Some take handfuls of petals for redistribution to friends and relatives who could not attend.

After finishing prayers, supplicants may 'wash' their faces with the saint's blessedness through appropriate gestures. Such actions, done with a clear heart would appear to allow for the penetration of the saint's gaze and the reception of blessedness. According to devotees, if such actions are performed correctly and properly, truly in the name of Allah or the saint and without trace of selfish or devious purpose, then the blessedness of the saint would fall upon the supplicant. Praying, chanting or merely being in the coffin room do not in themselves ensure the reception of blessedness. Rather, such actions, all regarded as cooling, clear the supplicant's animality from blocking the linkage between his spirit and that of the saint. Hotter aspects of the supplicant's human nature are dampened, constrained or overcome before the reception of blessedness can take place.[20]

Material offerings, as human actions, are generally accorded cooling properties. However, as with persons, material offerings must be processed so as to allow for the flow of blessedness. In the offering of flowers it is apparent that the newly brought flowers are not imbued with blessedness (i.e., are not *tabarak*). It is only after flowers have been in the presence of the saint that they can absorb his blessedness and become blessed material. Supplicants may physically ingest blessed material only after offerings have become so blessed. For material objects there are signs that a mixing of spirit and material has occurred – that blessedness has been substantiated in the object. For flowers this sign is typically the wrinkling and curling of petals. As fresh petals age, their heat is released and blessedness substantiated. In eating the petals, the supplicant is said to receive the blessedness contained in them.

This mixing process is also in evidence in the offering of sweets. The hard white sugar sweets are brought by supplicants to the anteroom. An attendant typically dumps the sweets into a large container in which previously given sweets have been deposited. The new sweets are mixed into the container and the attendant scoops out a volume of sweets roughly equivalent to what was brought. The supplicant receives sweets which have been in the presence of the grave, or the gaze of the saint for a sufficiently long time for blessedness to have become substantiated within them. The sweets are regarded as being blessed only when returned to the supplicant – not when given to the attendant. Supplicants then eat or distribute the sweets so their blessedness may be incorporated.

The offering and reception of oil follows the same pattern. Oil brought into the anteroom is deposited in a larger container. The new oil is stirred into the old, which is kept heated by a flame. An amount of oil is then drawn from the container and returned in blessed form to the supplicant for a skin or hair massage. The manipulation of incense is also similar. Incense brought by supplicants is lit by attendants or devotees and allowed to burn to ash. The ash, imbued with blessedness, is then collected and may be rubbed into the supplicant's skin. Food brought to the shrine as an offering is usually given to the devotees of the saint. It is often mixed with previously donated food, heated, or reheated, and eaten by the devotees or other supplicants as being blessed.

Cloth, money, and donated Qur'ans may also be redistributed in blessed form. Gifts of money may be made to attendants for the upkeep of the shrine, or directly to devotees, or may be placed in miniature cradles in the tomb. (Money placed in such cradles signals a desire of the giver to bear a child — a necessary component of which is the endowment of spirit [ruh] by Allah.) Money collected at the shrine and given in the name of Allah or Abdullah Shah Ghazi is regarded as blessed. Those who receive it do so under the gaze of the saint. Cloths, ragged and stained from the weight of flowers are redistributed after use and are also regarded as blessed. And the sounds of the verses of donated Qur'ans carry blessedness to the ears of their listeners.

According to devotees, other items may also be considered blessed but are not usually consumed by most supplicants. The dirt surrounding the graves of the saint's followers is regarded as blessed and is eaten by some devotees. The old dirt, having dried out, is attested to have absorbed the blessedness of the saint. The wash water from cleansing the coffin of the saint is also considered blessed and may be consumed. Another form of substantiated blessedness is the droppings of the pigeons which live in the shrine's towers . Supplicants may contribute grain for feeding the pigeons — a task usually performed by resident devotees. The pigeons eat the offering, digest it, and leave their droppings on the roof of the tomb. Although such droppings are usually not eaten, they are used as a medicine and are considered to be blessed.

THE CONSUMPTION OF BLESSEDNESS

Offerings — flowers, oil, incense, sweets, cloth, money, etc., are generally cool material objects. They are controlled and restrained in terms of their properties—capable of retaining blessedness and worthy of offering to the saint. In order to become blessed (*tabarak*), blessedness (*barkat*) itself must be substantiated in them. Mixing, burning, heating, and absorbing processes would seem to serve as the catalyst for the combination of the material offering with the spirituous blessedness. Ingested or otherwise incorporated by humans, the blessedness of the offering is thought to cool and relieve the supplicant, performing a wide variety of physical, emotional, mental, and spiritual purposes.

Similar results ensue with regard to human actions undertaken at the shrine. Certain actions may clear persons for the reception of blessedness. Blessedness thus received is thought to penetrate the supplicant's heart and go to the depth of his being—to his or her spirit. Reception of blessedness is above all spiritual connection, reconnection, or renewal; and yet due to the way in which the spirit and body are joined in the person, such renewal may have physical, emotional, and mental consequences—such as the curing of disease, the relief of worry, the heightening of intellective processes, etc. If blessedness is spiritual and gives one a measure of control over life energy, then the gaining, or regaining of control allows for the multifarious channelling of that energy—of one's own life and its attendant forces and manifestations.

Most supplicants visiting the tomb undertake cooling actions such as ablution, prayer, chanting or meditation to open themselves to the reception of blessedness. Yet the performance of these actions entails an emotional release—an intensely felt giving up of oneself. In the coffin room this is evidenced by the tears of supplicants, their body throbs, and their grasping for the coffin as they kiss and caress it. Supplicants speak of this as *'ishq*, an energetic, intense, giving, hot form of love. It is this emotion, rooted in the heart at the meeting point of body and spirit which seems to serve as the catalyst, as the means by which human action can be united with and felt as divinely blessed. The cool spirit of Allah, focused by the saint, and the spirit of the supplicant, under the gaze of the saint, are united by a heating process—in this case intense love. As the separation of each person's spirit from God proceeds from heated acts of parental copulation and conception, so too are separated spirits joined through heated means. Whereas parents join animal bodies in hot, erotic, but temporal, love so as to separate the spirit of their offspring from Allah, supplicants clear or separate their animal bodies from their spirit through hot, intense, but eternal love so as to join their spirit with that of Allah.

LIVING IN BLESSEDNESS

Devotees (*malang*) who live in the shrine on a daily basis may continually receive the blessedness of the saint. They assert that they are continually in a receptive state – being the beloved (*nyazi*)and servants (*khidmatgar*) of Allah. Some devotees also speak of themselves as true brides of Allah (*sada suhagan*). Anointed with earrings and other conventionally female appurtenances, these devotees argue that they are married to their master, true servants of his desires, and obedient to his commands. According to them, they have killed their animal natures (*nafs*) and put aside carnal and lustful desires which might block the flow of blessedness to them. Living their lives in accord with their spiritual nature, they undertake those activities which will link their spirit to that of Allah through the saint. Practising servitude, being dominated, and giving all of their lives to Allah, it is intense love (*'ishq*) which draws them toward and unites them with the source of all blessedness – reachable through the saint as well as through their own hearts.

EXORCISM THROUGH BLESSEDNESS

The courtyard behind the tomb of Abdullah Shah Ghazi is another locus of activity within the shrine complex. During the course of any Thursday night various groups may perform their music and song, concentrating upon devotional themes – emphasizing love (*'ishq*) of God, the love of the Prophet for God, and of God for the Prophet, the power of various saints to direct blessedness to people, etc. Audiences for the performances are strictly segregated. Males sit in the courtyard on the level of the musicians. Women occupy the rooftop of the shrine wall. The music is often said to be soothing and enjoyable – something which brings peace and tranquillity to its listeners. But it also moves them.

Many women come to the shrine to be exorcised of hot demons (*jinn*) which may inhabit their bodies; and cause them to do mischievous, lustful or vile things. Such women, as other supplicants, may perform ablutions and first visit the coffin of the saint before coming to the courtyard. They may pray, eat or ingest blessed offerings, and otherwise clear themselves for the reception of blessedness and the expurgation of the demon. Escorted by older women or family members, the possessed make their way to the courtyard roof. As the music plays, women, for the most part younger adults and post-pubescent adolescents flail their bodies in alternatively rapid and slow gyrations – heads rocking and hair swaying. Other women watch the possessed and keep them from falling over the roof wall, or injuring themselves.[21] Possessed women are said to enter a state of frenetic heated excitement (*josh*). This excitement brings forth the demon (*jinn*) as it makes its presence apparent in the woman's body. While the music serves as the catalyst for the excitation, it also serves as the vehicle of blessedness. The music is performed in the name of Allah, or the name of the saint. Indeed, males on the courtyard floor donate offerings of money to the musicians for such purposes. In invoking the name of Allah and the name of the saint the music constitutes a substantiated form of blessedness (*tabarak*).

The possessed woman, and by consequence the demon within her, hears the music. The music, as blessed, is thought to be very cool, tender, and tranquillizing. The demon, it is said, cannot stand the blessedness – it is too discomforting given the demon's fiery disposition.[22] Hence the demon departs from the body and flees the scene – leaving the woman free. The woman is subsequently relieved, or cooled as a result of having released the demon and having been infused with blessedness in its stead. Some women, after the exorcism may still be vulnerable to the re-entry of the demon once they leave the shrine. Hence, many such trips to the shrine repeated over long periods of time may be necessary so as to cool the body and make it an inhospitable place for the demon.

CONCLUSION

Blessedness is manipulated in many ways at the shrine of Abdullah Shah Ghazi. Nevertheless, the various actions and offerings at the shrine suggest a common pattern of communication between supplicants and Allah which in the process allow for their transformation.

All the offerings at the shrine have a somewhat dual nature. In one sense they are all cool. The material objects chosen as offerings are generally accorded cool humoral dispositions, the actions in the coffin room are commonly assessed as cooling ones, and even the body of a possessed woman – subjected to ablutions and experiencing a rejection of the 'possession' may be cool. Yet within each object, action or body is a hot component—regarded as baser and viewed as that to be overcome. Indeed, it is this very component that the supplicant seeks to override, undo or clear up by coming to the shrine. Material offerings, despite their coolness are nonetheless material, and therefore relatively hot when compared to the cooling light of Allah's or the saint's spirit. Various cooling actions are done for explicitly given general or specific lacks in the human condition coterminous with those actions. Such lacks are said to be due to the animalistic component of human nature. And the body of the possessed, despite preparations to receive the flow of blessedness is dramatically inhabited by a hot demon.

Offerings are a combination of components in tension. The manipulation of blessedness at the shrine may be seen as an attempt to resolve this tension by allowing for the control, relief or cooling of the unresolved condition. This resolution is accomplished by linking the offerer, through the offering, with Allah's spirituality through that of the saint. By affecting such a linkage, the lesser component is dominated by the greater component, the hotter by the cooler.

If resolution is to occur, the offering, whether as object, action or body, is subjected to a catalytic process—generally heating in character—which allows for the separation, release, or polarization of the hot and cold components. In the case of material objects, elemental heat may be lost as a result of burning, ageing, heating, absorbing, digesting, etc. In the case of actions, carnal and animalistic heat (associated with the *nafs*) is expended in the heated intense love directed to the saint. And in the case of a body, a demon may be separated and exorcised under the catalytic action of a frenzied and excited state.

This process is not merely a homeopathic one of burning off a hot element so as to create a cooled residue. A cotemporal allopathic process is also in evidence, one in which hot components brought to the fore are confronted by their opposite. Cooling blessedness is permeated into the offered object, action or body—spirit confronts material, spirituality animality, and spiritual control demonic intransigence. The means by which this blessedness is conveyed and the way in which it may permeate the person varies. Yet this blessedness seems to take the place of the residual component in much the same way as cool air is drawn in, and rushes under the flames of a hot fire. In the shrine, the reception of blessedness allows for the domination of the heated component by the cooled component. The offering is cooled (enspirited, controlled, and purged), the person cleared for easier transmission of blessedness from Allah, and more capable of resolving the unavoidable tensions of the human condition in directions deemed to be more desirable.

THE MANIPULATION OF BLESSEDNESS

Offering cool component/ hot component	Catalytic (heating) process	Separated or released unit (residue)	Vehicle of blessedness flow	Result	Means for linkage to spirit
cool material/ object materiality	burning, heating, warming mixing, absorbing	elemental heat	blessed material object	cooled (enspirited) material	ingestion
prayer, meditation, chanting/ lack	intense love	human animality	blessed sight	cooled (controlled) lack	heartfeltness
cooled body/ possessed demon	frenetic excitement	demon	blessed music	cooled (purged) body	infusion

Activities at the shrine and the ways in which blessedness is manipulated would seem to fit fairly well with models of ritual action described by Gennep[23] and Turner.[24] Offerings at the shrine of Abdullah Shah grow out of a state of human affairs in which basic conditions of objects, actions and bodies exist in dualistic form — combining materiality and spirit, hot and cold, control and intractability, humanity and animality. While such a state of affairs may be deemed normal or natural for those who live in it, it does not mean that such is accepted without some degree of equivocation. Some aspects of human states are deemed better or more desirable than others. In order to pass into more desirable states, the basic condition has to be altered and transformed. In the case of offerings, components are separated by catalytic action which pulls them apart and propels them toward other unities. In this case, cooler components are separated from baser ones and united with the spirit of Allah. The vehicles of this process — transubstantiation, radar-like sight, and sonar-like music allow for new unities. The new unity which permeates the person is made possible by the transformative ability inherent in the nature of blessedness (*barkat*). It is perhaps not surprising that the term for the shrine of a saint, *dargah* signifies a threshold.[25] In Turner's terms, the shrine may be regarded as a liminal place, a locus of transformation, where in this case, the spiritual can become personalized and substantiated, where humans can feel unity with God, and within themselves.

This hypothesis is enhanced by recent analyses of shrines[26] and tombs[27] which indicate that such are regarded as analogues of heaven. The threshold of the saint's coffin room may be regarded as a portal to heavenly paradise, and those who enter as spiritual beings being united with Allah. As illustrated in a previous analysis,[28] heaven is regarded as a cool place in contradistinction to a hot hell and mixed worldly life. If in the world the battle between the hotter elements of human animality and cooler spirituality is fought, in heaven the latter emerges victorious. The hotter elements, such as the body and its impurities are shed by death and afterlife in the grave so as to ensure the receptivity of cool spirit by Allah. Perhaps structurally similar to the ascent (*mi'raj*) of the Prophet, the supplicant's visitation to the shrine and participation in its blessedness allows him or her to glimpse and experience paradise, to reconstitute one's identity with its Godly source.

Unlike the Prophet who ascended to heaven, the supplicant usually returns to worldly life. In doing so, new-found or resurgent unity must be reformulated so as to allow the blessedness — constituted in spirit form — to penetrate to mental, emotional, and physical components of the person. After leaving the shrine, blessedness devolves back upon the initial condition — it becomes differentiated and assimilated.[29] If the flow has been good, and the unity firmly effected, the condition may be resolved and a passage or transformation achieved. If, however, the flow has been weak due to some blockage, or the unity effected only a temporary one, then the conflict may re-emerge, the tension reappear, and another trip to the shrine may be necessary. For those, such as saints and devotees who experience no blockage of flow, who are continually effecting the union of their bodies, actions and objects with Allah's blessedness, there is no such tension or conflict.

In his book on maraboutism in Morocco, Eickelman[30] argues that inter-relationships at a shrine may be paradigmatic of relationships within the society at-large. Gellner[31] in considering such a view suggests that maraboutism not only mirrors relationships within the wider society but also complements them by providing alternatives to dominant social relations. This paper makes a parallel point. Relationships enacted at the shrine of Abdullah Shah are paradigmatic of those thought to exist between humans and God as well as within persons themselves. Basic units and relationships of humanity, animality, divinity, personhood, and transformation are defined and distinguished. And yet at the same time the shrine offers the opportunity to go beyond the limitations of daily existence and to enact relationships in a way more appropriate to the spiritual life of heaven than the spiritually infused materiality of the world. The shrine, in this sense, not only encapsulates the problematic of human existence but also posits a means for its solution—if indeed only a temporary one.

NOTES

1. Arnold, T.W., *The Preaching of Islam*, Shaikh Muhammad Ashraf, Lahore, [Orig. 1896], 1961.

2. Pfleiderer, Beatrix, 'Mira Data Dargah: The Psychiatry of a Muslim Shrine', *Ritual and Religion among Muslims in India*, Imtiaz Ahmad (editor), Manohar, New Delhi, 1981.

3. Jeffery, Patricia, 'Creating a Scene: The Disruption of Ceremonial in a Sufi Shrine', *Ritual and Religion among Muslims in India*, Imtiaz Ahmad (editor), Manohar, New Delhi, 1981.

4. Mayer, Adrian, 'Pir and Murshid : An Aspect of Religious Leadership in West Pakistan', *Middle Eastern Studies*, 3, 1967, pp. 160-7.

5. Eaton, Richard, 'The Political and Religious Authority of the Shrine of Baba Farid', *Moral Conduct and Authority: The Place of Adab in South Asian Islam*, Barbara Metcalf (editor), University of California Press, Berkeley, 1983; and 'The Profile of Popular Islam in the Pakistani Punjab', *Journal of South Asian and Middle Eastern Studies*, 2(1), 1978, pp. 74-91.

6. Gilmartin. David, ' Shrines, Mosques and Gurdwaras: A Comparative View of the Growth of Muslim and Sikh Communalism', paper presented at the 34th Annual Meeting of the Association for Asian Studies, Chicago, 1982; ' Shrines, Succession and Sources of Moral Authority', *Moral Conduct and Authority: The Place of Adab in South Asian Islam*, Barbara Metcalf (editor), University of California Press, Berkeley, 1983.

7. Ewing, Katherine, 'Sufism, Cosmology and the Pakistani Government', paper presented at the 77th Annual Meeting of the American Anthropological Association, Los Angeles, 1977.

8. Maududi, S. Abul, A'la, *Islamic Way of Life*, Islamic Publications, Lahore, 1976; and *Fundamentals of Islam*, Islamic Publications, Lahore, 1975.

9. Thanvi, H.M.A., *Bahushti Zevar*, Medinah Publishing Company, Karachi, n.d.

10. O'Brien, Aubery, 'The Mohamaddan Saints of the Western Punjab', *Journal of the Royal Anthropological Institute* 41, 1911, pp. 511-18.

11. Geertz, Clifford, 'Conjuring with Islam', *New York Review of Books*, 29(9), 1982, pp. 25-28.

12. Turner, Victor, *Revelation and Divinity in Ndembu Ritual*, Cornell University Press, Ithaca, 1975, and *The Ritual Process*, Aldine, Chicago, 1969.

13. Marriott, McKim and Manuel Moreno, 'The Physics of a South Indian Pilgrimage', paper presented to the 10th Annual Wisconsin South Asia Conference, Madison, 1981.

14. Shajarah, Tibba, *Shajarah Tibba*, Iqbal Book House, Karachi, n.d.

15. Gellner, Ernest, *Saints of the Atlas*, University of Chicago Press, Chicago, 1969 points out that *barkat* is socially legitimated charisma that is treated as though it were a material substance. The analytical strategy here requires that *barkat* be considered in the way it is treated—that is in terms of the actors and not the analyst. What significance does it have for those manipulating it is the operative question—not what 'it' 'really' is. Jeffery's description of the concentration and dispersal of blessedness by the *pirzada* of the Dargah of Nizamuddin in Jeffery, Patricia, 'Creating a Scene: The Disruption of Ceremonial in a Sufi shrine', in *Ritual and Religion among Muslims in India*, Imtiaz Ahmed (editor), Manohar, New Delhi, 1981; Ewing, Katherine, analysis of the power of Lahori *Pirs*, in 'Sufis and Adepts: The Islamic and Hindu Sources of Spiritual Power Among Punjabi Muslims and Christian Sweepers', *Anthropology in Pakistan: Recent Socio-Cultural and Archaeological Perspectives*, Stephen Pastner and Louis Flam (editors), South Asia Occasional Papers and Theses, No. 8, South Asia Program, Cornell University, 1982; and Fusfeld's account of the flow of blessedness at the *khanqah* of Mirza Mazhar in Fusfeld, Warren, 'Connectedness, Structure and Change in a Sufi Tradition' paper presented to University of Pennsylvania Ethnohistory Workshop, Philadelphia, 1982, generally support the assertions made here concerning the features of *barkat*.

16. Schwerin in analyzing the shrine of Salar Masud describes such activity as worship. If such is the case then the concept of worship requires much clarification. The liturgical services of many Euro-American religious institutions do not occasion worship in quite the same way. Perhaps the closest homologue in mainstream Western tradition is the manipulation and meaning of the communal eucharist of the Roman Catholic church. Schwerin, Kerrin, 'Saint Worship in Indian Islam: The Legend of the Martyr Salar Masud Ghazi', in *Ritual and Religion among Muslims in India*, Imtiaz Ahmad (editor), Manohar, New Delhi, 1981.

17. The representation of blessedness in the form of light is quite common. In a dramatic example, devotees and other suppliants point to an incident during World War II when Karachi was under a blackout. The light bulb atop the tomb continued to burn despite attempts to switch it off. And while the area was heavily bombed and the nearby port damaged, nothing of the shrine was touched. It is clear that the light bulb radiated more than electric light, and that such light was protective and of greater power than material forces.

18. The means by which blessedness may be dispensed in relation to a particular locale was raised in a possible anomaly discussed with resident devotees. On visiting Thatta and shrines of that area I observed a small tomb which I thought bore the name of Abdullah Shah. Upon returning to Karachi I asked the devotees whether or not the Thatta tomb might be the shrine housing the actual coffin and the shrine in Karachi a mere memorial. Perhaps, so I argued, the body of the saint was not in Karachi, but in Thatta. The devotees found the issue briefly interesting but not very intriguing. If indeed the body was in Thatta it did not matter, for the

blessedness of the saint was evidenced in Karachi, at the shrine. After all, they said, just as a gaze could be reflected in a mirror, so too could the spiritual sight of the saint, if directed from Thatta, easily be focused to arrive in Karachi.

A supportive example utilizing the same principle is offered by Pfleiderer, op.cit., 1981, 215, who notes that attendants at the shrine of Mira Data may transfer the power of the tomb to other sites through the use of lighted lamps which share in the light, or blessedness of the central shrine. Fusfeld (n.d.) writing of the replication of a central shrine notes how satellite shrines are generated from and encapsulate the power thought to be manifest in the original shrine.

19. Shrines in Pakistan differ as to their procedures with regard to women coming into contact with the tomb of the saint. For most of the shrines I have visited in Sind and southern Punjab, women are allowed full access to the coffin. Shrines in the north tend to be more restrictive, disallowing direct contact. The logic of the prohibition concerns menstruation as a perceived impurity which blocks the flow of blessedness. In those shrines allowing access to women, it is often understood that menstruating women should restrain themselves from touching the tomb. According to supplicants at more restrictive shrines, outright externally imposed prohibition for all women is necessary as menstruating women are so weakened as to be deficient in rational ability and hence not be in a position to control (i.e., restrain) themselves.

20. There are two major strategies for doing this as many devotees and supplicants point out. One, a fiery strategy (*jalali*) is to perform very hot actions—sexual, violent, and over indulgent ones in order to 'burn out' or become cool by expending all of one's heat. The other, a controlling strategy (*jamali*) is to perform cool and restraining actions so as to conserve, stifle, and channel heat energy. Dramatic examples of both are to be witnessed at the shrine of Abdullah Shah—Qalandaris who burn their flesh and attain states of ecstatic intoxication (*must*), and a supplicant who had encoiled himself in chains and padlocks in order to 'control and contain his animal nature'.

21. I am indebted to my wife Allyn Bland, for her observations of and inquiries about rooftop behaviour.

22. Pfleiderer, op.cit., 1981 pp. 225-6 finds a similar type of relation with regard to the phenomenon of ghost (*bhut*) possession in Gujerat.

23. van Gennep, Arnold, *The Rites of Passage*, M. Vizedom and G. Caffe (translators), University of Chicago Press, Chicago, 1960.

24. Turner, op.cit., 1969.

25. Cf. Jeffery, op.cit., 1981, p.163.

26. Eaton, op. cit., 1983.

27. Begley, Wayne, 'The Myth of the Taj Mahal and a New Theory of its Symbolic Meaning', *Art Bulletin*, 61 (1), 1979, pp.7-37.

28. Kurin, Richard, 'Muslims in Paradise: Morality, Personhood and the Exemplary Life', *Moral Conduct and Authority: The Place of Adab in South Asian Islam*, Barbara Metcalf (editor),   University of California Press, Berkeley, 1983.

29. Blessedness, regarded in substantial (i.e., non-transcendent) form as light or ethereal vapour may be considered as having greater generative power than any other substance. Its devolution, due to material admixture (and attendant catalytic processes) allows for its degeneration or differentiation into such components as mind (*zamir, 'aql*), psychobiological energy (*nafs*), and body (*jism*).

The heart (*dil*) seems to play a key role in this devolutionary process. Such a view is quite consistent with the theory of spirit (*ruh*) advanced in the indigenous humoral medical system (Qarshi, Alama, *Mukhtasar al Kuliyat*, Ashraf Press, Lahore, 1974). It might be noted as a parallel that semen (*tukhum, bij*) undergoes a similar devolution in the formation of blood, its derivative fluids (humors) and bodily organs in indigenous theory.

The consideration of blessedness in humoral terms, and its conceptual linkage to worldly objects and forces is widespread in Pakistan (for example, *ruh afza*, a popular cooling summer drink) and is well illustrated by Pastner, Stephen, in 'Power and Pirs among the Pakistani Baluch' (in chapter 13 of this volume), in his treatment of Baluchi *pirs*.

30. Eickelman, Dale, *Moroccan Islam*, University of Texas Press, Austin, 1976.
31. Gellner, Ernest, *Muslim Society*, Cambridge University Press, Cambridge, 1981, pp. 214-18.

11

A Social Structural and Historical Analysis of Honour, Shame and *Purdah* in Baluchistan[1]

Carrol McC. Pastner

The ideological basis of sexual roles and norms of male and female conduct is intricately connected with the widest categories of behaviour
and institutional arrangements in a society. The mutual effects of
sexual role allocation on the functioning of society and of social structure on the ideology of role definitions is perhaps most apparent in
those cultures which emphasize an extreme dichotomization between
the sexes. Middle Eastern or Islamic culture is one of the most
prominent examples of such an extreme duality, although some of the
broad outlines of sexual role functioning there are common to other
situations. This paper focuses upon a specific example within the Middle East, although some of the elements discussed, such as the value
system of honour and shame, are relevant not only to that culture area,
but parts of the non-Middle Eastern and non-Islamic world as well.

The paper has three main goals: (1) to describe a specific code of
honour and shame; (2) to relate this ideological focus to social organization – kinship and stratification in particular; (3) to document
historically the elaboration of an ideology based on honour and shame
into the ritual of *purdah* as an example of the interaction between a
'great' and a 'little' tradition. The assumption behind these goals is
twofold. First, it is understood that the role of ideology (in this instance,
the framework of relationships between men and women and the
statuses and roles of women) has numerous repercussions within the
totality of social behaviour. Second, the incorporation into a 'great'
tradition involves factors other than the merely cultural. That is, there
are important structural components in the interaction between 'little'
and 'great' traditions and the social organization of cultural traditions.

THE SOCIAL AND CULTURAL SETTING[2]

The oasis of Panjgur lies in the north-west part of Makran District in Baluchistan, Pakistan. Makran is the south-western-most administrative district in Pakistan, bounded on the west by Iranian Baluchistan and on the south by the Arabian Sea. Its position has long been that of a geographical link between Persia, the Persian Gulf, the Arabian Peninsula, and the Indo-Pak subcontinent, as attested by the numerous groups which have passed through the area.[3] While the barren terrain of Makran has resulted in a dominant pastoral nomadic adaptation, several oasis centres have seen the development of irrigated agriculture and date cultivation in particular. Panjgur is the second largest of the oases in Makran.

The details of the history of Panjgur and the relationship between agriculture, kinship, and politics there have been discussed elsewhere.[4] Supporting a population of about 11,000, the oasis consists of a series of villages and hamlets which depend upon date cultivation made possible by intensive irrigation methods based on the use of surface and sub-surface water. There is one major *bazaar* which serves as the central market for the entire region. Panjgur is also the political centre for the same area.

While the indigenous populace subscribes to what can be termed Baluch culture, including the speaking of the Baluchi language and common kinship structures, the political structure of Panjgur traditionally has been composed of ascribed social strata organized along feudal lines. The three major groupings are the Hakim, the Baluch, and the Hizmatkar. As the traditional ruling class, the Hakim consists of a number of aristocratic families which have always constituted the largest land and water holding group. The Baluch represent a broad middle layer of small landowners, while the Hizmatkar traditionally have been either non-landowning tenants or slaves attached to the leading elite families. Ethnic distinctions cross-cut these caste-like groups since many of the Hizmatkar are negroid in origin in contrast to the predominantly Iranian stock of the other two groups.

The traditional social structure of Panjgur was based on revenue and tribute extraction and the predominant use of patron-client ties. This resulted in the sublimation of lineage organization although patrilineality continues to be important to the question of recruitment into each of the social strata. Similarly, endogamy within each group relates to the hierarchical aspect of stratification, with hypergamy also being recognized and hypogamy seen as shameful. However, due to historical forces which will be outlined below, there is now confusion between ethnic and economic criteria with regard to the categorization of these social groups and the jural rules governing the association between them. The traditional functioning of the social order has become challenged, particularly due to political and economic factors and the opening up of avenues out of status categories. As will be shown, the ambiguity created out of the introduction of new and different criteria relevant to social stratification has resulted in a compensatory, although culturally consistent, concern about the status and behaviour of women.

This concern is related as well to other aspects of social organization in Panjgur. In spite of the presence of strong cultural ideals of agnation and kin endogamy, actual social structuring reflects the predominance of non-kin corporate groups and a low rate of kin endogamy. An irrigation economy and a political system based on patron-client ties have been largely responsible for inhibiting the development of large scale kin corporations.[5] Nonetheless, cultural values continue to reinforce overt ideals of kin solidarity and endogamy which are directly related to the central question of the position of women. The ideology of honour and shame plays an important role in the perpetuation of this contrast between overt ideals and actual social structure.

HONOUR AND SHAME

The general features of an ideology of honour and shame are relevant to a broad range of societies, but have been discussed particularly with reference to Middle Eastern and Mediterranean cultures.[6] In each case, honour and shame relate to concepts of correct conduct, especially the sexual conduct of women which is seen to reflect upon the status of male relatives. The ideology has much to do with the overall functioning of society and not just the nature of relationships between men and women. 'Like all ideologies, honour and shame complement institutional arrangements for the distribution of power and the creation of order in a society. And ... concern with honour arises when the definition of the group is problematic'.[7] In the Middle East, the responsibility of males to control the 'shame' and defend the honour of their women is in keeping with the male centrism of Islam and the need for agnatic solidarity. However, while the notions of shame and personal and family honour ideally involve the widest limits of kinship, with the absence of strong lineage organization, the concepts relate more to the personal realm of honour and shame, particularly with regard to female sexual honour.[8] This is essentially the case in Panjgur. Although notions of male honour (*gherat* or *mayar*) exist, including such ideals as generosity and bravery, due to sanctions arising in the non-kinship realm and the abolition of martial activities, it no longer functions vitally in social control and the creation of equilibrium between kinship units. However, honour as it relates to women continues as an important focus in Baluch culture and social organization.

Notions of honour and shame, as they have existed both in the past and present, are similar to those in other Middle Eastern societies. Honour (*izut*) and shame or modesty (*luj*), as conceived by men,[9] relate to the behaviour of women which is seen to reflect upon the latter's male kinsmen — husbands, fathers, and brothers in particular. The stress on the physical modesty of women reflects the highly sexual connotation of these values. Two of the major methods of preventing the breach of modesty lie in limitations on the physical mobility of women beyond the home and the establishment of sexual 'invisibility' through such items of clothing as the *burkah* and the shawl. These instruments of seclusion are commonly known as *purdah* in the Islamic world. The use of *purdah* in Panjgur coincides with a general Pakistani model.

> Women's proper behavior, as sheltered persons, becomes an important measure of the status of their protectors, and the achievement of symbolic shelter is valued by the man as a measure of control over his environment. In a culture where male pride is a very significant-and very fragile-element of identity and status, the seclusion of women is an important aspect of male control.[10]

In Panjgur, many aspects of honour and shame are seen by men to emanate from women: 'A woman's shame is the shame of her husband and kin; her honour is their honour.' Awareness of the constraints upon women can be summarized by one male's view: 'A man is a man — he can do anything, go anywhere. But a woman's leg is broken; she is blind and not free to go where she wants. A man can be bad and no one will say anything; but when a woman is bad, everyone knows.'

The general concept of modesty in Panjgur is similar to that found in other Islamic contexts[11] and stresses particularly the necessity of bodily coverage, certain ideal character traits of women, the polluting aspects of female physiology and the jural and moral superiority of men. The greatest breach of modesty, predictably, is adultery which in the past could lead to political activation in the form of blood feud. This is one important area where agnatic solidarity can still function in spite of its minimization in other areas of social life.

THE HISTORICAL DIMENSION OF *PURDAH*

The practice of *purdah* in Panjgur involves a number of overt rules relating specifically to the veiling and seclusion of women. A woman may be subjected to varying degrees of *purdah*, the most stringent being that of almost virtual isolation from the world beyond the home. Lesser degrees involve the wearing of veils and shawls and limitations on physical mobility and exposure to non-kin males. A corollary of this is the small degree to which females are permitted formal education, since it is at the time of puberty that *purdah* is first enforced and not relaxed until the time of menopause.

Adherence to the rules of *purdah* parallels certain economic and social structural factors. Only the wealthier men can afford to seclude their womenfolk totally, since this implies certain architectural accommodations (such as a separate guest room for the entertainment of males) and the use of servants (often male) to perform domestic duties such as shopping. However, most women do limit their activities outside the home, and in this respect most women are at least minimal participants in the system. One factor which accounts for this generalized participation is that there is no necessity for female agricultural labour. During the date harvest season, when the need for additional hands is the greatest, pastoral nomads have always come to the oasis to perform labour which ordinarily might be provided by the women of the oasis. This is an important circumstance since it allows the elaboration of a sexual division of labour convenient to the practice of *purdah* and at the same time obviates the necessity of making accommodations between the 'modesty code' and economic needs faced by some other groups in the Middle East.[12]

Many aspects of *purdah*, however, are historically recent introductions into Baluch culture. Local history maintains that before the second half of the nineteenth century only Hakim women were kept in full *purdah* (i.e., total seclusion and veiling), while today Baluch and even Hizmatkar women from families with sufficient funds and high social aspirations are subjected to full *purdah*. In fact, in former times, women in Panjgur were reported to not even wear a *shalwar* (the baggy trousers or 'pajamas' endemic to the subcontinent and parts of the Middle East). 'The women, in towns, of the wealthy classes may dress in (pajamas) and may affect to hide their faces on the appearance of a stranger; but these are practices arising from imitation, and contrary to Baluch custom, which...enjoins not the privacy of women'.[13] The growth of status mobility which has facilitated an increase in the use of *purdah* is the result of political developments on the oasis.

Before the nineteenth century, Panjgur and the rest of Makran had been largely autonomous with local elites (the Hakim) politically and economically in control but continuously engaged amongst themselves in the struggle for power. In the late nineteenth century, while the Hakim were still locally dominant, Makran became incorporated into the Brahui Khanate of Kalat with its capital far north and east of Makran in what is now Kalat District. Prior to, and during this era, the socio-political environment had concomitants in the physical layout of the settled areas of Makran. Architectural features were not conducive to full participation in a *Purdah* system. Permanent mud enclosures and forts, which could provide the physical seclusion for women necessary to full *purdah*, were occupied mainly by the minority chiefly elite. The majority of the populace apparently resided in less substantial mat huts or tents.[14] These settlement patterns reflected the feudal political order and the high physical mobility of a populace which frequently shifted its locale and political allegiance as aspirants to power rose and fell.

Full control over Makran by the Khanate of Kalat was not effected until the mid-nineteenth century when the British joined with Kalat in treaties mutually beneficial to both. With the aid of the British, Kalat was able to strengthen its hold on Makran. One of the effects of this more direct control was the movement of non-Baluch (Brahui, Pathan, Hindu, British) political agents and traders into the larger settled areas of Makran. The introduction of these outsiders and the accompanying political developments had a profound effect on indigenous culture and social structure. First, a more secure political order permitted the stabilization of much of the population and the construction of more permanent housing, a *sine qua non* of full *purdah*. Second, the already established and traditional ideal of preventing the exposure of women to strangers, i.e., non-Baluch, led to the increasing adoption of *purdah* by indigenous groups when the number of outsiders increased. Other factors further reinforced the use of *purdah* to conserve honour. The emancipation of slaves in the early 1920's led to fears on the part of non-slave males about the safety of their women since the ex-slaves were regarded as morally polluting. In addition, the introduction of non-Baluch residents created the availability of a model for the practice of *purdah*, since many of these administrators brought their families with them. This model was essentially that of the traditional form of *purdah* practised within urban Islam for many hundreds of years.[15]

When the Baluchistan States Union was incorporated into Pakistan in 1955, the impetus to the increasing use of *purdah* survived as it does today. Non-Baluch (Punjabis and Pathans in particular) are still predominant in the political life of Makran since the oases serve as the residence for the local arm of the Pakistan Government. The presence of these administrators has a dual effect as far as the adoption of *purdah* is concerned. First, non-Baluch persist in their role as a model for the correct form of *purdah* as an urban phenomenon. Second, their being 'outsiders' also continues to encourage the insulation of women by the indigenous population. This last can be viewed as politically significant, not only with regard to the relationship between cultural groups in Pakistan, but to the workings of honour and shame in a broad range of societies. Honour can be used to strengthen the identity of a group by defining its boundaries and thus defending it against competing groups.[16]

However, it should be stressed that there are important continuities which permit the adoption of *purdah* by the Baluch and represent the on-going continuity between 'little' and 'great' traditions. The indigenous and traditional value of hiding women from strangers and non-kin is congruent with more complex social situations involving groups other than the local and traditional. The notion of female modesty, also traditional, is transposed easily into more exaggerated means of enforcing such modesty as well as providing an additional measure of social worth for males. In other words, culture change was and is taking place, but such change has represented the adoption of attitudes and practices which are consistent with traditional values in Baluch culture.

All of these developments have resulted in a contradictory situation for the women of Panjgur. The women have been incorporated increasingly into a national legal system concerned directly with their civil rights. Simultaneously, they have become structurally alienated from access to such rights, including a set of Family Laws promulgated in Pakistan in 1961 which attempts to ensure the registration of marriages, the prevention of abuse in polygyny, the fixing of a minimum age for girls at marriage (age 16), and the facilitation of claims by the wife for her rights to maintenance. To a large degree the inaccessibility to such civil rights is because women are barred from participation in non-kin arenas of social activity and acquiesce to male authority. At the same time, however, the seclusion of women has permitted the partial insulation of Baluch culture from external influences, and this too might be seen as relevant to the political relationship between cultural groups in Pakistan. In many respects, as Baluch men become more 'modernized' due to their continuing exposure to a wider society, women at the same time are becoming more 'traditional' as they are increasingly isolated from non-Baluch culture.

IDEOLOGY AND KINSHIP

As noted above, there is a discrepancy between stated ideals and the actual role of kinship in Panjgur social organization. In spite of a predominant value orientation which stresses the significance of kinship (agnatic links in particular), most political and economic activity is marked by the presence of non-kin corporate groups and patron-client ties. In parallel fashion, kin endogamy is highly valued, while actual statistics reflect a very low rate of endogamy.

The persistence of a strong ideological stress on endogamy and kin solidarity is directly correlated with predominant attitudes about women and their statuses, since honour and shame are most effectively protected if women are exchanged only between kin and exposed only to kin. An agnatic bias in particular functions in relation to women; that is, agnatic kin concern themselves primarily with inheritance (especially the crucial question of the inclusion or exclusion of women), and the control over women as embodiments of honour and shame. By extension, the *de facto* rights of women lie within the realm of kinship, particularly as it is defined by agnation, but involving as well, affinal and matrilateral kin. For women, effective rights do not lie within any wider framework than locally-anchored kin groups which constitute the domestic sphere of society. This is particularly true for the widow or the divorcee whose reliance on kin is absolutely crucial to even her physical survival.

The connection between ideology and kinship is aptly illustrated by the function of bridewealth. Economic transactions at the time of marriage correlate with the degree of social distance between the bride and groom. Bride-wealth is reduced or even eliminated in cases of exchange marriage or very close kin endogamy; otherwise it is of absolute necessity. Marriage payments, however, do not erase entirely the traditional shame of giving away a woman since they do not involve a total transfer in the status of a woman. Rights and duties contingent upon natal kinship are not eliminated at the time of marriage, and the married woman continues to participate in the honour of her father and brother as well as that of her husband.

The question of inheritance also reflects upon the enmeshment of women in kin networks. In general, women in Panjgur do not receive inheritance in land or rights to irrigation from their fathers, in spite of encouragement from the civil branch of government. This correlates with two other factors. First, the low rate of kin endogamy is consistent with non-inheritance by women since endogamy is often an important means of offsetting the fragmentation of estates in the Middle East.[17] Second, the acquiescence of women in this regard is related to the security of their statuses as kinswomen. A pattern of forfeiting property rights in order to maintain rights in kinship is found in other areas of the Middle East.[18] In Panjgur such rights include a dowry (primarily clothing and household equipment), periodic gift exchange, mutual visiting patterns, the right of refuge in the father's home after marriage, and recourse to natal kin in the case of widowhood or divorce.

While in actuality men may attempt to abstain from responsibilities (e.g. financial) maintained with relation to their kinswomen, this is offset by the highly sanctioned nature of such responsibility and its important role in the communication of male status in both kin and non-kin arenas of male social intercourse. The significance of kinship in Panjgur is thus directly related to the treatment of women and the ideology of honour and shame, in spite of the fact that in actuality the most important political and economic activities on the oasis are oriented around non-kin corporate groups and ties based on patron-client relationships. Nonetheless, men have had available to them sanctioned alternatives to (for example) blood feuds in the form of cash compensation (codified at the turn of the century) which allow the perpetuation of agnatic responsibility but check the possibility of endless feuding due to the necessity for agnatic solidarity. This can be seen as one form of accommodation in the face of a stringent and demanding ideological focus in Baluch culture, both traditional and contemporary.

PURDAH AS RITUAL

Leach[19] has presented the idea that '. . . the structure which is symbolized in ritual is the system of socially approved 'proper' relations between individuals and groups'. By regarding it as the ritual aspect of the ideology of honour and shame, *purdah* can be seen as a symbolic statement about social order in its ideal form.

The absence of *purdah* for all but the Hakim prior to the period of Kalat and British administration indicated two things about social structure at that time. One was the fact that for the Baluch *et al.*, who did not practice *purdah*, the local elites were not regarded as strangers but as participants in Baluch culture. Second, the high status of the Hakim, the seclusion of their own women, their control over politics and economics and the deference owed to them in a feudalized social order, all conspired to prevent the use of a ritual aspect of honour and shame (i.e., strict *purdah*) by the Baluch as a particularistic way of making certain statements about the relation between the Hakim and the non-Hakim. In other words, in the realm of social organization, the non-practice of a ritual can be as symbolic as its practice. In addition, the use of *purdah* made the position of the local elite more meaningful in political terms since it served to contrast the elite as participants in a 'more advanced' tradition than those immersed in a 'little' tradition or 'catchment of the popular undercurrent'.[20]

With the intrusion of non-participants in Baluch culture and the introduction of more complex variables into the realm of social stratification, the ritual of *purdah* as a symbolic statement about a more ambiguous social order was adopted by other sectors of the population. Significant alterations in the traditional organization of discrete caste-like groups, such as the emancipation of the slaves and the development of feasible means of mobility out of rigid statuses, served to reinforce the use of *purdah* as a means of lessening the ambiguity of relations between groups which traditionally had been defined in an hierarchical manner.

The high status connotation of *purdah* provides another reinforcement to its continuing adoption by persons sufficiently mobile in the changing society of Panjgur. A direct relationship between the assumption of a higher economic status and the use of *purdah* is typical of other areas in Pakistan. In the Punjab, *purdah* correlates with economic status and is assumed by peasant women when their families become more prosperous.[21] The same has been noted amongst sedentary

Pathans.[22] In Pakistani cities, *purdah* is often used to signify status achievement by the 'lower middle class'.[23] In each of these instances, differential adherence to a cultural tradition is an important component in social stratification and mobility between strata.

CONCLUSION

This paper has been concerned primarily with the delineation of a code of honour and shame in one specific setting, its relation to several aspects of social organization, and the historical factors involved in its elaboration into the ritual of *purdah*. While the orientation thus has been largely that of social history, ultimately I have been dealing with the question of origins, not of the code of honour and shame, but of its ritual component in the form of *purdah*. In this endeavour it became clear that the ideology of sexual role allocation and the status of women are directly correlated with the most important features of social organization, including kinship and stratification. The case of Panjgur provides a specific example of this often repeated but seldom documented co-variance between ideology and structure.

Historically, there is demonstrable continuity between value orientations traditional to Baluch culture and the elaborate ritual of *purdah* typical of other, usually urban, settings in Pakistan and the rest of the Middle East. Significant developments in the political and social framework of the oasis permitted this important change in the cultural orientation of the oasis. The achievement of greater political stability, for example, facilitated the adoption of *purdah* not only by larger numbers but different social categories of persons.

While the historical events are particular to the case of Panjgur, many of the structural and ideological factors are not, suggesting that the processes discussed here might be relevant to other instances where honour, shame, and *purdah* are found. Further examples of the processual arrangement of these cultural foci might shed further light on a question specific to the Middle East, as well as the more general problem of the interplay between social organization, ideology, and the cultural assignment of sexual roles.

NOTES

1. Using the case of an oasis society in Baluchistan, Pakistan, an attempt is made to unravel the structural and historical reasons for the elaboration of a traditional ideology based on the concepts of honour and shame into the use of the institution

of *purdah*. By tracing the social organizational and cultural prerequisites for this development, it is possible to explain the reasons for the adoption of *purdah* and its interrelationships with ideology and social structure over an historically documented period of time. While the specifics of the case are consistent with many features of Pakistan and the Middle Eastern culture area, the general question of the relation between the ideology of sexual roles and social structure is pertinent to most societies.

2. Fieldwork on the oasis of Panjgur was carried out between December 1968 and May 1969. Library research was conducted in London, primarily at the British Museum, the India Office Library, and the School of Oriental and African Studies, London University. Financial support was provided by NIMH in the form of a Pre-Doctoral Fellowship and Research Grant. I would like to thank Stephen Pastner for his helpful suggestions and criticism in the writing of this paper.

3. Field, Henry, *An Anthropological Reconnaissance in West Pakistan 1955*, Peabody Museum, Cambridge, 1959.

4. Pastner, Stephen and Carroll McC. Pastner, 'Agriculture, Kinship and Politics in Southern Baluchistan', *MAN* 6(4), 1972.

5. Ibid.

6. Peristiany, J.G.(editor), *Honour and Shame: The Values of Mediterranean Society*, Weidenfeld & Nicolson, London, 1965; Antoun, Richard T.,'On the Modesty of Women in Arab Muslim Villages: A Study in the Accommodation of Traditions', *American Anthropologist*, 70, pp. 671-97, 1968; Schneider, Jane, 'Of Vigilance and Virgins: Honor, Shame and Access to Resources in Mediterranean Societies', *Ethnology*, 10(1) pp. 1-24, 1971.

7. Schneider, op.cit., 1971, p. 2.

8. Barclay, Harold B., *Burri al Lamaab: A Suburban Village in the Sudan*, Cornell University Press, Ithaca, New York, 1964, p. 51.

9. One major dimension of the case studied here is lacking, primarily because its significance and complexity warrant a great deal of attention in its own right. This is the role of women in the perpetuation of honour, shame and *purdah* as it is actually played by the women themselves. The behavioural and structural accommodations made specifically by women in the context of a highly sexually dichotomized society are important, not only to understanding the female sector, but indeed, to the fullest comprehension of the society as a whole. (Pastner, Carroll McClure, 'Sexual Dichotomization in Society and Culture: The Women of Panjgur, Baluchistan'. Ph.D.Thesis, Brandeis University, 1971). But for the purposes of the present paper, a 'normative'(male) view of ideology is utilized, since the focus here is on the long range historical and organizational features of honour and shame. It should be understood that the actual day-to-day functioning of the value system profoundly affects and is profoundly affected by behaviour on the part of women.

10. Papanek, Hanna, *'Purdah* in Pakistan: Seclusion and Modern Occupations for Women', *Journal of Marriage and the Family*, August 1971, pp. 517-530.

11. Antoun, op.cit., 1968.

12. Ibid.

13. Masson, Charles, *Narrative of a Journey to Kalat*, London, 1843.

14. Pottinger, Henry, *Travels in Beloochistan and Sinde*, Longman, Hurst, Reese, Orme and Brown, London, 1816; MacGregor, Maj. Gen. Sir C.M., *Wanderings in*

Baluchistan, W.H. Allen & Co., London, 1882; Pastner, Stephen, 'Ideological Aspects of Nomad-Sedentary Contact: A Case from Southern Baluchistan'. *Anthropological Quarterly*, 44 (3), pp.173-84.

15. The adoption of *purdah* by the Baluch under such circumstances can be likened to a similar process in Hindu India-'Sanskritization' as it has been described by Srinivas, M.N., 'A Note on Sanskritization and Westernization', *Far Eastern Quarterly*, 15(4), 1956, pp. 481-90. Lower castes are seen to take over the customs, rites and beliefs of higher castes in a chain reaction through which lower castes, by assuming the customs discarded by the Brahmans, become increasingly Sanskritized. However, as Srinivas indicates, this form of mobility through the caste hierarchy does not result automatically in higher status for a particular group; the claim of such may continue for a long time prior to acceptance by other groups. In addition, while economic betterment by the group going through Sanskritization can be assumed normally, not all cases are preceded by the acquisition of wealth. Srinivas, op.cit., 1956, p. 492.

16. Schneider, op.cit., 1971, p. 17.

17. Granqvist, Hilma, *Marriage Conditions in a Palestinian Village*, II, Societas Scientarum Fennica, Helsinki, 1935; Peters, Emrys, 'Aspects of Rank and Status among Muslims in a Lebanese Village'; In *Mediterranean Countrymen*, J. Pitt-Rivers, editor, Mouton & Co, Paris, 1963.

18. Rosenfeld, Henry, 'On Determinants of the Status of Arab Village Women', *MAN* LX, 66-70; Mohsen, Safia K., 'The Legal Status of Women Among Awlad 'Ali', *Anthropological Quarterly*, 40(3), 1967.

19. Leach, E.R., *Political Systems cf Highland Burma*, Beacon Press, Boston, 1965, p. 15.

20. Von Grunebaum, Gustave E.,'The Problem: Unity in Diversity', in *Unity and Variety in Muslim Civilization*, University of Chicago Press, Chicago, 1955, p. 28.

21. Honigmann, John, 'Women in West Pakistan', In *Pakistan: Society and Culture*, HRAF, New Haven, 1957, p. 160.

22. Vreeland, Herbert H., 'Pathans of the Peshawar Valley', in *Pakistan: Society and Culture*, HRAF, New Haven, 1957, p. 126.

23. Papanek, op.cit., 1971, p. 522.

12

The Social Structure of the Brahui and the Baluch

Yuri Gankovsky

A major part of the ethnic territory inhabited by the Baluchi people has been one of Pakistan's four provinces since 1970. The territory of the Baluchistan Province is 344,600 square kilometres. According to the 1981 *Census,* its population is 4,300,000 people[1]. It should be noted that its administrative borders do not coincide with the ethnic boundaries of the areas populated by Baluchis in Pakistan (described in detail).

PROFILE OF BALUCHI POPULATION

There are 4 to 4.5 million Baluchis in the world.[2] About 3 million of them are living in Pakistan. Baluchis also live in Iran (550-600 thousand) and Afghanistan. Baluchi migrants are also to be found in India and certain Persian Gulf countries. There are several thousand Baluchis in the southeast of the Turkmen Soviet Socialist Republic.

The Baluchis in Pakistan belong to two groups: Makranis in its south-west, who derive their name from the historical province of Makran (or Mekran) on the Arabian Sea coast; and Suleimanis, so called after the Suleiman Mountains in the north-east. In between the two is the Kalat District (or the Kalat Principality, as it was called until October 1955), which is inhabited by the Brahuis, a small Dravidian-speaking nationality of about 600,000 people.

The Makrani Baluchis, like the Baluchis of Iran and Afghanistan, speak the western dialects of the Baluchi language that belongs to the north-western sub-group of the Iranian languages. The Suleimani Baluchis speak its eastern dialects.

Most Baluchis in the world are Sunnite Muslims. The Makran region alone has several dozen thousand Shiites from the Zikri sect.[3] A major part of Makrani Shiite Baluchis belong to the Buledi, Biranjan, Kilkaur, Sajdi, and Sangur tribes. Most of them are urban dwellers in the district, while the rest are still nomads.

The administrative borders within Pakistan, including those of the Baluchi-inhabited areas, have changed more than once since 1947. This hinders comparison of the data accumulated in the *Censuses* of 1951, 1961, 1972, and 1981, both with each other and with those of the *Censuses* of the colonial epoch. The following data on the Baluchis in Pakistan are based on the administrative borders that existed during the 1972 *Census*. The population figures are those of 1980.

It can be seen from the data that, in the province of Baluchistan (see Table 12.1), the Baluchis are in the majority only in such districts as Kachhi, Kharran, Makran, Sibi, and Chagai. The Pashtuns prevail in the districts of Quetta-Pishin, Loralai and Zhob, in the province's north-east; the Lasbela District is mostly populated by the Sindhis; and the major part of Kalat's population is the Brahuis. In the province there are also the Punjabis (in the Quetta-Pishin, Loralai, Kachhi, and Sibi districts); the 'Muhajirs', who had migrated from India, and their descendants who speak Urdu (chiefly in the Quetta-Pishin District); the Hazaras, who had arrived from Afghanistan in the late nineteenth and early twentieth centuries; and the Parses, in the Makran District.

There are also many Baluchis in the Sind Province, chiefly in districts of the Upper Sind, such as Jacobabad, Larkana, Dadu, and Nawabshah. Their number increasing at a high rate, there are over 1 million Baluchis there at present. The Baluchis in the Upper Sind belong to the tribes of the Rinds, Buledis, Bijranis, Bughtis, Chandias, Jatois, Gabols, Khosas, Lunds, Marris, Jamalis, Legharis, and Magsis (Magasis). About 200,000 Baluchis live in the Karachi District.[4] It should be noted, though, that nowhere in Sind are the Baluchis in the majority (i.e., from 10 to 30 per cent of the population is in the Upper Sind Districts, and about 4 per cent live in the Karachi District). In addition to the Baluchis whose ancestors lived in Sind as far back as the pre-colonial epoch and those who migrated there in recent decades, a great number of Baluchis annually arrive in Sind as seasonal workers from the districts of Karachi, Lasbela, and Chagai; for instance, 30-40 per cent of all the able-bodied men from the Chagai District go to the Lower Sind District every winter in search of a living.

Table 12.1: **Baluchi Population in Baluchistan Province (1980 data)**

No.	District	Territory in Square miles	Population in thousands	Baluchis in thousands	Percentage	Main Baluchi Tribes	Other Ethnic Groups in thousands	
1.	Kachhi	5,599	400	300	75	Rinds, Magsis (Magasis), Dombkis, Umranis, Buledis, Khosas, Jatois, Kebaris, Mugharis, Dinaris, Chalgris.	Sindhis (Lasis) Punjabis	70 30
2.	Kharran	18,553	120	90	75	Nausherwanis, Rakhshanis Muhammadhasnis	Brahuis (Sasolis, Samalaris)	30
3.	Makran	23,640	400	350	88	Gichkis, Buledis (Zikris), Sangurs, Biranjans, Kilkaurs	Brahuis (Bizenjos) Parses	20 15
4.	Sibi	11,390	550	400	73	Marris, Bughtis, Rinds	Pashtuns (Kakars, Tarins, Panis) Brahuis Punjabis Sindhis	110 10 10
5.	Chagai	19,516	90	70	77	Sanjranis, Jamaldinis, Badinis	Brahuis (Mengals)	20
6.	Quetta-Pishin	5,314	650	60	9	Migrants from all main Baluchi Tribes	Pashtuns (Kakars, Tarins, Panis, Achakzais) Brahuis (Shahwanis, Lehris, Langars, Mengals, Raisanis, Kambraris, Nicharis, Muhammadshahis) Punjabis Hazaras 'Muhajirs'	350 70 60 30 30
7.	Loralai	7,364	250	50	20	Sayed, Legharis, Ghurchanis, Buzdars, Kaisranis	Pashtuns (Kakars, Panis, Tarins, Shiranis, Ustaranis, Ghilzais) Punjabis	150 50
8.	Lasbela	7,048	200	50	25	Gadris, Sungurs,	Sindhis (Lasis) Brahuis (Bizenjos)	130 20
9.	Zhob	10,475	220	–	–	–	Pashtuns (Kakars, Shiranis)	220
10.	Kalat	25,332	370	50	13	Zehris	Brahuis (Raisanis, Shahwanis, Bangalzais, Lehris, Langavs, Rustamzais, Mengals, Bizenjos, Kambranis, Mirwaris, Gurgnaris, Nicharis Sasolis, Khidranis and others)	320
Total		132,909	3,250	1,420	43.7		Brahuis – 490 (15.1 per cent) Pashtuns – 830 (25.5 per cent) Sindhis – 210 (6.4 per cent) Punjabis – 150 (4.6 per cent) Hazaras – 30 (0.9 per cent) 'Muhajirs' – 30 (0.9 per cent) Parses – 15 (0.5 per cent)	

Source: *Population Census of Pakistan, District Census Report,* Islamabad, 1976.

The Baluchis (mainly the Mazaris and the Dastis) also inhabit the districts of Dera Ghazi Khan and Muzaffargarh of the Punjab Province. There are 250-300 thousand Baluchis there, or 12-15 per cent of the districts' population.

Some of the Baluchis, who since their ancestors migrated to Sind and south-western Punjab several generations back have been living in isolation from their ethnic mass among people of another ethnic stock, have forgotten their mother tongues and speak Sindhi or Punjabi. In many cases this has even changed their ethnic consciousness, as compared to that of their ancestors.[5] Several thousand Baluchis belonging to the Leghari, Rind, Hot, Shahani, and Lashari tribes are living in the district of Dera Ismail Khan of the North-West Frontier Province (NWFP).

The establishment of capitalist relations in Baluchistan began about eighty years ago. Their development was speeded up by the laying of several spur lines in north-eastern Pakistan(1891-1905), expansion of the network of dirt roads and modernization of the ports of Gwadar and Pasni. Market orientation emerged in Baluchistan's agriculture as certain areas specialized more thoroughly in commodity production. First, industrial facilities appeared. Parallel with that, however, was the dispossession of land and the emergence of social differentiation among Baluchi farmers, both of which were speeded up by the land-taxation reforms introduced by the British colonial administration (including substitution of the duty paid in kind with taxes). The most fertile land gradually passed into the hands of landlords and usurers. Meanwhile there appeared vast strata of leaseholders and landless agricultural workers, their number and share of the total population growing with every decade.

Baluchistan's entry into the world capitalist market was accompanied by a steady increase in its import of manufactured goods, which along with the growing tax burden entailed the ruin of great numbers of local artisans.[6] Expropriation of direct producers, i.e., farmers and artisans, facilitated formation of the labour market and the population's migration to the more developed regions of Baluchistan. The number of nomads and semi-nomads kept slowly but unflinchingly decreasing. Townships (i.e., population points of the urban type) were developing. Economic ties among various regions of Baluchistan were growing stronger, and a Baluchi national market was gradually coming into being. However, the socio-economic development was most uneven, so that by the mid-forties the capitalist structure was only formed in Baluchistan's most developed (i.e., northern and north-western) regions as a derivative of the British monopoly capital functioning in the country. The rest of Baluchistan was dominated by feudal relations complicated by the survival of backward tribal forms of social organization.[7] Serfdom was only officially abolished in Baluchistan as late as 1926-29.

Development of capitalist relations in Baluchistan was also accompanied by the formation of the proletariat and the bourgeoisie, the basic classes of bourgeois society. But the formation of permanent proletarian *cadres* has been and is being hindered by Baluchistan's utter social, cultural and economic backwardness, the meagre wages paid to hired workers and hard labour conditions. Thus, the level of occupational injuries due to accidents was among the world's highest at the coal mines of Baluchistan in the 1970s.[8] Until the seventies, skilled workers from Punjab and Sind prevailed at the mines, railways, and the few manufacturing facilities, while the Baluchis accounted for the bulk of non-skilled workers (which to a large extent is also true today). The Baluchi proletariat was also being formed outside Baluchistan, in Punjab and Sind, as well as in Bombay and Husestan, areas to which thousands of Baluchis without means of subsistence were heading annually in search of jobs.

The situation in Baluchistan also obstructed the formation of the Baluchi bourgeoisie proper. This process has been and is being blocked by, among other things, the essentially monopolistic role on the home market played by big commercial and money-lending bourgeoisie from outside Baluchistan (i.e., from Gujarati, Punjabi, and Sindhi), often having close ties with foreign capital.

The development of Baluchi intellectuals was also extremely slow. In 1948 there were less than 2 per cent of local Baluchis among Baluchistan's teachers, which is about a score of people. Despite the fact that the schools in Baluchi never charged, according to some estimates, the total number of Baluchis who could read and write in their native language was as little as 132,000 in 1980.[9]

Development of capitalist relations and the formation of classes and social strata of bourgeois society, as well as transformation and erosion of formerly existing social classes, estates and groups connected with the pre-capitalist economic structures, were speeded up all over Baluchistan during World War II and the post-war period. The processes were extremely slow, however. Pakistan's ruling circles did not pay sufficient attention to the economic and social progress of the areas inhabited by the Baluchis. The enterprise of the growing Baluchi national bourgeoisie (despite certain advantages acquired when about 50,000 Indian merchants, usurers, and employers emigrated from Baluchistan in 1947) was restrained by the narrowness of the internal market and the ruinous competition from the big non-Baluchi bourgeoisie.[10] Baluchi intellectuals, in the process of formation as a strata of the population, could find no application for their knowledge. Nonproletarian pauperization of Baluchi farmers and livestock breeders, as well as of artisans, entailed, as mentioned above, their mass emigration to other countries.

Pakistan's Baluchi regions in the late seventies and early eighties still remained preserves of backwardness, poverty, feudal yoke, and lawlessness. Although capitalism is at present the leading socio-economic structure in Baluchistan's most developed areas (above all in Quetta, as well as in the quickly developing regions of Sui and Pat Feeder in the Sibi Division), a mixed character and diversity of structures are common aspects of the socio-economic system in Baluchistan, which is due to the uneven development of capitalist relations. A strong natural economic structure, and pre-capitalist methods and forms of exploiting the working people are still preserved there. The extremely low annual per capita income in Baluchistan testifies to its general economic and social backwardness.[11] Meanwhile, the bulk of the income is still created within the natural, small-scale commodity market, and petty capitalist sectors of the national economy.

Sixty-four per cent of Baluchistan's able-bodied population is employed in agriculture. As to industry(including the manufacturing and mining industries) and construction, these employ as little as 13 per cent of the able-bodied population.

According to the 1972 *Census* in Pakistan, the province of Baluchistan had only 32 townships, inhabited by about 399,000 people, or 16.4 per cent of the province's population (see Table 12.2). It should be noted here that according to the same *Census,* in 1961-72 one-half of Baluchistan's districts (Quetta-Pishin, Kalat, Sibi, Loralai, and Zhob) had lower growth rates of the urban population than those of the rural population, which is additional proof of the province's backwardness. Quetta was the only town with a population of over 100,000 people; however, most of its population was not Baluchi, but migrants from other Pakistani provinces(the Punjabis, above all), Muslim refugees from India and their descendants (Muhajirs), and the Hazaras who

Table 12.2: Urban and Rural Population of Baluchistan Province[1] (According to 1972 Census)

No.	District	Township	Urban Population in thousands	per cent	Rural Population in thousands	per cent	Total in thousands
1.	Kalat	Kalat, Mastung, Khusdar	20.2	6.2	306.7	93.8	326.9
2.	Kachhi	Bhag, Mach, Dhadar, Gandawa	22.3	8.4	242.8	91.6	265.1
3.	Lasbela	Bela, Uthal	9.0	6.7	125.7	93.3	134.7
4.	Kharran	Kharran	6.1	7.9	70.7	92.1	76.8
5.	Makran	Turbat, Panjgur, Pasni, Gwadar, Jiwani	74.4	24.5	229.6	75.5	304.0
6.	Sibi	Sibi, Usta-Muhammad, Harnai, Jhatpat, Shagrig Bazar, Ziarat, Sui	33.8	8.6	361.1	91.4	394.9
7.	Chagai	Nushki, Dalbandin, Nokhundi	11.2	17.2	54.1	82.8	65.3
8.	Quetta-Pishin	Quetta, Chaman, Pishin	189.0	37.7	312.5	62.3	501.5
9.	Zhob	Fort Sandeman, Muslim Bagh, Killa Saifullah	20.8	12.1	151.1	87.9	171.9
10.	Loralai	Loralai	12.6	6.7	174.7	93.3	187.3
	Total	32 townships	399.4	16.4	2,029.0	83.6	2,428.0

The farmers who own and cultivate their small plots,[2] account in Baluchi districts for less than one-fifth (19 percent)of the able-bodied rural population, with the shares for the Sibi and the Kharran Districts being respectively 12 and 30 per cent. However, even the Kharran figure is much lower than the average for the Province (i.e., 41.5 per cent). It should be stressed that in Baluchistan's Pashtun districts nearly 60 per cent of the able-bodied rural population are farmers who own upto 1 hectare plots of land, working in their natural or semi-natural economies.

[1] The Table was compiled on the basis of the *Population Census of Pakistan*, District Census Report, Islamabad, 1976.

[2] The average farmer's plot of land in Baluchistan is 0.7 hectare, according to official Pakistani sources.

had migrated from Afghanistan in the late nineteenth and early twentieth centuries.

The most numerous and proportionally biggest part of Baluchistan's working people are farmers (55.7 per cent of the population in the province). No less than one-sixth (17.5 per cent) are still nomads. The nomads' lowest proportion in the agricultural population is 7.5 per cent (the Quetta and Pishin districts), and the highest is 32.6 per cent (in the Chagai District of Baluchistan).[12] As to the Baluchi districts of the province (i.e., those with the Baluchis comprising the prevailing ethnic group), nearly one-quarter of the rural population (or 23.1 per cent) are nomads there.

About 6 per cent of the economically active strata of the rural non-nomadic population are landless agricultural workers. Their number is the lowest in the Pashtun districts of Zhob and Loralai (0.3 and 1.6 per cent, respectively), and the highest — in the Baluchi district of Makran, where they are called *darzadas* and *rayat-hamsayas* (41.4 per cent, or nearly one-half of the farmers there!). As to the Baluchi districts of the province, nearly every fifth farmer there (18 per cent) has by now lost his plot of land, thus becoming a farm labourer without any rights. With leaseholders who account for 40 per cent of the population employed in the agriculture of the Baluchi districts, the situation becomes one of almost three-fourths of the Baluchi farmers cultivating landlords' fields at present.[13]

BALUCHI SOCIAL STRUCTURE

The above aspects of the social structure of the Baluchi farmers (the overwhelming majority of 'leaseholders out of charity' and farm labourers) have resulted — in addition to the many consequences of British colonial domination still persisting in the province — from a number of aspects of Baluchistan's socio-economic development as part of Pakistan. There have been no agrarian reforms in Baluchistan since 1947. The 1959 reform, implemented by the government of M. Ayub Khan, officially did not involve Baluchistan;[14] only big Baluchi landowners in the district of Dera Ghazi Khan, the Punjab Province, lost about 40 per cent of their land. As to the agrarian transformations announced by the government of Z. A. Bhutto in 1972,[15] their implementation in Baluchistan was torpedoed by the powerful Baluchi *sardars* (tribal chiefs), who strongly resisted them. The outdated relations of production in agriculture — the paramount sphere of

Baluchistan's social production — also exerted a negative influence on the socio-economic development and the political situation in the province.

The so-called independent workers in the non-agricultural spheres of Baluchistan's national economy are numerically second to the farmers as a strata of working people in the province. Some of them are artisans who make rugs, footwear, bags, belts, ropes, baskets, plates and dishes, and who produce salt in the coastal areas or work in retail trade and the services. There are more than 100,000 of them at present. However, the Baluchis account for only a small portion (about 20,000) of them. According to official sources, the retail trade in the district of Lasbela in the seventies was in the hands of Indian Sindhis.[16]

Fishing has been developing in the coastal areas, above all in Makran, in recent decades. The bulk of the catches is exported to Eastern Africa and Western Europe.[17] However, this sphere of productive work is not in the hand of Baluchis, but of the Meds and the Khojas(i.e., the Sindhis and the Gujaratis).

In the late seventies and early eighties, about 140,000 hired workers (41,000 of them in the districts where the Baluchis were in the majority) were employed in Baluchistan's manufacturing and extractive industries at building sites and in transport. Meanwhile, according to the data at our disposal, the Baluchi proletariat has been and is being formed not so much on the territory of Baluchistan proper as outside it (above all in Karachi and other bigger towns and cities in Sind, and in the Punjab). According to official data, the Pashtuns accounted for the major part of skilled workers at Quetta's coal mines in the seventies, and the Punjabis at railroads. The Baluchis were chiefly employed as non-skilled labourers (i.e., such hired workers as navvies, road maintenance staff, loaders; their wages being one-third of those earned by non-Baluchi skilled workers).[18] At the same time, as noted in the press of Democratic countries, unskilled Baluchi workers had to give part of their meagre earnings to the chiefs of tribes, clans, and heads of families (i.e., the *sardars, muqaddams*, and *waderas*). There were high turnover rates among the labour force, which, along with the persisting ties of Baluchi workers with the countryside, hindered the formation of permanent Baluchi proletarian *cadres*.

Formation of the Baluchi intelligentsia, launched in the first quarter of the twentieth century, is also underway chiefly outside Baluchistan. Early in the sixties, the province's Baluchi districts together had as few as 205 medical workers, 477 teachers, and 1,819 public officers of all ranks. The first university in the province was opened in 1970. The top Baluchi intellectuals are mostly graduates of the universities in Karachi, Lahore, and abroad (above all in Britain and the United States). Unable to apply their knowledge in Baluchistan, these people are mainly working in Sind or the Punjab. As a rule, they come from well-to-do families of landlords and businessmen (the latter being in the minority). Some of them maintain ties with the landownership in the form of a personal union (i.e., 2.5 per cent of Baluchistan's landowners are teachers and physicians).

In Baluchistan in the seventies, there were as few as approximately 6,000 college students and senior formers at secondary schools(who are playing a significant role in the province's political life). As few as 830 of them lived in the districts where the Baluchis were in the majority.

The *Ulema* (Muslim theologians and clergymen) are comparatively few in Baluchistan — about 7,500 according to the data for the early eighties. The majority of them inhabit the province's Pashtun districts, while less than 20 per cent are in its Baluchi districts.

The *Ulema's* authority and influence are much weaker among the Baluchis (and the Brahuis) than among the Pashtuns in Baluchistan (the Zhob Quetta and Pishin Districts in particular) and the North-West Frontier Province. According to the available data, the *Ulema* and the *pirs* of various Sufi orders are also highly influential among the population of the coastal areas in Makran.

Through their living standards and their social and political ideals, the bulk of the *Ulema* are quite close to the well-to-do landowning farmers, artisans and petty tradesmen (thus to be seen as a kind of traditional intelligentsia). However, the *Ulema's* top figures (i.e., the *imams* and *mullas* of cathedral mosques; the *pirs* and *ishas* — heads of religious Muslim orders; famous theologians, instructors and heads of religious schools), with quite a few big landowners among them, are undoubtedly a group of the top layer of Baluchi society.

BALUCHI SYSTEM OF EXPLOITATION

The dominating top layer of Baluchi society is not numerically large. It consists of four main groups: the landowning aristocracy of Baluchi tribes; top Muslim theologians; the upper level of the Baluchi bourgeoisie, now in the process of formation; and the not very numerous representatives of the upper echelon of the civil bureaucratic apparatus. The key role is played by the *sardars*, *muqaddams*, and *waderas* (i.e., the chiefs of Baluchi and Brahui tribes, clans, and families), who are now big landowners, as well as members of former princely families that had been vassals of the British crown until August 1947.

In the district of Kalat, vast estates belong to the family of Kalat's former *khan*, Mir Ahmad Yar Khan (1902-77). Other big landowners in the district are Brahui *sardars*, such as Ataullah Khan Mengal, chief of the Mengal tribe, the most numerous in the district; Ghaus Bakhsh Bizenjo, chief of the Bizenjo tribe; Ghaus Bakhsh Raisani, chief of the Brahui Raisani tribe living in the vicinity of the Bolan Pass; and Doda Khan Zarakzai, chief of the Brahui tribes' union in Jalawan in southern Kalat. Nabi Bakhsh Zehri, the *sardar* of the Zehri tribe, is a major Baluchi landowner in the district.

In the Kharran District the biggest landowners are the *sardars* and *muqaddams* of the Nausherwani tribe (most famous among them is Mir Ghulam Mustafa Nausherwani); in the Makran District, those of the Gichki tribe; in the Sibi District, the tribes of the Bughtis (with Nawab Muhammad Akbar Khan Bughti as their *sardar*) and the Marris (Nawab Khair Bakhsh Marri as their *sardar*); and in the district of Chagai, those of the Sanjranis, the Jamaldinis and the Badinis. The official Pakistani report on the situation in the Chagai District in 1973 stated in part that those tribes' *sardars* were ruling the district and enjoying most of their old privileges.[19]

Baluchi *sardars* and *muqaddams* are not just large landowners. Their nearly absolute power and great influence on the territories inhabited by their tribes were ensured by the so-called *sardari* (or *sardari nizam*) system, which gave them the right to administer justice in the territory. Many *sardars* maintained their own jails and armed detachments that functioned as police and invoked the traditional 'sacred right' to demand a share of the population's income, to make people work for the *sardars* free, etc.[20] Central governments in Pakistan have more than once tried to abolish the *sardari* system, but in vain.

Throughout the past decades (the process gaining momentum in the fifties through the seventies), some *sardars* began investing their capital into trade and industries, thus becoming partners of big businessmen in Karachi and other cities and towns of the Sind and the Punjab Provinces. A local Chamber of Commerce and Industry was established in the town of Quetta in April 1964, and the above-mentioned *sardar*, Nabi Bakhsh Zehri, became its first President.

Tribal *sardars* are naturally distant from the only Baluchi social group whose members are becoming, in part, businessmen. The latter also includes former officials and servicemen(i.e., people belonging to the same landowner circles). Besides, many Baluchi employers are often both landowners and merchants at the same time.

Socially close to them is the bureaucratic uppermost layer of Baluchi public officers, which has increased numerically and consolidated its position since 1973, when over 3,600 Punjabi employers and officials who had occupied the overwhelming part of the civil administrative posts in the province of Baluchistan were returned to the Punjab. However, even in 1979 as few as 20.3 per cent or 181 of the 830 top officials in the province, were Baluchis.[21]

In analysing the social structure of the Brahui-Baluchi society, it should be stressed that the Baluchi, as well as the Brahui and the Pashtun, tribes in Baluchistan are at present but survival communities, preserved due to certain peculiarities in the historical development of the Baluchis and the Brahuis. The feudal Baluchi-Brahui aristocracy was interested in preserving these groups, since tribal traditions camouflaging the growing class contradictions enabled it to use the tribes' efficient men as guards in its own interests. Until recently their preservation was also to a certain extent in the interests of the Baluchi and Brahui working people — farmers, livestock breeders, artisans, and tradesmen — for the tribal organization guaranteed the defence of their lives and property from the predatory encroachments of the rulers of the neighbouring feudal states, and from the colonizers' invasions.

THE BRAHUIS OF CENTRAL BALUCHISTAN

The Brahuis that mainly inhabit central Baluchistan are, as mentioned earlier, a small ethnic group of 600,000 people who speak a Dravidian language. Most of them are living on the territory of the former Kalat Principality; and there are Brahui settlements in Quetta-Pishin, Sibi, Chagai, Kharran, and the northern Sind. (There are also small groups of Brahuis in Iranian Baluchistan and south-western Afghanistan.) It should be noted that the Brahui areas divide the Baluchis' ethnic territory into two isolated parts.

For centuries the Brahuis were surrounded on all sides by the Baluchis, and consequently were gradually assimilated.[22] The Brahuis' cultural and economic backwardness and absence of a written language of their own prevented the formation of clear-cut ethnic con-

sciousness. The recorded changes in the latter were due to the assimilation of the Brahuis by the Baluchis. That was also testified to by the
Brahuis active participation in the Baluchi 'national' movement.

Besides the historically close relations between the two
nationalities, this situation was due to the Brahui feudal-landlord top
strata's domination of Baluchistan since the mid-seventeenth century.
Therefore, isolation of the Brahuis from the Baluchis by declaring the
Brahui-inhabited territory an autonomous administrative entity could
only harm the top Brahuis' positions and interests. Along with that,
within Baluchistan proper the interests of the Brahui and Baluchi national bourgeoisie (still in the process of formation) have never
clashed, since there were no developed capitalist relations there.
Meanwhile, outside Baluchistan both Brahui and Baluchi dealers have
been suffering equally from the competition of the stronger, large Punjabi and Sindhi bourgeoisie or the Urdu speaking bourgeois migrants
of 1947-48 from India. This is why the Brahui personalities (many of
them leaders of the Baluchi movement) have never set up Brahui
organizations, nor proclaimed platforms different from those of the
Baluchis.

We should note, however, that the ethnic development of the
Brahuis in recent decades proves that their ethnic (national) consolidation is underway. They now have a written language, and periodicals
and books are published in the Brahui language. A group of Brahui intellectuals set up the Brahui Academy as far back as the early 1960s to
study the language and folklore of the Brahuis. An association of
Brahui writers has been established, which joined the Pakistan Writers'
Guild that was established in 1959. The Brahuis' ethnic consciousness
has acquired a more clear-cut form, since over the past decades they
have gained an idea about their own Brahui ethnic community against
the background of the mass of the Baluchi population. In addition,
since 1968 they have been urging recognition of the Brahui language
as a 'regional language' in Pakistan, like the Sindhi, Pashtu, Punjabi,
and Baluchi languages, as well as budget appropriations for development of the Brahui language.[23]

The social, economic, and cultural backwardness of Baluchistan,
the influence of the pre-capitalist traditions and concepts there, and
the fact that contemporary classes are yet incompletely formed all exert
a profound impact on the social and political processes among the
Brahuis and the Baluchis. Many tribal organizations established in the
past are functioning now. One example is the well-known Mazlum

Party (the Party of the Oppressed):[24] only Marri Baluchis are members of the party, which functions strictly within the territory of the Marri tribe. It was late in the seventies that the first peasants' organizations appeared in Baluchistan as a result of the establishment and development of the farmers' movement in Baluchistan, which involved in 1973-74 many clashes between farmer leaseholders and landowners in Kalat, Makran, Sibi, and elsewhere in the province. Only scant information is available on the activity of such organizations, but their very appearance and development are noteworthy, for they testify to the processes of class delimitation within the Brahui-Baluchi society.

BALUCHIS IN IRAN

The above description of the eastern (Pakistani) Baluchistan population's social structure can generally be applied to the Baluchis in western (Iranian) Baluchistan. This is to be explained by the common histories of the Baluchis living on both sides of the Iranian-Pakistani border, by continuous contacts among them, and by the similarity of the conditions under which traditional Baluchi social institutions in both countries are being transformed. More than 80 per cent of the Baluchis in Iranian Baluchistan are in the rural districts, employed in agriculture; they combine oasis farming with semi-nomadic livestock breeding, and with fishing in the coastal areas.

The agrarian reforms of the sixties and the large-scale building of roads have stimulated the growth of commodity production. In the sixties and seventies the urban population of Iranian Baluchistan increased nearly threefold; parallel with that the number of nomads decreased. Although far less than all the land, which was alienated from local landowners with redemption by the agrarian reforms, was given to Baluchi farmers (part of the land passed into the hands of the migrants from central Iran), the reforms have generally increased the number of Baluchi farmers with small plots of land. Along with that, the agrarian reforms facilitated the gradual transformation of some Baluchi landowners and well-to-do farmers into agricultural employers of the capitalist type: as early as the mid-seventies, half of the cultivated area there (60,000 of the 124,000 hectares) was being ploughed by tractors. At the same time, the number of landless Baluchi agricultural workers was on the increase.

The industries in Iranian Baluchistan were only taking their first steps in the sixties and seventies, while the territory possessed but few small enterprises working with local raw materials; therefore, the formation of the Baluchi working class started comparatively recently there, and the class is numerically small, as is the local Baluchi intelligentsia. Both the Baluchi proletariat and intelligentsia are mainly being formed outside their homeland, in the economically more developed regions of Iran and Pakistan. The young Baluchi national bourgeoisie was represented in the seventies in Iranian Baluchistan by owners of small commercial and artisan-industrial enterprises concentrated in the town of Zahedan (the province's administrative centre) and several townships. Its growth was hindered by the stronger and more experienced competitors of other ethnic groups, both from Iran and Pakistan (those from Pakistan having rather vast business interests in Iranian Baluchistan).

NOTES

1. Population Census of Pakistan, Census Bulletin No. 1, Islamabad, 1981.
2. According to Brook S. I., there were 2,780 Baluchis in the world in 1978. See *Population of the World,* Moscow, 1981, p.870 (in Russian). And according to S.S. Harrison, there were 5 million. See Harrison, S.S., *In Afghanistan's Shadow,* New York, 1981, p.10.
3. Zikri is derived from the Arab word *zikr*, or mentioning (Allah's name).   This is a branch of the Mahdawi sect, established late in the fifteenth century by Sayyid Muhammad of Jawnpur (1443-1504), who proclaimed himself the *Mahdi* or Messiah. Until recently the Zikris have been practicing the *taqiyya*, i.e., they concealed their belonging to the sect. (For more details see Qureshi, I.H., *Ulema in Politics*, Karachi, 1972, pp. 37-40, and Aziz Ahmad, *Islam in India*, Edinburgh, 1969, pp.27-9.)
4. Many Baluchis living in Karachi are seasonal workers who migrated from Iranian Baluchistan, as well as young Baluchis who came from Iran to study at general educational and at religious schools, since Iran is a Shiite state, whereas the Baluchis are Sunnites.
5. Judging by the family names of many an active participant of the Sindhis' national movement, they are not of Sindhi, but Baluchi origin. Similar processes are underway in Punjab.
6. Over the decade of 1921-31 alone the number of artisans in Eastern Baluchistan decreased by 63 per cent. See *Census of India, 1931*, Vol.IV, Pt.II, pp.66-7.
7. For details see Gankovsky, Yu.V., *Nations Inhabiting Pakistan*, Moscow, 1964, pp. 228-35, in Russian.
8. Harrison, op.cit., 1981, p.163.
9. For details see ibid., pp.10, 207.
10. For details see Gankovsky, Yu. V., *Nationalities Question and National Movements in Pakistan*, Moscow, 1967, pp.79-80, and Levin, S.F., *Formation of Big Bourgeoisie in Pakistan*, Moscow, 1970, pp.69-70 (both in Russian).

11. Pakistan's per capita GNP amounted to 252 dollars at current prices in 1979/80. According to Belokrenitsky, V., the figure was 343 dollars for Sind; 247 dollars for Punjab; and as little as 184 dollars for Baluchistan.

12. *District Census Report, Quetta-Pishin, Islamabad, 1976, and District Census Report, Chagai, Islamabad, 1976.*

13. Fifty-seven per cent of the residents in the Sibi District are leaseholders, and 45 per cent in the district of Harran. The proportion is also high in the Kalat District (49 per cent). Their share among the able-bodied agricultural population of Baluchistan is 35.5 per cent. Most of Baluchistan's leaseholders are the so-called 'leaseholders out of charity,' who do not own the plots of land they are cultivating, but have to give the landlord a large part of their crops and bear the burden of the many feudal requisitions.

14. The 1959 agrarian reform envisaged limiting the land estimates to 200 hectares of irrigated and 400 hectares of non-irrigated land. For details see Moskalenko, V.N., *Problems Facing Pakistan Today*, Moscow, 1970, pp.35-53, in Russian, and Ziring, L., *The Ayub Khan Era*, New York, 1971, pp.18-19, 169-70.

15. The limits established by the 1972 land reform were 60 hectares of irrigated and 120 hectares of non-irrigated land.

16. *District Census Report, Las-Bela*, Islamabad, 1976,p.6.

17. Mir Ahmed Yar Khan, *Inside Baluchistan*, Karachi, 1975, pp. 46-47.

18. Harrison, op.cit., 1981, p.164.

19. *District Census Report, Chagai op. cit.,p.7.*

20. For details see Baluch, Inayat, *Tribal System in Baluchistan, 'Siyasat-i' Pakistan*, London, April 1980, pp. 6-7.

21. In the late seventies and early eighties, 70 per cent of the policemen in Baluchistan were non-Baluchis (for details see Harrison, op.cit. 1981, pp.163-4.)

22. Rooman, A., *The Brahuis of Quetta-Kalat Region*, Karachi, 1960.

23. *Morning News*, Karachi, 9 April 1968.

24. *Imroz*, Lahore, 11 March 1957.

13

Power and Pirs Among the Pakistani Baluch[1]

Stephen L. Pastner

If one is a proponent of the traditional functionalist view that religion is a mirror of and charter for the secular social order, on the surface there can be no more contrary cases than the tribal enclaves of the Muslim world. In settings ranging from the hill country on the Pakistan-Afghanistan border, where Pathan factions coalesce and dissolve in competition over land and political retainers,[2] to the high valleys of Morocco where Berber tribesmen do much the same thing,[3] we find such turbulent secularity in juxtaposition to a normatively monolithic cosmology — that of Islam. From the Hindu Kush to the Atlas, tribesmen acknowledge that there is no God but Allah, and regard men of God as arbiters in the pervasive political factionalism. Indeed, such figures may emerge as political leaders themselves when unification against a common enemy is required and the kinship cum political system, by its segmentary nature, cannot itself provide such a nexus, *de jure* ideals of fusion of kinsmen against outsiders notwithstanding.

This phenomenon has been well documented for a number of areas. Evans-Pritchard[4] has shown how the Sanusi religious order served to mediate disputes between Bedouin clans in Cyrenaica and ultimately provided the leadership necessary to unify the nomads against invading Italians. Likewise Gellner[5] has suggested that among the Berbers 'saints' frequently serve as 'spiritual lords of the marches', keeping peace between hostile clans and sometimes themselves assuming secular authority.

Among the turbulent Pathans of the Swat Valley it was holy men like the nineteenth century Akhund who united the divided and faction-ridden tribesmen against the British[6] while in other settings figures like the late nineteenth century Sudanese Mahdi[7] and the 'Mad Mullah of Somaliland[8] again demonstrate the potency of Islam as an ideology.

Such accounts convey the impression that Islam and its specialist devotees have an almost teleological ability to counteract centrifugal tendencies in the secular arena and that in such settings religion, contra the classic functionalist view, is everything society itself is not. It has in fact frequently been suggested[9] that at its very inception Islam provided just such a unifying force in the face of an otherwise divided temporal social order.

However, since the time of the Prophet, the maintenance of local-level Islamic tradition has been in the hands of lesser men and it would be incorrect to assume that such figures, no matter how supposedly imbued with divine blessing or power (Arabic *baraka*; Indo-Iranian *barkat*) and the ascetic values of the medieval Sufis, from whom they derive their theological roots, are themselves always exempt from the same competitive drives that motivate their lay followers. We find, accordingly, in several of the accounts cited above that the holy man's role as mediator and unifier frequently co-exists with baser personal ambitions. Thus Barth[10] cites the case of the Swat Pathan saint who roguishly declared 'I look like a simple man; I live simply—but, Oh! the things I do!,' while Ahmed[11] also dealing with the Swat Pathans, has documented the intrigues of the quasi-religious figure who was to become the Wali or king of Swat in the early twentieth century. Likewise Gellner[12] has shown how Berber saintly lineages(*igurramen*) compete to see which can produce the most effective holy men.

Relying on data from the Baluch of Pakistan—primarily the maritime Baluch of coastal Sind—I hope to further explicate the ways in which the 'sacred' and 'profane' in Islamic 'little traditions' mirror, rather than contradict, each other.[13]

NORMATIVE BALUCH POLITICAL ORGANIZATION

There are variations in the jural forms of Baluch socio-political organization, two of which have been relatively well studied. In the first, centred in oasis areas of southern Baluchistan, a feudal stratified system has evolved, dominated by chiefly lineages (*hakim* in Pakistani Baluchistan; *hakomzat* in Iranian Baluchistan) who stand above free-born Baluch agriculturalists and nomads and a stratum of (ex) slave or menial negroid share-croppers and servant groups—the *hizmat-*

kar.[14] A second variety, found among the nomads of the Iranian Sarhad plateau studied by Salzman[15] and among the Marri and Bugti in character – i.e., all sections of the society – both ruler and ruled – trace common descent although often fictively to apical ancestors with segmentary lineage principles serving to regulate political life.

Still another variety of socio-political organization, is found among the Baluch from whom most of the present data are drawn. These are the Baluch fishermen of coastal Sind province in Pakistan who, although their ancestors were drawn from some of the most notable desert Baluch tribes (Mohammed Hassanis, Bizanjo, etc.), have transferred their primary orientation of self-identity from tribal or feudal idioms to a religious one. The fishermen studied were Zikri – members of a sect imported to Baluchistan sometime in the late fifteenth century or early sixteenth century.[16] Centred on belief in a Mahdi (Islamic messiah) called Nur Pak ('Pure Light'), whose teachings were believed to supersede those of the Prophet Muhammad (a belief anathema to orthodox Sunni Islam), by the mid-eighteenth century Zikriism had achieved the status of a virtual state religion in southern Baluchistan, with certain of the *sardars* or paramount chiefs acting as both temporal and spiritual heads of the religion. This brought it to the attention of Nasir Khan of Kalat – the head of a powerful tribal confederation among the Brahuis of eastern Baluchistan, and a fanatical Sunni Muslim. He mounted a jihad or holy war against the Zikris whom he considered infidels or *kafir* and Sunni Islam was reinstated as the dominant religion in southern Baluchistan, with Zikriism nowadays surviving there primarily among nomads in the more remote regions.

By the mid-nineteenth century numerous Zikris in Baluchistan subjected to the scorn of their Sunni neighbours (called *nemazi* by the Baluch), began to look toward coastal Sind and its capital at Karachi as a haven. At this time the British under Sir Charles Napier and his successors conquered the area from the Talpur Baluch *Mirs*, imposing the 'pax Britannica' and turning an unimposing settlement of Sindhi fisherfolk into a burgeoning port city. The infidel *farinji* provided a mantle of protection for the Zikris, who filtered down from the interior in increasing numbers, since the British were notably more tolerant in religious matters than the Sunni chiefs they had ousted. While many Baluch settled in Karachi itself, others followed a mixed economy of desultory herding, dry crop cultivation and beach net fishing, with the maritime emphasis assuming more importance as sailing and other techniques were learned from indigenous fishermen like the Mohanas, for whom the immigrant Baluch often crewed. Indeed a common Baluchi term for a Baluch fisherman is *paadi* – 'one who goes on foot' – referring to the crude beach netting techniques of the ancestral fishermen *cum* herdsmen, techniques now secondary to fishing from a variety of lateen sailed craft ranging in length from twelve to forty-five feet.

Ascribed class stratification is weak among Zikri fishermen, for – like hunting – fishing is governed by the 'law of the chase'; that is, one may be lucky one day and unlucky the next. Reciprocity is accordingly highly developed and a community ideology of *wat ma wat*, 'united amongst ourselves,' is the normative ideal. Endogamy among these co-religionists is also high, with 64 per cent of the 171 marriages sampled taking place between real cross or parallel cousins drawn from both within one's own village and from other Zikri fishing settlements and *mohallas* (neighbourhoods) of Karachi.

Yet despite such solidarity, ascribed political – if not economic – hierarchy does exist in Zikri fishing villages which are led by headmen called *wadera*. This position is hereditary within certain lineages. In our primary study site, it was confined to descendents of the village's founder who was a Brahui (a Dravidian speaking people of eastern Baluchistan, in contrast to the Indo-Iranian speaking Baluch proper). By the time of our fieldwork, however, this family had long been 'Baluchized' in both language and custom, using Baluchi as their mother tongue. In this particular kin-cluster 18 of 26 marriages were between patrilateral parallel cousins, a high percentage in comparison with statistics from the Muslim world generally and from their already highly endogamous co-villagers in particular. The position of *wadera*, while always within this lineage, did not follow any definite line of succession in the three times it has changed hands, due to the death of the incumbent, since the founding of the village. Rather, *jirgah*s or councils of all the male adults assessed the personal qualities of a number of possible leaders in the *wadera* lineage to determine who should 'tie the turban' of leadership.

Normatively the most important quality of the *wadera*, when dealing with his co-villagers, is held to be persuasiveness, since coercion is not considered appropriate among *wat ma wat*. 'If your tongue is sweet, the world is yours' *(agar gop shirin, mulk girin)*, is the intravillage mandate of the *wadera*. However, when confronted with opposition from outsiders, he is expected to be aggressive – violently if necessary – in furthering the interests of his followers. Such qualities of righteous strength and aggressiveness coupled with persuasiveness are variously labelled *zabr dost* and *tiar*.

REAL POLITICAL BEHAVIOUR

Despite the varieties of jural socio-political organization described above for the Baluch of oasis, desert and coast, common *de facto* political behaviours can be discerned. Ultimately these involve the idea that 'might makes right' and that he who holds power should be obeyed, often with marked obsequiousness, but only until there is a good chance of disobeying with impunity and/or the chance of gain. A corollary of currying favour with those higher in the status hierarchy is lording it over those below. Thus a sub-chief of the 'tribal' Marris states 'I touch the political agent's boots and get a thousand to touch mine'[17] while adages from southern Baluchistan and the Zikri fishermen proclaim:

'Strong water can flow uphill' (i.e., the mighty can violate natural law), or

'If your fortress is strong and your followers numerous, for you there shall be neither danger nor trouble,' or

'If you don't know who farted, blame the powerless.'

Behaviourally, the Baluch respect for power has its limits, and in places like the Makran region of southern Baluchistan authority was always being tested as members of the *hakim* stratum and desert Baluch chiefs, backed by mercenary retainers (*posht*), jockeyed amongst themselves for control of the oases and the revenues they represented through long established systems of taxation and tribute, such as *dahak* (10th shares of the crop) and an open ended *zar-i-shah* or 'rulers gold'.[18] In more recent Baluch history Matheson[19] has documented analogous political intrigues among the 'tribal' Bugti Baluch of eastern Baluchistan.

The seeming contradiction between obedience and rebelliousness among the Baluch is centred on the importance placed on the concept of 'guardianship' (*sambal* or *pannag*). A major attribute of a leader is to protect and guard his followers' interests against outsiders while at the same time using whatever means necessary to keep his followers' own unruliness from disrupting social order. A constant probing of the leader's abilities as watchman is therefore necessary—probing which becomes less cautious and more overt as evidence of a leader's weakness appears.

Thus the Zikri fishermen were initially staunch supporters of the ousted Pakistani Prime Minister Bhutto. However, they became increasingly disenchanted with him during the riots which followed the elections of March 1977, not because of (well-founded) allegations of vote rigging and brutality toward political rivals but rather because he was, in their view, too conciliatory toward opposition leaders in the chaotic election aftermath and not forceful enough in his role as guardian of order.

At the local level among Zikri fishermen the *de facto* role of the *wadera* can be analysed from a body of 73 cases of disputes and their settlements which I collected. We find from these that the *wadera* is generally quite effective as an aggressive partisan of his followers, *vis-a-vis* outsiders, the more so when sectarian rivalries are involved. One such clash occurred when Sunni Baluch villagers living on the plains behind the fishing village refused the Zikris permission to bury their dead next to the Sunni graveyard. An armed band of Zikri fishermen — many with guns — led by the *wadera*'s son, with his father's blessing — marched toward the Sunni village, forcing the Sunnis to back down.

While this aggressiveness is in keeping with 'ideal' *wadera* behaviour toward outsiders, the headman is supposed to be more conciliatory when dealing with conflicts within the village. Yet it appears that when he is confronted with intra-village conflicts in which he or his close kin have a direct interest the *wadera* quickly sheds any attempt at mediation and instead becomes an active disputant, ultimately requiring outsiders — the *waderas* of other villages or religious figures — to heal the rift in *jirgah* councils. I cite two of the ten such cases which exemplify this pattern:

CASE 1:

During the headmanship of A, the village lacked the several standpipes which now bring drinking water from Karachi, and water was either fetched from distant wells or was sporadically sent by a water truck of the Fisherman's Co-operative Society. While the women were lined up to fill their pots from the water truck the wife of headman A quarrelled with the wife of B over who was first in line. Headman A himself appeared on the scene and struck B's wife. Normatively this would have been an intolerable offense to B, as Baluch *izzat*, or honour, demands rigorous protection of womenfolk. But **B**, having a keen sense of his place in the political pecking order, did not himself respond directly. Instead he went to his wife's brother — a fish buyer in Karachi — who was a far more influential and powerful man. This brother in turn loudly proclaimed that *wadera* **A** was without honour to strike a woman and simultaneously threatened to press charges to the police. A number of other Zikri *waderas* and religious leaders then intervened and ultimately settled the case by imposing a five-thousand rupee *dand*, or fine, on the hot-tempered *wadera* **A**.

CASE 2:

The captain of boat **A** accused the captain of boat **B** of ruining **A**'s fishing by means of *nizar* ('envy' which can act like the 'evil eye'). This led to a violent fight between the 2 crews which was finally stopped by other men. The captains seemingly reconciled. Yet, patrilateral cousins of **A**'s captain still harboured resentment against captain **B** and ambushed him, beating him seriously. Seeing the fight, the patrilateral cousins and uncle of **B**'s captain ran over to help their agnate. The *wadera*, being the father-in-law of one of **B**'s cousins, instead of trying to mediate the conflict urged side **B** on to victory and only the intervention of a mass of men, women, and children stopped the melee. Even then much ill-will existed on both šides and a final settlement (a fine on captain **A**'s cousins) was only imposed when a number of outside Zikri *waderas* held a *jirgah*. The *wadera* in whose jurisdiction the conflict occurred remained non-conciliatory to the end.

Clearly then, although the Zikri *waderas* do from time to time fulfill their normative role as arbiters, particularly if they have no direct stake in a dispute, they are on the whole a microcosm of the turbulent political leaders found throughout Baluch history.

The *waderas* even today rely more on 'clout' than consensus in holding their position. For example, they may themselves become clients of powerful non-Baluch political figures in Karachi, promising to deliver people for political demonstrations in return for various rewards both for themselves and the village itself. (This is the widespread Pakistani practice of *chimcha* or 'spoon', i.e. 'you feed me and I'll feed you'). Likewise without a retinue of loyal kinsmen and/or deputies (*wazir*) no *wadera* is likely to stay in office long no matter how 'sweet tongued' he may be.

PIRS AND POWER

Against the backdrop of secular partisanship and self-aggrandizement is juxtaposed the Baluch reverence for Islam and its human figureheads—the *pirs* (saints) and other lesser holy men. Both Zikri and Sunni Baluch *pirs*, like their counterparts elsewhere in Islamic 'little traditions', are heirs to the Sufi belief in the ability of the individual mystic to attain union with God without the mediation of the Ulama or 'official' learned clergy representing 'Great Tradition' Islam.[20]

Baluch *pirs*, like other Muslim saints, often come from lineages claiming *sayyid* status. In the Sunni context this means descent from Muhammad's Arabs. Among the Zikris, saints are also said to be drawn mainly from *sayyid* or *pirzada* (descendants of saints) families but to the Zikris, whose reverence for Muhammad is subordinate to that of their Mahdi, Nur Pak, *sayyids* are the descendants of the mysterious *Khoda Dad* (see note 16,) who is said to have taught the Baluch the ritual of the Zikr and the belief in the Mahdi. To Zikris, only members of Khoda Dad's line can be true *pirs*. Other men, equally devout but not as noble, become *mians*.

Despite this element of ascription the Baluch *pir* is a spiritual virtuoso who has obtained *barkat* (divine blessing or power) through communion with God. This is most usually achieved by means of periodic forty-day fasts *(chillag)* in isolated deserts or mountains, or in designated *chillag khana*, edifices set aside for such meditations. The central ideal of *pir*-like behaviour involves 'killing' worldly desire which emanates from the baser recesses of the soul (Baluchi *nasp*; Arabic *nafs*). In turn the more elevated aspects of the spirit are supposed to be strengthened and *pirs* exhort their lay devotees *(murids)* to similarly renounce evil, carnality and greed (Baluchi *tobo kanag,* from Arabic *tauba,* 'repentance').

A holy man's reputation doesn't end (and indeed it sometimes only really begins) at his death. Ground that has been consecrated with the *barkat* of a living saint can become a *tik-khana* or 'house of curing' after his death, with geophagy often a feature of such cures, as the *barkat*-saturated earth is mixed with water or tea. Similarly the burial places of other saints become *ziarat* or shrines.

Unlike *waderas* who, at least in their dealing with outsiders, are supposed to be of 'hot' (*garm*) temperament (some informants use the Arabic word *tasir* or 'effect,' a term more commonly applied to foods, based on ancient Greco-Arabic homeo and allopathic medical concepts), the holy man should be 'cool' and meditative (*sard tasir,* a label that in other contexts would be pejorative, e.g., as in a person who has an energy-sapping ailment).

Like other Islamic saints, Zikri Baluch *pirs*, often act as mediators in secular conflicts, particularly when *waderas* themselves become disputants. This is amply borne out in the 73 conflict-cases mentioned above. But other, perhaps more important, dimensions of the *pirs'* role emerge from a corpus of 48 stories about the deeds of Zikri *pirs* and other holy men—both living and dead. These cases can be evaluated against the normative picture of the *pir,* just as the dispute cases were contrasted to the *wadera* ideal.

We find the following breakdown in the major themes of these *pir* stories.

Table 13.1: **Breakdown of Themes in Case Studies of Barkat (holy power) use.**

		Number of examples
I	Use of *barkat* for curing disease, finding lost objects and telling the future	15
II.	Use of *barkat* for economic-ecosystemic benefits (ending drought, finding fish, etc.)	9
III.	Use of *barkat* in competitive contexts:	
	a) contests of divine power (*Chikasag*) with other holy men	14
	b) use of power to defeat secular enemies (own or followers)	6
	c) use of power against a Jinn (spirit)	2
	d) contests of power between men and women	2
	Total	48

Clearly the largest category, and indeed half of all the cases, falls into the category of competitive use of spiritual power with *chikasag* or holy power contests between rival *pirs* the largest sub-category. This emphasis on competition is further strengthened by the fact that one of the curing stories deals with how a Zikri *pir* effected a miracle when Sunni holy men had failed, a theme which recurs in one of the 'economic' stories as well.

Of the fourteen *chikasag* eight were contests between Zikris and Sunnis with six between Zikris. The motif of sectarian rivalry between

Zikri and Sunni, while only hinted at in the *chikasag* stories, is considerably strengthened by the six stories in which divine power was used against secular enemies, all of which involved Zikri *pirs* versus lay Sunnis, and by cases like that of the graveyard incident cited earlier from the secular arena.

Several examples of competitive or partisan use of spiritual power can be offered:

CASE 1:

Barkat used against a lay rival. A turn-of-the-century Zikri *pir* had a beautiful female servant. The Jam or ruler of Las Bela (a former princely state, now an administrative district of Baluchistan), hearing of her beauty, ordered the saint to send him the woman. The saint refused and the Jam sent a *lashkar* or troop to force the holy man to give her up. The saint got word of the approaching force and went into the hills far to the west of the Jam's capital at the town of Bela. He fired off his pistol and so great was his power that the bullet wounded the Jam in his distant capital.

CASE 2:

A Power-Contest between Zikri and Sunni Pirs. A Sindhi pir — a Sunni Muslim — threatened to steal the *barkat* of a famous pir (a common theme), and force him to embrace Sunni Islam. The Zikri accepted the challenge, mounted his camel and travelled to Hub, the river marking the border of Sind and Baluchistan, where the Sindhi was waiting. As soon as the Zikri came into view the Sindhi's limbs grew rigid and he became mute, unable to return the *salaam* of the Zikri. The grandfather of a prominent Zikri in our village was witness to the event. At the time he was himself a Sunni, but on seeing the power of the Zikri he converted.

CASE 3:

Test of Power between Zikris (also involving revenge on a Sunni). Not long ago a Zikri pir — still living — travelled to Koh-i-Murad, the mountain in southern Baluchistan said to be the site where their Mahdi once sat and which, rather than Mecca, is the primary goal of the Zikri Hajji or pilgrim. When he arrived, he learned that the *chunda* or golden offerings to the shrine had been stolen. Chiding the other holy men present for not having sufficient *barkat* to recover the gold he announced that his power would cause a snake to attack the guilty party. That night a Sunni Baluch in the oasis of Turbat, near the holy mountain, was bitten by a cobra. He surrendered the gold and begged the Zikri to cure him. The saint replied that he was destined to die for his crime — and so he did.

CASE 4:

A Pir helps a client (sort of!). Several years ago a well known leader of the Baluch guerrillas, who were waging a sporadic war for independence from Pakistan, came to a Zikri pir for a charm that would render him invulnerable to the weapons of the government soldiers. This guerrilla was himself a Sunni but, like many Muslims, was eclectic enough to avail himself of any means — even a Zikri — to achieve his ends. The *pir* gave him a special turban which, he said, would turn aside the bullets of the Pakistani troops.

One night, while the rebel was sleeping in his home in the remote mountains of Jhalawan (S.E. Baluchistan) a force of government commandos attacked. The hut and the guerrilla himself were shot to pieces. However, the turban itself survived unharmed.

Unlike comparable figures elsewhere (e.g. the Sudanese Mahdi) Zikri Baluch *pirs* only infrequently take up arms in their quest for reputation and followers (Case 1, cited above, is unusual in this regard). Yet their willingness to use *barkat* to gain their ends or those of their followers can still be seen as a reflection of the competition found in the secular arena.

For the *pirs*, *barkat*-derived status is often more than symbolic. A *pir*'s regular followers or *murid* frequently bestow gifts and wealth upon him, as do non-*murid* for specific services rendered, such as cures. Baluch *pirs* spend much time making the rounds of their *murids'* homes which may be quite widely separated. During our period of fieldwork among the maritime Baluch on the Sind coast, several Zikri *pirs* from the distant Makran coast — a rough overland trip — arrived for visits during which they were feted quite lavishly. *Pirs*, like *waderas*, can also exert influence via the *chimcha* or patronage system, and much of the Baluch fishermen's enthusiasm for ex-Prime Minister Bhutto could be traced to the fact that a major Zikri *pir* had urged such support in return for a promise from Pakistan People's Party officials that one of the *pir*'s close relatives would be given a plum position in the bureaucracy.

The Baluch, however, have no *pirs* that compare in this regard to the hereditary Pir Pagaro ('Saint of the Turban') of Sind – an individual whose mantle of inherited charisma co-exists with secular power and affluence on a grand scale. The incumbent Pir Pagaro is a race-horse owner, official of a major political party and *murshid* or leader of a band of murid – the Hurs (The 'Free') – whose violence potential has frequently been a threat to both Pakistani regimes and the British before them.[21]

It is, of course, irrelevant as to whether or not a *pir* actually performs the miraculous feats attributed to him (many of the stories involve such themes as changes of bodily form, levitation and 'second sight'). The point is that a saint's followers believe he did the deeds and the saints themselves do little to discourage embellishments on their reputations. Indeed, despite the normative ideal of the *pir* as a person devoid of worldly ambition, a good case can be made for the argument that until he has validated his *barkat* in the competitive arena an aspiring *pir*'s claims to holiness are non-availing, successful *chillag* or forty-day fasts notwithstanding. Thus one man, who was to become a well known Zikri *pir*, completed several *chillag* but only secured his reputation when, the story goes, he used his *barkat* to halt a train on which he had been refused a seat.

In his competitive persona, the Zikri saint can be seen in the photograph of one notable *pir* which graces numerous Zikri homes. The saint stares haughtily at the observer, bedecked not in the Sufi's wool cloak, or with the staff of the mendicant, but rather in a bullet-filled bandoleer.

DISCUSSION

In a recent discussion that has already generated considerable debate,[22] Akbar Ahmed[23] addresses himself to that other turbulent folk of Pakistan's frontier – the Swat Pathans – with the aim of modifying Barth's[24] by now classic portrayal of them which Ahmed views as a caricature of border wild men. Maintaining that Barth's analysis has over-emphasized the point of view of the secular political leaders, the khans, Ahmed contends that the Pathans' deep ideological attachment to Sufic traditions and their spokesmen is at the basis of Swat polity, with the emergence of Swat State itself being more a theocracy than the creation of 'profane' leadership. To Ahmed, the Pathan is 'religious man' as well as the 'political man' emphasized in Barth's account.

However, the present discussion, and indeed much of Ahmed's own data on such religious leaders as the nineteenth century Akhund of Swat (the leader of the tribesmen against the British in the 1863 Ambela campaign) and Miangul Wadud (who became the first *Wali* of Swat after killing his cousins), clearly indicate that the boundaries between 'sacred' and 'profane' motives and behaviours are fuzzy at best along the South Asian frontier. Despite their role as spokesmen of the one unifying God, the Baluch *pirs*, like those of the Pathans are products of a cultural matrix steeped in ideologies of revenge *(badl)*, aggressive defense of personal honour *(izzat)*, the need to support friends and kin (until they in turn became enemies), and a distrust of people unlike oneself, recently referred to by Gulick[25] as the mentality of 'peril and refuge'.

Having thus pointed out the similarities between sacred and secular personnel and behaviours among the Baluch, I would like to suggest a further analogy between the Baluch *pir* and the Baluch secular leader on a more purely symbolic level, based on Leach's[26] intriguing discussion of the role of the human head and headgear as symbols of secular and sacred power.

The main points of Leach's thesis are:
1) The phallus is a widespread symbol of diety.
2) The human head is often a symbolic substitute for the phallus.
3) Head hair is thus a symbol of 'sexuality'.
4) With elaborate, ritualized headgear a ruler or ecclesiastic calls attention to the 'potency' i.e., power — of the individual.

Among the Baluch, both saints and *waderas* have the turban as the primary symbol of office. Investiture of a secular chief involves a ritual 'tying of the turban.' Living saints, too, are often marked by their elaborate head-dress; but it is in shrines to dead *pirs* where the role of the turban is most pronounced, resting at the head of the bier in the *mazars* where famous dead saints are said to lie, and crowning the patently phallic piles of stones dedicated to lesser *pirs* on remote desert mountaintops.

A particularly favoured form of turban for both secular and religious 'big men' is the so-called Mashadi style (named for the holy city in Iran). This consists of either a high conical cap embroidered in gold or silver thread around which the turban-cloth is wound and tied so as to leave a high upright fan (called a *bul* in Baluchi) or else a large turban *(sans* cap) of fine cloth, again with a conspicuous *bul*. If one follows Leach's reasoning that the headgear of the politically and sacrally powerful accentuates phallic imagery (as in a bishop's mitre), this particular form of turban may have significant implicit symbolism. It is, in fact, also to be seen on non-political or religious personnel who nonetheless represent power and responsibility in other areas — for example, the *chowkidars* or watchmen of important households or public places.

With a slight permutation of Leach's argument, it is further possible to see the normative roles of both *wadera* and *pir* as symbolizing control over the rampant and animal in mankind (represented by the concept of *nasp* — base desires of the soul — that the saint is said to 'kill' in himself and the *wadera* supposed to placate in others via reasoned arbitration). The turban thus simultaneously covers, and thereby contains (contra Leach), the baseness (i.e., sexuality and by extension, *nasp*) represented by the hair of the saint or headman. At the same time it accentuates the stature (and hence heroism) of the figure of *wadera* or *pir* who is seen as fighting the battle with *nasp* on behalf of the more noble aspects of the human spirit.

When we turn to the real (as opposed to the ideal) behaviours of *waderas* and saints, an even purer application of Leach's thesis can be brought to bear. In the *de facto* world of secular and sacred competition the turban, which on other individuals may serve mainly to prevent sunstroke, becomes, on *wadera* and *pir*, the symbol of potency exercised in political and spiritual contexts respectively (cf. *pir* Case 4 cited above).

NOTES

1. The original version of this paper was read at the 1978 meeting of the North Eastern Anthropological Association. I would like to thank Carroll Mc. C Pastner for her helpful criticisms and Richard Kurin of the University of Chicago for his stimulating companionship while in Pakistan and his suggesting certain of the lines of inquiry dealt with here.

2. Barth, F., *Political Leadership Among Swat Pathans,* Humanities Press, New York, 1959(a) and 'Segmentary Opposition and The Theory of Games', *Journal of the Royal Anthropological Institute*, 1959(b), 80, pt.1.

3. Gellner, E., *Saints of the Atlas,* University of Chicago Press, Chicago, 1969; Benet, F., 'Explosive Markets: The Berber Highlands', in *Trade and Market in the Early Empires,* Polanyi, K., Arensberg, C., and Pearson, H. (editors), The Free Press, New York, 1957.

4. Evans-Pritchard, E.E., *The Sanusi of Cyrenaica* , Oxford University Press, London, 1949.

5. Gellner, op. cit., 1969.

6. Ahmed, A., *Millenium and Charisma Among Pathans* Routledge and Kegan Paul, London, 1976.

7. Holt, P.M., *The Mahdist State in the Sudan 1881-1898*, Clarendon Press, Oxford, 1958.

8. Lewis, I. M., *A Pastoral Democracy*, Oxford University Press, London, 1961.

9. For example, Aswad, B., 'Social and Ecological Aspects in the Formation of Islam' in *Peoples and Cultures of the Middle East*, Sweet, L. (editor), Natural History Press, New York, 1970.

10. Barth, op. cit., 1959, p. 98.

11. Ahmed, op. cit., 1976.

12. Gellner, op. cit., 1969.

13. 12 months of fieldwork among the Pakistani Baluch were conducted on two separate occasions in collaboration with my wife, Carroll Mc.C Pastner. In 1968-69, 5 months of research among Baluch oasis villagers and nomads in the Makran region were supported by Fellowships and Grants from the National Institute of Mental Health. Research among the Zikri Baluch fishermen on the Sind coast was carried out during a seven month period in 1976-77 with the support of the *American Institute of Pakistan Studies*.

14. Pastner, S., 'Ideological Aspects of Nomad Sedentary Contact: A Case from Southern Baluchistan', *Anthropological Quarterly 44*, 1971, pp. 173-84; Pastner, S. and C.Mc. C Pastner, *'Agriculture, Kinship and Politics in Southern Baluchistan'*, *Man 7*, 1972, pp. 128-36 and 'Adaptations to State -Level Politics by the Southern Baluch', in *Pakistan : The Long View*, Ziring, L., Braibanti, R., and Wriggins, W.H. (editors), Duke University Press, Durham, 1977; Spooner, B., 'Politics, Kinship and Ecology in South East Persia', *Ethnology 7* (2), 1969, pp. 139-52.

15. Salzman, P.C., 'Adaptation and Political Organization in Iranian Baluchistan', *Ethnology 10* (4), 1971, pp. 433-44.

16. The few published references to the origin of Zikrism (for example, Field, H., *An Anthropological Reconnaissance in West Pakistan, 1955*, Peabody Museum Cambridge, 1959, who follows the turn of the century Baluchistan District Gazetteer Vol. VII) identify its founder as Sayyid Mahmud of Jaunpur who in his Indian homeland had proclaimed himself a Mahdi by the early sixteenth century and is considered to be the founder of the Mahdavist sect which still survives there and in Pakistan. Zikrism which arose in Baluchistan at about this time is said to have been brought to the area either by the Sayyid himself or his followers.

At the Zikri Baluch village level, however, the name of the Jaunpauri Sayyid is virtually unknown and instead the Mahdi is identified as *Nur Pak* ('Pure Light') who is said to have been created by God before Adam. He will return, at the apocalypse *(AkerZaman)* to restore the true faith. The teachings of the Mahdi and the founding of the Zikri sect are attributed to another mystery-shrouded figure, Khoda Dad (Gift of God) said to have been born not of man and woman at some unspecified time in the not too remote past and to be the forebear of the dominant lineage of Zikri pirs. I believe it is possible that this Khoda Dad can be identified with either Sayyid Mahmud Jaunpauri or whichever of his disciples is responsible for introducing Mahdiism to the Baluch.

Whatever its specific origins Zikrism is an offshoot of the Sufic movement and has as its central ritual the Zikr or repetitive chants in praise of God and the Mahdi. The Zikri *shahdat* or profession of the faith, with which the Zikir are prefaced, says (in Arabic) 'There is no God but God and *Nur Pak*, the Mahdi, is the prophet of God'.

The Qur'an is replaced as the holy book by the Zikr Illahi—a compendium of chants in Persian, Arabic and Baluchi—and the pilgrimage to Mecca by a Hajj to Koh-i-Murad, a holy mountain in southern Baluchistan said to be the throne (*takht*) of the Mahdi.

17. Pehrson, R., *The Social Organization of the Marri Baluch,* Wenner Gren Foundation, New York, 1966, p. 26.
18. Pastner and Pastner, op. cit., 1972 and 1977.
19. Matheson, S., *Tigers of Baluchistan,* Arthur Barker Ltd., 1967.
20. Schimmel, A., *Mystical Dimensions of Islam,* University of North Carolina Press, Chapel Hill, 1975.
21. Mayne, P., *Saints of Sind,* John Murray, London, 1956; Lambrick , H.T., *The Terrorist*, Ernest Benn Ltd., London, 1972.
22. Cf. *Current Anthropology.,* Vol. 18, No. 3.
23. Ahmed, op. cit., 1976.
24. Barth, op. cit., 1959 (a) and 1959 (b).
25. Gulick, J., *The Middle East: An Anthropological Perspective*, Goodyear Pub. Co., Pacific Palisades, 1976.
26. Leach, E., 'Levels of Communication and Problems of Taboo in the Appreciation of Primitive Art', in *Primitive Art and Society*, Forge, A. (editor), Oxford University Press, London, 1973, pp.227-230.

Index